CROAT

IST

WITH RIJEKA & THE SLOVENIAN ADRIATIC

RUDOLF ABRAHAM
THAMMY EVANS

www.bradtguides.com

Bradt Guides Ltd, UK
The Globe Pequot Press Inc, USA

Bradt GUIDES
TRAVEL TAKEN SERIOUSLY

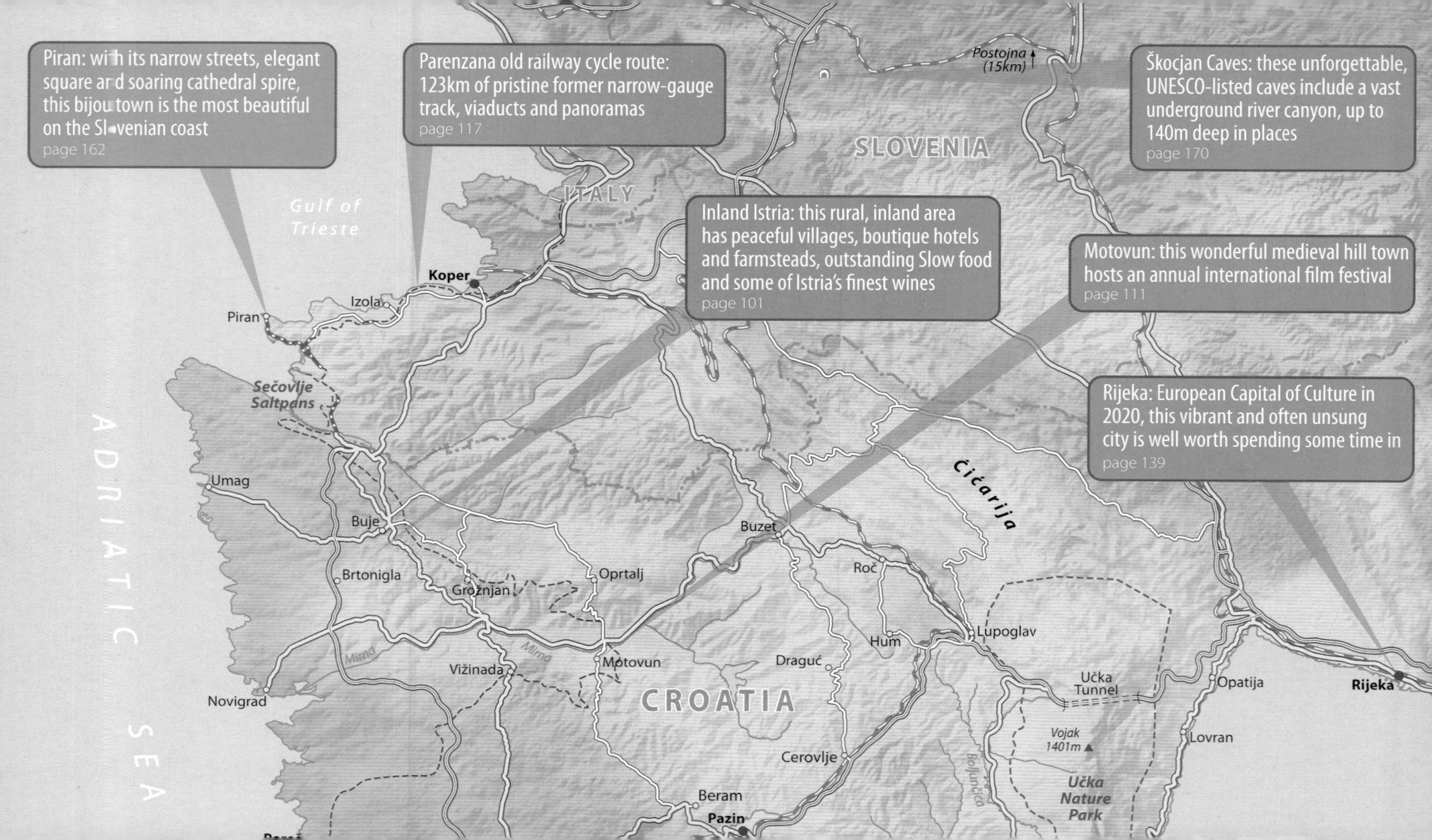
Piran: wi h its narrow streets, elegant square ar d soaring cathedral spire, this bijou town is the most beautiful on the Sl venian coast
page 162
Parenzana old railway cycle route: 123km of pristine former narrow-gauge track, viaducts and panoramas
page 117
Škocjan Caves: these unforgettable, UNESCO-listed caves include a vast underground river canyon, up to 140m deep in places
page 170
Inland Istria: this rural, inland area has peaceful villages, boutique hotels and farmsteads, outstanding Slow food and some of Istria's finest wines
page 101
Motovun: this wonderful medieval hill town hosts an annual international film festival
page 111
Rijeka: European Capital of Culture in 2020, this vibrant and often unsung city is well worth spending some time in
page 139
SLOVENIA
ITALY
CROATIA
Postojna (15km)
Gulf of Trieste
ADRIATIC SEA
Koper
Izola
Piran
Sečovlje Saltpans
Umag
Buje
Brtonigla
Grožnjan
Oprtalj
Motovun
Mirna
Vižinada
Novigrad
Buzet
Roč
Hum
Dragué
Cerovlje
Beram
Pazin
Lupoglav
Ćićarija
Učka Tunnel
Vojak 1401m
Učka Nature Park
Boljunčica
Opatija
Lovran
Rijeka

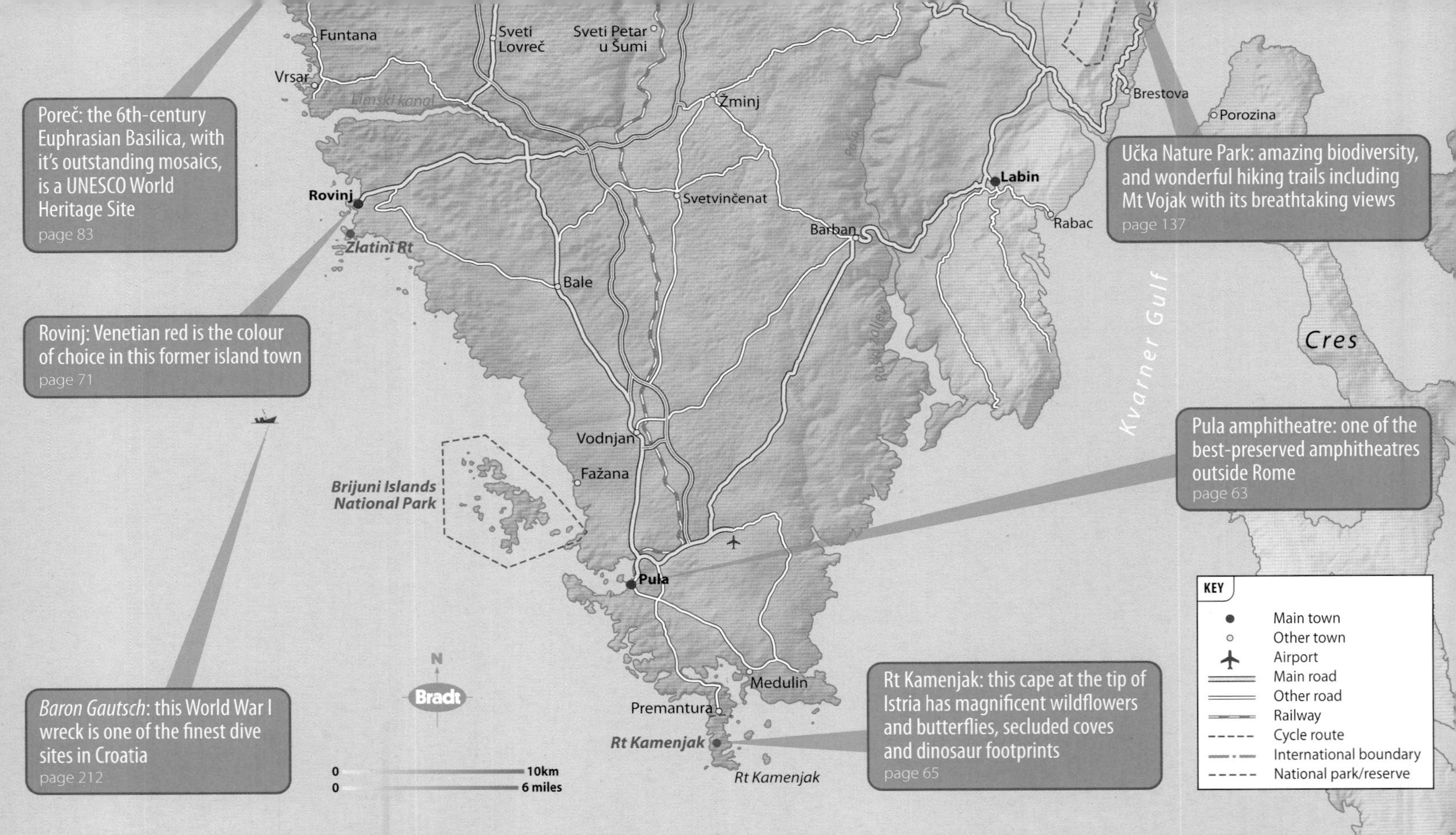
Poreč: the 6th-century Euphrasian Basilica, with it's outstanding mosaics, is a UNESCO World Heritage Site
page 83
Rovinj: Venetian red is the colour of choice in this former island town
page 71
Baron Gautsch: this World War I wreck is one of the finest dive sites in Croatia
page 212
Učka Nature Park: amazing biodiversity, and wonderful hiking trails including Mt Vojak with its breathtaking views
page 137
Pula amphitheatre: one of the best-preserved amphitheatres outside Rome
page 63
Rt Kamenjak: this cape at the tip of Istria has magnificent wildflowers and butterflies, secluded coves and dinosaur footprints
page 65
Funtana
Vrsar
Sveti Lovreč
Sveti Petar u Šumi
Limski kanal
Žminj
Brestova
Porozina
Rovinj
Zlatini Rt
Svetvinčenat
Labin
Rabac
Barban
Bale
Raša
Raški zaljev
Kvarner Gulf
Cres
Vodnjan
Fažana
Brijuni Islands National Park
Pula
Medulin
Premantura
Rt Kamenjak
Rt Kamenjak
N
Bradt
0 10km
0 6 miles
KEY
Main town
Other town
Airport
Main road
Other road
Railway
Cycle route
International boundary
National park/reserve

ISTRIA
DON'T MISS...

INLAND ISTRIA
The hill towns and villages of Istria's interior are full of charm. Here, a narrow street in Grožnjan PAGE 115
(JD/ITB)

ROMAN ARCHITECTURE
Pula's amphitheatre, dating from the 1st century AD, is one of the largest and best-preserved Roman amphitheatres in the world PAGE 63
(J/S)

FESTIVALS
Traditional singers at the Subotina festival in Buzet
PAGE 121
(IZ/P)

SUN AND SEA
Whether you are a weathered sea dog or a novice swabbie, sailing along the Istrian peninsula is a delight. Pictured here: the Brijuni Islands
PAGE 68
(ja/S)

FOOD AND DRINK
From superb seafood to the famed truffle dishes of inland Istria – it's worth coming to Istria just to eat. Pictured here: slicing local *pršut* at Konoba na kapeli in Tinjan PAGE 109
(RA)

ISTRIA IN COLOUR

left (I/S) — The medieval old town in Rovinj shows off its Venetian heritage PAGE 71

below left (RA) — Built in 1882 and known as the 'Adria Palace', the Jadrolinija building's sheer grandeur is one of the finest reflections of Rijeka's pre-eminent maritime history PAGE 150

below (JD/ITB) — Motovun, a hill town in central Istria, viewed across the surrounding vineyards PAGE 111

Most visitors miss the little town of Pazin, which is a shame as it has a cracking castle, a dramatic gorge and literary associations aplenty PAGE 101 above left (JD/TBCI)

Detail of one of the magnificent, UNESCO-listed Byzantine mosaics in Poreč's Euphrasian Basilica PAGE 93 above right (TBP)

Once the capital of Istria, the coastal town of Poreč is a beautiful and quite typical Croatian old town PAGE 83 below (TBP)

AUTHORS

Rudolf Abraham (w rudolfabraham.com) is an award-winning travel writer, photographer and guidebook author specialising in Croatia, Slovenia and central and southeast Europe. He first visited Croatia in 1998, lived in Zagreb for two years, and continues to spend several weeks a year in his favourite country in Europe. He is the author of over a dozen books including the first English-language guide to hiking the Alpe-Adria Trail through the mountains of Austria, Slovenia and northern Italy, as well as the first English-language hiking guides to Croatia and Montenegro, the Peaks of the Balkans Trail, the Juliana Trail, and several other guides to Austria, Montenegro, Patagonia and Slovenia, and his work is published widely in magazines. He lives in London with his wife and daughter, though is just as likely to be found in Zagreb, the mountains of Slovenia or on a small island somewhere on the Croatian Adriatic.

Thammy Evans, born in London of Welsh and Peranakan parents, has travelled and lived abroad for 25 years. Her first overseas trip was to Malaysia at the age of eight, and she has been dabbling in numerous foreign languages ever since. Among many other travels, her most memorable are the Trans-Mongolian Railway from Tianjin to Moscow in 1991, mountaineering in Bolivia in the summer of 1999, and doing the field research for her second Bradt travel guide *Great Wall of China* in 2005.

She has also written the Bradt guide to North Macedonia. She and her family now divide their time between France and a small stone house by the sea in Istria.

DEDICATION

Rudolf Abraham – To Ivana and Tamara
Thammy Evans – To Plamenka, Dalibor and Korvin

Third edition published June 2023
First published 2013
Bradt Guides Ltd
31a High Street, Chesham, Buckinghamshire, HP5 1BW, England
www.bradtguides.com
Print edition published in the US by The Globe Pequot Press Inc,
PO Box 480, Guilford, Connecticut 06437-0480

Project Managers: Laura Osborne, Rebecca Gurney & Anna Moores
Editor: Faye Winsor
Cover research: Pepi Bluck, Perfect Picture

ISBN: 9781784779429

British Library Cataloguing in Publication Data
A catalogue record for this book is available from the British Library

Photographs Rudolf Abraham (RA); Croatian National Tourist Board: Ivo Biočina (IB/CNTB), Aleksandar Gospić (AG/CNTB); Dreamstime.com: Peewam (P/D); Istria Tourist Board: Julien Duval (JD/ITB), Goran Šebelić (GS/ITB), Roey Yohai (RY/ITB); Photonet: more about Lovran (m/P), Igor Zirojević (IZ/P); Shutterstock.com: AAR Studio (A/S), aquapix (aq/S); Inu (I/S), jarino (ja/S), jasomtomo (J/S), Igor Karasi (IK/S), Kayo (K/S), Peter Klampfer (PK/S), Anna Maloverjan (AM/S), Milan Z81 (M/S); Slovenian Tourist Board (www.slovenia.info): Jošt Gantar (JG/STB), Nikola Jurišič (NJ/S); Superstock.com (SS); Tourist Board of Central Istria: Julien Duval (JD/TBCI), Renco Kosinožić (RK/TBCI); Tourist Board Poreč (TBP)
Cover The houses of Rovinj's old town in early morning light (RA)
Back cover Clockwise from top left: The village of Draguć (JD/TBCI); Pula's Roman amphitheatre (RA); cycling the Parenzana (AG/CNTB); *Pršut* (dry-cured ham) is a local speciality (JD/TBCI)
Title page From left: Vineyards near Butonigla (JD/ITB); Aerial shot over Labin (IB/CNTB); Traditional music in Istria (JD/ITB)

Maps David McCutcheon FBCart.S

Typeset by Ian Spick, Bradt Guides
Production managed by Jellyfish Print Solutions; printed in India
Digital conversion by www.dataworks.co.in

AUTHORS' STORIES

RUDOLF ABRAHAM My first contact with Croatia came at the age of four, when living opposite the former home of author Rebecca West in the village of Ibstone, Bucks – and through recipes from my mother's copy of *The Balkan Cookbook*, which have evidently shaped my taste buds forever. Many years later I met my wife, who is Croatian, while trekking through the mountains of eastern Turkey, and moved to Zagreb soon afterwards. In the 25 years or so that I've been visiting, living in, writing about or photographing Croatia and Slovenia, the prospect of spending some time in Istria – whether visiting its medieval hill towns, cycling along its bike trails and backroads, or enjoying its more than heavenly food and wine – has never lost its appeal, or its magic. Thanks Thammy for helping me put one of my favourite parts of Croatia in the spotlight – I hope we've come somewhere near to doing it justice.

THAMMY EVANS Already a Balkanophile, I was drawn to Istria a decade ago. As a spit of land, it has been bandied about between various nations, yet has borne all this in its stride with pride. As a result it is remarkably cosmopolitan, even in its village life, and so I feel very at ease there. Istria evokes a feeling of warmth: a warm sea in the summer, a warm hearth in the winter and yes, warm-hearted people. I was hiding away there in the summer of 2011, in our lovely Istrian farmhouse, when Adrian Phillips, then Publishing Director at Bradt, asked me whether I would be interested in co-writing a guidebook on Istria. Part of me did not want to write about the place where I go to escape, nor to write about the many secrets best known only to those who live there. But my desire to see it better represented in more than just a few pages appended to the rest of Croatia's glory got the better of me. Thank you, Rudolf, for disturbing my peace.

FEEDBACK REQUEST

At Bradt Guides we're aware that guidebooks start to go out of date on the day they're published – and that you, our readers, are out there in the field doing research of your own. You'll find out before us when a fine new family-run hotel opens or a favourite restaurant changes hands and goes downhill. So why not tell us about your experiences? Contact us on 01753 893444 or e info@bradtguides.com. We will forward emails to the author who may post updates on the Bradt website at w bradtguides.com/updates. Alternatively, you can add a review of the book to Amazon, or share your adventures with us on Facebook, Twitter or Instagram (@BradtGuides).

Acknowledgements

RUDOLF ABRAHAM Firstly I must thank Thammy, for sharing her knowledge of and enthusiasm for this little wedge at the top of the Adriatic, and for making co-authorship such a straightforward and enjoyable process. For this third edition I would like to thank Darija Reic, Director of the Croatian National Tourist Office in London; Marko Marković, former Marketing Manager at the Istrian Tourist Board; Tanja Augustinović at the Kvarner Tourist Board; Iva Balen at the Rijeka Tourist Office; Aleksandra Lipej, Global Communications Manager at the Slovenian Tourist Board; Tine Murn, formerly Head of Communications at the Slovenian National Tourist Board in London; Lučka Peljhan, Director of the Vipava Valley Tourist Office; Tina Sračnjek at Taste Slovenia; Nika Krajnović at PP Učka; Jani Pejhan at Wajdušna; Đurđica Beletić of Al Torcio Olive Oil; Ingrid Savarin at the Novigrad Tourist Office; Luana Fernetich Ladavac at San Rocco; Ivana Braut at Hotel Navis; Anamaria Ružić at Jadra Hoteli; Nikola Benvenuti at Benvenuti Wines; Željka and Ivan Damjanić at Damjanić Wines; Marko Fakin at Fakin Wines; Vesna Cattunar at Cattunar Wines; Zoran Užar at San Crianzo; Tomaž Kavčič at Dvorec Zemono; David Ličen at Golden Ring Cheese; Pension Sinji Vrh; Peter Lisjak at Lisjak 1956; Matej Pelicon and Anita Lozar at Pelicon Brewery; and Damir 'Mrle' Martinović in Rijeka. Last but very much not least, I must thank my wife Ivana and daughter Tamara, who have shared in several Istrian adventures over the years – and have yet to tell me they're fed up with hearing about just how amazing the food was on my most recent trip.

THAMMY EVANS For my part, the secrets of Istria that have made it into this book would not have become known to me without the wonderful hospitality of my good neighbours Teta Ita, Plamenka, Dalibor and Korvin, and my good friends Deborah, Mauricio, Viktor and Petar. I thank the entire crew of Commodore Travel for a wonderful ferry trip from Rovinj (Aldino Vlašič Žiga, the captain Nikolas Korić, Danijela, Mareg, Miran, Mirna, PT, et al). For help with matters diving, I thank Miloš and Olwyn Trifunac, Lars, Stipe, and Damir of Poreč Diving Centre, and Filip Vušič of Puffer. Katie and Andy have helped with Rovinj; Paul and Anne with Piran; Bridget Jordan for lots of the east coast. I must also thank my mother again, not least for looking after our Dani, and for dropping everything at the last minute to assist. Finally, as ever, I thank my husband, Vic, for conducting last-minute primary and secondary research. And for her contribution to a second guidebook I must thank my daughter, Daniella (aged five), for doing the field research on travelling with children. *Hvala svima.*

Contents

Introduction

Long the seaside playground of the central, landlocked-Europeans, Istria's attractions are becoming increasingly well known and popular with English-speakers. While Croatia's Dalmatian coast has topped the list of tourist destinations in Croatia in terms of visitor numbers for a while now, it is little Istria's proximity and accessibility that attract those who want to stay and play a while and really appreciate what life on the Adriatic has to offer. A large, wedge-shaped peninsula at the head of the Adriatic, Istria has some of Croatia's most famous sites, including Pula's Roman amphitheatre, UNESCO-protected Byzantine mosaics in Poreč, picturesque medieval hill towns and hidden frescoes, and Brijuni Islands National Park, home to Tito's former summer residence. Renowned for its cuisine (and food-related festivals), in particular its truffles, game, first-rate pasta, seafood, wine and olive oil – and a whole host of earthy peasant stews – Istria also hosts Croatia's two most famous international film festivals (Pula and Motovun), while Rijeka, on the edge of the Istrian Peninsula, boasts the second-largest carnival in Europe after Venice, and was European Capital of Culture in 2020, the first city in Croatia to be awarded this title.

And that's just a taste of the cultural stuff. Then there's the outdoors – both above and below the water. A mix of Mediterranean and continental fauna adorn the peninsula, as well as some rare endemic species. Istria's cuisine is a further testament to the wealth of the soil here, and its geographic diversity for such a small area is matched only by the region's variety in outdoor sports which includes well-marked and well-trodden hiking trails, the Parenzana long-distance cycle route, one of Croatia's best spots for windsurfing at Rt Kamenjak, paragliding from the slopes of Ćićarije and Učka, and diving among World War I wrecks.

This brand-new edition of what was the very first guidebook to Istria is not bound by national boundaries, but looks at the whole of geographic Istria, including the Slovenian Capodistria region, which offers hot-spring spas, glorious castles and beautifully lit caves, and the corner of the Kvarner Bay region in Croatia. All these are within a day trip from anywhere in Istria, meaning you can happily stay in one location if you wish, making it ideal for families and for making the most of the beach. Distances in Istria are small, and within half an hour's drive you can move from the labyrinthine streets and Venetian splendour that is Rovinj, to rolling olive groves punctuated by traditional stone shepherd huts.

Both of this book's authors are happiest in Istria, sipping a glass of Malvazija wine with local dishes while looking out over the sea, be that from up high in an Istrian hill town, down on the shore or from a gently bobbing yacht. We hope you'll enjoy it too.

LIST OF MAPS

KEY TO SYMBOLS

International boundary
Motorway/dual carriageway
Main road
Minor road
Track
Footpath
Featured hike
Railway
Ferry
Airport
Railway station
Bus station
Car hire/taxi
Filling station/garage
Tourist information office
Museum/art gallery
Important/historic building
Historic castle/fortification
Town gate
Statue/monument
Roman site

$ Bank/ATM
Post office
Hospital
Pharmacy/clinic
Hotel/guesthouse
Camping
Restaurant
Café
Bar/pub
Internet access
Church/cathedral
City wall
Historic site
Dive centre
Vineyard
Beach
Viewpoint
Lighthouse
Cave
Other attraction
Urban market
Urban park
National park

HOW TO USE THIS GUIDE

AUTHORS' FAVOURITES Finding genuinely characterful accommodation or that unmissable off-the-beaten-track café can be difficult, so these authors' favourites will point you in the right direction. They are marked with a ✱.

PRICE CODES Throughout this guide we have used price codes to indicate the cost of those places to stay and eat listed in the guide. For a key to these price codes, see page 32 for accommodation and page 34 for restaurants.

MAPS

Keys and symbols Maps include alphabetical keys covering the locations of those places to stay, eat or drink that are featured in the book. Note that regional maps may not show all hotels and restaurants in the area: other establishments may be located in towns shown on the map.

Grids and grid references Several maps use gridlines to allow easy location of sites. Map grid references are listed in square brackets after the name of the place or site of interest, with page number first, eg: [123 C3].

ABBREVIATIONS

bb (*bez broja*)	used in street addresses to indicate a house or other building with no number
IDS (*Istarski demokratski sabor*)	Istrian Democratic Assembly (the main political party in Istria)
np (*nacionalni park*)	national park
pp (*park prirode*)	nature park
Ul (*ulica*)	street

Part One

GENERAL INFORMATION

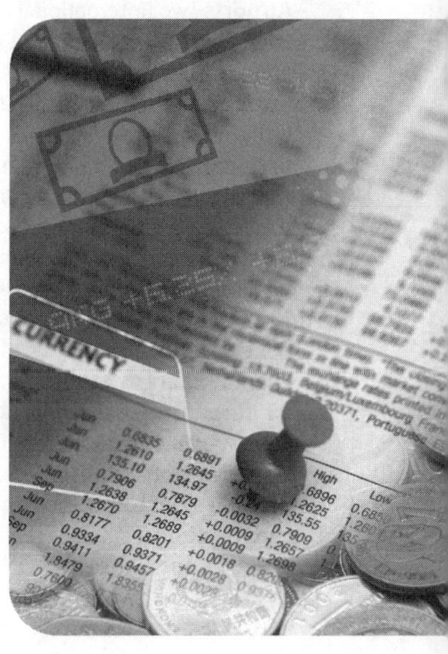

ISTRIA AT A GLANCE

Country name The Republic of Croatia (Republika Hrvatska)
Region name Istria (Istra)
Location A peninsula at the head of the Adriatic. Bordered by Slovenia to the north and the Kvarner region of Croatia in the northeast.
Official language Croatian
Other languages and dialects Italian, Istriot, Istro-Romanian, Venetian
Population of Istria County: 195,794 (2021 census)
Religion Roman Catholic
Župan (equivalent of mayor) Boris Miletić
Main political parties Istarski demokratski Sabor (IDS), Hrvatska demokratska zajednica (HDZ), Socijaldemokratska partija (SDP)
Regional capital Pazin (population 8,306) (2021 census)
Economic centre Pula (population 52,411) (2021 census)
Other major towns Poreč, Rovinj, Labin, Buzet, Umag
Local government units 41 (ten towns, 31 municipalities)
Area 2,820km^2
National parks Brijuni Islands
Nature parks Učka
Nature reserves and other protected areas Rt Kamenjak, Zlatni rt, Limski kanal, Palud
UNESCO World Heritage Sites Euphrasian Basilica, Poreč; Škocjan Caves, Slovenia
Total length of coast 441km
Airports Two (international airport, Pula; local airfield, Vrsar)
Highest point Vojak (Mount Učka), 1,401m
Time GMT+1
Currency As of 1 January 2023, the Kuna (HRK, usually written as kn) was replaced by the euro (€)
Exchange rate £1 = €1.14 (March 2023)
Average net monthly salary €1,275 Croatian Bureau of Statistics, 2021)
International telephone code +385
Electricity 220 volts AC. Sockets are round two-pin.
Local symbols Goat and *boškarin* ox
National holidays 1 January (New Year's Day); 6 January (Epiphany); Easter Sunday and Easter Monday; 1 May (Labour Day); Corpus Christi (60 days after Easter Sunday); 22 June (Day of Anti-fascist Struggle); 25 June (Statehood Day); 5 August (Victory and Homeland Thanksgiving Day and the Day of Croatian Defenders); 15 August (Assumption of the Virgin Mary); 8 October (Independence Day); 1 November (All Saints' Day); 25 and 26 December (Christmas)

1

Background Information

GEOGRAPHY

A wedge-shaped – some might say, heart-shaped – peninsula at the head of the Adriatic, Istria covers an area of around 2,820km^2, and is bordered by Slovenia in the north and the Kvarner region of Croatia in the northeast. The Istrian coast, like that of the rest of Croatia, is highly indented and riddled with small, rocky coves, and runs to a total length of some 441km – roughly double the distance as the crow flies. Most beaches are pebble or rocky, though there are some notable exceptions such as the broad, sandy Bijeca, near Medulin.

The Limski kanal, often incorrectly described as a fjord (it's actually a drowned river valley), cuts deep into the west coast, while the Raški zaljev makes a prominent break in the southeast coast. Just off the west coast near Pula are the Brijuni Islands, now a national park, and further north towards Rovinj another scattering of islands lies just off the coast.

The hilly Istrian interior is divided from the east coast by the Učka and Ćićarija mountains, which rise steeply from the Opatija Riviera to an altitude of 1,401m and 1,272m respectively. These form part of the Dinaric Alps, an extended chain of mountains that stretches southeast through Croatia parallel to the coast, down through Montenegro and Albania and into northern Greece. In the west the transition between the interior and the coast is more gentle. Inland Istria is bisected by three main rivers: the Mirna and the Dragonja in the north, both running from east to west, and the Raša in the east, running more or less north to south. A large lake in the northeast, Butoniga jezero, is actually a manmade reservoir. Like elsewhere in Croatia and Slovenia, the karst limestone is pierced by caves, such as Mramorinca near Brtonigla and Baradine near Nova Vas.

The Istrian landscape is remarkably green when compared with some of the islands of the nearby Kvarner and northern Dalmatia, with well-cultivated soils supporting grape vines, olives, corn and other crops, and around 35% of Istria is covered by forest.

Despite Istria's predominantly rural character, around 70% of the population live in towns.

FOREST FIRES

Like much of the rest of Croatia, Istria's hot, dry climate makes it particularly prone to forest fires. High temperatures in the summer frequently combine with dry winds and a lack of rain, leaving forests and grasslands tinder-dry, and easily ignited by a carelessly discarded cigarette. Owing to the risk of forest fires you should *never* light an open fire in the wild.

KARST

Istria – like much of Croatia – is predominantly a karst landscape. Karst is formed through the gradual action of rainwater on limestone (rainwater contains carbon dioxide, making it mildly acidic, and able to slowly dissolve a soluble rock such as limestone). Cracks in the rock and surface drainage holes are enlarged as the acidic water seeps downwards, leading over millennia to the creation of a distinctive surface texture, pockmarked and scored by vertical fissures, and a profusion of caves and sinkholes. An elaborate subterranean drainage system develops, as a consequence of which most surface water rapidly disappears underground, to flow as subterranean streams, which may later re-emerge as karst springs, only to vanish into the rock once more further along their course.

Istria's deepest cave is found at Rašpor in the Ćićarija Mountains – though at 365m it's still relatively small by Croatian standards (a cave in northern Velebit plunges over 1,400m into the depths of the mountain, making it one of the 15 deepest caves in the world). It has been estimated that there are at least 1,000 caves and sinkholes in Istria, perhaps double this number.

Among the most prominent karst features in Istria accessible to visitors are Baredine Caves near Poreč (page 93), and Pazinska jama or 'Pazin abyss' (page 106), a cave and sinkhole at one end of a gorge below Pazin Castle, into which the River Pazinčica disappears. Near the inland entrance to the Učka tunnel is a small canyon called Vranjska draga, with some spectacularly slender rock pinnacles. The new Poklon Visitor Centre in Učka Nature Park (page 138) is a good place to learn more about karst landscapes.

The term 'karst' is derived from the limestone Kras region in neighbouring Slovenia – an area that formed the basis of early studies into karst from the late 17th century onwards, in particular Cerkniško jezero, a huge intermittent lake which fills over the winter, only to drain away gradually through a labyrinth of sinkholes during the summer. This part of Slovenia is also home to one of the world's most-visited caves, Postojnska jama (page 176).

CLIMATE

As along the rest of the Croatian coast, Istria is characterised by warm, dry summers and mild winters. In comparison with the Dalmatian coast, Istrian summers tend to be a couple of degrees cooler, reaching 30–34°C from mid-June to the end of August, when it's very unlikely to rain. August tends to be slightly cooler than July, in part due to the slightly shorter days, and so the evenings are likely to be quite cool such that you might even need a light jacket. Correspondingly, winters are usually a few degrees warmer than on the Dalmatian coast, with the Opatija pocket in particular being especially sheltered. With the exception of the Učka and Ćićarija mountains, Istria rarely sees snow, or frost, and if it does it dissipates quickly in the morning sun. It is almost always sunny.

The peninsula is characterised further by three winds in particular. The *maestral* is the summer breeze blowing from east to west; the *jugo* brings warm air and rain from the south; and the *bura* reigns from the northeast bringing cold winds, which can whip up the sea. Although the *bura* can appear at any time of year, when it arrives characteristically around October, it signals the end of summer.

NATURAL HISTORY AND CONSERVATION

FLORA AND FAUNA With almost 40,000 taxa of wildlife already formally identified in Croatia as a whole, the count continues and final numbers are estimated by the State Institute for Nature Protection (**w** dzzp.hr) to possibly lie somewhere between a minimum of 50,000 to over 100,000. Istria used to be densely wooded until much of it was used during Venetian rule for shipbuilding. Nonetheless, a lot of Istria remains wooded – mainly deciduous forest, with downy oak, beech, oriental hornbeam and sweet chestnut, as well as areas of conifer forest, predominantly spruce and black pine – and is still favoured for picking wild asparagus and other local delicacies, as well as for gathering truffles, and seasonal hunting. Outside the towns you will often see various species of deer in the fields, especially at dawn and dusk, and it is not uncommon to see plenty of other species of **wildlife** – buzzard, kestrel, goshawk, hoopoe, rock partridge, owls (little owl and scops owl among other species), alpine swift, blue rock thrush and several species of woodpecker are just some of the birds you have a good chance of seeing, with Palud and Sečovlje on the coast being particularly good for waterfowl and wading birds, including little egret, great white egret, purple heron and little grebe. There are many species of bat present, including greater horseshoe bat and Geoffroy's bat. Croatia's rocky karst landscape makes a perfect habitat for **reptiles**, and Istria is no exception, with several species of wall lizard, as well as Dalmatian algyroides, green lizard, slow worm and glass lizard, and several species of snake such as dice snake and four-lined snake.

The only potentially fatally venomous animal in Istria is *Vipera ammodytes*, known in English as the **nose-horned viper**, known in Croatian as *poskok*, meaning 'something that jumps', because it is known occasionally to lurch from the ground to catch its prey. It is mostly found on rocky or stony ground, but can also be encountered in drystone walls or grass, and only becomes a threat if trodden on while basking in the sun or when it is protecting its eggs or young during the summer. For the most part, *poskok* are lethargic (hence you might tread on one) and unaggressive. Most will slither away if disturbed, some might hiss and expect you to slither away, and every now and again one will bite, especially if you step on it. If you are unlucky enough to get bitten by one, try to remain calm, keep the affected part below the level of your head and heart and phone emergency services (112) immediately. Do not attempt to suck out the venom – it has been shown to be completely ineffective. The **common viper** or **adder** (*Vipera berus*) is also found in Istria but is much less venomous. Make sure you wear sturdy boots and long trousers if hiking in the summer. Wide tracks can suddenly become remarkably rough and narrow in Istria.

Another venomous creature in Istria that people tend to fear is the **scorpion** (*Euscorpius italicus*). No species of *Euscorpius* is considered dangerous and its effects are usually localised (mainly pain at the sting site). At only 4–5cm in length, what little venom they have can stun a fly or a small grasshopper, but can't kill

BOŠKARIN

Native to Istria is the ***boškarin*** cow, a distinctive-looking animal with its long horns and allegedly one of the oldest breeds in Europe. It used to be a working animal until the tractor arrived and replaced it, and almost became extinct. It is now protected and while it is no longer used to plough fields or pull carts, it is farmed for its meat, which is considered a delicacy.

ENDANGERED FISH OF THE MEDITERRANEAN

Fish stocks have been on the decline globally since industrialisation brought about the freezer and a rise in the human population has outstripped the rate at which fish can reproduce to meet human consumption demands. In trying to reverse this trend, and stop the extinction of now vulnerable fish species, the International Union for the Conservation of Nature (IUCN) has produced Red Lists of all animals and where they rate on the continuum of Extinct to Least Concern. Croatia has also produced national lists.

Owing to differences in local tastes, fishing trends and national laws, some fish might be threatened in some areas of the world but not in others. Fish farming has started to make up for stocks in some species, but there is a vast difference between farming from spawn, and farming from wild catch – the latter being very inefficient due to the high death rate among trapped fish. Fish quotas and international fishing rights are big politics and affect the lives of many local fisherpeople as well as big businesses. Enforcement of the law is difficult, especially once the (by then dead) fish make it to market or the restaurant table. Below is an overview of some of the most commonly found endangered fish along the Adriatic, and suggested alternatives for consumption. See also page 208.

SHARK The common Croatian name for all shark species – which are, among other things, defined by the cartilaginous skeleton to their classic fish shape – is *morski pas*. Almost all shark species in Adriatic waters are at least Near Threatened with others being Endangered, and some even Critically Endangered. The only shark species that is of Least Concern is *Scyliorhinus canicula*, the **small-spotted catshark**, known locally as *mačka bljedica*. While there is a high chance that this is the *morski pas* that is served up at the local market and the many fish festivals, you might prefer not to take the risk. An alternative to the large flaked, sweet white flesh of the shark is swordfish *Xiphias gladius*, or *sabljan* in Croatian. Data is, however, deficient on the vulnerability of swordfish in the Adriatic, although some sources say that it is overfished generally in the Mediterranean. So far, we have not seen swordfish served in Istria.

it. Some people might be allergic, but are still unlikely to die from the venom of *E. italicus*. These scorpions do tend to like rocks and crevices, and in the dry summer season can be found in houses. They are not at all aggressive unless you provoke them seriously. I usually just brush them into a dustpan when I find one, and it sits there waiting for me to throw it out.

On a friendlier note, you'll find a spectacular number of **butterflies** (50 species have been recorded on Rt Kamenjak alone, compared with 56 species in the whole of the UK), including scarce swallowtail, southern swallowtail, small blue, Cleopatra, large tortoiseshell and southern festoon. Look out for plenty of dragonflies, too.

In the Učka and Ćićarija mountains wild boar are common, and chamois, red and roe deer, foxes and rabbits are also to be seen, as well as pine marten and dormouse, although you are highly unlikely to come across the protected brown bear.

The native ***Učkarski zvončić*** (*Campanula tommasiniana*) with its lilac-blue bell-shaped flowers can only be seen in the Učka Mountains, and is protected, as are all the varieties of **native orchid**, which can be found more commonly nearer the sea. Rt Kamenjak (*rt* means 'cape' or 'point' in Croatian) alone is home to at least 28

SKATE OR RAY *Raža* in Croatian, skate and ray species are mostly Near Threatened or Data Deficient. The only ray of Least Concern in the Adriatic is *Raja miraletus*, or *raža modropjega* in Croatian. Again it's hard to find an alternative to skate in Croatia, as even flounder *Bothus podas* (*razok* in Croatian) is Near Threatened. *Microchirus ocellatus*, **sole** or *list* in Croatian, is a smaller flatfish alternative with very fine sweet flesh.

JOHN DORY *Zeus faber* in Latin and German, *kovač* in Croatian, the John Dory is a Near Threatened species. This big disc-shaped fish with large spiky fins and a characteristic black circle on its side can be found served occasionally in restaurants. It's expensive precisely because it is rare. **Dentex** (*zubatac*) or sole are good alternatives.

SCORPIONFISH *Scorpaena scrofa* in Latin, *škrpina* in Croatian, the scorpionfish is also Near Threatened. It is not commonly eaten in the UK, but is very popular along the Mediterranean. In Istria it is a key ingredient for *brodet* fish soup, because it is a firm-fleshed fish that does not fall apart in a soup. Monkfish or angler *Lophius piscatorius*, or *grdobina* in Croatian, would be a good alternative if it wasn't also Near Threatened. The **black-bellied angler** *Lophius budegassa*, or *grdobina žutka* in Croatian, is of Least Concern and can be safely used as an alternative.

Other **fish to avoid** are turbot *Psetta maxima* (*oblič*; Near Threatened); brill *Scophathalmus rhombus* (*romb*; Near Threatened); black sea bream *Spondyliosoma cantharus* (*kantar*; Near Threatened); northern bluefin tuna *Thunnus thynnus* (*tunj*; Data Deficient); and **all forms of whitebait** – a generic term used for the juvenile fry of fish – because eating fish fry before maturity is detrimental to the sustainability of their species. The Adriatic sturgeon (*Acipenser naccarii*) is now Critically Endangered, and possibly Extinct.

Fish to eat, you'll be glad to know, include the ubiquitous sea bass (*brancin*) and gilthead sea bream (*orada*), as well as mackerel (*škomber* or *skuša*) and fresh sardines (*sardele*).

species of orchid, many classified as facing extinction and two of them endemic to southern Istria (*Serapias istriaca* and *Serapias x pulae*). The last recorded sighting in Croatia of the Critically Endangered **Mediterranean monk seal** (*Monachus monachus*), of which fewer than 700 individuals survive in the wild, was off the coast of Istria (for more information on this elusive species, see **w** monachus-guardian.org). It's also worth noting that within easy striking distance of Istria is the last Croatian stronghold of the griffon vulture, at Beli on the island of Cres.

The karst caves and subterranean rivers of Istria are home to a fascinating cave fauna, including the **olm** or cave salamander (*Proteus anguinus*), the distribution of which is limited to the karst landscapes of Slovenia, Croatia, northeast Italy and Bosnia (page 177).

ENVIRONMENTAL EFFORTS Croatia has taken steps to protect many of those species currently known to be under threat in the country, and has created Red Books specific to Croatia (an ongoing process). These are not yet all published, online or in English, but some can be found at **w** dzzp.hr. There are over 2,300 highly protected species in Croatia, meaning that they must not be deliberately

WHAT TO DO IF YOU SEE A DOLPHIN

Nine species of cetaceans (dolphins and whales) are known to visit the Adriatic, all of which are strictly protected in Croatia. Only the bottlenose dolphin lives in Adriatic waters, and they are often seen around Istria, especially in deeper waters. With increasingly frequent sightings, the State Institute for Nature Protection issued the following guidelines for conduct when encountering a dolphin or whale:

- Do not chase the dolphins or drive your boat directly towards them.
- If you wish to approach the dolphins, do it very slowly, keeping parallel to their course, and avoid sudden changes of direction or speed, which could confuse or disorientate them.
- It is better to give animals the choice of approaching you. The motor should be maintained in neutral or switched off.
- Do not make sudden noises, especially with the engine, as these could alarm the animals.
- Ensure that no more than one boat is within 100m of the dolphins, or three boats within 200m.
- Do not stay with the dolphins for more than 30 minutes.
- For your safety and theirs avoid diving or swimming with them, never offer them food or try to touch them.
- Leave the area, accelerating gradually when the boat is more than 100m from the animals.
- Do not throw litter overboard or leave it on the beach; plastic bags can accidentally be swallowed by the dolphins, causing their death.
- Any deliberate disturbance of dolphins or whales must be reported to the Directorate for Inspection of Nature Protection and the local police.
- Findings of injured, sick and dead animals must be reported on the emergency number (112).

disturbed, never mind killed. A further 800 or so are simply protected and may not be hunted or harvested without licence.

Istria has its fair share of nature reserves, which include the Učka Nature Park (page 137); Limski kanal (page 99), between Vrsar and Rovinj; Palud bird sanctuary (page 82), south of Rovinj; Brijuni Islands National Park (page 68), off the west coast; Rt Kamenjak (page 65), on the southern tip of Istria; and Sečovlje saltpans (page 169), Škocjanski Zatok nature reserve (page 159) and UNESCO-listed Škocjan Caves (page 170), all of which lie in Slovenia. The difference between a national park (*nacionalni park*, abbreviated np) and a nature park (*park prirode*, pp) in Croatia is mainly the level of protection it is accorded, with national park being the highest level of protection.

For more on protected fish species, see page 6.

Environmental contacts in Istria

HAOP (Ministry of Economy and Sustainable Development) Radnička cesta 80/7, Zagreb; 01 4886 840 ; e zavod@mongos.hr; w haop.hr. The central institute dealing with nature conservation in Croatia, now (strangely) altered & amalgamated from the former DZZP (State Institute for Nature Protection).

Natura Histrica Riva 8, Pula; 052 351 528; e info@natura-histrica.hr; w natura-histrica.hr. Founded in 1996 with the aim of protecting, maintaining & promoting protected areas in Istria.

Zelena Istra Gajeva 3, Pula; 052 506 065; w zelena-istra.hr. Zelena Istra (Green Istria) is a non-governmental, non-political & non-profit environmental organisation founded in 1995, with the aim of protecting the environment & natural resources.

HISTORY

FROM PREHISTORY TO THE ILLYRIANS Some 4,000–8,000 years ago, **Neolithic** man wandered through the wooded landscape of what is now the Istrian Peninsula. These early farmers and hunters tended flocks, and later began cultivating cereal crops. They left traces of their passing at several sites across Istria, in the form of pottery, stone flakes and polished stone tools – including Vižula near Medulin, and in caves such as Pupićina and Vela in Vela draga, a steep-sided valley in the Učka Mountains, near the inland entrance to the Učka tunnel. Evidence of much earlier human habitation has been found in the Sandalj Cave near Pula, dating back to the lower Palaeolithic, perhaps as early as one million years BC.

Istria takes its name from the **Histri**, an **Illyrian** tribe which inhabited the region in the centuries before the Roman conquest, from around 1000 BC. Another Illyrian tribe, the Liburni, also inhabited parts of the coast, while the Japodes inhabited the area inland to the northeast, including Trsat, above modern Rijeka.

ROMAN ISTRIA The **Romans** conquered Istria in 177bc – it took them two military campaigns – when they took the Illyrian settlement of **Vizače** (Roman Nesactium) at Valtura, near Pula's present-day airport, defeating the Histrian king Epulon (who, according to the Roman writer Tito Livio, stabbed himself and threw himself from the town walls rather than be captured alive). Following the Roman conquest, Roman settlements were established at Polentium (Pula), Parentium (Poreč), Tarsatica (Rijeka) and elsewhere (it took the Romans a further 150 years to defeat the Illyrian tribes further south in Dalmatia, which then became part of Roman Illyricum, with its capital at the old Illyrian stronghold of Salona, near Split). Istria became an important source of olive oil and wine for the Romans, as well as limestone and other resources; you can still see the remains of olive oil production and storage on Brijuni (page 68), and there's a permanent exhibition in the passages below Pula's 1st-century Roman amphitheatre (page 63).

BYZANTINE AND MEDIEVAL Following the collapse of the Roman Empire in AD 476, the Istrian Peninsula was successively overrun by the Visigoths, Huns and Ostrogoths, before **Byzantium** established control over the Istrian and Dalmatian coast in the 6th century, under the emperor Justinian I. It was during this period of reasonably extended peace that Bishop Euphrasius built the large basilica in Poreč named after him, the exquisite mosaics of which are listed as a UNESCO World Heritage Site. This peace was interrupted towards the end of the 6th century when the **Avars** swept into the region, causing widespread destruction (including, further south, sacking the former Roman capital of Dalmatia at Salona in AD 612), before Byzantium once again regained control. Also during the 6th and 7th centuries the **Slavs**, a people originally from an area north of the Black Sea, began migrating into the valleys of the Danube and the Sava, reaching the Adriatic by the early 7th century. Istria was taken by the **Lombards** in AD 751, before falling back into the hands of the Avars only some 25 years later, and was annexed by the Frankish ruler **Charlemagne** in AD 789, becoming (along with almost all of Dalmatia by AD 812) part of the **Carolingian Empire**.

The Franks initially attached Istria to the **Duchy of Friuli**, but from the end of the 8th century it became one of several marches or **margraviates**, established – along with Carniola (in what is now Slovenia) and Verona – as a frontier defence against attack or invasion of Frankish Italy from the northeast. Following the division of the Carolingian Empire Istria became part of the Middle Frankish Kingdom ruled by Lothair I, after which it was passed backwards and forwards between various Bavarian and Carinthian dukes and the Patriarchs of Aquileia.

Meanwhile, further south in Croatia during the 9th and 10th centuries, a series of increasingly powerful **Croatian dukes**, and then kings, succeeded in wresting control of a large part of what is now modern Croatia from Byzantine and Hungarian control, with Zvonimir (1075–89) having the title King of Croatia and Dalmatia conferred upon him by Pope Gregory VII. It was during this period of increasing autonomy that **Glagolitic** (the written form of Old Church Slavonic) was adopted instead of Latin (which much of the local population was unable to understand) by local priests. Croatia's brief 'golden age' was cut short in 1091, when **Hungary** invaded northern Croatia and installed a Hungarian *ban* or governor.

VENETIAN RULE In 1267 the increasingly powerful **Republic of Venice**, which had anyway already been in control of much of the peninsula's west coast since the 9th century, annexed Istria. Only a small area around **Pazin** remained part of the Duchy of Carniola, which in turn belonged to the Austrian House of Habsburg, and Austria also gained **Rijeka** in the 15th century.

A legal document has survived from 1275 (with some additions from the 14th century, which show that it was still used at that time), known as the ***Istrian Book of Boundaries*** (*Istarski razvod*). Originally written in Latin, German and Glagolitic (though only later transcripts of the Glagolitic version have survived), the document defines the borders between the different spheres of rulership in Istria at that time – the Patriarchate of Aquileia, the Principality of Pazin and the Republic of Venice.

Sometime between the 10th and 14th centuries, **Vlachs** (mercenaries and their families from what is now Transylvania and elsewhere) were settled in the northeastern part of Istria to defend the borders of Austria, and in the 17th century the **Uskoks** of Senj – famed pirates who had been the bane of both Ottoman and Venetian shipping in the Adriatic, in the pay of Austria – were settled here after being forcibly disbanded. During the 17th century outbreaks of **plague** devastated the population of Istria, with the town of Dvigrad being abandoned, and Pula reduced to a mere 300 inhabitants.

NAPOLEON AND AUSTRIA The Venetian Republic was extinguished with the arrival of **Napoleon** at the end of the 18th century, and in 1797 the Treaty of Campo Formio awarded Venice's Istrian territories to Austria – until 1805, when Napoleon's victory over Austria at Austerlitz resulted in Istria and Dalmatia being taken into his Illyrian Provinces. In 1815 Istria, along with the rest of Croatia, became part of Austria's Küstenland or Austrian Littoral, which included Trieste and the Kvarner Islands, and then Austria-Hungary, with the Istrian capital established at Poreč from 1861.

This period saw the Istrian coast, in particular the northeast around **Opatija**, develop into an extremely fashionable resort for the well-heeled Austrian elite – visitors included the composer Gustav Mahler, and the emperor Franz Joseph I himself, who purchased a villa in nearby Voloska for his mistress. Rijeka became the site of the Austro-Hungarian Naval Academy, and rail connections between Rijeka and Budapest and between Trieste and Vienna opened in the 1880s. On the west coast the formerly malarial swamps of the **Brijuni Islands** were transformed into a luxury health resort by wealthy businessman Paul Kupelweiser in the 1890s.

THE 20TH CENTURY After **World War I**, the Treaty of Rapallo (1920) gave Istria to the Kingdom of Italy, while Rijeka was annexed by the Italian poet Gabriele D'Annunzio, who set up his own, short-lived regency there, from 1919 to 1921. On 1 December 1918, partly in response to fears that Croatian territory would be bartered as part of the post-war settlement, the first communal Yugoslav state – the Kingdom of Serbs, Croats and Slovenes – was founded, later called the Kingdom of Yugoslavia. It was to last until 1941, although was never recognised by the Treaty of Versailles. Rijeka was formally handed to Italy with the Treaty of Rome (1924). During this period the border between Italy and the Kingdom of Serbs, Croats and Slovenes ran down the River Rječina in Rijeka (Italian Fiume).

The 1920s and 1930s and the rise of Italian **fascism** witnessed a policy of forced Italianisation in Istria, with the closure of a number of Croatian and Slovenian schools, a suppression of local language and culture, and the torching of the Narodni dom (People's House or Cultural House) in Pula and Trieste. In response, the militantly anti-fascist group Trst Istra Gorizia Reka (TIGR), considered one of the earliest anti-fascist movements in Europe, was established in Slovenia, and was active in Istria.

Following the outbreak of **World War II**, Italy annexed further parts of Croatia, establishing concentration camps (including one on the island of Rab), while the rest of Croatia and the Kingdom of Yugoslavia were occupied by Nazi Germany. Armed resistance was organised by the Partisans under Josip Broz Tito. The Italian surrender in 1943 and the defeat of Germany in 1945 were accompanied in Istria by reprisal killings and massacres, most notoriously the 'foibe massacres', in which the bodies of Italians were disposed of in karst sinkholes (*foiba* means 'sinkhole' in Italian) – a practice in fact perpetrated throughout the war to some degree or another by all sides, German, Partisan and Italian. In any case, between 1943 and 1954 a significant proportion of Istria's Italian population moved to Italy in several waves – through fear of persecution, economic uncertainty and with encouragement from both Italy and Yugoslavia. This **Istrian exodus** is estimated to have amounted to 230,000–350,000 people, a figure that includes Italians from both Istria (Croatia) and Slovenia, and a significant number of anti-communist Croats and Slovenes.

From 1945 Istria, along with the rest of Croatia, became part of Tito's **Federal Republic of Yugoslavia**, which endured for several years after Tito's death in 1980, until its bloody collapse in the early 1990s.

In May 1991 Croatia held a referendum, in which over 90% voted in favour of **Croatian independence**, which was formally declared on 25 June. In response, Serbs in the Krajina region of Croatia held their own referendum and voted to remain part of Yugoslavia. In June 1991 heavy fighting broke out in Krajina and eastern Slavonia, after which the Serb-dominated JNA (Yugoslav People's Army) increasingly intervened on its own authority in support of Serbian irregulars. In the three months following 25 June a quarter of Croatian territory fell to Serb militias and the JNA, and by December 1991 thousands of people had died in the fighting in Croatia, and more than half a million fled their homes. Unlike many other parts of Croatia, Istria emerged largely unscathed from the 1991–95 Homeland War (Croatian War of Independence).

Over the past two decades Croatia has seen tourism soar, a new network of motorways has been built and foreign property buying has boomed. Croatia achieved candidate status in its bid for EU membership in 2004, finally joining the EU on 1 July 2013.

GOVERNMENT AND POLITICS

Istria is one of Croatia's 20 counties or prefects. Known locally as *županija*, counties emerged as administrative districts only after the Homeland War ended in 1995. The county is headed by a *župan*, akin to a mayor (at the time of updating this guide in 2022, this was Boris Miletić, who assumed office in June 2021), but there is also a Regional Assembly, which in Istria's case comprises 45 councillors, including a president and two vice presidents, who serve a term of four years after being sworn in, in both Croatian and Italian. The Regional Assembly represents Istria's various government units – both towns (Buje, Buzet, Labin, Novigrad, Pazin, Poreč, Pula, Rovinj, Umag and Vodnjan) and municipalities – and performs various tasks within the region's jurisdiction, including adopting the regional budget. The Istrian Democratic Party (IDS) has been the strongest party by far for many years as the region has never been particularly nationalistic – around half of the councillors in the Regional Assembly are members of the IDS, while those belonging to Croatia's two main political parties, the Social Democrats (SDP) and Croatian Democratic Union (HDZ), number fewer than five each – although this picture does not necessarily translate into national politics, where in the 2020 Croatian parliamentary elections the IDS took only three seats in the Croatian parliament, compared with 66 for the HDZ and 41 for the Restart Coalition.

ECONOMY

If you think the Istrian economy is primarily about tourism, you wouldn't be entirely wrong. It gathers about a third of all the tourists in Croatia each year – in 2021 there were some 23.5 million overnight stays in Istria, of a total of 84.1 million across Croatia. Other industries are present, and unsurprisingly prominent among them is fishing – both commercial fishing in the open Mediterranean and also fish and mollusc farming close to shore. Istria also has a solid agricultural sector – as legions of vineyards and olive groves attest. Around 10% of Istria is covered with vineyards. Also unsurprisingly, shipbuilding leads Istria's production sector with Pula's Uljanik shipyard building several ocean-going vessels per year.

The entire Croatian economy suffered during the break-up of Yugoslavia, but overall Istria wasn't hit as hard as other regions that suffered both material damage and loss of economic activity. Unemployment in Istria in 2021 stood at 3.2% – over 50% less than the average unemployment rate across Croatia. Alongside tourism, road construction has been a key source of economic activity in Istria and elsewhere in Croatia as the government has built hundreds of miles of new highway in the past 20 years.

The Covid-19 pandemic had a huge impact on tourism in Croatia and the economy more widely, and Istria was no exception. However, Croatia has recovered relatively quickly in terms of tourism, with visitor numbers in 2022 almost up to the record levels seen in 2019.

PEOPLE

Vo se veživa za roge, a čovik za besidu (An ox is tied to his horns, man to his word)

Istrian proverb

The 2021 census shows the population of Istria to be 76.4% Croatian, 5.01% Italian, 2.96% Serbian, 2.48% Bosnian, 1.05% Albanian, 1% Slovenian, plus several other nationalities listed below 1%. It's worth pointing out that just because someone lists their nationality or ethnicity as Italian, for example, doesn't necessarily mean they consider themselves any less 'Istrian'. Before the end of World War II, the number of Italians living in Istria was much higher (page 11).

Istrians – whether of Croatian, Italian or other ethnicity, and whatever their mother tongue – are in the experience of both authors an incredibly warm, friendly and open people, justifiably proud of their peninsula's rich cultural heritage, superb wine and delicious cuisine. A testament to this is how often different ethnicities live side by side, and despite having gone through a period of fascism and an exodus in the first half of the last century, Istrians remain open-minded and forward-looking.

LANGUAGE

The official language in Istria is Croatian, though much of the population (particularly on the west coast) is bilingual, with Italian as a second language, attesting to centuries-long historical and cultural ties (according to the 2011 census, over 6.8% of the population in Istria described Italian as their mother tongue). The area with by far the highest proportion of people describing Italian as their first language is the municipality of Grožnjan – some 56% of the population in 2011 – followed by Brtonigla (39%), Buje (33%) and Oprtalj (28%). In contrast, the equivalent figure for the town of Rovinj – despite the fact that it's frequently seen as the most 'Italianate' place in Istria – is only around 10%.

Most Croatians in Istria – at least, those within the areas more frequented by tourists – speak excellent or at least reasonable English, so getting by without speaking any Croatian isn't usually a problem unless heading well off the beaten track, though you will undoubtedly get most out of your visit if you can learn a few words of Croatian. In addition, there is a small scattering of places where Istriot and Istro-Romanian are still

ISTRIA'S ENDANGERED LANGUAGES

Istriot, which has been variously classified as a sub-dialect of the Venetian language (see below) or an entirely separate Romance language, is spoken by fewer than 1,000 people (roughly 400 who speak it as a first language, plus another 400 who claim only to speak it as a second language) in just six towns in Istria: Vodnjan, Rovinj, Šišan, Bale, Fažana and Galižana. **Istro-Romanian** is an eastern Romance language, related to Romanian, which most probably owes its presence in the region to mercenaries and their families from what is now Transylvania (a people now more generally referred to as Vlachs, not only in Istria but also in several areas of southeast Europe), who were settled in the northeastern part of Istria sometime between the 10th and the 14th centuries to defend the borders of the Austrian Empire. It is now estimated to be understood or spoken by only around 300 people, in two small areas of Ćićarija and Učka, in particular the villages of Žejane and Šušnjevica (for more information, see w istro-romanian.com and w istro-romanian.net). **Venetian** is spoken by around two million people in and around the Veneto region of northern Italy, as well as in Istria and Slovenia. It is related to Vulgar Latin but was influenced by several other languages in the region, and attained the status of a lingua franca under the Republic of Venice. Both Istriot and Istro-Romanian are classified as severely endangered on the UNESCO list of endangered languages, Venetian as vulnerable.

spoken – both of them distinct local languages (sometimes referred to as languages, sometimes as dialects), now spoken by only a handful of people and in danger of becoming extinct – see page 13. Croatian belongs to the south Slavonic branch of the Indo-European family of languages, and is similar to, though not entirely the same as, Serbian and Bosnian. The relationship between Croatian and Serbian since the break-up of the former Yugoslavia, following almost 50 years of the two being amalgamated as Serbo-Croatian, is variously seen as similar to that between British and American English, or as that between two wholly separate and distinct languages, depending very much upon on one's particular point of view.

For more information on language, pronunciation and vocabulary, see page 217.

RELIGION

With close ties to Italy and the Austro-Hungarian Empire, Istria is of course Roman Catholic. In 1900 Istria had a population of 344,000, 99.6% of whom were Catholic, under the ecclesiastical jurisdiction of three bishops. Under communism and socialism, religion died down to a degree across the country, and the Catholic population of Istria is now around 75%. Church services are regular and welcome tourists. The service in the Euphrasian Basilica (page 93) is particularly popular. Less than 3.5% of Istria is Orthodox Christian.

There are around 5,000 practising Muslims in Istria according to the Medžlis Islamic community in Pula, and a smaller number of non-practising Muslims, making a total of just under 4.8% of the peninsula. The Medžlis Islamic community run prayer services in the Islamic community building (Medžlis islamske zajednice Pula; Leonardo da Vinci 11; 052 211 175; e medzlis@medzlis.org; w medzlis.org), not far from the Roman amphitheatre.

EDUCATION

Literacy in Istria is slightly higher than the average for Croatia, which is 99.8%. Compulsory education starts at age six or seven, and continues to the age of 18. Many schools teach Italian as a second language, and certainly on the coast most Istrians are bilingual Croatian/Italian, with many also speaking German.

Pula University (w unipu.hr) specialises in humanities, economics, tourism, music, educational science, Italian and marine science. The University of Rijeka (w uniri.hr) was founded in 1973 from the amalgamation of a number of other tertiary-education facilities in the area. It traces its earliest educational roots, however, to the 17th century when there was a Jesuit high school in Rijeka. The university specialises in science and technology. There are also polytechnics in Pula and Rijeka. The Ruđer Bošković Science Institute in Zagreb also has a branch in Rovinj, which, among other things, manages the Rovinj aquarium.

CULTURE

Istria's rich, multi-layered culture is apparent everywhere – the critical tools required to appreciate it are simply eyes and ears.

LITERATURE Among the most prominent figures in Istrian literature are the poet and novelist **Mate Balote** (1898–1963), who was born near Pula, and the poet and playwright **Drago Gervais** (1904–57), who was born in Opatija. You'll find busts of both men in Žminj (page 109), beside the *kula* (tower). The most popular literary association in Istria, however, is ***Veli Jože***, the story of a kind-hearted giant living near Motovun, written by the great Croatian poet and politician **Vladimir Nazor** in 1908.

Some parts of Istria, along with the nearby island of Krk, were centres of **Glagolitic** learning during the medieval period, and one of the most important Glagolitic inscriptions in Croatia was discovered at **Plomin**. Churches in Roč, Hum and elsewhere in the Istrian interior still bear traces of Glagolitic graffiti among their frescoes, and a series of sculptures inspired by letters of the Glagolitic alphabet can be found along the road between Roč and Hum (page 123).

Istria is also linked to the names of several foreign novelists, including the likes of **Jules Verne** (who set part of his novel *Mathius Sandorf* in Pazin Castle, Pazinska jama and the Limski kanal), **James Joyce** (who taught English in Pula for a short period, at which time he worked on some of the material which would later become his novel *Portrait of the Artist as a Young Man*) and **Dante Alighieri** (who visited Pazin and possibly based the entrance to Hell in his *Inferno* on Pazinska jama).

ART There are some beautiful and little-known medieval **frescoes** hidden away in the Istrian interior, many dating from the 15th century. You'll find them in churches in Roč, Hum, Draguć, Oprtalj and elsewhere (including over the Slovenian border at Hrastovlje) – though it is undoubtedly the *Dance of Death* scene at **Beram** that is the most striking (page 107), painted in 1474 by Vincent of Kastav. The churches are usually locked, but a local keyholder will be happy to come and let you look inside – see details of individual churches in *Chapter 6*.

Istria has some superb Roman and Byzantine **mosaics**, including a large and mostly intact Roman floor mosaic in Pula illustrating the *Punishment of Dirce* (page 60), and of course the magnificent Byzantine mosaics at Poreč (page 93), the latter on a par with the Byzantine mosaics at Ravenna and in the Hagia Sofia in Istanbul.

The work of **Dušan Džamonja** (1928–2009), one of the best-known sculptors of the former Yugoslavia, can be seen in a sculpture park at **Vrsar** (page 98), where Džamonja had a house. Vrsar had a strong influence on another contemporary Croatian artist, **Edo Murtić** (1921–2005), who spent much of his time there and included its landscapes in a number of his paintings. In **Brtonigla**, there's a gallery dedicated to the work of Zagreb-born sculptor and painter **Aleksandar Rukavina** (1934–85), who lived in Istria from the 1970s. The sculptures of the so-called **Glagolitic Alley** between Roč and Hum are the work of Croatian sculptor **Želimir Janeš** (1916–96).

If you're in Rovinj on the second weekend of August there's a big outdoor art fair on Grisia Street, when local artists exhibit and sell their work, and in September Grožnjan holds an art festival, Extempore (page 116).

MUSEUMS AND GALLERIES Istria does not contain the phenomenal concentration of museums and galleries you'll find in the Croatian capital, Zagreb, but it does have several important collections.

To see the most extensive collection of Istria's prehistoric and Roman past, you should visit the **Istria Archaeological Museum** in Pula (w ami-pula.hr; page 62). The **Pazin Museum** (w central-istria.com) and the **Ethnographic Museum of Istria** (w emi.hr), both housed in Pazin Castle (page 106), are also well worth visiting. Other museums and galleries include the **Maritime and Historical Museum** (w ppmhp.hr) and the new **Sugar Palace** (part of the Rijeka City Museum; w muzej-rijeka.hr), both in Rijeka (page 148), the **Magical World of Shells** in

Piran (**w** svet-skoljk.si; page 166), the **Istrian Museum of Contemporary Art** in Pula, the **Aleksandar Rukavina Memorial Gallery** in Brtonigla, the **Naval Museum** in Novigrad (page 96), the **Batana Boat Museum** in Rovinj (page 79) and the **Museum Olei Histriae** in Pula (page 62).

ARCHITECTURE Istria's architectural heritage belies its historical ties with Venice, while at the same time evoking its periods of Roman, Byzantine and Austro-Hungarian rule – together with some distinctively Istrian elements.

Rovinj is perhaps the most familiar symbol of the area's **Venetian** past, with its Renaissance and Baroque palaces and narrow, cobbled streets. Less well known but equally evocative are the small towns of Sveti Lovreč and Svetvinčenat, with their clear medieval street patterns and Venetian loggias.

Roman remains in Istria (or anywhere else in Croatia for that matter) don't get much more impressive than the 1st-century **amphitheatre** in **Pula** (page 63), one of the six largest Roman amphitheatres in the world. Many of the region's Roman

ISTRIA'S LIGHTHOUSES

Istria has nine lighthouses. Eight were built during the 19th century and remain active. Three have accommodation available (**w** lighthouses-croatia.com; see page 97 for the accommodation at Savudrija).

The very first lighthouse was built by the Venetians in 1403 on the island of St Nicholas just off Poreč. At 15m high, it originally just burned a fire at the top to warn passing ships of the rocks below. Later, in the 17th century, the fire was replaced by a lantern which required less tending and was not so susceptible to the wind. The lighthouse was abandoned at the end of the 18th century, but was restored in 2014.

The first of the currently active lighthouses is at Rt Savudrija. At 29m high, it was officially opened by Emperor Francis I of Austria in 1818. It was also the first lighthouse in the world to be powered from coal and was financed by the Trieste Stock Exchange.

The next to be built was the lighthouse at Porer, a small islet south of Rt Kamenjak. It is the southernmost of all Istria's lighthouses, and at 35m high it is also the tallest.

St John's lighthouse, built in 1853, is on the outermost of Rovinj's archipelago of 13 islands. It is 23m high, with an octagonal tower, and is permanently staffed because it has no electricity supply from the mainland grid and relies instead on a generator.

Next, the lighthouse at Rt Zub (Cape Tooth) on the mouth of the River Mirna was built in 1872. It is more like a traditional stone house than a lighthouse, but on one corner facing the sea is the light. The following year, Istria's shortest lighthouse, at 5m tall, was built at Rt Crna south of the village of Skitača near Labin.

In 1877, the southernmost tip of Veliki Brijun Island gained its own lighthouse atop a two-storey building; another was built in the same year south of Pula at Rt Verudica opposite the island of Veruda. Both these lighthouses now run on electricity and are automated, so do not need to be permanently manned.

Istria's last lighthouse was completed in 1880. Named Marlera lighthouse, it is on Punta Grkova on the eastern side of Medulin.

remains are now held in the Archaeological Museum in Pula. Istria's – and Croatia's – finest **Byzantine** remains are in Poreč, where the dazzling 6th-century mosaics of the **Euphrasian Basilica** (page 93) are a UNESCO World Heritage Site. Smaller Byzantine monuments include the 6th-century Chapel of St Mary Formosa in Pula. In **Opatija** (page 125) and **Rijeka** (page 139), you'll find some wonderfully opulent **Secessionist** architecture, which hints at this part of Istria's former Austro-Hungarian grandeur.

Istria has some impressive **castles**, in particular **Pazin Castle** (which sits perched on the edge of a dramatic gorge; page 106), **Trsat Castle** in Rijeka (page 150), and the surprisingly large **Grimaldi Castle** at Svetvinčenat (page 110), while just over the border in Slovenia the iconic **Predjama Castle** (page 178) is built into an overhanging cliff. On a smaller scale but no less impregnable in appearance are the stout towers or ***kula*** that can still be found in some towns, sometimes as remnants or more extensive fortifications – there is a good example in **Žminj** (page 109).

Although the slender bell towers of Rovinj's St Euphemia Cathedral and Vodnjan's St Blaise Church might seem transplanted from the Piazza San Marco (St Mark's Square) in Venice, there are many smaller **churches** in the region that remain distinctively Istrian. The square, simple porch and single bell of these churches will soon become familiar to anyone who goes in search of frescoes in the Istrian interior.

Out in the countryside of central Istria, along with plenty of stone farmhouses, you might see ***kažuni*** – small, circular stone huts with a conical roof, which are built, like the drystone walls (***suhozid***) in the fields around them, without any mortar. These humble but beautifully constructed *kažuni* – just as much as 'Venetian' Rovinj or 'Roman' Pula – have become more or less emblematic of Istria.

MUSIC AND DANCE Istrian **folk music** is based on a distinctive six-tone musical scale (the so-called Istrian scale), and the peninsula's two-part, slightly nasal **singing** – sometimes with words replaced by emphatic syllables such as *ta-na-na* (a widespread variation known as *tarankanje*) – is inscribed on the UNESCO List of Intangible Cultural Heritage. Traditional **instruments** include the *roženice* (a woodwind instrument, similar to an oboe) and the *mih* (a type of large bagpipe made from a goat's skin). There are a number of traditional Istrian **folk dances**, the best known being the ***balun***, in which several couples dance in a circle while executing different steps and twirls.

The Istrian scale was first recognised and studied by the Lovran-born composer **Ivan Matetić Ronjgov** (1880–1960), who went on to write music in the style of local folk music. One of the biggest names in Istrian music these days is musician and ethno-musicologist **Dario Marušić** (w dariomarusic.com), whose clean, sometimes jazz-infused musings on Istrian folk music have earned him great critical acclaim.

A good opportunity to catch performances of local folk music is in Pazin, when **TradInEtno** run concerts and workshops during the summer months (page 104). Istria also hosts several international **music festivals**, including an outstanding jazz festival in Opatija and several large festivals in Pula (page 58).

2

Practical Information

WHEN TO VISIT

The best times to visit Istria are undoubtedly spring and autumn: it's warm during the day, cool in the evening and the madding crowds of summer are absent. It's sunny almost all year round, and even the winter sun brings warmth. Even in winter, cafés often have outside terraces open for customers to benefit from the sun's rays (and for smokers since smoking inside was banned – although, in winter, you might just find everybody smokes inside). T-shirt weather – at least during the main part of the day – can start as early as March and go into October. Cyclists wanting to take advantage of the lack of people on the roads combined with beautiful sunny days often come as early as February and as late as November. July and August are hot – usually over 30°C – and very busy with tourists (at least along the coast), but for those with families, this is of course the only time they can take their summer holidays.

If you're looking for particular festivals, see page 39.

HIGHLIGHTS

FOOD AND WINE Oh, where to start? From superb **seafood** on the coast to the famed **truffle** dishes of inland Istria (especially around Buzet and Motovun), excellent local ***pršut*** (dry-cured ham) and delicious homemade pasta – it's worth coming to Istria just to eat. Istria also produces some of the best **wine** in Croatia – in particular its signature white, **Malvazija**, though the red **Teran** is also pretty good – and its superb **olive oil** is winning an increasing number of international accolades.

See page 33 for more on food and wine in Istria.

CULTURAL AND ARCHITECTURAL For many, **Rovinj** (page 71) is one of the highlights of Istria. Its medieval old town – once an island – shows off its Venetian heritage among steep, narrow cobbled streets and the largest replica of Venice's St Mark's campanile. **Koper** (page 154) and **Piran** (page 162), in Slovenia, actually display a grander Venetian style and are well worth a day trip. Equally impressive is Istria's UNESCO World Heritage Site, the 6th-century Euphrasian Basilica and mosaics in **Poreč** (page 93). **Pula** is home to a magnificent and very well-preserved amphitheatre (page 63), and unlike some other towns on the coast remains a vibrant, busy city throughout the year – while the medieval hill towns of the Istrian interior (page 101) offer a completely different picture of Istria, dotted with churches and little-known frescoes.

COASTLINE While Istria has few sandy beaches, it has a lot of coastline for a small place, and almost everyone goes there for its crystal-clear waters. Sometimes wrecks at 20m can be seen from the surface. Some of the best beaches and coastline to enjoy are along the 12km **coastal walk** from the spa town Opatija beneath the mass of the Učka Mountains to Lovran (page 130), and the beaches in **Rt Kamenjak** coastal reserve (page 65).

INLAND The **hill towns** and villages of the Istrian interior – Motovun, Buzet, Draguć, Hum and others – should not be missed, and remain beautifully unspoilt. There are hidden frescoes at Beram, Roč and Hum, and the area around Buzet and the Mirna Valley is renowned for its **truffles.** In Slovenia don't miss the opportunity to see the phenomenal underground world of stalagmites and stalactites at the **Postojna Cave** (page 176).

OUTDOOR Istria has some wonderful **cycling** opportunities (page 196), with extremely little traffic in spring and autumn for those wanting to ride on the roads. Off-road tracks, including old Roman roads and the Parenzana (page 117) are simply delightful, and a good introduction for younger members of the family. There are some great **hiking** trails on the Učka and Ćićarija mountains (page 187) as well as elsewhere, and several exceptional **climbing** areas including Raspadalica (page 122), and paragliding and balloon flights.

WILDLIFE The **Brijuni Islands** (page 68) are a national park, and the former summer residence of Yugoslavia's former president Tito (complete with safari park), while the **Učka Mountains** (page 137) are a natural park. **Rt Kamenjak** (page 65) has an astonishing flora including several rare or endemic orchids, as well as numerous butterfly species, and you can often see **dolphins** off the Istrian coast or even in the Limski kanal. Both **Učka** and the **Ćićarija** mountains offer a good chance of seeing wildlife, from deer to raptors. **Sečovlje saltpans** (page 169) in Slovenia is a haven for birds (and for ornithologists) and holds the region's only Salt Museum.

DIVE Wreck diving is a real highlight of Istria with some wrecks as low as 28m, well within recreational diving capabilities for advanced open-water divers, and some of the larger wrecks at technical diving depths. Moreover, marine life is varied, making this a great place for expanding your diving experience (page 205).

SUGGESTED ITINERARIES

ONE OR TWO DAYS Rovinj, to see this old Venetian-era town – which was once an island – with its replica of Venice's St Mark's campanile, and/or Pula with its extremely well-preserved Roman amphitheatre. If you have your own transport you could even take a quick spin into the Istrian interior for half a day to visit the medieval hill town of Motovun.

ONE WEEK Rovinj, Pula, Poreč, Motovun and Buzet, plus a visit to one of the nature reserves or national/nature parks, such as the Brijuni Islands (Tito's former summer residence) or Rt Kamenjak, and finally maybe a hike up to Vojak on Mount Učka if you're not too busy sunbathing and swimming on the local beach. Make a trip over the border to Piran on the Slovenian coast. Take a boat trip to one of the islands, or to the Limski kanal, or to see Rovinj by night.

TWO WEEKS As above, plus a longer trip to the Slovenian coast, especially Piran, along with Postojna and Škocjan Caves and/or Lipica Stud Farm, and the Vipava

Valley. More time can be spent in central Istria to discover the best of Istria's vineyards, and bike the Parenzana old railway line. Go scuba-diving at one of the many dive centres if you have Istria's wrecks high on your list of things to do; or indulge in some of the best spas in Europe – eg: those at Lone Hotel in Rovinj or Kempinski Palace in Portorož, or Hotel Kaštel in Motovun. Take in some of the concerts and festivals of which there will be many over the summer: check on w istra.hr/en/attractions-and-activities/events, and at the local tourist office as soon as you arrive.

THREE WEEKS TO A MONTH If you've got this much time to spend in Istria (lucky you), then you're bound to want to make the most of the sea, and probably to travel a little further afield along the Dalmatian coast and into the rest of Croatia, and perhaps to take a day trip to Venice. The Bradt guide to Croatia (page 231) offers more for further afield, and for hikers there are two pertinent guides, *Islands of Croatia* and *Walks and Treks in Croatia* by Rudolf Abraham (page 231). All the main towns on the west coast have ferries to Venice during the summer (see individual towns for more information) and every ferry company provides plenty of information about Venice on the 2½-hour journey.

TOUR OPERATORS

ISTRIAN TRAVEL AGENTS AND TOUR GUIDES

In addition to the following selection of local travel agents, most hotels will be able to offer a variety of excursions.

Istra Line Partizanska 4, Poreč; ☎052 427 062; e info@istraline.hr; w istraline.hr. Offers accommodation bookings.
Istriana Travel Vrh 28, Vrh nr Buzet; m 091 541 2099; e istrianatravel@gmail.com; w toursistria.com. Agency based in the village of Vrh offering truffle hunts, fresco workshops & various excursions.
Marco Polo Tours Ivana Mažuranića 21, Rovinj; e info@marcopolo.hr; w marcopolo.hr. Offers excursions, transfers & accommodation booking in Istria (& the rest of Croatia), Slovenia & elsewhere.
Montona Tours Kanal 10, Motovun; ☎052 681 970; e info@montonatours.com; w montonatours.com. Offers a range of private accommodation.
Paragliding Tandem Istria e info@istraparagliding.com; w istraparagliding.com. Offers paragliding tandem flights from €100 pp for a 15–20min flight.
Tour Istra Tržni centar Katoro bb, Umag; ☎052 741 808; e info@touristra.hr; w touristra.hr. Specialises in accommodation throughout Istria.

CROATIAN TOUR OPERATORS AND TOUR GUIDES

Croatian Culinary Tours e info@culinary-croatia.com; w culinary-croatia.com. Zagreb-based agency offering culinary tours throughout Croatia, including Istria & the Kvarner.
Zagreb Tours ☎01 482 5035; e info@zagrebtours.com; w zagrebtours.com. Zagreb-based operator offering a 5-day Istria tour, & others that include Istria in the itinerary.

UK OPERATORS

Balkan Holidays ☎020 7543 5555; w balkanholidays.co.uk. Long-standing southeast Europe specialist offering a number of itineraries in Istria.
Completely Croatia ☎0800 970 9149; w completelycroatia.co.uk. Offers 1-week breaks in Istria.
Croatia Gems ☎0117 409 0850; w croatiagems.co.uk. Hand-picked villas, rooms & apartments, including Istria.
Croatian Villas ☎020 8888 6655; w croatianvillas.com. Apartments & villas in Istria & elsewhere in Croatia.
Freedom Treks ☎01273 224066; w freedomtreks.co.uk. Hiking, cycling & sailing tours in Croatia including an Istrian coast bike tour.

Headwater ☎ 01606 218846; **w** headwater.com. Offers a 1-week cycling tour in Istria & a 'castles to coast' walk.
Leger Holidays ☎ 01709 787463; **w** leger.co.uk. Offering tours of Poreč & the Istrian Riviera & Rovinj for singles.
Sunvil ☎ 0208 568 4499; **w** sunvil.co.uk. Sunvil offers short & longer stays in Istria, combining the inland valleys with a seaside escape.

US OPERATORS

Adriatic Tours ☎ +1 310 548 1446; **w** adriatictours.com. Offers escorted tours, pilgrimages & cruises, sometimes including Istria.
Friendly Planet Travel ☎ +1 800 555 5765; **w** friendlyplanet.com. Offers a 10-day Croatia package including Istria.

TOURIST INFORMATION

The **Istrian Tourist Board** (**w** istra.hr) has made an enormous and highly successful effort to promote the region, with a wealth of information available online as well as in local tourist information offices. In fact it would be pretty safe to say that no other region in Croatia has so much practical, accessible and useful information available online to the potential visitor – from detailed cycling routes with maps (**w** istria-bike.com) to food and wine (**w** istria-gourmet.com). Further information is available online from local tourist board websites (see individual chapters and page 232) and the **Croatian National Tourist Board** (**w** croatia.hr), as well as from offices in Istria's main towns and tourist centres, where you will be able to pick up local or town maps, find out more on what the town or region has to offer, and (usually) book accommodation. The **Taste Slovenia** website has plenty of information on Slovenian food and wine (**w** tasteslovenia.si/en), and there's further useful information on the main **Slovenian Tourist Board** website (**w** slovenia.info). Excellent English is spoken in every local tourist office we have visited. For other useful websites, see page 232.

Town **maps** are available free at local tourist information centres (and most hotels and other accommodation will have them available as well), usually along with regional maps, sometimes with hiking and cycling routes marked, and the excellent Istria Bike (**w** istria-bike.com) maps. There's also a useful foldout map of Croatia, which is free. Larger Istria maps can be bought in bookshops, or before you travel through the excellent The Map Shop (**w** themapshop.co.uk) or Stanfords (**w** stanfords.co.uk). These include *Kompass: Istria* (1:75,000) and *Freytag & Berndt: Istrian Peninsula & Pula* (1:100,000).

For information on hiking maps, see page 186.

RED TAPE

PASSPORTS/VISAS Nationals of EU countries do not need a visa to stay in Croatia and Slovenia, and will merely need to show a valid form of identification such as a passport or an ID card. Happily, the same rules apply for UK nationals despite the country's exit from the EU, although documentation requirements may change, so do check before travelling. Most nationals of other countries may visit Croatia and Slovenia for up to three months within a six-month period starting from the first day of entry. You can easily essentially extend this to six months by popping over the border into a non-EU neighbouring country (such as Serbia or Bosnia) for a day or two, then returning to Croatia, where you will be entitled to stay for another three months. If you want to stay for longer, you'll need to apply for a temporary residence permit (*privremeni borovak*) at the Croatian embassy in your home country. This is supposed to take up to 12 weeks, but don't be surprised if it takes longer. As of 2021, Croatia has also offered digital nomad permits for non-

EU nationals, which are effectively a form of residency permit for a period of up to one year, after which you must leave the country for at least six months before applying for a new one (**w** mup.gov.hr/aliens-281621/stay-and-work/temporary-stay-of-digital-nomads/286833). Full details of who does and doesn't need a visa for Croatia, as well as up-to-date addresses and phone numbers of all the Croatia diplomatic missions worldwide – and foreign diplomatic missions in Croatia – can be found on the Ministry of Foreign and European Affairs' website (**w** mvep.gov.hr).

Make sure you keep your passport with you at all times, as the failure to produce an identity document to a police officer can incur a fine or imprisonment (although, given that Croatia is quite used to tourists and you conceivably might have left your travel documents at a hotel reception, this is unlikely to happen).

REGISTRATION The *Law on Aliens* governs the stay of foreigners in the country. It is essentially based on the old Yugoslav law and is similar in all the former Yugoslav republics. Under Article 150 a foreigner must be registered with the police at the latest within 48 hours of arriving in Croatia. If you are staying in a hotel or other licensed accommodation (including licensed private accommodation and campsites), then the hotelier or owner will do this for you and must register you within 24 hours of your arrival at the hotel. The hotel will fill out the necessary *potvrda* (certificate) for you and you need do nothing except provide your passport for your identification details. You are entitled to keep your section of the *potvrda* (normally returned with your passport at the end of your stay) and it is advisable to make sure you keep your copy, because if you can't prove your official registration for any part of your stay in Croatia then you could be subject to deportation and a restriction on your return to Croatia.

If you are staying in private accommodation, with friends or in your own home bought in Croatia, then your host must register you within 24 hours of arrival at the accommodation. Your host should register your details at the nearest tourist office if there is one in the local town, or at the nearest police station. There is a sliding scale of tourism tax per day ranging from €1.10 to €1.60 depending on the time of year. This is included in your accommodation costs if you are renting.

Foreign homeowners in Croatia staying in their own home (*korisčenje nekretnine*) are exempt from the tourist tax outside the peak tourism season (15 June–15 September) and pay a reduced tourist tax during the peak tourism season. If as a homeowner you will be using your property a lot during the summer season, you can pay a reduced lump sum for the entire period, saving you the hassle of going in and out of the tourist office. This will register you in the country for 90 days, however, and you will then not be able to return for a further three months. You will need to bring proof of your ownership of the property in order to qualify for home ownership exemptions/reductions to the tourist tax.

In case you first read this section while waiting for a delayed bus after you've already been in Croatia a while and, therefore, have not yet registered, you'll find that most unregistered tourists will probably get away with just a discretionary warning. Application of the law is likely to be much stricter, however, if it is evident someone has been deliberately avoiding registration. The *Law on Aliens* and a summary of useful information is available at the Ministry of Interior's website (**w** mup.gov.hr).

EMBASSIES

CROATIAN DIPLOMATIC MISSIONS ABROAD There is a useful list of contact details for Croatian diplomatic missions abroad at **w** mvep.gov.hr/en – click 'Embassies and Consulates'.

FOREIGN DIPLOMATIC MISSIONS IN CROATIA Most English-speaking countries have embassies or consulates in the capital, Zagreb, while the UK also has consulates in Dubrovnik and Split. For a comprehensive click-through list of all embassies and consulates in the Croatian capital, go to **w** zagreb-touristinfo.hr, and select 'Diplomatic Representatives' from 'Other Information' which is under 'Travel Plan' in the menu, or see **w** mvep.gov.hr/en and click 'Embassies and Consulates'.

GETTING THERE AND AWAY

BY AIR Istria has one international airport, at Pula, or, more accurately, 7km northeast of Pula near the village of Valtura (Valtursko polje 210; ☎ 052 550 926; **w** airport-pula.hr). Airlines operating flights to and from Pula airport include:

British Airways **w** britishairways.com. Operates flights from Pula to London Heathrow twice weekly during the summer.
Croatia Airlines **w** croatiaairlines.com. Operates daily flights from Pula via Zagreb to London Heathrow & Gatwick, as well as to several other European cities.
easyJet **w** easyjet.com. Operates flights from Pula to London Gatwick, Luton, Glasgow & Bristol as well as Paris, Berlin & other airports.
Norwegian **w** norwegian.no. Seasonal flights from Pula to Oslo Gardermoen & several other European airports.
Ryanair **w** ryanair.com. Runs direct flights from London Stansted to Pula.

Getting to and from Pula airport

A **shuttle bus** departs Pula's bus station for the airport (for timetables see **w** airport-pula.hr/en/passenger-info/shuttle-bus/). Tickets cost €6.10. **Taxi** drivers usually mill around the exit of the arrivals area, and will charge around €20 for the journey into Pula. There are also car-hire offices in the arrivals area.

Other airports

Rijeka also has an international airport (**w** rijeka-airport.hr), though it's actually on the island of Krk so is less convenient for Istria. Croatia Airlines and Ryanair operate routes from Rijeka. A shuttle bus connects the airport with Rijeka and Opatija (for timetables, see **w** rijeka-airport.hr/en/bus).

Croatia's other main airports include Zagreb, Zadar, Split and Dubrovnik, the most convenient of which as a staging post for Istria is **Zagreb** (**w** zagreb-airport.hr), from which Croatia Airlines has flights to destinations throughout Europe including London, Paris, Frankfurt, Munich and Amsterdam, and British Airways (**w** britishairways.com) also operates flights to London. From Zagreb's main bus station (**w** akz.hr) there are fast bus services to Rijeka, Pula, Poreč, Rovinj, Pazin, Buzet and elsewhere in Istria, and trains to Rijeka. Over the border in Slovenia, easyJet (**w** easyjet.com) and Wizz Air (**w** wizzair.com) are among the airlines operating flights from **Ljubljana** (**w** lju-airport.si) to the UK and Europe. From Ljubljana there are bus services to Istria and during the summer months a fast train from Maribor to Pula. Ryanair (**w** ryanair.com) and other airlines operate direct flights from the UK to **Trieste** (**w** aeroporto.fvg.it), just over the border in Italy and easily reached from Istria or the Slovenian Adriatic coast either by bus or boat (page 24).

BY TRAIN Rijeka is easily reached by train from Zagreb, as is Koper from Ljubljana. Pula can also be reached by train from Ljubljana, with a change at Hrpelje-Kozina. There are around five trains a day from Ljubljana to Koper (journey time 2½ hours), via Postojna and Hrpelje-Kozina, with some sections having been replaced by bus transfers for several years now; likewise from Buzet to Divača public transport is currently limited to a fairly spartan bus service (one service daily, journey time around 1hr). The fastest service from Ljubljana to Koper, the IC 503, departs at 09.00, arriving at 11.28. The train has ample cargo space for bicycles and its most up-to-date timetable can be found at w potniski.sz.si/en.

Direct trains between Zagreb and Rijeka were reduced to one service a day at the time of writing (journey time at least 4½hrs) due to work on some sections of the line, with other trains requiring a change at Ogulin – check current timetables at w hzpp.hr/en. Unless you're on the direct train, taking the bus is definitely a better choice. From Rijeka it's possible to take a bus which connects with the train in Lupoglava, either towards Pula or Buzet; however, this is fairly impractical, and you'd be better off simply getting a direct bus from Rijeka to Pula to start with. For train times in Croatia see w hzpp.hr/en, and for international destinations check at Deutsche Bahn (w bahn.com).

Travelling from the UK to Croatia by rail is easier than you might expect. The fastest route is by Eurostar to Paris, followed by a TGV to Stuttgart, then either the 'Lisinski' overnight sleeper train to Zagreb, or the overnight sleeper from Stuttgart to Rijeka. Booking is easiest through w thetrainline.com or through Deutsche Bahn (w bahn.com) which gives the option of including a 24-hour stopover along the route, and of course you won't have any baggage fees to add to the fare. The most useful website for information on train travel within Europe is the excellent w seat61.com.

If you're travelling across Europe by train and including a visit to Istria or elsewhere in Croatia, an **InterRail pass** could be the way to go (w interrail.eu). InterRail **multi-country passes** are valid in up to 30 countries in Europe (including Croatia) and are available for five days' travel within a ten-day period, ten days' travel within a period of 22 days and other variations. InterRail passes, once a privilege of those under the age of 26, are now available for all ages. In addition to the price of the pass, you'll need to pay for seat reservations on most international trains. A **one-country pass** for Croatia is also available, valid for three, four, six or eight days' travel within one month – though this won't save you any money if you're only visiting Istria, and train tickets are cheap within Croatia anyway.

BY BUS The Istrian coast is well connected to the rest of Croatia and several international destinations by bus. Pula has buses to Trieste, Ljubljana, Belgrade and Frankfurt, while Rovinj and Poreč have services to Trieste, Ljubljana and Belgrade. Rijeka has international services to Trieste, Ljubljana and Munich, and is well connected to most places in Istria by bus. If you're travelling from Zagreb by bus try to get one of the direct services, as these have only a couple of scheduled stops and are quite a bit faster – for example Zagreb–Pazin or Zagreb–Rovinj. For bus routes and timetables, see w akz.hr, w arriva.com.hr/en-us/home and w brioni.hr/en-gb.

BY BOAT During the summer, international ferry routes operate between both Trieste and Venice in Italy, and Poreč, Rovinj and Pula in Istria, as well as to Piran in Slovenia, making it quite possible to ferry-hop between several towns on the coast. **Liberty Lines** (w *libertylines.it/en*) sails from Trieste to Rovinj via Poreč. **Venezia Lines** (w *venezialines.com*) sails between Venice and Pula, via Rovinj via Poreč, and to Piran in Slovenia. **Adriatic Lines** (w *adriatic-lines.com*) sails from Venice to Pula, Poreč, Rovinj and Umag. **Jadrolinija** (w *jadrolinija.hr*) has sailings from Rijeka to the islands of Cres and Rab, and from Brestova to Porozina (Cres).

BY CAR Istria is easy to reach by car. For those flying in, or arriving by boat, major car-rental companies such as Europcar, Budget and Sixt are available at the main airports serving onward travel to Istria. These also allow you to pick up in one country and drop off in another if you wish (at a cost). See page 26 for the specifics of driving in Istria.

The Učka tunnel near Rijeka can sometimes see tailbacks, but rarely – although current work on a second tunnel, which is expected to continue until at least September 2023, means that traffic is stopped several times a day for 20 minutes or so while drilling takes place. What is more common is the closure of certain high bridges, especially when the *bura* (page 4) blows. These closures are announced in several languages, including English, on the radio stations HRT1 and HRT2.

HEALTH *With Dr Felicity Nicholson*

Istria has reasonable health services and some good private doctors. There is a hyperbaric chamber for diving-related accidents at Pula (page 207). All the major towns have some hospital services, with Pula being the main hospital for Istria (page 59). Larger facilities are available in Rijeka (page 146), with the country's best services of course in Zagreb. From Slovenia, the best services are in Ljubljana. Croatia already has very good public health services for tourists, which are available at most hospitals. Travellers from the EU and Switzerland can use their EHIC to access free or discounted public health care in Croatia – UK nationals currently need to show their passports along with their GHIC or EHIC card to access free emergency treatment in a hospital. Private health care is not included, nor is the cost of repatriation or routine monitoring of pre-existing conditions, therefore additional health insurance is still strongly recommended.

MOSQUITOES These are prevalent in Istria from April to November, and in the height of summer they'll get busy as early as midday. However, there is no risk of malaria. Istria has particularly vicious tiger mosquitoes, which are black-and-white striped, so ensure any repellent you buy is good for repelling this kind of mosquito. Mosquito-repellent creams, sprays, smoke coils and electric plug-in repellents are ubiquitous, and usually state if they are good for tiger mosquitoes, sometimes by showing a drawing of a black-and-white striped mosquito. If you prefer the wristbands or solar sonic repellents, you'll need to bring these from home (but they might not be so effective against the tiger mosquito). Natural repellents such as Citronella are not as easy to find in Istria and are best brought from home (though they may be less effective against tiger mosquitoes).

FIRST-AID KIT As with any travels away from your medicine cabinet at home, it's good to have a small first-aid pack with you. You can buy these ready made from any good pharmacy at home, such as Boots in the UK, or Walgreens in the US, or you can just make up a small kit yourself from the following items: plasters/Band-Aids; painkillers (eg: aspirin, paracetamol or Tylenol); lipsalve; sunscreen; antiseptic cream (or diluted tea-tree oil); mosquito-bite cream; spare contact lenses if relevant; and a small sewing kit.

VACCINATIONS There are no compulsory vaccinations for Croatia, and as of July 2022 it is no longer necessary to present an EU digital Covid certificate to enter the country (any updates can be found on **w** mup.gov.hr/en). You should be up to date with tetanus, diphtheria and polio, which comes as the all-in-one vaccine Revaxis

TICK REMOVAL

As elsewhere in Europe, ticks are present in Croatian forests, particularly during late spring and summer, and tick bites carry the risk of infection – including Lyme disease and European tick-borne encephalitis. Not all ticks carry the bacteria leading to these diseases, and a bite will not necessarily lead to infection; however, if you do find a tick attached to you, it should be removed as soon as possible, as leaving it on the body increases the chance of infection. Ticks should be removed with special tick tweezers that can be bought in good travel shops (the O'Tom Tick Twister is widely available or can be ordered from w otom.com/en), which you twist gently at a right angle to your skin – the tick will come away completely as long as you do not jerk or twist it. If possible, douse the wound with alcohol (any spirit will do) or iodine. Do *not* try to pull at the tick's abdomen as this will crush it, causing it to regurgitate and therefore increase the risk of infection. Likewise irritants (such as Olbas oil) or lit cigarettes should *not* be used to try and dislodge them. It is best to get a travelling companion to check you for ticks and if you are travelling with small children remember to check their heads, and particularly behind the ears. An area of spreading redness around the bite site, or a rash or fever coming on a few days or more after the bite, would require a trip to the doctor. For more information, see w masta.org/tickalert.

and lasts for ten years. Hepatitis A vaccine may be recommended for travellers with underlying medical conditions such as chronic liver disease or haemophilia.

While Croatia is classed as a high-risk country for rabies, Istria – like northeast Italy – will probably be low risk. Nevertheless, a rabies vaccination may be recommended for all travellers, particularly for longer trips. Rabies is spread through the saliva of an infected animal, usually through a bite or scratch. It can be carried by any warm-blooded mammal though dogs and related species and bats are the most likely carriers. Having the vaccine before travel removes the need for rabies immunoglobulin (RIG) and reduces the number of post-exposure doses of rabies vaccine. Washing the wound with soap and water for a good 10 minutes will help to stop the virus entering the nervous system and is the first thing that should be done. RIG is not always available which is why pre-exposure vaccine is a sensible precaution to take: if you contract rabies and RIG is unavailable, then the virus is almost 100% fatal.

SECURITY AND SAFETY

Emergency number (including police, ambulance, fire and roadside safety) 112

PERSONAL SAFETY The security situation in Istria is completely safe – even theft and pickpocketing seem to be largely unheard of. As with any travel abroad, ensure you let someone at home know your itinerary, or register or update your details with your national foreign ministry for the period of your travel abroad. Americans can do the latter through the **Smart Traveler Enrollment Program (STEP;** w *step.state.gov/step*).

DRIVING AND ROAD SAFETY Istrians are generally very good and courteous drivers. Istrian roads are also reasonably well kept, with several modern highways and little traffic outside the peak summer season. Speed restrictions are enforced with limits being 50km/h in built-up areas, 90km/h outside built-up areas, 110km/h on dual carriageways, and 130km/h on motorways.

Seat belts must be worn in the front and back seats of a car if fitted. Children under the age of 12 are not allowed in the front of cars, and suitable child seats are required for children under the age of six. The blood alcohol limit is 0.05% (50 milligrams of alcohol per 100 millilitres of blood, as opposed to 80 per 100 in the UK). For those driving under the age of 24, the limit is zero. Visibly drunk people may not travel in the front of a vehicle. Dipped headlights during the day are compulsory. As with the rest of Europe, certain minimum equipment must be held in your car in case of emergency, and specific winter equipment (such as chains and a shovel) as well as winter tyres once there is risk of ice and snow. Crash helmets are compulsory for motorcyclists. For more details on Croatian driving regulations, see w rac.co.uk/drive/travel/country/croatia.

If you get into an accident or breakdown, the **Croatian Automobile Club (HAK;** 1987; w hak.hr/en) can assist. Its website also has links to webcams and gives regular updates on the traffic state at border crossings.

WOMEN TRAVELLERS Sexual harassment is not usually a problem in Istria and it is not considered strange to be a woman traveller on your own. Dress for women here is as in the rest of western Europe, but take care not to be in swimwear or skimpy attire in churches.

As with anywhere in the rest of the world, if you are a single female driver and an unmarked police car indicates that you should pull over, you should turn on your hazard lights and drive slowly to a public area such as a petrol station before stopping. You could also phone the police on 192 to check whether the police car is genuine.

LGBTQIA+ TRAVELLERS The LGBTQIA+ scene is very limited in Istria although it is more accepted throughout Croatia and Slovenia than in other parts of former Yugoslavia. This said, the most popular gay resort this side of Zagreb is Rovinj. While the town itself may not offer much overtly to visitors belonging to the LGBTQIA+ community, Punta Križa Beach north of Rovinj town, between Amarin and Valalta campsites, is the renowned gay mecca. As an extension of the Valalta nudist camp, it is full of bronzed males perfecting every last inch of their tan.

TRAVELLERS WITH A DISABILITY Istria is not so easy to get around for those with mobility problems, in part because of a lack of public transport in small towns and because of the steep cobbled streets in most of the seaside towns, and the hill towns of the Istrian interior. Poreč, being at least flatter, is easier to get around. Disabled car-parking spaces are common, however. Pula airport has ramps until

INFORMATION ON TRAVELLING WITH A DISABILITY

The UK's **gov.uk** website (w gov.uk/government/publications/disabled-travellers/disability-and-travel-abroad) has a downloadable guide giving general advice and practical information for travellers with a disability (and their companions) preparing for overseas travel. The **Society for Accessible Travel and Hospitality** (w sath.org) also provides some general information. **Disabled Holidays** (w disabledholidays.com) offer trips to Istria.

you enter the plane itself. For the blind or partially sighted, there is little assistance. Modern hotels, and those of the large conglomerates are more accustomed to clients with mobility problems and do have some specially fitted rooms, at least with walk-in showers.

TRAVELLING WITH CHILDREN Istria, being Mediterranean in nature, is very tolerant of children, who will be welcome in all restaurants, and are expected to be out in the late evenings when it is cool. Croatian children, who are in nursery till they are six or seven years old, have a 2-hour siesta at nursery; hence they are all still awake at 22.00. Finding washrooms with baby-changing facilities or restaurants with highchairs is more difficult, so bring with you travel change mats and portable booster seats. Big hotel restaurants are better equipped.

Every medium to large town and resort along the coast has a burgeoning funfair, known as a *luna park* in Croatian (from the name of the first amusement park to be opened at Coney Island in the US in 1903), with lots of amusement rides and games to fritter your money away. Every town and village also has a free play park with the usual slides, swings and a climbing frame. The major seaside towns also have small aquariums and glass-bottom boats, and most resorts also have an aquapark of inflatables out in the cordoned areas of the sea. Go-karting and paintballing are also popular across Istria. Funtana (page 98) has a dinosaur theme park, and there are numerous caves, including one to abseil down (Baredine, page 93), which children find fascinating – in particular the vast, seemingly magical underground world at Postojna (page 176) and UNESCO-listed Škocjan (page 170) in the Slovenian karst. The aquarium at Pula (page 64), with its marine turtle rehabilitation programme, and Piran's Magical World of Shells (page 166) are also fantastic places to visit with children. The Parenzana cycle route provides excellent cycling for kids, much of it being along traffic-free gravel tracks with only a very gentle gradient (pages 117, 197, 199 and 202).

Should your child need paracetamol in suspension, the local brand is called Lupocet. This is a quarter of the price in Croatia of international brands such as Calpol.

WHAT TO TAKE

You don't need to bring a great deal with you when visiting Istria, or Croatia in general, at least during the summer – and it's easy enough to buy anything you might have forgotten when you're there. Light summer clothes, and a light sweater or similar for the occasional cool evening (or if visiting caves, which tend to be quite cool), should suffice. Suncream and a sunhat will be indispensable sitting around on the beach during the summer, and if you're travelling with small children or a baby, bring some sort of collapsible sunshade for the beach. Sandals are definitely worth bringing, not least for wandering around rocky beaches. Something with longer sleeves, long trousers or long skirt are more appropriate for visiting churches (where swimwear or skimpy attire will not usually be acceptable). Reading material in English is a good idea, this being available only from bookshops in larger towns and cities. Mosquito repellent of some sort or another (page 25) may also prove useful. If you're hiking, make sure you have adequate footwear, a waterproof jacket (Gore-Tex or similar material) and a warm fleece in case the weather changes, as well as a sunhat, small first-aid kit, whistle (for attracting attention in an emergency) and reflective 'space blanket' – and make sure you carry plenty of water. The best fabric strip plasters for protecting your feet against blisters are those made by Hansaplast, available locally in pharmacies such as DM. Don't forget to bring an adaptor for phone chargers, etc. The electricity supply in Istria is the same as in the rest of mainland Europe, at 220V and 50Hz. Croatian plugs are the familiar round two-pin type, also the same as the rest of Europe.

MONEY AND BUDGETING

MONEY Since 1 January 2023, the Croatian currency has been the **euro**. This replaced the kuna (officially abbreviated HRK but usually written as kn), which was in use from 1994. Prices are set to be displayed in both currencies until the end of 2023. For the record, kuna notes came in denominations of 10, 20, 50, 100, 200, 500 and (less commonly) 1,000 kuna, and there were 1, 2 and 5 kuna coins. Each kuna consisted in turn of 100 lipa, though the smaller denominations of lipa went out of circulation several years ago.

ATMs (*bankomat* in Croatian) are easily found in larger towns and cities, though don't necessarily expect to find them in small towns and villages, especially in inland Istria. **Credit cards** are widely accepted in hotels, restaurants and larger shops, but not for private accommodation, or in smaller shops and cafés. Smaller shops tend not to carry a lot of change, so don't expect to be able to pay with a large note every time – try to always carry some notes in small denominations.

Changing money Foreign currency is best exchanged in **exchange offices** (*mjenjačnica* in Croatian) – banks almost always involve a lot of queuing. These can be found throughout larger towns and cities, and should have daily exchange rates posted at the counter. If you're carrying travellers' cheques you'll need to exchange them in banks. The most widely accepted are American Express.

BUDGETING Istria and Croatia are fast catching up with the rest of western Europe in terms of prices. Once you've got to Istria, you can expect to pay at least €40 per day per person on food and lodging (in private accommodation), more if you add bus fares, a bit less if staying in hostels. At the upper end of the scale, you can easily pay over €200 per person per day to stay at the five-stars, eat at the best restaurants and drink the best wine. Most accommodation is almost double the price in high season compared with low season, so you can make considerable savings on the figures quoted above if you visit outside July and August. You can also make good savings if you book for a week or more in the same accommodation – and as Istria is small, it is possible to visit most places in a day, even by public transport.

At the time of writing these are the shop prices for:

1½ litres water	€0.85
½ litre local beer	€3.50
Loaf of bread	€0.90
Street snack	€2
Postcard	€0.60
Litre of petrol	€1.50–1.80
Local city bus ticket	€1.50
Intercity bus ticket (Rovinj–Pula)	€7.40 (Rovinj–Pula), €14 (Rijeka Poreč)
Train ticket (Pula–Pazin)	€4.60
Cup of coffee (espresso) in café	€1.10
Pizza in pizzeria	€6–9
Museum/gallery entrance ticket	€3 (Pazin City Museum), €7.90 (Rijeka City Museum)

If you're hiring a car in Croatia, you'll find petrol and diesel are quite a bit cheaper than in Italy, but it's still not cheap.

TIPPING It is normal in Istria to round up to the nearest couple of euros on a reasonably large bill, or to leave an additional coin for smaller drinks. More upmarket restaurants increasingly charge *kuvert*, usually around €2 per person, which includes the ubiquitous bread, often a small starter to put on the bread, and occasionally a *rakija* (local brandy) at the end. If you know you're definitely not going to want all of that (eg: if you're allergic to wheat) then let the waiter know as soon as they take your drinks order, so that it can be omitted from the bill.

GETTING AROUND

BY TRAIN Train travel within Istria is limited to the Pula–Pazin line, which continues to Lupoglav from where some services continue north to Buzet. From Pula there are eight daily trains to Pazin (1 hour 10 minutes) via Vodnjan and Sveti Petar u Šumi, continuing to Lupoglav (1 hour 40 minutes) with six continuing to Buzet (2 hours 10 minutes) – the station for which, by the way, is nowhere near the town. Rijeka is well connected to Zagreb by rail (though works on the tracks in 2022 and 2023 have reduced the number of direct trains significantly, albeit only temporarily).

Rail fares are very reasonable in Croatia, eg: Pula–Pazin costs €4.50, Rijeka–Zagreb €7.70. There are four categories of train in Croatia: ICN (high speed, currently only Zagreb–Split); IC (fast intercity); *brzi* (fast); and *punički* (slow – stops at every station), though (with the exception of the service running to Ljubljana and Maribor during the summer) you'll only encounter the last two when travelling in Istria.

You need to buy train tickets (*karta*) before you travel (ticket office is *prodaja karta* in Croatian), but you don't need to validate them by stamping them in a machine before travelling as in Italy or France. Buying a train ticket doesn't give you a seat reservation, which costs just a little extra, but is very unlikely to be required on most trains except the faster intercity or international services, where it is sometimes mandatory. A return ticket (*povratna karta*) will be cheaper than two singles, and two people travelling together can get a joint ticket, which is slightly cheaper but means you must travel together. For timetables, see **w** hzpp.hr/en.

BY BUS Bus is the most convenient means of public transport in Istria, with frequent, fast services between all main centres on the coast. Pazin also has a good, fairly regular bus timetable, but most other places in inland Istria do not (most notably Motovun, despite being by far the most visited town in the Istrian interior).

You can buy tickets at the bus station (advisable, since it will guarantee you a seat) or on the bus itself. Return tickets include a seat reservation for the outward journey, but not the return – if you want a seat reservation on the way back (and you probably do, to make sure get a place on the bus if it's busy), you need to buy one at the ticket office once you get to your destination. Return tickets also mean coming back with the same bus company. Bear in mind, however, that once you've reserved a seat for your return journey it will tie your otherwise 'open' return ticket (albeit limited to the same bus company) to that specific time; if you change your mind you may be allowed on an earlier or later bus operated by the same company, but it's very much at the driver's discretion.

You need to pay for luggage (except small bags, etc, which you can carry on the bus) when you put it in the hold, usually €1 per bag. You'll be given a small receipt to match the tag on your bag.

For timetables, see w buscroatia.com, w arriva.com.hr/en-us/home, w brioni.hr/hr-hr and for services originating in or going through Zagreb w akz.hr/en. A few local bus services only run during school term times (so not, for example, during the summer holidays which last from mid-June to early September), but you're unlikely to encounter many of these.

Sample (one-way) bus fares: Pula–Rovinj €7, Pula–Poreč €8.60, Pula–Rijeka €15, Rijeka–Opatija €2.50, Rovinj–Zagreb €26.

BY BOAT Travelling by ferry is a lovely way to get around the Croatian coast, and tickets for foot passengers are a bargain (although if you're taking a car on the ferry it's another matter). The state ferry company Jadrolinija (w jadrolinija.hr) operates services from Rijeka to the islands of Cres and Rab, and from Brestova to Porozina on the island of Cres. During the summer several companies operate services from Italy to Poreč, Rovinj and Pula, and these can be used to travel between these cities (for details, see page 24). Small boats run a regular service between Fažana and the Brijuni Islands. Boat tours are offered from major centres such as Pula, Rovinj and Poreč to numerous places around the coast, including the Limski kanal (page 99) and the islands around Rovinj (page 72).

See page 44 for information on sailing off the Istrian coast.

BY CAR Istria is very easy to get around by car, and the peninsula has been on a tarmacking spree in recent years (though a few of the smaller minor roads in the interior are still dirt tracks, called *makadamska cesta* or *bijela cesta*). Istria's only motorway, known locally as the *ipsilon* because of its 'y' shape, is a toll road like all motorways in Croatia. You can pay in cash or by credit card. In 2022 the fee from Lupoglav to Pula was €5.60, the Učka tunnel crossing cost €4.40 (w bina-istra.com/en). The old road over the Učka Mountains is, of course, much more scenic, and longer.

Cars are easy to hire once in Istria, although in the summer you will need to book several days or preferably even weeks in advance to be sure of getting the type of car you want, especially if you're looking for a seven-seater for the family. Car-hire companies are listed in individual chapters. In addition to the major car-rental companies such as Europcar, Budget and Sixt, the local company **Vetura** (w vetura-rentacar.com) is also very good. For more on driving safety, see page 26.

BY TAXI Taxis are plentiful in the main towns on the coast (Rovinj, Poreč, Pula, etc), with several taxi companies operating in each, and a smaller number of operators in towns in inland Istria (Buzet, Pazin, etc). Taxi prices here, and elsewhere in Croatia, used to be somewhat extortionate – but the arrival of **Taxis Cammeo** a few years ago saw the introduction of much, much lower fares, initially causing outrage among other taxi companies and leading to strikes and protests, but finally forcing them to lower their fares as well (though, in general, Cammeo fares are still significantly lower). Cammeo (w cammeo.hr/en) now operates in several towns and cities across Croatia, including **Rijeka** (051 313 313), **Pula** (052 313 313) and **Rovinj** (052 313 300). Cammeo don't use taxi stands, so you'll need to call or flag them – or better still, download their app (which is in English) and book and pay there.

BY BIKE Cycling can be a great way to travel in Istria, particularly some of the inland areas where public transport is minimal. See page 196 for more information on cycling and a selection of sample routes.

HITCHHIKING Hitchhiking is not a particularly good way to get around Croatia, particularly on the main coast roads where few people are likely to stop (you may have more luck inland, but don't hold your breath) – nor can it ever be recommended as entirely safe. The Croatian online forum for finding a ride in Croatia and the wider region is **w** gorivo.com.

ACCOMMODATION

Not surprisingly for a region which hosts several million tourists per year and over a third of all overseas visitors to Croatia, there is certainly no shortage of places to stay in Istria. These range from humble bed and breakfasts to luxurious five-star hotels, and from small boutique establishments to earthy farmhouse accommodation, and campsites beside the clear blue waters of the Adriatic.

Stays of fewer than three nights, especially in private rooms and apartments, will usually incur a surcharge of 30%, and many rooms and apartments are only available on a weekly basis during high season.

Accommodation (*smještaj*) in Croatia carries a small (around €1 – that's per stay, not per night) **tourist tax**, which is usually not included in the price of a room but is added on to your bill at the end. It may sound obvious but if you're travelling in the peak months of July and August, many places will be fully booked, so make sure you book in advance. **Registration** with the Croatian police (page 22) – a compulsory and frankly annoying legacy of the former Yugoslavia which is very much at odds with Croatia's bid to attract more visitors – will be carried out automatically by your hotel, private accommodation or campsite. Most hotels offer **free Wi-Fi** for guests, as do the more upmarket private rooms and villas.

HOTELS Istria offers a range of hotels to suit most tastes and budgets, including new headliners such as the Grand Park in Rovinj and the exceptionally swish Hilton Costabella in Rijeka, as well as older though still charming Secessionist buildings in Opatija and Rijeka, oozing Austro-Hungarian opulence. On many parts of the coast, the larger hotels and resorts are dominated by local chains – Maistra in Rovinj, Arena in Pula, for example. If it's something more along the lines of a resort you're after, the large complexes at Rabac, Medulin and elsewhere will more than suffice. Many (though still not all) of the large and less inspiring hotel complexes built during the 1970s have received a much-needed facelift, while an increasing number of small, boutique or design hotels such as San Rocco in Brtonigla, Hotel Navis in Volosko or Villa Tuttorotto in Rovinj can be counted among the nicest places you could hope to stay anywhere in Croatia.

Hotel **prices** tend to be comparatively high by Croatian standards, particularly in the high season (August), though dropping slightly in the mid (July) and shoulder (June and September) seasons. Prices drop considerably during the low season and

ACCOMMODATION PRICE CODES

Based on a double room per night in high season

Exclusive	**€€€€€**	€180+
Upmarket	**€€€€**	€100–180
Mid range	**€€€**	€70–100
Budget	**€€**	€50–70
Shoestring	**€**	up to €50

winter, with many places offering large **discounts**, sometimes up to 50%. Online booking, where available, will frequently net you special deals well below the standard rates, especially off-season. Hotels usually include **breakfast** (*doručak*) in the cost of a room (*noćenje i doručak*), and **half board** (*polupansion*) is often available for very little additional cost. Some have exceptionally nice **spa** and wellness centres (eg: the Hilton Costabella in Rijeka, and Hotel Kaštel in Motovun). Many hotels close over the winter (November to March), in particular some of the large resorts.

PRIVATE ACCOMMODATION Private accommodation – either rooms (*sobe*) or apartments (*apartman*) – is the most common form of holiday accommodation in Croatia. It is popular with Croatians (who typically book an apartment *na moru* – by the sea – for one or two weeks during the summer) as well as foreign visitors, and is usually quite a bit cheaper than hotels. Expect to pay around €40–80 per night for a double room on the coast in high season, €70–90 for an apartment, around €10 less in shoulder seasons. Weekly bookings usually run from Saturday to Friday (which adds a corresponding increase in traffic to, and from, the coast on the respective days).

Rooms and apartments can be booked through local tourist offices and travel agencies, as well as websites such as w apartmanija.hr. People offering rooms (both licensed and unlicensed) often congregate at bus and train stations. If you haven't already booked something and you're offered a room on the spot, it's better to establish the price, and exactly where it is (some places might be located quite a way from the old town, beach or tourist attractions that you've come here to see), before you go trudging off with the owner and your bags.

AGRITOURISM The past decade or so has witnessed a notable and very welcome increase in agritourism or village tourism (*seoski turizam*) in Istria, and in Croatia as a whole. Staying in a traditional old stone home, you will often get to see a much more genuine slice of Istrian life than in a hotel or resort on the coast, and enjoy home-cooked food (often including homemade wine and cheese, and home-cured *pršut*). Some farms offer horseriding (eg: Ranch Goli Vrh, near Umag; page 97) or other activities.

CAMPING Camping is enormously popular in Croatia, and Istria is no exception. Campsites are usually large – and sometimes, huge – and very well serviced, with electricity, showers, kitchens, barbecue areas and all manner of other conveniences, and cater either to motorhomes and caravans or tents, or both. They can get extremely busy in the summer so book in advance. Many of those by the coast have their own beaches. Wild camping, on the beach or elsewhere, is prohibited in Croatia.

Istria is also well known for its **naturist** (nudist) campsites, including the largest in Croatia (and purportedly the biggest in Europe) near Vrsar on the northwest coast. Naturist campsites generally have their own beach (nudist beaches are often called FKK after the German expression *Freikörperkultur – free body culture*), though sometimes a naturist campsite is combined with a non-naturist beach, or vice versa. To avoid confusion, non-naturist campsites are often described as 'textile'.

For more information on camping in Croatia, see w camping.hr.

EATING AND DRINKING

FOOD **Breakfast** for many people in Istria is a fairly light affair and might just include fruit and yoghurt, and perhaps bread, cheese and ham – though hotels usually offer a far more substantial buffet-style continental or cooked breakfast.

Otherwise, buying a pastry from a bakery and sitting outside a café to eat it while you drink your coffee is quite acceptable (providing the café doesn't serve food). For most people, **lunch** is the main meal of the day, often starting with soup of some kind or another (most traditionally, *maneštra*; see below), followed by meat or fish, with homemade pasta possibly being served in between this and the soup, or replacing the main course. **Dinner** is again lighter, at least when eating at home.

The words *restoran* and *konoba* are both used to describe places you can eat out in Istria. A *konoba* is usually the slightly more homely of the two – though that in no way implies the food is inferior (in fact, many of the best restaurants I know in Istria are in fact *konobas*).

A quintessential Istrian recipe is ***maneštra***, a thick, delicious **soup**. There are several versions; one of the best known is made with potatoes, fresh or ground corn, beans, chickpeas, fennel and cabbage, and sometimes *špek* (bacon) – simple, filling and delicious.

Seafood is very popular, especially along the coast, with freshly caught gilthead bream (*orada*) and sea bass (*brancin*) jostling for position on the menu with shellfish (*školjke*) from the Limski kanal, lobster (*jastog*), mackerel (*skuša*), octopus (*hobotnica*, either roasted or served as a cold salad made with potato, olive oil, garlic and parsley), 'black' risotto with cuttlefish (*sipa*), and fish stew (*brodet*). Grilled fish is traditionally served with boiled potatoes and Swiss chard (*blitva*), drizzled with olive oil, garlic and parsley.

Meat is as popular in Istria as it is elsewhere in Croatia, from the proverbial *roštilj* (mixed grill) to tender beef carpaccio. The ***boškarin*** or native Istrian ox is considered a great delicacy. **Game** (*divljač*) is often found on the menu in Istria, either venison (*srnetina*) or wild boar (*vepar*), the latter being fairly widespread in the Ćićarija Mountains, where it is hunted. *Fuži* (a traditional type of Istrian pasta) with a sauce of wild game (*fuži sa šugom od divljači*) is fantastically rich and highly recommended. Istria is also renowned for its excellent *pršut* (dry-cured ham, similar to Italian prosciutto), especially that produced around the village of Tinjan (page 108).

Vegetarians may find Istria slightly easier to travel in than some other parts of Croatia, with plenty of pasta and truffle dishes to choose from, and salads (*sezonska salata*) – although here, as elsewhere in Croatia, fish, sausages or even turkey might not be considered 'meat' by some. Say *Ja sam vegetarijanac* (*Ja sam vegetarijanka* if you're a woman) – meaning 'I'm a vegetarian' – or *Imate li nešto bez mesa?* ('Do you have something without meat?'). There are now several good vegetarian and vegan restaurants in Istria, including Vegan House in Pula (100% plant based), Mint in Premantura and Bistro Artha in Poreč, and an increasing number of otherwise quite meaty restaurants and bars include at least a vegetarian or plant-based burger on the menu. Some of the excellent Michelin-listed restaurants like Konoba Buščina in Umag and Konoba Malo Selo near Buje offer some wonderful vegetarian dishes, and in many hotels you'll find a choice of non-dairy milk alternatives at breakfast

RESTAURANT PRICE CODES

Based on the average price of a main course

Expensive	€€€€€	€20+
Above average	€€€€	€15–20
Mid range	€€€	€7–15
Cheap and cheerful	€€	€5–7
Rock bottom	€	up to €5

ISTRIAN OLIVE OIL

In 2022, Istria was declared the best olive oil region in the world by Flos Olei, the world's most influential olive oil guide – a title it has held for seven years in a row. Olive oils from Istria also regularly sweep the board at the New York International Olive Oil Competition, one of the world's largest and most prestigious competitions for extra virgin olive oils.

You'll usually find several fine Istrian olive oils on your table in the region's top restaurants (Badi in Umag and Navis in Volosko for example), and you can also visit olive oil producers for tastings and to buy bottles – sample sets containing several different olive oils are often available. Alongside well-known international varieties Leccino, Pendolino and Frantoio, there are several local olive varieties found in Istria such as Bjelica and Rosulja. Among the very best Istrian olive oils to seek out are:

Al Torcio Strada Contessa 22a, Novigrad; ☎ 052 758 093; w altorcio.hr/en; page 96

Ipša Ipša 10, Livade; ☎ 052 664 010; w ipsa-maslinovaulja.com/en; page 114

Mate Romanija 60/A, Zambratija, Savudrija; ☎ 052 759281; w mateoliveoil.com/en

Negri Giuseppina Martinuzzi 11, Labin; m 098 219 524; w negriolive.com

Oleum Viride Belić Creska 34, Rabac; ☎ 052 872 189; w oleabb.hr/en

(in small boutique as well as luxury hotels, though less so in some of the old-style chains). If you're searching for vegan or gluten-free ingredients, Zagreb-based Bio&Bio also has branches in Rijeka and Pula and is a good place to start. **Fruit** and **vegetables** are plentiful, from wild asparagus (in season during spring) to corn, figs, chestnuts and cherries.

Pasta is an important part of Istrian cuisine, with several distinct local homemade varieties, the best known of which is *fuži,* as well as gnocchi (*njoki*). **Pizza** is another favourite, thin-based, delicious and extremely good value. **Polenta** (*palenta*) is a traditional Istrian staple – and then there are the truffles (*tartufi*) for which Istria is justifiably famous (page 38).

Traditional Istrian **cakes** and desserts include *fritule* (small, doughnut-like pastry balls), *kroštule* (fried sweet pastry ribbons, dusted with icing sugar) and *pinca* (a traditional sweet Easter roll). **Ice cream** (*sladoled*) is available in myriad different flavours and is almost always excellent.

Snacks include various sandwiches and sliced pizza ('*pizza cut*', vastly inferior to the real thing), and ***burek***, a very tasty cheese-filled (*burek sa sirom*) pastry, available from some bakeries (usually in the morning) and particularly around markets (it's also available with meat, *burek sa mesom*, or with spinach and cheese, *burek sa špinatom*). Also around markets, bus and train stations you are likely to find places serving ***ćevapčići***, small grilled meatballs, although they may be less easy to come across than elsewhere in Croatia.

DRINKS Istria produces some exceptionally good **wine** (see overleaf), some of which might be counted among the best in Croatia. A traditional Istrian drink is ***supa***, red wine (usually Teran) heated with olive oil, sugar and pepper, and served in a *bukaleta* (traditional pottery jug) with slices of toasted bread on top.

ISTRIAN WINE

Istria's signature grape is **Malvazija** (though it is not unique to Istria, with other varieties growing elsewhere in the Mediterranean), a lovely crisp white with hints of acacia, while its best-known red is the autochthonous **Teran** – though Chardonnay, Cabernet Sauvignon, Merlot and several other varieties are also produced, including Refošk (Italian Refosco, as grown in the Veneto). Many vineyards offer tastings and *degustations*, and can also sell wine by the litre if you turn up with your own empty plastic bottles.

Vineyards are widespread across Istria; however, the finest *terroir* is arguably in the northwest (which is where almost all the vineyards in the list below are located) – the blend of *terra rossa* soil (*crljenica*) and humus (*crnica*), rolling hills and sea breezes, producing various microclimates and some spectacular wines. Vineyards in Istria are for the most part small and family-run.

Istrian wines tend to be drunk quite young – though there are awards at the big annual Vinistra wine fair for *zreli/zrela* (aged or mature) as well as *mladi/mlada* (young) wines, and a good Malvazija aged in oak or acacia for eight months or more is definitely not something to be merely sniffed at. In style, some Istrian (and Croatian in general) whites can be slightly heavier than visitors may be used to, and some of the reds slightly lighter. Of course, you can be unlucky and end up with a mediocre bottle of wine here just as anywhere else in the world (particularly if it has been poorly stored in a supermarket). But the chances are that, whether buying a litre of homemade wine from someone's neighbour, or a finely crafted boutique label from a *vinoteka* (wine shop), you'll get something very much more than drinkable.

As for wine from **Slovenian Istria**, well there's plenty of that too – and it's also extremely good. One of Slovenia's best wine regions, the Vipava Valley, which runs northwest from the karst landscape between Škocjan Caves and Postojna, is also included in this book (page 178), along with some recommended vineyards (page 180).

A few particularly noteworthy Istrian wineries (all of them offering tastings) are:

Benvenuti [map, page 102] Kaldir 7, Motovun; m 099 354 1281 e info@benvenutivina.com; w benvenutivina.com. The Benvenuti family includes 3 winemakers – brothers Albert & Nikola, & their father Livio – & their wines have been awarded a whole slew of gold medals at Vinistra. Their Malvazija istarska is simply wonderful, but move up to their Malvazija Anno Domini, which is aged for 12 months in oak & is superb. Santa Elisabetta is a stunning monster of a wine – 100% Teran, aged for 30 months in Slavonian & French oak – while their Corona Grande is luscious dessert wine, which took gold at Vinistra 2022. The star of the show for this author however is their Muškat San Salvatore, the 2017 vintage of which won platinum at Vinistra 2022, and simply knocks the socks off any other dessert wine I have ever tried – heaven in a glass.

Cattunar [map, page 84] Nova Vas 94, Brtonigla; 052 720 496; e info@vina-cattunar.hr; w vina-cattunar.hr. Cattunar stands at the boundary between 4 terroirs – & if you taste the 4 Malvazijas in their 4 TERRE series, each from a single vineyard in one of these

Istria's local brand of **beer** (*pivo*) is Favorit, which is brewed on the outskirts of Buzet, and there are some really good craft beers too such as San Servolo from Buje and Bura Brew from Poreč. Other Croatian beers include Ožujsko and Karlovačko. Local beers are cheap, whether on tap (*točeno*) or bottled, though imported beers cost more.

different soil types, you'd hardly know they were the same grape. Best aged Malvazija at Vinistra 2016. They also offer accommodation (10 dbls).

Damjanić [map, page 87] Fuškulin 50, Poreč; 052 654 120; e visit@damjanic.eu; w damjanic.eu/en. Superb wines from young couple Ivan & Željka Damjanić who quite literally sold everything to buy a small plot of what had been some 80 years earlier an award-winning family vineyard. Winemaker Ivan's Clemente blanc was awarded 96 points by Decanter in 2019, & took a gold medal at Vinistra 2022; his Akacija (the author's favourite) is an absolutely lovely aged Malvazija which has spent 8–12 months in acacia barrels.

Dešković [map, page 102] Kostanjica 58, Grožnjan; m 098 197 7985; e info@vina-deskovic.hr; w vina-deskovic.hr. Vinistra awards have included best aged Teran in 2012 & best young Malvazija in 2022.

Fakin [map, page 102] Bataji 20, Brkač, Motovun; m 092 239 9400; e info@fakinwines.com; w fakinwines.com. Along with an excellent young Malvazija (which has been awarded best young Malvazija at Vinistra, & won a gold medal from Decanter), Marko Fakin makes a delicious barrique-aged Malvazija, La Prima, matured for 12 months in acacia (gold medals from Vinistra and Decanter, and silver in the International Wine Challenge), a Muškat Žuti (bronze from Decanter) and a particularly good Rosé. Just a short way from Motovun, with a great little tasting bar.

Franc Arman [map, page 102] Narduči 5, Vižinada; 052 446 226; m 091 574 04 98; e info@francarman.hr; w francarman.hr. Wines from Franc & Oliver Arman include an excellent, crisp Malvazija, the lovely Malvazija Classic (oak-aged for 9 months), & a robust Teran (*barrique*-aged for 12 months).

Kozlović [map, page 102] Vale 78, Momjan; 052 779 177; e info@kozlovic.hr; w kozlovic.hr. Kozlović have won numerous awards – their Santa Lucia Malvazija, oak-aged for 18 months, took the award for best *zrela* (aged) Malvazija at the 2022 Vinistra (and not for the first time), & was also awarded Best in Show, & they also won best young Teran in 2022. The award-winning Muškat Momjanski is a particularly lovely dessert wine.

Roxanich [map, page 102] Kosinožići, Nova Vas; m 091 617 0700; e info@roxanich.hr; w roxanich.hr. Mladen Roxanich has won several awards – his Teran Ré & Merlot tend to be particularly good.

Tomaz [map, page 102] Kanal 36, Motovun; 052 681 717; m 098 335 769; e tomaz.klaudio@gmail.com; w vina-tomaz.hr. Wines include Malvazija Avangarde, & Teran Barbarosa, aged in oak for 12 months (the 2020 vintage was awarded Best Young Teran at Vinistra 2021).

Trapan [map, page 52] Veruda 10, Pula; m 098 244 457; e info@trapan.hr; w trapan.hr. Bruno Trapan's wines include a Malvazija Potente & Malvazija Uroborus, the latter (aged in acacia barrels) having taken Best Aged Malvazija at Vinistra, & a good aged Teran, Terra Mare.

Vinakoper [map, page 156] Šmarska cesta 1, Koper; +386 5 663 01 00; e vinakoper@vinakoper.si; w vinakoper.si/en. This Slovenian vineyard had been winning a string of awards at Vinistra, including platinum for their Capris Refošk in 2022 (along with gold for three other Refošks the same year).

Rakija, a potent local spirit, comes in several guises including *loza* (made with grapes, and similar to grappa), *šljivovica* (made with plums) and the deceptively easy-to-drink *medovača* (*rakija* with a smidgen of honey to take the edge off).

TARTUFI (TRUFFLES)

No visit to Istria would be complete without sampling the truffles, or *tartufi*, for which the deciduous woodlands of the Istrian interior (and in particular, the area between Buzet, Motovun and Oprtalj) are famed. You'll find *tartufi* on the menu in most parts of Istria – in pasta sauces, infusing local cheeses, shaved over the top of steaks, even in ice cream (which is actually much tastier than it might sound) – and they are generally cheaper here than their counterparts in Italy and France (indeed, plenty of Italians come to Istria to eat, or buy, truffles).

Truffles are tubers which grow among, and in symbiosis with, the roots of oak, hazel and beech trees, about 10–15cm beneath the surface. They are invisible from above ground, but when ripe can be sniffed out by specially trained dogs. The largest, most intensely flavoured (and also the most highly priced) variety are white truffles (*Tuber magnatum*), the 'white gold' of Istrian woodlands which sell, depending on size and quality, for around €800 per kilo for small ones or, for larger ones over 120g, over €2,000 per kilo. Black or 'summer' truffles (*Tuber aestivium*) are smaller, but still sell for around €600 per kilo. The white truffle season lasts from September to January, while black truffles can be gathered throughout the year.

In November 1999, **Giancarlo Zigante** and his dog Diana discovered what was at that time the largest white truffle ever recorded, near Buje. Weighing 1.31kg and measuring nearly 20cm in diameter, it gained a place in the *Guinness Book of Records* (though since then an even larger one has been discovered in Italy, weighing 1.5kg). Instead of selling his 'Millennium' truffle, as it came to be known, Zigante used it to prepare an elaborate banquet for 100 carefully selected guests. He now sits at the centre of what might be described as a small empire as far as truffles are concerned, with shops all over Istria and beyond (w zigantetartufi.com).

Karlić tartufi in the village of Paladini, near Buzet (Paladini 4; \ 052 667 304; m 091 754 4618; w karlictartufi.hr), can take visitors out on truffle hunts in their local woods, after which they'll make an omelette with fresh truffles. They also sell some excellent cheese and sausages infused with truffles. See page 40 for truffle festivals.

Homemade **lemonade** (*limunada*) is available in many cafés, and traditionally comes in a tall glass with a spoon and a sachet of sugar to add to your own taste. **Fruit juices** are widely available – unless you have a particularly sweet tooth, try to get one without added sugar (*bez dodanog šećera*). The **coffee** in Istria is almost always excellent, and you'll never be far away from a café with tables spilling out on to the street, or a pleasant terrace, perhaps overlooking the sea or in the shade of ancient chestnut trees.

There are plenty of **wine roads** in Istria, usually well signposted as *vinska cesta* (though in Istria a wine road doesn't necessarily imply that there are numerous wineries on that particular route, perhaps only a handful). For more information on some of the wine roads in Istria, see w istra.hr/en/gourmet/wine.

PUBLIC HOLIDAYS AND FESTIVALS

PUBLIC HOLIDAYS On these days, expect banks and most shops to be closed. Public transport will operate to a reduced Sunday timetable, or not at all.

1 January	New Year's Day
6 January	Epiphany
Easter Sunday and Easter Monday	9 and 10 April 2023, 31 March and 1 April 2024, 20 and 21 April 2025
1 May	Labour Day
Corpus Christi	60 days after Easter Sunday
22 June	Day of Anti-fascist Struggle
25 June	Statehood Day
5 August	Victory and Homeland Thanksgiving Day and the Day of Croatian Defenders
15 August	Assumption of the Virgin Mary
8 October	Independence Day
1 November	All Saints' Day
25 and 26 December	Christmas

FESTIVALS

February to May The **Rijeka Carnival** (w visitrijeka.hr/rijecki-karneval) is the second-largest carnival in Europe, and should be considered unmissable if you're here in **February** (page 147). Lovran's two-week **Asparagus Festival**, held in **mid-April** during the wild asparagus season, sees all manner of asparagus dishes on the menu at local restaurants, and culminates in the preparation of a giant omelette in the town's main square, made with 30kg of wild asparagus. The village of Roč holds an **Accordion Festival** in **mid-May** (Z armoniku v Roč, International Meeting of Diatonic Accordion Players). The Lighthouse Festival (w lighthousefestival.tv) is an underground electronic music festival held north of Poreč near the Lanterna campsite in May.

June Pazin's **TradInEtno Orchestra** put on traditional folk music concerts and workshops in Pazin during the summer months (page 104). Lovran's **Cherry Festival**, which takes place in the second week of June, celebrates (as you might have guessed) the delicious cherries which grow in the area (they were probably introduced around 100 years ago), and culminates in the preparation of a giant cherry strudel. In mid-June, Pazin's **Jules Verne Days**, which has been running since 1998 to celebrate the connection between the town and Jules Verne's 1888 novel *Mathius Sandorf*, sees balloon and helicopter flights, theatre performances and even a treasure hunt for kids (page 104).

Istra Inspirit (w istrainspirit.hr) sees a series of events taking place across Istria from late June to early September, celebrating the history, myths and legends (and of course, cuisine) of the region.

July The **Pula Film Festival** (w pulafilmfestival.hr) is Croatia's largest film festival and runs for two weeks, with screenings of Croatian and international films in the amphitheatre and elsewhere in town. The festival has been running since 1953, making it one of the world's oldest (page 58). The **Motovun Film Festival** (w motovunfilmfestival.com) kicked off in 1999, and is also enormously popular. The festival runs for five days, and showcases mainly small budget films and world cinema (page 113). The **Istra Open** is Croatia's top paragliding championship, and takes place at Raspadalica, a cliff just east of Buzet (page 121). The **International Jazz Festival** (w jazzisbackbp.com) in Grožnjan has been voted among the world's best boutique jazz festivals (page 116). The **Svetvinčenat Festival** (w svetvincenatfestival.com) sees open-air performances of dance and theatre within the impressive castle of this beautiful little town.

August The annual **Tilting at the Ring** (Trka na prstenac) in Barban, first held back in 1696, sees horsemen charging about and competing to spear a large ring (page 137). **Velika Gospa** or **Assumption Day** (15 August) is one of the most important feast days in Croatia's religious calendar. Expect celebrations of some kind or another wherever you are. Opatija's excellent **Liburnia Jazz Festival** (w liburniajazz.hr) takes place on the first weekend of August, with concerts all over town. Labin's **Art Republika** (f Labin Art Republika) runs through July and August, with theatre, music and dance performances taking place all over town.

September One of Istria's most colourful festivals is the **Subotina**, held in Buzet on the second weekend of September. Expect traditional and period costumes, music, and stalls selling local handicrafts and produce. On the previous night, to celebrate the opening of the truffle season, a giant omelette is prepared in the lower town from over 2,000 eggs and 10kg of truffles. You get to eat it, too (page 121).

Giostra, the medieval re-enactment festival held in Poreč, is also gaining in popularity. Here you can see jousting on horseback along the seafront, colourful period dress, and the usual offer of great Istrian food (page 90). Grožnjan's festival of the arts, **Extempore**, also takes place in September (page 116).

October **Pršut Festival**, Tinjan. Istria produces some of the finest *pršut* (air-cured ham) anywhere in Croatia, and the best of it comes from the area around Tinjan, which celebrates its pre-eminence with a festival on the first weekend in October (page 108).

The **Chestnut Festival** (Marunada) is Lovran's biggest festival and has been running since 1973. Expect limitless cakes, pastries and other dishes – all prominently featuring chestnuts of course – to be available throughout the town. There's also local folk music and other entertainment. The tiny settlement (technically a town, and loudly proclaimed to be the smallest town in the world) of Hum holds a **Rakija Festival** in October (page 123).

November Buzet's **Truffle Festival** or 'Weekend of Truffles' takes place on the first weekend in November and is the biggest truffle-related event in the region (page 121). **Sv Martinje Festival** celebrates the patron saint of Vrsar on 11 November – it's when locals taste the first of their wine harvest, and you'll find up on their big square one of the biggest fish festivals of winter. **Sv Maurus Festival** in Poreč (page 90), complete with brass bands and chamber music, starts on 21 November, and is definitely worth a visit if you're in the region.

December Mid-December is the time to see, or take part in, the **Parenzana** bike tour (w parenzana.net). There are also many Christmas markets throughout Istria's towns, one of the best being in Sveti Lovreč, near Poreč, where the whole of the old town turns into a Bethlehem scene. Drinks and snacks are free!

SHOPPING

There are plenty of large supermarkets (Konzum, Diona, Plodine, etc) and chemists (DM, etc) in Istria where you can buy whatever you need for a self-catering holiday, or things you may have forgotten to bring from home. You'll also find no shortage of clothes (and shoe) shops, including plenty of designer labels – though don't expect prices to be any cheaper than at home.

OPENING HOURS Shops are generally open 08.00–20.00 Monday–Friday, with supermarkets (especially larger ones) often open longer hours (07.00–21.00), and a number of shops including bakeries as well as cafés open from 06.00 or 06.30. On Saturday supermarkets keep the same hours as during the week, but other shops may close earlier. On Sunday supermarkets open 08.00–15.00 or similar; a few shops may be open on Sundays in larger towns, but most will be closed. The exception to this rule is large shopping malls (Tower Centre in Rijeka, etc), which open late on Sundays as well. During the week and on Saturday smaller shops and those in smaller towns and villages may also close for an hour or two at lunchtime. Markets are usually open from early (07.00) and are at their busiest before lunchtime, with some closing (or at least partly closing) by 14.00. Opening hours (for example, on some museum or restaurant websites) are sometimes listed as summer/winter rather than specific months – in which case you can usually take 'summer' to mean April to October or similar.

See page 39 for a list of public and bank holidays in Croatia, when you can expect to find most shops closed.

SOUVENIRS OF ISTRIA When it comes to buying typical Istrian products to take home, you won't be short of choice. Istrian wine, olive oil, *pršut*, spirits, truffle paste, honey, lavender and other products can be bought in various boutique shops in most major towns in Istria – **Aura** is one example, with several branches including in Buzet and Hum, and **Zigante** has branches of its truffle shops seemingly around every corner. **Hafne** wine bar in Pula is a great place to try Istrian wine before buying a bottle or two.

Better still, you can buy wine and olive oil direct from many producers (although this may not be possible during harvest or *berba* – September for grapes, mid-October for olives). For some of Croatia's best **wines**, head for wineries such as **Benvenuti** (Kaldir 7, Motovun; m 099 354 1281 e info@benvenutivina.com; w benvenutivina.com), **Cattunar** (Nova Vas 94, Brtonigla; ☎ 052 720 496; e info@vina-cattunar.hr; w vina-cattunar.hr), **Damjanić** (Fuškulin 50, Poreč; ☎ 052 654 120; e visit@damjanic.eu; w damjanic.eu/en), **Fakin** (Bataji 20, Brkač, Motovun; m 092 239 9400; e info@fakinwines.com; w fakinwines.com) and **Kozlović** (Vale 78, Momjan; ☎ 052 779 177; e info@kozlovic.hr; w kozlovic.hr) – see page 36 for more details on which wines to look for at these and other wineries. For some of the world's finest **olive oils**, make a trip to **Al Torcio** (Strada Contessa 22a, Novigrad; ☎ 052 758 093; w altorcio.hr/en) and **Ipša** olive oil (Ipši 10, Livade; m 091 206 0538; e info@ipsa.com.hr; w ipsa-maslinovaulja.hr), where you can buy several types of oil which will quite likely knock the socks off any olive oils you've ever tasted (see page 35).

There are many small shops selling local handmade **jewellery**, including Venetian (murano) glass, and local art. A ***bukaleta***, the distinctive painted pottery jug which wine is often served in, makes a good souvenir. Traditional handmade baskets can be bought on markets and at festivals such as the Subotina in Buzet.

ARTS AND ENTERTAINMENT

It can be hard on first arriving in Istria to see beyond the tourist kitsch and the budding modern art, which is popular in the region. However, Istria's primary cultural claim has to be its musical heritage. The Istrian scale is a unique musical scale, made up of six non-equal tempered tones and half-tones, and is inscribed in the UNESCO List of Intangible Cultural Heritage (for more, see w ich.unesco.org). It is most prevalent in Istrian and Kvarner folk music, and may have been experimented with by Tartini (page 167) and by Haydn in his String Quartet in F minor, Op 20 No 5. The scale was first noted by the Istrian composer Ivan Matetić Ronjgov at the beginning of the 20th century, and as a result of fathoming the scale he was able to document local folk songs and compose new works based upon it.

The townsfolk of Rovinj are also known for their *bitinada* and *aria da nuoto* (night aria). The *bitinada* is a choral vocal accompaniment to a soloist, whereby the choir or *bitinaduri* imitate string instruments by repeating onomatopoeic phrases in a waltz-like manner. This style of improvised folk singing is said to have been developed by local fishermen during the long hours they were out on the water fishing or on the shore repairing their nets. You can hear a *bitinada* live during the many summer performances in Rovinj. The *aria da nuoto* is more formal, and is closer in style to sacred music. Both forms use improvisation and are now very much a part of Croatia's cultural heritage.

Music schools are many in Istria, and the town of Grožnjan itself (page 115) becomes a summer school every year. Musical concerts abound, often held outdoors in the summer, or in the many medieval churches or town squares. Attending a concert in Pula's Roman amphitheatre shouldn't be missed. Jazz festivals are also popular.

OUTDOOR PURSUITS

HIKING Istria is a lovely area for hiking, from the high peaks of the Učka and Ćićarija mountains in the northeast, to easy walks around hill towns, and balmy coastal walks such as Rt Kamenjak and the Opatija Riviera. See *Chapter 10* for more details and a selection of hiking routes.

CLIMBING Istria has some fine areas for climbing, in particular the series of cliffs and crags east of Buzet and Roč – **Raspadalica**, **Nugla**, and best of all **Kompanj** which has nearly 100 routes graded up to 8c. The cliffs on the hillside above Mošćeniška Draga are also good. **Vranjska draga** (also known as Vela draga) is a small canyon and nature reserve near the inland entrance to the Učka tunnel, with slender rock pinnacles – but the rock is increasingly unstable, so maybe just come for a hike. Spring and autumn are the best times of year for climbing – August may be a little too hot. Routes on sea cliffs include the walls of the Limski kanal, the overhanging sea cliffs near Brseč, and Zlatni rt near Rovinj.

CYCLING Istria is the best area for cycling in Croatia, with comparatively little traffic in inland areas, a wealth of information (including detailed route maps and descriptions) available online at **w** bike-istria.com, and at least one route, the excellent **Parenzana** (**w** parenzana.net), which now has an international reputation. See *Chapter 11* for more details and a selection of routes.

PARAGLIDING Istria's best area for paragliding is in the northeast, on the inland slopes of the Ćićarija Mountains, especially the area above Gornja Nugla just east of Buzet. Gornja Nugla is home to a large paragliding festival in July. Go to **w** istra.hr, 'Attractions and activities', 'Sports' then 'Paragliding' for a list of take-off sites in northeast Istria, and **w** istraparagliding.com for information on a local paragliding club offering tandem flights.

CANOEING AND KAYAKING There is little scope for canoeing in Istria itself (the largest lake in Istria, Butoniga jezero, is a reservoir so is off-limits). However, the Limski kanal and Rt Kamenjak are good spots for canoeing and sea kayaking.

PHOTOGRAPHY

Istria is a highly photogenic part of the world and abounds in subjects at which to point a camera, from gorgeous architecture to bustling markets, stunning coastline and colourful festivals.

Nevertheless, however beautiful a scene might be, lighting conditions will make a huge difference to whether a photo captures something of that beauty. You can't control the weather of course, but you can choose to return at a better time of day for photography if necessary. In general, the harsh sun in the middle of the day and early afternoon will produce flat, rather lifeless images – the best times of day to shoot are early in the morning and in the late afternoon/early evening – the golden hour, as it's sometimes called. Using a circular polariser can be helpful in bright sunshine, particularly on the coast, to reduce reflections on water and other surfaces, and darken and add contrast to skies (but take it off in less bright conditions since it reduces the 'speed' of your lens by a couple of stops).

Some people, particularly in rural areas (and including market stalls in major towns), may be reluctant to have their photo taken, and in general when photographing people – unless it's a candid shot from across the road or similar – it's always preferable to seek permission first. Ask *Mogu li slikati?* ('Can I take a photo?') or *Smeta li vam ako slikam?* ('Does it bother you if I take a photo?'). Of course they might decline, but if you can engage someone a little in conversation the chances are you'll end up with a much more intimate and compelling portrait than you would snapping something quickly halfway behind their back. Having said that, I've generally found people in Istria to be much less bothered about having their photo taken than in some other parts of Croatia.

WINDSURFING The best spot for windsurfing in Istria is Premantura in the south which, given its position at the tip of the Istrian Peninsula, is more or less guaranteed good winds. For further information, see **w** windsurfing.hr.

MEDIA AND COMMUNICATIONS

MEDIA Istria has its own television station, TV Nova (**w** tvnova.hr), several local radio stations (which also broadcast partly in Italian), and its own newspaper *Glas Istre* (**w** glasistre.hr), which gives all the local ins and outs of what's going on among the few big players who control the region's business. Otherwise, the two main newspapers in Croatia are *Jutarnji list* and *Večernji list* (published in the morning and evening respectively). A fascinating website called Istarske novine online (**w** ino.com.hr) has put all of the newspapers ever published in Istria online for all to read. Starting from as early as 1850 and going to as late as 1938, the range of newspapers published in Istria cover Croatian, Italian, German and Slovenian.

German and Italian newspapers are still very easy to get in Istria, but English ones are more difficult.

POST The postal system is improving in Croatia, and while not superfast, mail between Istria and the rest of Europe usually takes one week (postcards take longer). Allow two–three weeks for the rest of the world. Stamps can be bought at local kiosks as well as at the post office. A town's main post office opens 07.00–

SAILING THE SHORES OF ISTRIA

The freedom of the open sea beckons. Whether you are a weathered sea dog or a novice swabbie, there is an unmatched serenity in wind-powered motion – gliding over the blue mirror that is the Adriatic. Coasting along the Istrian Peninsula seaside, one can explore inlets and the Limski kanal (complete with pirate's cave; page 99), as well as the incomparable towns – peninsulas in their own right – of Pula, Rovinj, Poreč and Novigrad. Or simply enjoy some sunshine, lounging on deck with a *gemišt* (white wine spritzer). Sailing brings out some of the best Istria has to offer.

WHEN TO GO Sailing is year-round in Istria, but the best times are spring and autumn (early May and mid-October). April, May and October have the best wind conditions for the real yachtsman, while the remaining months, with gentler breezes, are better for learning or for a relaxing family cruise.

WHO CAN SAIL As in the rest of Croatia, sailing in Istria offers something for everyone. From sailing lessons at all levels, to boat rentals for licensed captains (known as 'bareboat'), and chartered boats that include a captain (particularly helpful if you're not good at manoeuvring large floating objects into small spaces). For those who like being driven and served, a captain with crew are available. Most charters offer a diving option.

FOR BEGINNERS The larger coastal cities in Istria have sailing clubs (*škola jedrenja*) where would-be captains can learn the ropes, literally. A list of sailing clubs in Istria is on page 229. Special courses are offered on a weekly basis for kids aged seven to 14, and are very reasonably priced. Adults should check at the marina for courses. In Poreč, Horizont Sailing Club (Jedriličarski klub Horizont; w jk-horizont.hr) offers weekly beginners and advanced courses including both theory and practical, from mid-June to the end of August (either course costs €100).

CHARTERING Hiring a boat (chartering) comes in many forms. You can hire a boat and a crew, the boat only (bareboat) or just get a cabin. Then there are the myriad types of boat: sailing yachts, catamarans, motorised yachts, and *gulets* (largish, crewed wooden boats with several cabins – usually taking groups). After the type, boats are usually classified by their length in metres. A six-berth cruising-yacht (eg: a Bavaria 37, referring to the length of the boat in feet) can cost around €3,500 per week (bareboat) in the high season. In addition, a skipper can cost €1,050 per week, or €150 per day, and a crew €125 per person per day, for whom you will need to provide food, drink and a berth on the boat or onshore. A charter pack is mandatory (€140), and you will also have to leave a deposit of €1,000–1,500.

Croatian Yachting ☎ 021 332 332; w croatia-yachting-charter.com. Sailing & motor boats for charter.

Sail Croatia ☎ +44 20 4525 7534; w sail-croatia.com. Offers group cruises on larger boats, plus yacht charters.

19.00 Monday–Friday and 07.00–13.00 Saturday. Sub-post offices only open until 17.00 Monday–Friday. To have post sent to you at the post office, have it addressed to you at Poste Restante, Pošta, postcode of the town and the town name, Croatia.

Sails of Croatia m 095 921 3495;
w sailsofcroatia.com/en/sailing-regions.
Sailing & motorboats for charter.

MOORING For those with their own boat sailing into Istria, you can rent a berth in any of the peninsula's public marinas – and there are dozens of them, at least one in each city. Fees are set annually and vary from marina to marina. They also relate to the size of your boat's beam and its length (size matters) – or at least the space along the pier your boat occupies. For example, in Pula Marina in 2022, a 10m boat that's under 4m wide cost €68 per day to moor in the port in May–October, and €59 outside these months. Monthly berths cost roughly €815 in May–October, €535 in other months. The same boat can be stored on land throughout the year for about €250 per month. During July and August it's a good idea to phone ahead and reserve a berth. If you get caught out, dropping anchor for the night out in a bay is usually free, but some harbours might charge you a fee for an extended stay, although the fee should include some service such as rubbish collection (get a receipt). Marinas in Croatia are open year-round, but the fuel depots might only work mornings in the winter. Water and electricity are available in all marinas. They all also have at least basic repair services and most have a crane and offer winter drydocking. The larger marinas also offer cleaning and maintenance services year-round. For contact details of Istria's marinas and details of their facilities, see *Appendix 2*.

REGULATIONS Croatian sailing regulations are not unlike those elsewhere. The law requires at least one person on the boat to be a licensed skipper – which means both a navigational and a VHF licence. There must also be an accurate 'crew list' on board, and any changes must be recorded and a new list issued. Speciality activities like diving or fishing require their own licences.

WHAT TO BRING For those unfamiliar with sailing, if you do decide on a sailing holiday, bear in mind that the cabins are not large. You will want to bring the minimum, but there are a few essentials: don't bring hard suitcases, but rather cloth or canvas (foldable) bags which can be more easily stored in tight spaces. Clothing should include waterproof outerwear, with long sleeves a must. You'll also want a jumper or other warm outerwear for the evenings – as the breeze off the water at night can be chilly even after the hottest of days. Otherwise, light cotton items are good, some short and long sleeved shirts, shorts or trousers. Think carefully about your footwear. You want waterproof, protective sandals or deck shoes – especially good is footwear that can be used on board, in the water and on the rocky shores. Newport H2 sandals, made by Keen (w keenfootwear.com) are perfect. Don't forget a good hat (with a strap!), your sunscreen and lip balm. You may also want to bring beach towels and/or a mat, your snorkelling gear and extra batteries for all your electronics. A small torch and a deck of cards are also helpful.

PHONE The international telephone code for Croatia is +385. The dial-out code from Croatia is 00 and then your country code (eg: +1 for Canada and the US, +44 for the UK, +61 for Australia, +64 for New Zealand). Despite the dominance of mobile phones, public phones are still generally available in Istria, both outdoors and in the post office, taking coins, telephone cards and, increasingly, credit cards. Calls are cheaper in the evenings (19.00–07.00) and on Sundays than during the day on weekdays and Saturdays. Following the UK's exit from the EU and the return of roaming charges by several UK networks, it's generally cheaper to use a Croatian SIM (which you can pick up in a mobile phone provider shop) to call, text or use 4G within Croatia than it is to use the existing SIM on your home mobile phone (although do check if your network offers EU roaming as part of your package; some still do). Mobile phone operators in Croatia include T-Mobile, VIP, Telemach and Tele 2, and some of them offer a 'tourist package' which can work out as good value at around €10 – although, depending on your package, it might still be cheaper to use your own SIM to phone home. Check with your home mobile phone provider before making a call. Croatian SIM cards and top-up cards come in various amounts (valid for three months).

Useful telephone numbers in Croatia are:

General information ☎ 18981
Local directory ☎ 11888
International directory enquiries ☎ 11802

TIME Croatia and Slovenia are 1 hour ahead of Greenwich Mean Time, 6 hours ahead of New York, and 8 hours behind Sydney. Croatian Summer Time falls at the same time as British Summer Time.

INTERNET Istria has extensive internet coverage. Most hotels and many restaurants offer free Wi-Fi to their guests, as do many (though not all) cafés. It's not too unusual for some Croatian small business websites to switch off out of season – but in most cases this is only temporary.

BUSINESS

Business hours in Istria vary a lot between winter and summer, with summer hours for shops extending often until 22.00, but perhaps taking a siesta for a couple of hours in the afternoon. In the winter most businesses open 08.30–16.30. Government offices and utilities will be open 07.00–10.30 and 11.30–14.00.

Work culture in Istria is very much shaped by the sea. Within the tourist industry it's perfectly normal to go to a meeting in just board shorts and flip-flops. For more formal meetings, a short-sleeved shirt is acceptable and long trousers. Istrians are not particularly timely, but that's no reason to keep them waiting, of course.

With only a few exceptions (such as antique markets), bargaining is no more acceptable than in western Europe – prices are posted and un-negotiable.

CULTURAL ETIQUETTE

Istrians are proud of their peninsula and like to see it kept clean and tidy. They are also very courteous to visitors and, for instance, will generally stop at a zebra crossing for pedestrians (not something that can be said for the whole of Croatia!), and expect the same from foreigners.

If invited to an Istrian house, you should never turn up empty-handed, but bring a small gift of food, even if it's only local biscuits or chocolates. You'll be more than reciprocated during your visit, and usually offered homemade *rakiju* or coffee, which would be considered rude to turn down. If you're ever handed a plate of food or cakes to take back to your apartment, never return the plate empty, but make sure that you return it with cake or chocolates.

On the Istrian coast, skimpy dresses and bare chests are completely the norm. Some beaches are nudist (naturist), and even on the non-nudist beaches, it is not uncommon for women to be bare-bosomed. Most restaurants, except those right on the beach, will expect people to wear some sort of top when eating. Wearing swimming costumes or excessively revealing clothing will be considered unacceptable for visiting churches.

Drugs, on the other hand, are not acceptable. While, of course, they can be found, the penalties for drug possession, sale or smuggling are harsh.

INTERACTING WITH LOCAL PEOPLE Istrians are very well versed in interacting with international visitors, and so you'll find them friendly and helpful, not least because tourism is the main employer in the region. In the height of the season, most Istrians will be too busy working to spend too much time with you, never mind invite you to their house.

The cosmopolitan heritage of Istria means that, compared with the rest of Croatia, you will be on much safer and more neutral ground if you want to enquire into the break-up of Yugoslavia. Otherwise, even Istrians can be quite conservative; homosexuality, for instance, remains largely taboo despite being legalised in 1977.

TRAVELLING POSITIVELY

As with anywhere in the world, you should try to buy local and think global. Even within Istria, there are four or five big businesses that run almost everything, making it very difficult for small businesses to thrive, offer variety and provide true competition. So the more you can do to support small family-run hotels, apartments and businesses or local guides the better, especially outside the main tourist season. Agritourism (page 33) is one good way to ensure you are doing this.

To help or support the environment in Istria, check out **Zelena Istra (Green Istria)** (**w** zelena-istra.hr), who run lots of campaigns and activities to educate the public, raise awareness and change behaviour for the better.

If the sea is your true love, then you might be interested in contributing towards Pula's **turtle rescue centre** (**w** aquarium.hr/sea-turtles). There you can adopt a rescued turtle until it is released back into the wild, by donating to its care and rehabilitation at the centre.

Part Two

THE GUIDE

3

Pula and Southern Istria

PULA

Located towards the southern tip of the Istrian Peninsula, Pula often (quite undeservedly) receives less attention than neighbouring Rovinj and Poreč. Yet it is a thriving city, as becomes the largest urban area and economic centre of Istria, with some of the finest Roman ruins anywhere in Croatia – most spectacular among these is its huge amphitheatre, one of the six largest Roman amphitheatres to have survived anywhere in the world. There are popular beaches south of the centre at Medulin, Premantura and Stoja, cosy bars in town where you can acquaint yourself with a variety of local wines or listen to live jazz, a terrific open market, and Istria's main archaeological museum. Croatia's largest film festival is held in Pula in July.

HISTORY Legend tells that Pula was founded by Jason (he of the Golden Fleece) and the Argonauts, following their pursuit by the enraged Colchians. There was certainly an Illyrian settlement here from at least 500BC, and Roman Pula – or to give it its full title, Colonia Julia Pollentia Herculanea – was probably founded by the emperor Augustus around the middle of the 1st century BC. It rapidly grew into a flourishing commercial city, with an estimated population in its heyday of 25,000–30,000 inhabitants. After being plundered by the Ostrogoths in the 5th century and sacked repeatedly during the struggle between Venice and Genoa in the 13th and 14th centuries, the population was further devastated by plague in the 17th century, when only some 300 inhabitants were left. It was converted into a major port by Austria in the 19th century, but lost its importance under Italy following World War I, and was later bombed by both the Germans and the Allies in World War II. These days, Pula is Istria's main economic centre.

GETTING THERE AND AWAY

By air Pula's international airport (Valtursko polje 210, Ližnjan; ☎ 052 530 105; w airport-pula.hr) is around 7km northeast of the city at Valtura. Easyjet (w easyjet.com), British Airways (w britishairways.com) and Ryanair (w ryanair.com) have direct flights between Pula and London Gatwick, Heathrow and Stansted respectively; Croatia Airways (w croatiaairlines.com) has daily flights from Pula to London Heathrow and Gatwick via Zagreb. Swiss, Eurowings and Norwegian also all operate out of Pula. See page 23 for more information.

Getting to and from the airport A **shuttle bus** runs between the airport and Pula's bus station, daily except Thursday, though its timetable does not always coincide particularly well with arrivals (for timetables see w airport-pula.hr/en/passenger-info/shuttle-bus). Buses leave from outside the arrivals area, and depart from Pula's bus station. The timetable has been known to change (and varies on different days), but as a rule of thumb buses depart the airport 30 minutes after flights have landed. Tickets cost €4 to the city centre. There are also three other shuttle bus services running from the airport to Rabac, Medulin and Umag via Poreč and Rovinj, operated by Brioni (w brioni.hr). The information on shuttle bus routes is listed under the dropdown menu for 'passenger transport' w brioni.hr/en-gb/passenger-transport/shuttle-bus/prices-and-stops, with buses leaving the airport 30 minutes after a flight has landed (hasn't anyone ever heard of having to go through passport control and wait for checked bags to arrive?). Prices include €18 to Rovinj and €39 to Umag, with a small discount for online bookings (which are, however, impossible to do on Brioni's website). **Taxi** drivers congregate around the exit of the arrivals area, although Cammeo (w cammeo.hr/hr/gradovi/pula; page 31) will work out cheaper (it's worth downloading their app and making bookings through that ahead of time). Otherwise, fares into Pula's town centre are likely to be around €16, slightly more if you haven't booked in advance – try Taxi Hodak (w taxi-hodak.com), or Taxi Pula Airport (w taxi-airport-pula.com) which helpfully has a list of transfer fares online. **Car-rental** offices at the airport include Europcar (w europcar.com.hr) and Sixt (w sixt.com) – there's a list on the airport website (w airport-pula.hr/en/passenger-info/rent-a-car). You can expect to queue for quite a while at the offices after a flight has arrived.

By train Pula is connected by rail to Pazin (1 hour) and other stations inland, including Vodnjan and Sveti Petar u Šumi (timetables at w hzpp.hr/en), with some services continuing to Lupoglav (from where there are connecting bus services to Rijeka) and Buzet. Pula's **railway station** [54 A5] (Željeznički kolodvor; Kolodvorska 5) is a 10-minute walk north of the amphitheatre: from the amphitheatre continue along Flavijevska towards the bus station, then turn left at the roundabout and head downhill past the Hotel Riviera. The last stretch is apt to be a bit dark, so you may not want to walk there late at night.

By bus Most people arriving in Pula by public transport, whether from Istria or elsewhere in Croatia, will do so by bus. Pula has frequent bus services to Rovinj (45 minutes), Poreč (1½ hours), Pazin (45 minutes–1 hour), Rijeka (2–2½ hours), Zagreb (4 hours or more) and cities on the Dalmatian coast (eg: Zadar 7 hours). International services connect Pula to Trieste (w flixbus.co.uk/bus-routes/pula-trieste; 2hrs 35mins), Ljubljana (w flixbus.co.uk/bus-routes/pula-ljubljana; 4hrs 15mins) and elsewhere. Pula's **bus station** [54 A3] (Autobusni kolodvor, Trg 1, Istarske brigade bb) is a 10-minute walk northeast of the amphitheatre (if you're staying out at Verudela, take local bus #2a).

By boat **Venezia Lines** (w venezialines.com) and **Adriatic Lines** (w adriatic-lines.com) sail between Venice and Pula in the summer months (Apr–Oct). Tickets cost €60/€30 adult/child one-way, €69/€35 return, under sixes go free.

By car Pula is a 1½-hour drive from Rijeka, 45 minutes from Rovinj, 45 minutes from Pazin, 4 hours from Zagreb and 2½ hours from Ljubljana.

GETTING AROUND Local **bus** services are run by **PulaPromet** (☎ 052 222 677; w pulapromet.hr) and are cheap, frequent and reliable. Useful services from the bus station (Trg 1, Istarske brigade bb) or the city centre include #1 to Stoja, #2a to Verudela (travelling towards Verudela, #2a also stops at Giardini, near the Sergius

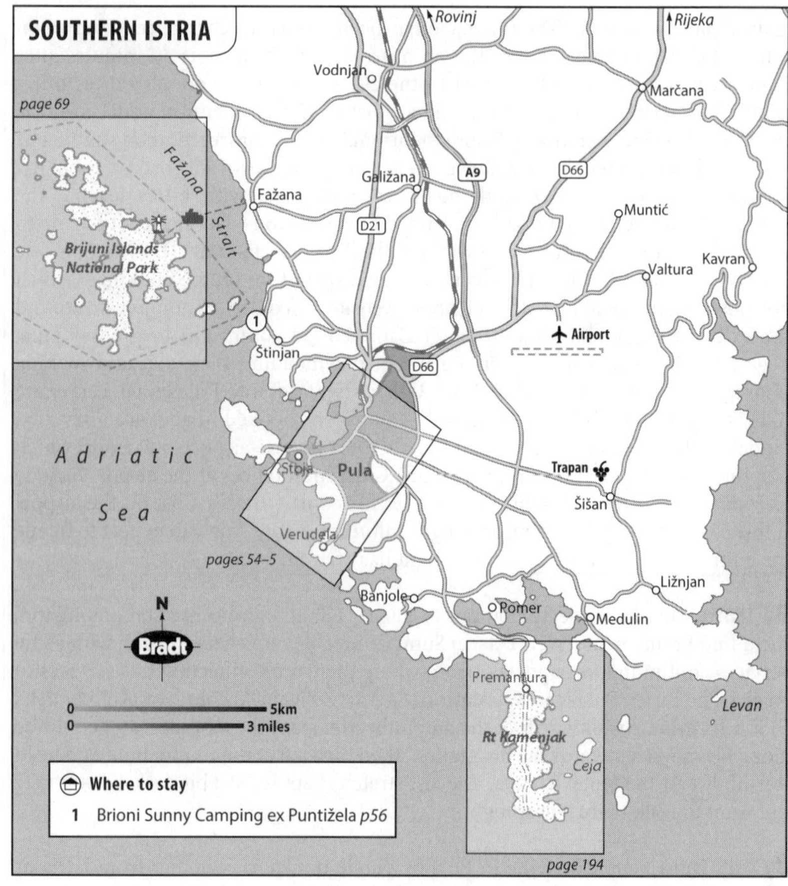

Arch; returning from Verudela, #3a will take you to the bus station, or you can take #2a to Trg Republike, near the market and the old town, or to Koparska from where it's only a short walk to the bus station), and #5 for Štinjan and Puntižela. See **w** pulapromet.com/en/gradske-linije-eng for a map of routes (or look under *Linije* then *Gradske linije* on the Croatian language version) where there's also a useful link to timetables (*vozni red*). Tickets bought on the bus cost around €1 for journeys within zone 1 (which includes Verudela), €2 for zone 2 (including Premantura), or around 30% less if you use a prepaid contactless card which you can buy and load up at the bus station. You can also get a daily ticket for €4 that is valid for 24 hours across all three zones, which works out as good value if you're taking the bus a few times, and there are three- and seven-day ticket options available too. Suburban services (*Prigradske linije*) include #21 to Fažana (for Brijuni), #22 to Vodnjan, #23 to Valtura, #24 and #25 to Šišan, #25 to Medulin, #26 and #28 to Banjole and Premantura (for Rt Kamenjak). For **taxis** call **Cammeo** (☎ 052 313 313, **w** cammeo.hr/hr/gradovi/pula) or **Taxi Pula** (**m** 098 440 844; **w** taxipula.com).

TOURIST INFORMATION Pula's **tourist information office** [59 C4] (Forum 3; ☎ 052 219 197; **e** tz-pula@pu.t-com.hr; **w** pulainfo.hr; ⏰ Jul/Aug 08.00–21.00 Mon–Fri, 09.00–21.00 Sat/Sun, Jun/Sep 08.00–20.00 Mon–Sat, 09.00–20.00 Sat/

Sun, May/Oct 09.00–18.00 Mon–Fri, 10.00–18.00 Sun, Nov–Mar 09.00–16.00 Mon–Fri, 10.00–14.00 Sat) is conveniently located on the forum, and has maps and plenty of local information.

WHERE TO STAY Pula has no shortage of places to stay, from larger and boutique hotels to hostels and campsites. As well as a good number of long-established hotels out of town at Verudela (including the reliable Park Plaza Histria and Park Plaza Arena), there is an increasing choice of places to stay in the city centre itself, including several hostels to choose between.

Hotels

Grand Hotel Brioni Pula Radisson Collection [54 H2] (227 rooms & suites) Verudela 31; 052 378 000; e info@grandhotelbrioni.com; w grandhotelbrioni.com; all year. Newly opened in 2022, this is now the height of luxury on the Verudela Peninsula, with smart modern rooms (still not huge at 23m2) with sea or garden views, spa facilities & a price tag to match. **€€€€€**

Hotel Amfiteatar [59 B3] (16 dbls, 2 sgls) Amfiteatarska 6; 052 375 600; e info@hotelamfiteatar.com; w hotelamfiteatar.com; all year. Boutique hotel positioned squarely between the arena & the old town, with an excellent new vegan restaurant (page 57). **€€€€**

Hotel Milan 1967 [54 F4] (12 dbls) Stoja 4; 052 300 200; e hotel@milanpula.com; w milan1967.hr; all year. Family-run for 3 generations, the Milan lies on the southern edge of town near the Naval Cemetery, at the base of the Stoja Peninsula, & is well known for its standout seafood restaurant (page 56). **€€€€**

Hotel Oasi [54 G1] (9 dbls) Pješčana uvala X-12a; 052 397 910; e info@oasi.hr; w oasi.hr; all year. Small, modern hotel just south of Verudela with smart rooms, own restaurant & spa. **€€€€**

Park Plaza Arena [54 H2] (175 rooms, 7 suites) Verudela 31; 052 375 000; e ppapres@parkplazacroatia.hr; w arenahotels.com; all year. The renovated Arena, on the opposite side of the peninsula from Verudela, has lovely rooms, many with balconies overlooking lush green trees which are the only thing dividing the Arena from a nice pebble beach (& some suites have the added bonus of a private jacuzzi on the balcony). The existing structure of the building means that rooms, though wonderful & still quite spacious, are technically a smidgen too small to earn the hotel what would otherwise very clearly be a 4-star rating– which is actually good news since it gets you what is essentially 4-star accommodation at a slightly lower price tag than at the nearby Histria. Restaurant, bar, pools & direct beach access – & hugely popular, so book ahead in high season. **€€€€**

Park Plaza Histria [54 G1] (241 dbls) Verudela 17; 052 590 000; e pphpres@parkplazacroatia.hr; w arenahotels.com; all year. The spruced-up Histria, associated with the Park Plaza brand, is still one of the nicest options on Verudela (the other being the Arena), & one of the best places to stay in or around Pula. The rooms have small balconies & swish bathrooms, & there is a large terrace area with comfortable lounge chairs, as well as indoor & outdoor swimming pools at the hotel & another (as well as a kids' pool) 5mins' walk away, & a nice pebble beach a few mins beyond that – not to mention a huge waterslide nearby which kids will never want to leave. The rate for half board is not too much more than that of a room with b/fast, & the buffet-style restaurant is excellent – so unless you plan to spend all your evenings in Pula itself, this is well worth considering. There is also a good à la carte restaurant, Istrian Taverna. **€€€€**

Scaletta [59 A3] (12 dbls) Flavijevska 26; 052 541 599; e info@hotel-scaletta.com; w hotel-scaletta.com; all year. Stylish (& very popular) German-owned boutique hotel close to amphitheatre, with its own, highly rated restaurant. **€€€€–€€€**

Hotel Galija [59 B2] (10 dbls) Epulonova 3; 052 383 802; e info@hotelgalija.hr; w hotelgalija.hr; all year. Small, long-standing & decent value 3-star. **€€€**

Hotel Modo [54 F5] (12 dbls) Valovine 42; 052 219 490; e modoresort@gmail.com; w booking.com/hotel/hr/modo-pula.en-gb.html; all year. Small new hotel out near the beaches at Valovine. **€€€**

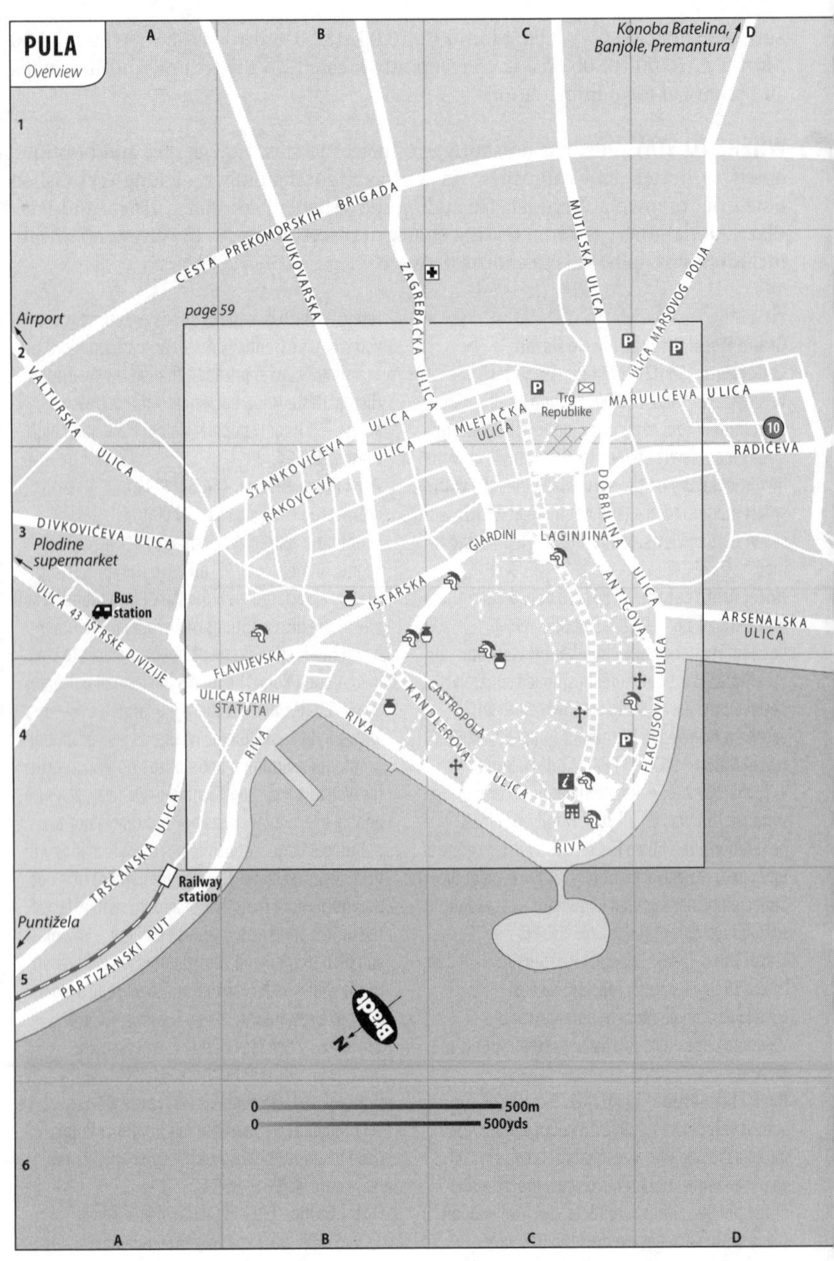

Hotel Riviera Guesthouse [59 A4] (67 dbls) Splitska 1; 052 211 166; e arenariviera@arenahotels.hr; w arenaturist.com; May–Oct. In a grand old Secessionist building just a few mins' walk from the bus & train stations, the Riviera is now long overdue for an overhaul. At present it is somewhat overpriced for what it actually is – a 1-star establishment, offering 5 floors of faded grandeur, & no AC. **€€€**

Monvidal Residence Guesthouse [59 A2] (5 dbls, 1 apt) Ilirska 2; w booking.com/hotel/hr/rezidencija-monvidal.en-gb.html; all year.

Small modern guesthouse 500m from the arena with bright, clean rooms & pool. €€€

Hostels There are now quite a few hostels to choose from in Pula, see w pulainfo.hr/accommodations for more.

Boutique Hostel Joyce [59 C2] (21 rooms) Trg Portarata 2; m 099 324 2224; e hostel.joyce@gmail.com; w boutiquehostel-joyce.com; all year. Located, as the name suggests, in a building once housing the Berlitz school where James Joyce taught, right by the Sergius

Arch, with smart rooms – clean, bright & spacious. **€€–€**

Hostel Pipištrelo [59 D4] (30 beds, inc 2 dbls) Flaciusova 6; m 095 913 0290; e hostel.pipistrelo@gmail.com; w pipistrelohostel.com; ⏲ all year. Excellent hostel just around the corner from the forum, with stylish, themed rooms, shared kitchen, Wi-Fi, friendly, helpful staff, several dorms as well as 2 en-suite dbls. **€€–€**

Pula Youth Hostel [54 F3] (152 dorm beds) Zaljev Valsaline 4; ☎ 052 391 133; e pula@hicroatia.com; w hicroatia.com/en/hostel/hi-hostel-pula; ⏲ all year. Simple, well-priced dorm beds at Valsaline, a bay at the base of the Verudela Peninsula (buses #55/#3, or take the #2a to the crossroads before Verudela). A further 64 beds in mobile homes with private bathrooms, each sleeping 4; & a campsite in the pine trees. **€**

Private rooms

Plenty of stylish new apartments have appeared in recent years, many of which you'll find on w booking.com, & you'll also find private rooms & apartments listed on w pulainfo.hr.

Apartments Arena [59 A3] (4 apts) Flavijevska 2; ☎ 052 506 217; m 098 486 109; e booking@pula-apartments.com; w pula-apartments.com. Comprises 4 large – no, huge – renovated apartments, with AC, right next to the amphitheatre (some apartments overlook it), within easy walking distance of old town & bus station. 2 apartments sleep 3, 1 sleeps 4 & the other sleeps 5. Excellent value. **€€€–€€**

Casa dei Fiori Sonja [59 D2] (4 apts) Tartinijeva ul 6; m 099 348 3349; w booking.com/hotel/hr/casa-dio-fiori.en-gb.html; ⏲ all year. Stylishly decorated apartments owned by a Dutch-Swedish couple, in a quiet street 200m from the Sergius Arch. **€€€**

Deluxe Rooms and Apartments Korzo [59 C2] (2 apts) Giardini 10; w booking.com/hotel/hr/deluxe-rooms-and-apartments-korzo.en-gb.html; ⏲ all year. Stylish boutique apartments right in the old town centre, with free use of bikes & free pickup from Pula airport. **€€€**

Camping

The most popular camping area for Pula is the **Stoja Peninsula**, 3km west of the city centre. Alternatively, there is camping at **Medulin** (page 64) & **Premantura** (page 65). One of the cheapest places to camp is Pula's **youth hostel** at Valsaline, with 50 simple pitches for €10.70 pp with a tent in summer; you can also hire a tent for €2.

Brioni Sunny Camping ex Puntižela [map, page 52] Puntižela 155; ☎ 052 456 000; w eurocamp.co.uk; ⏲ Mar–Nov. Around 7km northwest of the city centre at Puntižela & overlooking the Brijuni Islands, this site has holiday cabins in 3 levels of comfort (despite the name, it's no longer a campsite with pitches). 2 night min stay. **€€€**

Arena Stoja Camping Homes [54 G5] Stoja 37; ☎ 052 529 400; e arenastoja@arenacampsites.com; w arenacampsites.com/en/mobile-homes-istria/mobile-homes-arena-stoja; ⏲ Mar–Sep. Camping villas & glamping tents from €200 (3 night min stay) plus a few lots for caravans or motorhomes.

WHERE TO EAT AND DRINK

Pula has plenty of choice when it comes to eating out, both in the old town itself and along the coast at Verudela – though the better tables in the town centre tend to be fairly well hidden off the main drag, whereas the obvious concentration of restaurants around the forum and towards the west end of Sergijevaca cater mainly to tourists and have been uniformly unmemorable, in our experience. Among the nicest places to eat in town are the family-run **Vodnjanka**; **Jupiter**, on the road up to the fort; and **Kantina**, behind the main market. **Milan 1967**, out at Stoja, has been winning accolades for years, while further out of town at Banjole, you'll find the excellent **Konoba Batelina**.

Restaurants

Milan 1967 [54 F4] Stoja 4; ☎ 052 300 200; w milan1967.hr; ⏲ 11.00–midnight daily, closed Sun during winter. Top-rated seafood restaurant at the base of the Stoja Peninsula, with a wide range of freshly caught fish & shellfish & an extensive wine cellar. **€€€€€–€€€€**

Ribarska Koliba [54 F2] Verudela 3 5; m 091 600 1269; e info@ribarskakoliba.com; w ribarskakoliba.com/en; ⌚ 08.30–16.30 daily. Long-standing traditional mainly seafood restaurant out at the resort of the same name, out at Verudela, which has more recently gained a recommendation in the *Michelin Guide*. €€€€€–€€€€

✷ **Konoba Batelina** [54 D1] Čimulje 25, Banjole; ☎ 052 573 767; ⌚ 17.00–23.00 Mon–Sat. This superb Michelin-recommended seafood restaurant in the village of Banjole, a few km southeast of Pula, is run by the friendly Skoko family, with a menu featuring whatever was brought ashore in that day's catch. Dishes include a range of imaginatively prepared & classic entrées, from lightly dressed crab meat served in its shell, to succulent scallops or a light mousse made from conger eel, & homemade pasta, while for mains there could be *brodetto* with polenta, or perfectly grilled sea bass. It's extremely popular so reservations are definitely advised. Buses #26 & #28 will take you out to Banjole from Pula, otherwise a taxi shouldn't set you back much more than getting to the airport. €€€€

Kantina [59 C1] Flanatička 16; ☎ 052 214 054; f Kantina Pula; ⌚ 07.00–23.00 daily. A great place next to Pula's large open market, with a wide range of dishes served in a lovely vaulted stone interior. €€€

Vegan House [59 B3] Amfiteatarska 6; m 091 615 6086; w veganhousepula.com; ⌚ midday–23.00 daily. Pula's first fully plant-based restaurant, which opened in late 2021 at the Hotel Amfiteatar. €€€

✷ **Vodnjanka** [54 D2] D Vitezića 4; ☎ 098 175 7343; ⌚ summer 09.00–23.00 Mon–Sat, winter 09.00–17.00 Mon–Sat. Lovely family-run restaurant with an emphasis on traditional Istrian dishes, such as *fuži* with game, as well as plenty of seafood dishes – & seasonal dishes such as steamed dandelion leaves with hard-boiled egg. About as close as you're likely to get to genuine home cooking without being invited to somebody's house. €€€

Jupiter [59 C3] Castropola 42; ☎ 051 214 333; w pizzeriajupiter.com; ⌚ midday–23.00 Mon–Fri, noon–23.00 Sat, 13.00–23.00 Sun. Excellent place hidden away from the main drag on the road leading up to the fort, with a range of dishes, from legendary pizzas to great portions of succulent grilled squid served with lashings of *blitva*. Friendly & unpretentious & deservedly popular with locals. €€

Agrippina [59 D4] Sergijevaca 5; w agrippina-street-food.business.site; ⌚ 11.00–22.00 daily. Friendly new place with a street-food-style menu in a sit-down setting, including highly rated veggie burgers. Tasty, relaxed & good value. €

Fresh Sandwich & Salad Bar [59 D2] Anticova 5; f Fresh Sandwich & Salad Bar; ⌚ 08.30–16.30 daily. Fresh salads, sandwiches & juices to take away, with plenty to choose from for both vegetarians & vegans. €

Bars and cafés You'll rarely be short of a place to stop for a coffee or a drink in Pula, but here are a few favourites:

Caffe Diana [59 C4] Forum 4; ⌚ 07.00–22.00 daily. There's no shortage of cafés on & around the forum, but this has always proved a reliable choice.

Caffe Milan [59 C2] Narodni trg bb; ⌚ 07.00–20.00 Mon–Fri, 07.00–14.00 Sat/Sun. Nice café right beside the covered market, packed with locals, with a large covered terrace, impeccable coffee & plenty of shade.

Caffe Uliks [59 C3] Trg Portarata 1; ⌚ 07.00–23.00 daily. Small café tucked on a corner behind the Sergius Arch, where you can combine a stop for a coffee with the requisite look at the James Joyce sculpture sited outside (page 60).

Slastičarnica Charlie [59 C2] Flanatička 17; ⌚ 08.00–20.00 daily. A popular choice for ice cream near the market, with plenty of tables outside.

ENTERTAINMENT AND NIGHTLIFE

Bass Bar Pula [54 F3] Širolina 3; f Bassbarpula; ⌚ 08.00–midnight Sun–Wed, 08.00–02.00 Thu–Sat. Out towards Verudela, with plenty of beers, luscious cocktails, a big terrace, & DJs.

Rock Bar Mimoza [59 B1] Vukovarska 15; f Caffe.Mimoza; ⌚ 08.00– 01.00 Mon–Thu, 08.00–02.00 Fri/Sat, 17.00–01.00 Sun. As the name implies – classic rock & metal, with live music from local acts several times a week, & around 40 types of beer.

PULA FILM FESTIVAL

Croatia's largest film festival (w pulafilmfestival.hr) runs for two weeks in July, with screenings of Croatian and international films in the amphitheatre and elsewhere in town (venues include the fort/Historical Museum of Istria and Valli Cinema or Kino Valli). Tickets for screenings in the arena cost €3.50, or €22 for all arena screenings; screenings elsewhere are free. Tickets can be bought from an information office on Giardini during and a few days before the festival (🕘 09.00–22.00), as well as from in front of the arena during the festival (🕘 18.00–midnight), and online through the festival website. The festival will be in its 70th year in 2023, making it one of the world's oldest film festivals (Venice is the oldest, having started in 1932; Cannes got underway in 1946), and it was the most important film festival in the former Yugoslavia. The festival draws a huge number of visitors to Pula, so book your accommodation way in advance if visiting at this time of year. The same applies for opening- or closing-night tickets. It also attracts plenty of international celebrities (past festivals have been attended by the likes of Ben Kingsley, Ralph Fiennes and John Malkovich).

Arena As well as constituting Pula's star attraction and providing a venue for the Pula Film Festival, the city's Roman amphitheatre is also used as a venue for large, high-profile concerts, from Croatian singers such as Oliver Dragojević to international acts such as Seal, Elton John and Sting.

FESTIVALS Pula has a long history of hosting huge music festivals – Fort Punta Christo, situated on the Štinjan Peninsula just north of the city, leapt into the limelight as one of Europe's hottest festival locations with the arrival there of Outlook in 2008. Although Outlook, Seasplash and Dimensions have all moved elsewhere in the past couple of years (to Tisno down the Dalmatian coast, in case you were wondering), there are still plenty of festivals in Pula.

GoatHell Metal festival held in Pula in Jul (w goathell.eu).
Pula Film Festival Held in Jul. (See above.)
Pula Music Week Techno & House festival in the arena in the first week of Jul (w pulamusicweek.com).
Spectacula Antiqua w spectaculaantiqua.com. Staged gladiator combat in the arena in Jun. Part of Pula's 'days of antiquity' (also known as Pula Svperiorvm) which take place in the forum, in front of the Golden Gate & elsewhere, & include music & theatre, an antique crafts fair & plenty of entertainment for kids.

SHOPPING Pula's large, busy main **market** [59 C1] (*tržnica*, sometimes referred to as the *placa;* Narodni trg; w trznica-pula.hr; 🕘 07.00–14.00 (fish & meat) & 07.00–15.00 (vegetables & other stalls) Mon–Sat, 07.00–midday Sun) is only a 5-minute walk from the Sergius Arch, and has stalls selling all manner of fresh fruit and vegetables as well as local honey and other produce, and a covered area selling seafood and fresh and cured meat. There's a large Plodine **supermarket** [54 A3] northwest of the bus station, near the junction of 43 Istraske divisije and Prekomorskih brigada (Jurja Žakna 12, Šijana; 🕘 08.00–21.00 Mon–Sat, 08.00–13.00 Sun), and several other large supermarkets nearby; smaller, local supermarkets (Konzum, Plodine, Diona, etc) are dotted around town. If you're staying at Verudela, the nearest supermarkets are a long hike away in Nova Veruda.

OTHER PRACTICALITIES

General Hospital [54 C2] (Opća bolnica) Zagrebačka 30; 052 376 000/500; w obpula.hr

Istarske ljekarne w istarske-ljekarne.hr. Has branches on Giardini 14 [59 C2] (052 222 544; 07.00–20.00 daily plus a night shift) & near the arena [59 A3] (Flavijevska 28; 07.00–20.00 Mon–Fri, 07.30–13.00 Sat). For other branches & opening times, see website.

Post office [59 D1] Trg Republike 1; 08.30–17.00 Mon–Fri

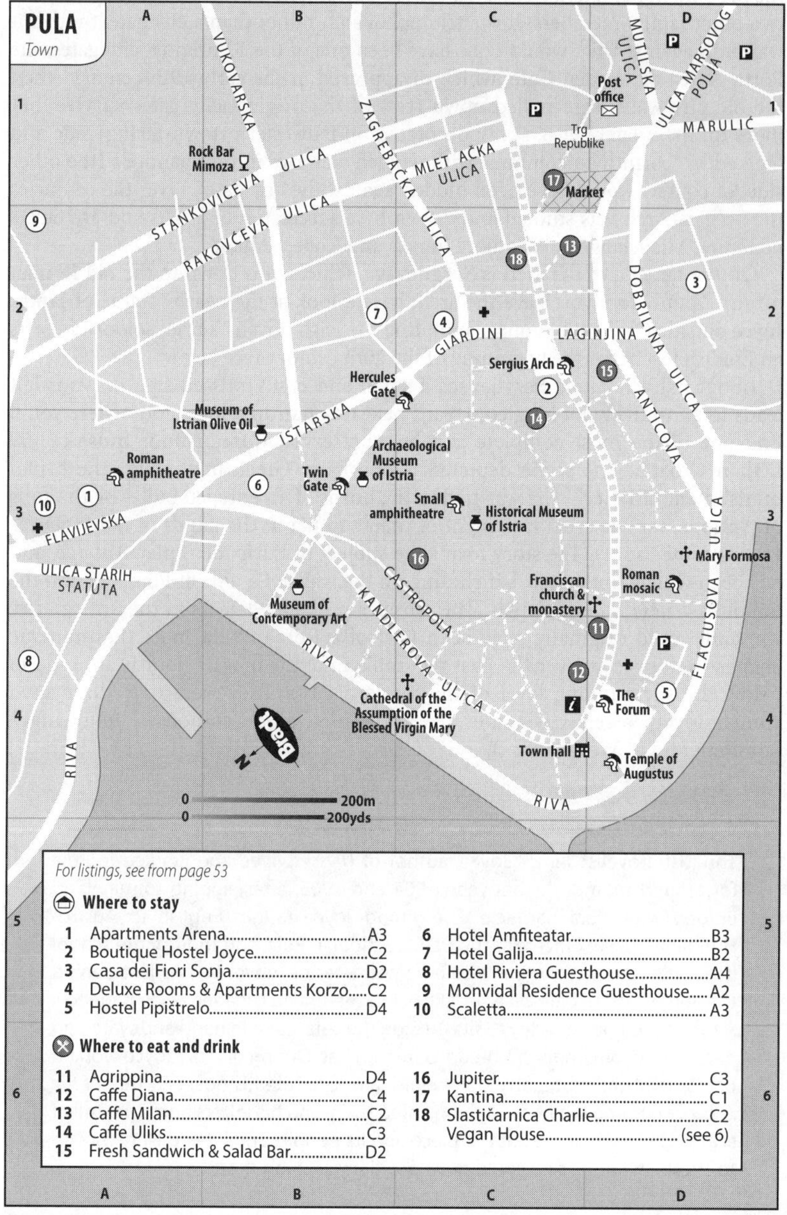

WHAT TO SEE AND DO

A walking tour of the old town All of the main sights in Pula are concentrated within a relatively small area and can easily be explored on foot. For the amphitheatre, see page 63.

For a walking tour of Pula's old town centre, start at the Sergius Arch on Trg Portarata. The **Sergius Arch (Slavoluk Sergijevaca)** [59 C2] probably dates from the years 29–27BC, and was commissioned by Salvia Postumia Sergi, a member of the prominent Sergi family, as a tribute to her husband Lucius Sergius Lepidus and two other family members. It is a triumphal arch rather than a city gate, though it was built against what would once have been one of the 12 original city gates, the Porta Aurea or Golden Gate, which disappeared in the early 19th century when the old city walls were pulled down (two of the original city gates survive, but more on them later). It is richly decorated on its western (town-facing) side and flanked by Corinthian columns, with winged victories in the spandrels (the other side, of course, would have been hidden against the city gate). Over the centuries the Sergius Arch was studied and drawn by a succession of artists and architects including Michelangelo, Palladio, Piranesi and Robert Adam.

On the far side of the arch is **Sergijevaca**, which runs down to the old Roman forum – but before you leave the arch, have a look at the nearby statue of **James Joyce** outside Café Uliks, commemorating the Irish novelist's brief sojourn here as an English teacher at the beginning of the 20th century (see below).

About halfway along Sergijevaca a small and easily missed sign on your left leads to an unlikely looking courtyard next to a hairdressing salon, where you'll find one of the most complete and best-preserved **Roman floor mosaics** [59 D3] in Croatia. The scene depicted is one from Greek mythology, the brutal punishment of Dirce – she was tied to the horns of an enraged bull – by the sons of Antiope, for the cruel treatment of their mother at the hands of Dirce (Dirce was Antiope's aunt). The story forms the subject of Euripedes's play *Antiope*, and has been widely illustrated – including on the walls of a villa at Pompeii, and the famous *Farnese Bull* in Naples. The mosaics probably date from the 3rd century AD, and would originally have been part of a Roman villa (note the dramatic change in floor level over the past two millennia: the mosaic floor is around 2m below the surrounding level of the modern city). They were only discovered comparatively recently – under the ruins of a block of houses, following a bombing raid in World War II.

JAMES JOYCE

The Irish novelist James Joyce, author of *Ulysses*, lived and worked in Pula for around six months between 1904 and 1905, after eloping to mainland Europe with Nora Barnacle. The young Joyce taught English to Austro-Hungarian naval officers at the Berlitz school in Pula, and though the school itself is long gone, there is a café named after his novel *Ulysses* just behind the Sergius Arch (Café Uliks – Uliks being the title in Croatian – see page 57). A bronze sculpture of Joyce sits outside the café, cane in hand and watching passers-by from under his broad-brimmed hat. During his stay Joyce worked on some of the material which would later become his novel *Portrait of the Artist as a Young Man* – though he hated Istria, and his letters home are full of scathing comments about the place and its people, and he and Nora moved to Trieste as soon as he could get a position teaching there.

Before returning to Sergijevaca, continue from the mosaics towards Flaciusova ulica, where you'll find the small 6th-century **Chapel of Mary Formosa (Kapela sv Marije Formoze)** [59 D3], which once formed part of an enormous Byzantine basilica (much of which was apparently used as building material by the Venetians, and according to some, finding its way into St Mark's). The chapel is usually locked, but some of the surviving floor and wall mosaics from inside can be seen in the Archaeological Museum (page 62).

A little further along Sergijevaca, a street on the right leads up to the 14th-century **Franciscan church and monastery (Crkva i samostan Sv Franje)** [59 D3] (Sv Franje; 🕘 10.00–19.00 Mon–Sat; entry €1.30), built in Romanesque style with some Gothic elements and an attractive cloister.

At the far (western) end of Sergijevaca you'll find a large square which was once the **Roman forum** [59 D4], now surrounded by cafés with tables spilling out on to the square. Two temples once stood here, one of which, the Temple of Augustus, is still standing. Built in the years 2BC–AD14 (there's an inscription with the date on the architrave), and dedicated to the goddess Roma and the emperor Augustus, the **Temple of Augustus (Augustov hram)** [59 D4] (forum; w ami-pula.hr; 🕘 Apr–Sep 09.00–20.00 daily; entry €1.40) is an exceptionally beautiful building, with refined, slender proportions, and tall columns with Corinthian capitals. It was converted into a church under Byzantine rule, and later the Venetians used it as a theatre, before its fortunes waned and it came to be used as a granary, and – not that you'd guess looking at the building now – was completely blown to bits in a bombing raid during World War II. Painstakingly restored to its former glory between 1945 and 1947, it now houses a small though interesting collection of Roman stonework and sculpture, including statues of several emperors and a fragment of a rather wild-eyed medusa. The **Temple of Diana (Dijanin hram)**, which once stood next to the Temple of Augustus, was incorporated into the back of the **town hall (Gradska palača)** [59 C4] during the 13th century – walk around the back of the latter building and you'll find its outline still clearly visible in the wall. An inscription on the town hall gives the date of its construction as 1296, though it probably existed in an earlier form before that, and the façade dates from the 16th century. It was the seat of the local duke during the Venetian period, and is still used by the mayor.

Walking northwest from the forum along Kandlerova ulica leads you to the **Cathedral of the Assumption of the Blessed Virgin Mary (Katedrala uznesenja Blažene Djevice Marije)** [59 C4]. The cathedral was built during the 5th century, on the foundations of an even earlier building, but following a fire in 1242 and other damage during the conflict between Venice and Genoa for control of the city, several parts of it were rebuilt over the next four centuries. The Renaissance façade dates from the 16th century, but traces of the earlier 4th-century building can be seen in the back wall. Inside you'll find re-used Roman and Byzantine columns and fragmentary 5th- or 6th-century floor mosaics, and a 3rd-century sarcophagus masquerading as an altar – which, some say, contains the relics of the 11th-century Hungarian king Solomon (who officially died on the battlefield near Edirne in modern Turkey, but according to legend escaped and ended his life as a monk in Pula). Note the lintel dated 857 embedded in the south wall. The bell tower dates from the late 17th century, and includes a large amount of building material pillaged from the arena, including a number of seats in its foundations.

Turning right on to Ul Sv Ivana, you'll find the **Museum of Contemporary Art of Istria** [59 B3] (MSUI/Muzej suvremene umjetnosti Istre; Ul Sv Ivana 1; 📞 052 351 541; w msu-istre.hr; 🕘 summer 10.00–22.00 Tue–Sun, winter 10.00–17.00 Tue–Sun; entry €2.60) with its collection of modern and contemporary art from

THE MUSEUM OF ISTRIAN OLIVE OIL

[59 B3] Museum Olei Histriae (Istarska 30; m 099 4105 002; w oleumhistriae.com; ⌚ 10.00–18.00 daily, with extended hrs Jun–Sep), opened in 2017 and subsequently moved to within 50m of the arena, highlights the history of olive cultivation and olive oil production in Istria over the past two millennia. Housed in a former textile factory, it is divided into three parts – a permanent exhibition, an area for olive oil tasting, and a shop selling some of Croatia's finest olive oils. There's an audio guide in 12 languages, plus a kids' corner. Tickets cost either €6.60/€3.30 including entry to the permanent exhibition plus an audio guide, €12/€6 including a guided tasting session (50 minutes), or €17.50/€8.60 including an extended tasting session with five of Istria's top olive oils plus a surprise dessert (60–70 minutes).

the second half of the 20th century up to the present. Bearing left after crossing Amfiteatarska ulica takes you towards the **Museum of Istrian Olive Oil** (see above) which is well worth seeing.

Continuing up Carrarina ulica you'll find the first of the two surviving city gates, the Porta Gemina or **Twin Gate** (**Dvojna vrata**) [59 B3], which dates from the 2nd or 3rd century and leads to the **Archaeological Museum of Istria** (**Arheološki muzej Istre**) [59 B3] (Carrarina 3; w ami-pula.hr), which has been closed for renovation for several years. There's little consensus on when it will finally re-open, but when it does – Istria's most important museum has extensive Roman and prehistoric collections, with objects from Pula as well as sites all over Istria (including the former Histrian capital Nesactium, Buzet, Dvigrad and Parentium, better known these days as Poreč), ranging from early floor mosaics to classical sculpture and Roman funerary monuments, pottery, glass and jewellery. There's also a medieval collection with stonework including fragments from the lost Byzantine complex of Mary Formosa.

On top of the hill at the centre of the old town is the 17th-century **Venetian fort**, restored by Napoleon and then under Austro-Hungary, with a star-shaped plan and four bastions. You can walk up to the fort from the Twin Gate, but it's not really the most impressive part of Pula, and our advice is to leave it until last. The fort now houses the **Historical Museum of Istria** (**Povijesni muzej Istre**) [59 C3] (Gradinski uspon 6; 052 211 566; w ppmi.hr; ⌚ Apr–Sep 09.00–21.00 daily, Oct–Mar 09.00–17.00 daily; entry €5.30), interesting mainly for the views of the city below from its ramparts. The hill was probably the site of an earlier, pre-Roman settlement, and there's also a **small Roman amphitheatre** up here, one of three that originally provided the city's entertainment (one of the others is probably the reason you've come to Pula; the third disappeared long ago, but once stood on the slopes of Montezaro, southeast of the city walls).

Continue up Carrarina, passing fragments of the old **city walls**, to the **Hercules Gate (Herkulova vrata)** [59 C2], built in 47–44BC and now flanked by two medieval bastions. At the top of the arch is a worn relief of Hercules with his club, and an inscription which includes the names of the two Roman officials, Lucius Calpurnius Piso and Gaius Cassius Longinus, entrusted by the Roman Senate with the duty of founding a colony at Pula.

Finally, turn left on to Istarska and follow this down to Pula's number-one star attraction – its exceptionally well-preserved Roman **amphitheatre** [59 A3] if, that is, you haven't abandoned this itinerary and headed there first.

Pula amphitheatre (Pulska Arena) [59 A3] (Flavijevska; 052 219 028; w ami-pula.hr/en/collections-on-other-locations/amphitheater; Apr–Oct 08.00–23.00 daily (last entry 22.00), Nov–Mar 09.00–17.00; entry adult/child €9.50/€4.60) Pula's amphitheatre was probably built during the first few years of the 1st century AD, during the reign of the emperor Augustus, and was completed in its present form under Vespasian (AD69–79), making it roughly contemporary with Rome's Colosseum. It is one of the six largest surviving Roman amphitheatres in the world, slightly elliptical in plan and measuring some 132m x 105m, with an estimated capacity of around 20,000 spectators. Its remarkably intact outer walls reach a height of some 32m, with two tiers of arches surmounted by a third tier of rectangular apertures, and on the landward side (where the ground level is higher), only two levels. The walls also incorporate four towers, each with a spiral staircase that gave access to the seating areas, and with a water storage tank (supplied by an aqueduct), from which water was then distributed around the arena by channels. The underground passages, through which unfortunate gladiators once made their way into the arena to undertake bloody, mortal combat, now hold an exhibition of wine and olive oil production in Roman Istria. The arena itself now holds major concerts and operas, and some screenings of the Pula Film Festival (page 58), with seating for 5,000–8,000. It stands just outside the city walls on Flavijevska or Via Flavia, formerly the Roman road leading to Poreč and Trieste.

Over the centuries the arena has been pillaged for its fine, locally quarried stone (the cathedral's 17th-century bell tower being just one example of its re-use in other buildings). In fact the arena came close to disappearing altogether in the 15th century, when the Venetian Senate decided that the whole thing should be dismantled and reassembled in Venice – an idea fortunately thwarted by a Venetian senator, Gabriele Emo, whose name is commemorated on a plaque on the northwest tower of the arena. As a friend from the nearby town of Šišan once commented in horror at the idea, 'Just imagine – what would we do without our arena?!'

Beyond the old town centre Out towards Stoja near the Hotel Milan 1967 is the **Naval Cemetery (Mornaričko groblje)** [54 F4] (between Stoja & Ulika Rikarda Katalinića Jeretova), dating from 1866, a leafy green oasis which is the final resting place of some 150,000 soldiers from the Austro-Hungarian navy. There are also several little-known Austrian **forts**, in various stages of decay, scattered around the headlands surrounding Pula.

BEACHES Pula's best beaches for **swimming** are a short distance north and south of the town centre, at **Štinjan** (in particular the pebbly Vile Beach, which might sound like an unfortunate choice of name until you know that it means 'fairy' in Croatian; bus #5) and **Stoja** (pebbly, quite busy as it's also the main camping area; bus #1) respectively, and at **Verudela** (pebble beaches such as Ambrela and 'Hawaii'; bus #2a). A little further south are the sandy (and very popular) Bijeca Beach at **Medulin** (bus #25) and the rocky coves of **Rt Kamenjak** (beautiful and remote feeling, but the currents can be quite strong so it's not advisable for kids; buses #26 or #28 to Premantura, then hire a bike or walk down the cape; page 193). If it's a **windsurfing** beach you're after, then head south to Premantura and Medulin for some of the best conditions anywhere in Croatia – Stupice has a windsurfing school and hire facilities (w windsurfing.hr), Pomer or Bijeca beaches have slightly more sheltered conditions, so are particularly suitable for beginners, and for experienced windsurfers who want to catch the full force of the *bura* wind, there's Kuj Beach at Ližnjan.

MARINE TURTLE RESCUE CENTRE

Though they are endangered, it is estimated that each year around 6,000 marine turtles (mostly loggerhead) get accidentally caught in fishing nets in the Adriatic, around 2,500 of those in its eastern part. Many of these animals drown, since once in the net they are unable to come to the surface to breathe. Turtles also accidentally swallow plastic bags and other waste, not to mention fishing hooks, and since they spend a comparatively long time at the surface while breathing they are prone to being struck by powerboats and other motorised craft.

The Marine Turtle Rescue Centre at Pula Aquarium was founded in 2006, following the establishment of the Pula Marine Educational Centre in Verudela the previous year, and is the first centre of its kind in Croatia. Apart from the care and treatment of injured sea turtles, its activities include tagging turtles in the wild, and working to increase awareness among locals and fishermen of the dangers posed to turtles.

If you find an injured sea turtle in the wild, contact the aquarium staff who will send someone to collect it, and in the meantime try to cover it with wet rags or a wet towel to prevent it drying out. You can also **adopt a marine turtle**, which goes directly towards the work of the rescue centre – see the aquarium website (below) for details.

STOJA AND VERUDELA Just beyond the southern edge of Pula are the **Stoja** and **Verudela** (often written Verudella) peninsulas, the former Pula's main camping area and the latter home to several of its larger hotels. Both have pleasantly indented coastlines, with plenty of coves and rocky or pebble beaches and wooded areas, and are easily accessible by local bus (page 51).

Verudela is also where you'll find the excellent **Pula Aquarium** [54 H2] (Fort Verudela; 052 381 402; e infos@aquarium.hr; w aquarium.hr; Jul/Aug 09.00–22.00 daily, Jun/Sep 09.00–21.00 daily, May–first half Oct 09.00–20.00 daily, second half Oct–Apr 09.00–18.00 daily, Nov–Mar 09.00–16.00 Mon–Fri & 09.00–17.00 Sat/Sun, last entry 1 hour before closing; entry adults/children 7–18/3–6/under 3s €17.50/€13.50/€9.30/free), which is a must for those travelling with children, partly as recompense for having dragged them around Pula's Roman monuments. The aquarium is housed in a late 19th-century Austro-Hungarian fort, and was transformed into its present use in 2002. There are about 60 tanks, with a wide range of species and several interactive displays for kids, and on the first floor the **Marine Turtle Rescue Centre** (see above).

A little way past Verudela, near Uvala Soline, is the Roman quarry site where the stone for the Pula amphitheatre was quarried. Known as **Cave Romane** [54 G1] it is now open as a festival site for summer concerts (w caveromane.com).

SOUTH FROM PULA

MEDULIN The small town of Medulin is these days a large, busy holiday resort, with one of those coveted and fairly rare things in Croatia – a big, sandy beach. **Bijeca Beach** is popular with families as well as with windsurfers, and you can expect it to be packed in the summer. **Bus** #25 runs between Pula's bus station and Medulin. The **tourist information office** (Brajdine 43; 052 577 145; e info@tzom.hr; w medulinriviera.info; Jun–Sep 08.00–21.00 daily) offers information on hotels and beaches plus detailed information on local walks and cycling routes.

You can also get out to some of the ten uninhabited islands of the **Medulin archipelago**, including Ceja and Levan, both of which have restaurants – and Levan also has a small sandy beach. Taxi-boats run between Medulin and several islands as well as Rt Kamenjak. For example, Taxi Boat Dijana departs for Ceja from near the Hotel Holiday at 09.30, 10.30, 11.30, 13.30 and 14.30 and returns at midday, 14.00, 17.00, 18.00 and 19.00 daily (return ticket adults €7, children €3).

Where to stay and eat There's no shortage of accommodation in Medulin. **Camping** options include **Campsite Piccolo** (Vinkuran Centar 9, Medulin; 052 866 995; w camping-piccolo.com/en) – a nice little family-run place opened in 2020 (small and family-run being rare things among Croatian campsites) – and the (much, much larger) **Camp Arena Grand** (Kapovica 350; 052 577 277; w arenacamps.com; 31 Mar–21 Oct), which has 965 lots and 2km of beach including a separate naturist beach. There are more campsites listed at w medulinriviera.info/accommodation/camping.

Park Plaza Belvedere Medulin (190 dbls) Osipovica 33; 052 572 001; e ppbm@pphe.com; w radissonhotels.com/en-us/hotels/park-plaza-belvedere-medulin. Renovated 4-star with pools & a fitness centre; all rooms have balconies. Close to Bijeca Beach. **€€€€**

Tui Blue Medulin (ex Sensimer) (180 dbls) Osipovica 31; 052 572 601; e medulin@arenahotels.hr; w tui-blue.com/en/en/hotels/tui-blue-medulin. Next door to the Park Plaza Belvedere, 100m from the beach. **€€€**

Villa San Rocco B&B (ex Zibi) (13 dbls, 1 suite) Brajdine 99a; 052 577 218; w booking.com/hotel/hr/villa-zibi.en-gb.html. Small B&B just north of the marina, only a 10min walk from the beach, with good-sized b/fasts, a roof terrace with swimming pool. **€€€**

Konoba Casa Mia & Enoteka Selo 127a, Premantura; m 098 995 8393; w konoba-casa-mia.eatbu.hr; 18.00–23.45 Tue–Sun. Small konoba with a good choice of seafood, pasta & other dishes including several vegetarian options. **€€€**

RT KAMENJAK AND PREMANTURA [map, page 194] Rt Kamenjak (Cape Kamenjak) meanders out into the waters of the Adriatic between Medulin and Banjole – a slender, highly indented peninsula that constitutes the southernmost tip of Istria. **Premantura**, the small town at the base of the peninsula, can be reached by **bus** #26 and #28 from Pula's bus station. The nearest **tourist information offices** are in Medulin, and another small kiosk at Banjole.

There are several **campsites** around Premantura, including the large **Camp Stupice** [map, page 194] (Selo 250; 052 575 111; e arenastupice@arenacampsites.com; w arenacampsites.com/en/campsites-istria/camping-arena-stupice; 30 Mar–4 Nov) with around 1,000 lots, and **Camp Runke** [map, page 194] (Runke 60; 052 575 022; e arenarunke@arenacampsites.com; w arenacampsites.com/en/campsites-istria/camping-arena-runke; 20 Apr–16 Sep) which is much smaller, with 'only' 247 lots, set amid pine trees. There are no hotels or campsites in the southern half of the peninsula – fortunately, since it's a nature reserve (see below) – though there is a small no-frills bar, **Safari Bar** [map, page 194], at Mala Kolombarica, and it's possible to book a stay in a lighthouse on the tiny island of Porer (page 16).

The southern half of **Rt Kamenjak** is a nature reserve and one of the most beautifully unspoilt stretches of coastline anywhere in Croatia. Some 530 plant species have been recorded on Kamenjak, including at least 28 species of orchid, many of them classified as rare or endangered and two of them endemic to the southern part of Istria; there are numerous butterfly species; and one of the only sightings of the Critically Endangered Mediterranean monk seal in Croatia in recent decades was in these waters – an animal now reduced to only around 600 individuals. The nature reserve is administered from a small office in Premantura (Javna ustanova Kamenjak, Selo 120; 052 575 283; e info@kamenjak.hr; w kamenjak.hr) and is the place to go if you want to find out more about the flora, wildlife and marine life on and around Rt Kamenjak. The best time of year to visit Kamenjak for wildflowers is June, or March/April for orchids. There are also **dinosaur footprints** on the rocky northwest coast of Kamenjak, with an educational trail and dinosaur models – great fun for kids. Also, there are educational programmes for kids, and guided walks can be arranged.

Hike from Premantura to Mala Kolombarica (page 193).

There are seemingly endless rocky coves and bays along the length of Kamenjak, so there's no shortage of places for a **swim**, but be aware that the currents are quite strong here – don't swim too far out to sea, and don't let kids swim alone. A couple of the bays have small bars, including the Safari Bar at Mala Kolombarica. The best way to explore Kamenjak is by bike or on foot (page 193), and access is free for those on foot and cyclists; those determined to bring a car into the nature reserve will need to pay a fee (€5.50 per day for a car, €10 for a camper van) to drive on Kamenjak.

The east coast of Rt Kamenjak is also one of the best **windsurfing** spots in Croatia, since it is exposed to all the different winds experienced in the northern Adriatic – the *bura, burin, maestral* and *jugo*. There's a well-established **windsurfing centre** at Camp Stupice, Premantura (contact Boris Ivančić; m 091 512 3646; e bivancic@yahoo.com; w windsurfing.hr), which opened back in 2000, where you can rent or buy equipment, or join classes (in several languages, including English) from beginners to advanced level. They also rent mountain bikes. The best seasons are spring and autumn since they have the highest percentage of days with winds, though for beginners summer is preferable, since the water is warmer, and the more moderate *maestral* will be blowing.

NORTH FROM PULA

FAŽANA The small fishing village of Fažana lies around 8km north of Pula (bus #21), and its lively little harbour is the departure point for boats to the Brijuni Islands (page 68). During the Roman period, Fažana lay on the Via Flavia between Pula and Trieste and was an important pottery centre. The town produced large **amphorae** that were used to transport Istrian wine and olive oil to various parts of the Roman Empire including the Danube region and northern Italy, and a Roman kiln has been excavated in the town centre. The **Parish Church of SS Cosmas and Damian** (**Župna crkva sv Kuzme i Damjana**) (Fažana's patron saints) dates from the 15th century and has a *Last Supper* by Zorzi Ventura of Zadar (1598), as well as traces of 16th-century frescoes; the 14th-century **Church of Our Lady of Mount Carmel** (**Crkva bl Djevice Marije od Karmela**) contains fragmentary remains of 15th-century frescoes and a 14th-century wooden statue of the Virgin Mary. Fažana holds several foodie **festivals**. In July local women prepare *maneštra* and a variety of other traditional Istrian stews, and in early August there's a festival celebrating the humble **sardine** or pilchard, which is fished in the straits between here and the Brijuni Islands and can be eaten freshly grilled on the waterfront. The Brijuni Islands National Park Office is on Brioska, near the jetty from where the boats to Brijuni depart (Brionska 10; 052 525 888; e brijuni@np-brijuni.hr; w np-brijuni.hr).

Where to stay and eat Most people pass through Fažana on the way to and from Brijuni, but if you want to stay there's plenty of accommodation, and great views of the islands from the waterfront. The **tourist information office** (43 Istarske divizije 8; 052 383 727; Jul/Aug 08.00–22.00 daily, Jun–Sep 08.00–20.00 daily, Oct–May 08.00–15.30 Mon–Fri) can give details of private accommodation, otherwise there are a couple of hotels – including the beautiful, boutique Villetta Phasiana – and a hostel.

Villetta Phasiana (19 dbls, 2 sgls) Trg sv Kuzme I Damjana 1; m 091 887 9313; e info@villetta-phasiana.hr; w villetta-phasiana.hr. Small boutique hotel housed in a renovated 16th-century villa, with its own spa & a nautical-themed bar, shaped like the prow of a ship. **€€€€**

Apartments Dante, Medea & Dama (3 apts) Ul Ruže Petrović 62; m 095 3942 700; e edita.bgc@gmail.com; w visitfazana.com. Spacious, nicely decorated apartments on the north side of town, sleeping 4–7. **€€€**

Heritage Hotel Chersin (9 dbls) Piazza Grande 8; m 095 398 5350; e hotelchersin@gmail.com; w hotel-chersin.com. Small boutique hotel, beautifully renovated (exposed stone & brightly painted furniture) & right on the waterfront, with its own restaurant. **€€€**

Hostel Vala (51 beds in 15 rooms) Mala Vala 38, Valbandon; 052 520 028; e zuljanic@gmail.com. Bike-friendly hostel between Fažana & Štinjan. **€€**

Konoba Feral Boraca 11; 052 520 040; w restaurant-feral.com; midday–23.00 daily. Popular waterfront *konoba* with plenty of seafood on the menu, including Fažana's speciality, sardines. They also now have a small pension with 4 rooms (**€€€**). €€€€–€€

VODNJAN Around 10km northeast from Pula on the old road to Pazin, or just off the *ipsilon* (the main road between Pula and Rijeka), Vodnjan (Dignano) is a quiet little town with narrow, cobbled streets and some grand Venetian and Baroque architecture – not to mention a rather macabre collection of mummified saints.

The neo-Baroque **Parish Church of St Blaise** (**Župna crvka sv Blaž**) was built between 1761 and 1808 on the site of an earlier Romanesque church destroyed in 1760, and is the largest parish church in Istria, with a 25m-high dome. The 62m-high bell tower, which is clearly modelled on the one in Venice's Piazza San Marco, is the tallest in Istria and was built between 1815 and 1882 after designs by Antonio Porta of Trieste. The most interesting thing about the church, however, is its mummies. Hidden in a curtained, dimly lit room behind the main altar are six glass cases containing the intact bodies of three saints – St Leon Bembo (a chaplain in the Doge's Palace in Venice, who died in 1188), St Giovanni Olini (died 1300) and St Nicolosa Bursa (a Benedictine nun who died in Venice in 1512) – as well as various body parts of three other saints (St Barbara, St Sebastian and St Mary of Egypt). The bodies are clothed, and the skin and fingernails have darkened, giving them a strange, almost wooden appearance. Exactly how or why the bodies – which were not embalmed – have failed to decompose remains a mystery (the body of St Nicolosa is particularly well preserved and is often described as the best-preserved mummy in Europe). They were brought to Vodnjan from Venice in 1818 by the artist Gaetano Gresler. In total the church holds some 370 relics, belonging to 250 different saints.

Vodnjan is also a really good place to see ***kažuni***, traditional Istrian dry stone wall shelters (page 17) – there's a group of restored *kažuni* just outside town on the road to Bale. More recently Vodnjan has become quite a hotspot for **street art** with new works popping up all over the place during the Street Art and Boombarstick festivals – you can download a map of street art locations from the tourist office website w https://vodnjandignano.com/en/murals/stranica/62.

Vodnjan makes an easy day trip from Pula, either on **bus** #22 (runs every 90 minutes or so on weekdays, less frequently at weekends; journey time 30 minutes) or on the **train** heading towards Pazin. The helpful **tourist information office** is on the main square (Narodni trg 3; 052 511 700; w vodnjandignano.com; Oct–May 08.00–15.00 Mon–Fri, Jun–Sep 08.00–15.00 Mon–Fri, 09.00–13.00 Sat, Jul/Aug 08.00–20.00 Mon–Fri, 09.00–13.00 & 18.00–20.00 Sat, 09.00–13.00 Sun). Finally, if you head north from Vodnjan towards Bale and then turn towards the coast, you'll come to the extensive **Meneghetti winery**, which offers wine tastings, along with accommodation in a beautiful set of stone villas (Stancija Meneghetti 1, Bale; 052 528 800; reception@meneghetti.hr; w meneghetti.hr; **€€€€€**).

Where to stay, eat and drink There are several places to stay in Vodnjan itself and its surroundings (see w vodnjandignano.com/en/smjestaj/vodnjan/city/1), as well as some good places to eat, including the outstanding Vodnjanka.

B&B Tocà la Luna (4 dbls) Gradina 12; m 098 182 8726; w booking.com/hotel/hr/b-amp-b-toca-la-louna.en-gb.html. Nice little B&B with communal kitchen (min 2-night stay). **€€€**

✷ **Vodnjanka** Istarska bb; 052 511 435; w vodnjanka.com. 11.00–midnight Mon–Sat. If you're eating in Vodnjan, you won't find much better than this lovely restaurant where dishes include homemade pasta with truffles & steak with porcini & truffles, & wonderful seasonal asparagus dishes. Deservedly popular so booking is advised in the summer. **€€€–€€**

BRIJUNI ISLANDS

The Brijuni (Brioni) Islands lie around 3km offshore from the village of Fažana (page 66), north of Pula. National park, state residence and modern safari park, they have both Roman and Byzantine remains (and a golf course), and are an extremely popular day trip from the Istrian coast. The Brijuni islands are hugely popular – although if you have a limited amount of time in Istria, there are frankly plenty of other places which are much more rewarding to visit, in the opinion of at least one of the authors.

Brijuni National Park (Nacionalni park Brijuni; Brionska 10, Fažana; 052 525 888; e brijuni@np-brijuni.hr; w np-brijuni.hr – an often frustrating website that fails to prioritise basic information like entry fees, and it's been that way for more than a decade without improvement) is one of eight national parks in Croatia, and the only one in Istria (though there's a nature park, Učka, and several protected reserves). It covers all 14 islands and a larger area of the sea around them – a total area of just under 40km^2, 7.4km^2 of that comprising land. The largest island, by a long way, is Veliki Brijun ('Big Brijun').

There was a Bronze Age hillfort on Veliki Brijun, above Verige Bay, and the island was settled both during the Roman period and under Byzantium. The largest Roman site on the island is the settlement of **Kastrum**, on the west coast. A villa was built here during the 2nd–1st century BC, which later developed into a small walled settlement where olive oil and wine were produced and stored – the storage areas and channels through which the olive oil flowed can still be seen clearly. The

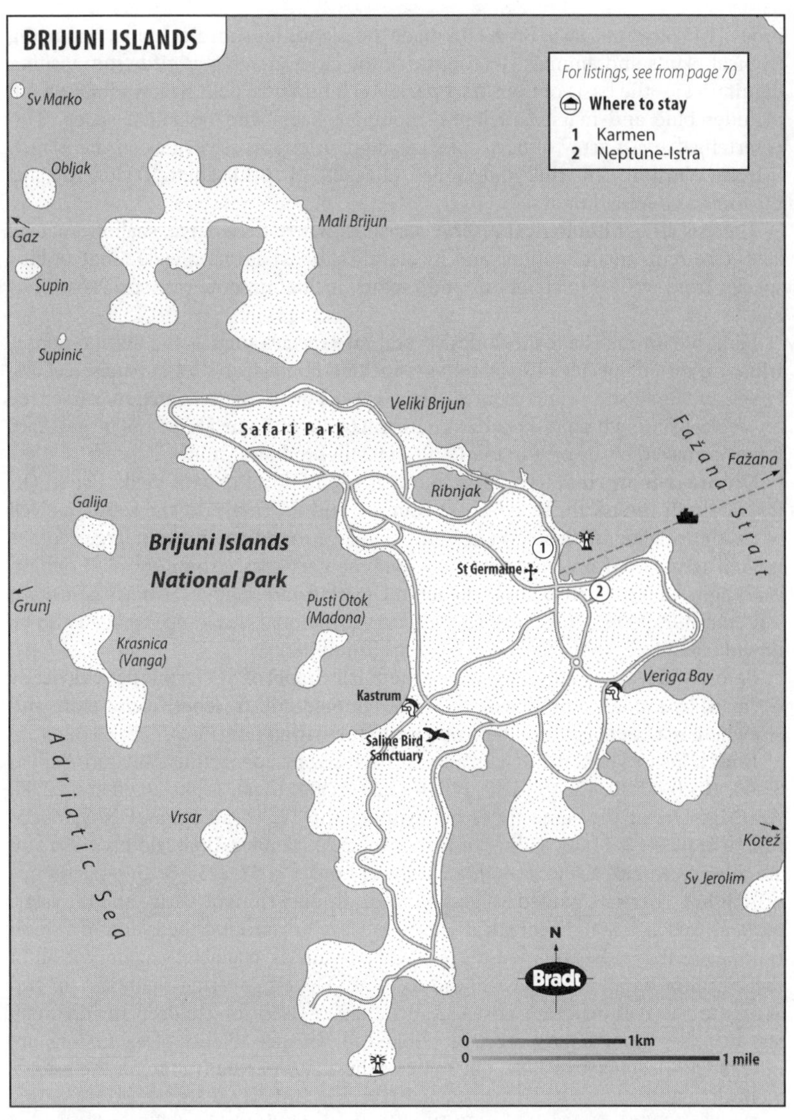

site continued to be inhabited through the Byzantine and Carolingian periods, and was still in use under Venice. There are remains of an early (5th–6th century) basilica nearby. There are also remains of a Roman villa at Verige Bay.

In 1893 – by which time they were largely overgrown and rife with malaria – the islands were purchased by Austrian businessman **Paul Kupelwieser**. Within a relatively short time, Kupelwieser eradicated the malaria and converted Veliki Brijun into a luxury health resort, complete with fine hotels, heated pools, a zoo and even an ostrich farm. Kupelwieser's resort became immensely fashionable, with everyone from George Bernard Shaw and Thomas Mann to the Austrian archduke Franz Ferdinand coming to stay on the island (on just one day in 1911 no fewer than 16 princes and princesses as well as 15 counts and countesses were in residence).

From 1949 onwards, **Josip Broz Tito** made the islands his summer home, importing tropical plants and animals (with more of the latter arriving as gifts from visiting dignitaries) – the basis of the **safari park** you'll find on Veliki Brijun today, which includes blue and marsh antelopes, mountain zebra and Somalian sheep. Tito entertained a vast array of heads of state, dignitaries and celebrities on the islands – from Winston Churchill and Queen Elizabeth II to Elizabeth Taylor, Richard Burton and Sophia Loren.

There is an **ornithological reserve** at Saline, where three large, shallow, marshy lakes (the remnants of antique and medieval saltpans) attract a wide range of bird species from waders to songbirds and raptors, including some rare species such as black stork.

Plant life on the islands includes several rare species such as the marine poppy, while imported species of exotic plants include Himalayan and Lebanese cedars, Greek and Spanish firs and sequoia. There's also a giant, twisted, **ancient olive tree** on Veliki Brijun which radiocarbon dating has shown to be about 1,600 years old. It was damaged by a storm in the 1970s, but still produces fruit.

Dinosaur footprints have been found at several locations on Veliki Brijun (Rt Pogledalo in the north, Rt Ploče, Rt Kamnik and Rt Trstike in the south, as well as on the smaller islands of Vanga and Galija), formed when these large reptiles walked across tidal and mud flats – now sedimentary rock – some 100–115 million years ago. An informative little booklet in Croatian and English, *Šetalište dinosaura – Promenade of Dinosaurs*, is available from the national park office and can also be downloaded free from their website (w np-brijuni.hr).

Before you leave Brijuni, step inside the small **chapel of St Germaine** (**Crkvica sv German**) by the museum, where the copies of medieval **frescoes** from Beram and elsewhere may persuade you to venture into the Istrian interior.

Boat trips to Veliki Brijun run all year from Fažana, departing daily Jun–Sept at 09.00, 10.00, 11.30, 12.30, 13.30, 14.30, 15.30, 17.00, 18.00, 19.00, 20.00 and 22.00, Apr/May/Oct at the same times but without the 12.30 sailing, and November–March at 09.00 & 11.30. Sailing time is around 20 minutes. Boats do fill up so you are advised to call a few days in advance to book (☎ 052 525 882/3; e izleti@np-brijuni.hr). There are guided excursions to the Roman ruins at Verige and the safari park, as well as the archaeological museum, travelling around the island in a small train, as well as other themed tours, and cycle hire is available – again, for all of these, call or email a few days ahead to book. Tickets covering the boat trip and access to the national park cost €33 for adults, €16.50 for children in Jun–Sept, less in other months, and must be booked in advance. Plenty of excursions are offered from agencies in Pula, but some of these don't actually stop on the islands – check first.

Divers might be interested in Rt Peneda, the only place where diving is allowed in the national park (page 214).

It's also possible **to stay on the islands** [map, page 69], in one of a small number of (frankly very overpriced for what you get) hotels (including the three-star **Neptune-Istra €€€€€**, close to where the boats arrive, or the two-star **Karmen €€€€€**) and rental apartments (w np-brijuni.hr/en/accommodation/villas-of-the-brijuni-islands; **€€€€€**) – contact the national park office in Fažana to book (e brijuni@np-brijuni.hr). There's a large restaurant close to where the boat arrives, though you're better off eating back in Fažana or Pula.

4

Rovinj

For many, Rovinj is the pearl and the envy of Istria. Favoured by the Venetians when it was ruled by the Republic of Venice, it was also a favourite of the touring classes of the Austro-Hungarian Empire. The colourful hues of Rovinj's houses hail from these influences, especially the dominant Venetian red. Often overwhelmed with visitors in the height of summer – when it's popular with tours from Poreč and Pula, where it is easier to get accommodation – in the winter it is almost deserted. The tightly packed houses of Rovinj's old town form some of the narrowest of cobbled streets, which pop out atop the hill of the once-upon-a-time island to a magnificent vista from the generously wide courtyard of the equally generously endowed St Euphemia Church. Being so popular, the town understandably has a couple of Istria's best restaurants, festivals and enviable bars.

HISTORY

As an island Rovinj was inhabited by man in the Bronze and Iron ages. It was known later to the Romans as Mons Rupineum, one of four islands of the Rovinj archipelago to be inhabited at the time, along with St Catherine, St Andrew and Cissa. The last, mentioned by Pliny the Elder in his writings in AD1, no longer exists, having sunk in an earthquake in the late 8th century.

By the 4th century, a fortification named Castrum Rubini was built on Mons Rupineum, and this grew gradually into the town known today as Rovinj. Mons Rupineum maintained a large level of autonomy until 966 when, under the Patriarch of Aquilea, it was annexed to the Bishopric of Poreč. From 1188 Rovinj threw its allegiance in with Dubrovnik in today's southern Croatia, signing the Renovatia pacis, which brought it into conflict on several occasions with cities further to the north in today's Slovenian Adriatic.

By 1283, however, Rovinj followed the lead of Poreč and other Istrian towns in joining the Most Serene Republic of Venice (known as the *Serenissima*). This in turn brought Rovinj into conflict with inland Istria, which was ruled by the Counts of Gorizia and then by the Habsburgs from 1374. Rovinj was fortunate to survive the plague of 1312 which dramatically reduced the populations of other towns and cities in Istria, but Rovinj continued to see destruction in Venice's war with Genoa in 1379, and then later from marauding pirates.

By the end of the 16th century, immigrants fleeing Ottoman rule further south started to settle in big numbers in Rovinj, and its population almost doubled over a period of 60 years to 5,000 by 1650. By 1775, Rovinj's population had grown to over 13,000, slightly higher than today, and it was during this period of expansion that the town came to look as it does today. It was also during this period that Rovinj grew as an important shipping base and producer of stone for building Venice. The latter's taxes on the town were high though, and Rovinj's competitiveness began to wane, especially after the Habsburg Empire proclaimed Rijeka and Trieste to be free ports with considerably relaxed taxes. Thereafter the *Serenissima* had to quell several town uprisings.

In 1763, the isthmus between the island and the mainland was filled in as the town grew to well beyond the town walls. With the abdication of the Grand Council of Venice in 1797, Rovinj joined the rest of Istria, ruled first by Austria, then briefly by Napoleon from 1809. Under Austrian rule again from 1813, industrialisation brought numerous factories to Rovinj, including today's still-dominant tobacco factory Adria, and the railway arrived in 1876.

GETTING THERE AND AWAY

BY BUS Rovinj **bus station** [76 D3] (Trg na Lokva bb; ☎ 052 811 453; ⏲ 06.30–22.00 daily) is very centrally located on the edge of the pedestrian zone, with a taxi stand and Bike Planet both within a stone's throw. There are daily buses to Ljubljana, Belgrade and Trieste, and several buses a day to Zagreb, Pula, Poreč and Rijeka.

BY BOAT Rovinj runs two summer services to Italian ports, all arriving and leaving from Veliki mol pier [80 D3] next to the harbour master's office.

Venice **Venezia Lines** (w venezialines.com) sails from St Basilio port in Venice to Rovinj at 17.15 between April and October via Piran and Poreč, arriving at between 21.00 and 22.30 in Rovinj. For sailing times from Rovinj, see w venezialines.com. This boat has no outdoor seating. Single tickets cost from €55/€39 for adults/kids. Returns are the same price as two singles. **Adriatic Lines** (w adriatic-lines.com) sails from Venice to Rovinj between mid-May and early October, departing Venice at 17.00 and arriving in Rovinj 19.30– 20.00, and returning from Rovinj at 08.00; one-way tickets cost €60 for adults, €30 for children, returns €69/35.

GETTING AROUND

The old town of Rovinj has no public transport and is perched on a steep hill, with the flagstones on the main street of Grisia up to St Euphemia Church being quite polished from use, making them slippery, particularly in the rain.

BY BOAT Taxi-boats are available from Mali mol pier [80 D2]. Regular passenger boats ply between the main resorts.

Sv Katerina Boats leave Rovinj's Delfin pier [76 C4] every hour on the half-hour 05.30–00.30. The timetable is listed on the Maistra website (w maistra.com/properties/island-hotel-katarina/boat-schedule). Guests of hotels on the island travel for free. Return tickets are purchased at the kiosk on the island near the pier or at the reception of Hotel Istra: adults €8, children half price.

Sv Andrija (Crveni otok) Crveni otok ('Red Island') isn't actually red and is in fact composed of two islets, Sv Andrija and Maškin, connected by an isthmus. Boats leave the Delfin pier [76 C4] every hour on the half-hour (05.30–00.30; €10.60 return, children half price); see w maistra.com/properties/island-hotel-katarina/boat-schedule for timetables. Guests of Island Hotel Istra travel for free.

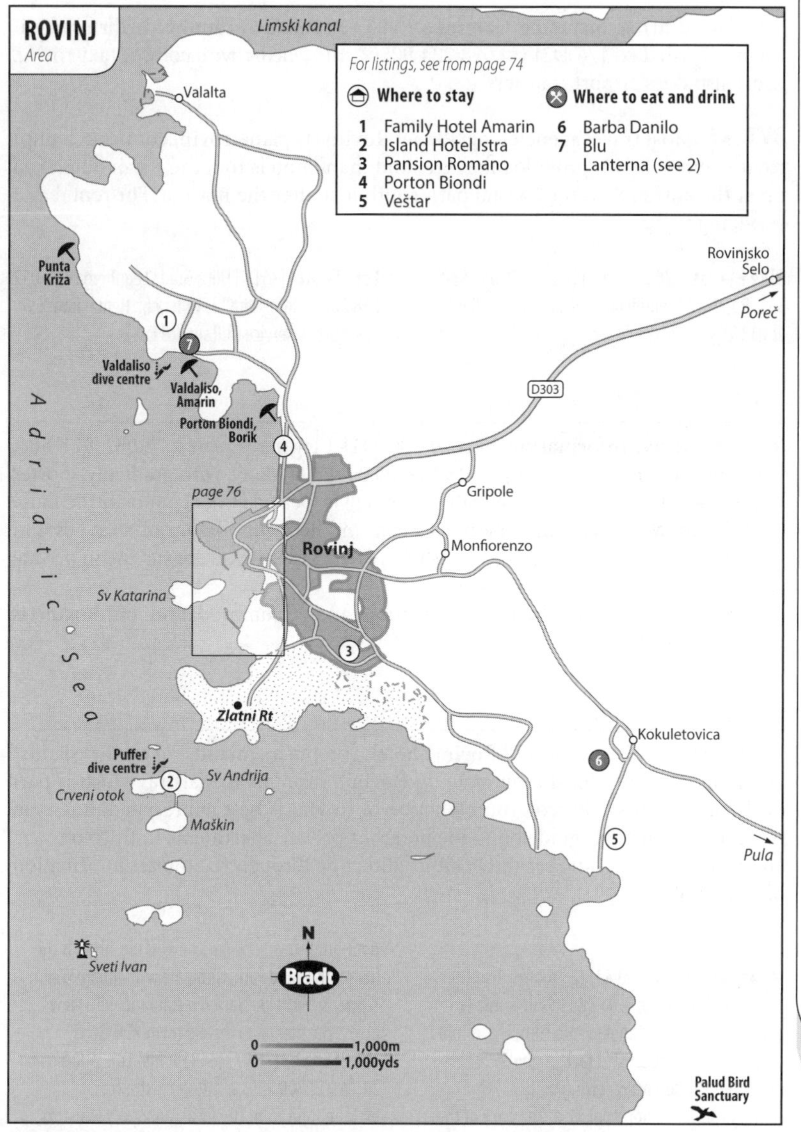

CAR HIRE Services are available through most travel agencies, or you can go direct to:

Sixt [76 D3] Hermana Dalmatina 8; 052 685 073; **w** sixt.com

Vetura-rentacar [76 C5] Vladimira Nazora bb; 052 815 209; **m** 091 730 4408; **w** vetura-rentacar.com. Can provide cars equipped with winter tyres (a legal requirement in the winter in Croatia), child seats & Garmin GPS.

BY TAXI Taxis wait round the corner from the bus station [76 D3] at Trg na Lokva. See **w** rovinj-tourism.com/en/plan-your-journey/service-informations/taxi, for a list of local firms, including **Cammeo** (☎ 052 313 300; **w** cammeo.hr/hr/gradovi/rovinj). Flash Taxi [76 D3] (**m** 098 224 905; **e** info@taxi-rovinj.com; **w** taxi-rovinj.com) also does airport transfers.

BY BIKE Most travel agencies, eg: Planet Rovinj (**w** planetrovinj.com/index.php/rovinj-rent-a-bike), provide bike hire, and many hotels too; these can be picked up at the entrance to the coastal path south just after the marina. For rental and servicing try:

Bike Planet [76 C3] Trg na Lokva 3; ☎ 052 830 531; Run by 2 friendly brothers. Rental available at €13/day.

Lera Sport [76 D4] Ulica Grada Leonberga 4; ☎ 052 818 225; **e** info@lera.hr; **w** lera.hr. Rental from €9/day, parts & service (full service €25).

TOURIST INFORMATION

Rovinj's **tourist information bureau** [80 D1] (Trg na mostu 2; ☎ 052 811 566; **w** rovinj-tourism.com; ⏲ 15 Jun–15 Sep 08.00–21.00 daily, with gradually shorter hours towards the winter, closed Sun in winter) is located almost opposite the Balbi Arch. Here, online and in person, you can find accommodation of all types and some fairly useful information. This is where to register if you are staying in private accommodation or on your own boat.

Another useful website for information and accommodation on Rovinj is **w** rovinj.info.

WHERE TO STAY

As elsewhere in Istria, most of Rovinj's hotels (on the mainland and on the islands) are dominated by a local monopoly: in Rovinj's case this is Maistra, which is part of the local Adris tobacco group. The joy of Rovinj is best appreciated, however, from one of the high-grade boutique hotels or private apartments in the old town, and so it is worth going for these, either direct or through the tourist information office, see above.

HOTELS

✷ **Angelo D'Oro** [80 A1] (26 rooms, 1 suite) Vladimira Švalbe 40; ☎ 052 853 920; **e** info@angelodoro.com; **w** angelodoro.com. This might only be a 4-star because it lacks a pool & fitness room, but the service & setting in this 17th-century former bishop's palace at the back of the old town are my favourites by far. Bijou & exquisite, it has the tiniest of spas, a miniature library corner & top-floor terrace. Here you're transported back to how travel could be for the Venetian classes, complete with antique furniture pieces (OK, minus the Wi-Fi, TV & AC now available here). Painted in Venetian red, it has a cavernous dining room, which is always cool in the summer. **€€€€€**

Grand Park Hotel [76 C5] (209 rooms & suites) Antonia Smareglia 1a; ☎ 052 800 250; **e** hello@maistra.hr; **w** maistra.com/properties/grand-park-hotel-rovinj. Rovinj's newest big-hitter is the luxurious Grand Park, complete with Albaro Wellness & Spa, & Michelin-starred restaurant, with views across the marina to the old town. **€€€€€**

Hotel Lone [76 C7] (248 rooms) Luje Adamovica 31; ☎ 052 800 250; **e** info@maistra.hr; **w** lonehotel.com. The local monopoly Maistra's 5-star über-stylish designer hotel that looks like a cruise ship. Modern with all the trimmings, from rooms with private terrace infinity pools to staff uniforms by Croatian designer I-GLE. **€€€€€**

✷ **Hotel Spirito Santo Palazzo Storico** [76 C1] (7 rooms) Augusta Ferrija 44; **m** 099 435 4333; **w** hotel-spiritosanto.com. Stunning new boutique hotel housed in 3 beautifully converted houses, formerly owned by a prominent local Italian family. Plenty of exposed stone, wooden beams & glass panels, & some of the rooms come with a small terrace. There's a lounge bar & wine cellar housed in a converted water cistern, where the excellent breakfast is served & where you can order food in the evening (**€€€€**), & there's a lovely little enclosed courtyard where you can sit with an impeccably made coffee or cocktail. Highly recommended. **€€€€€**

Monte Mulini [76 C7] (113 rooms) Antonia Smareglia bb; ☎ 052 800 250; **e** info@maistra.hr; **w** montemulinihotel.com. Another Maistra high-end hotel & only 300m from the Lone. Has a full spa service open to non-hotel guests. Standard chic. **€€€€€**

Casa Garzotto [80 C2] (4 rooms) Garzotto 8; ☎ 052 811 884; **e** casagarzotto@gmail.com; **w** casa-garzotto.com. This lovely little boutique hotel is in the centre of town, & offers 4 studio apartments in a renovated house with polished wooden floors & beams, & exposed stonework. **€€€€**

Family Hotel Amarin [map, page 73] (276 rooms, 4 suites) Val de Lesso 5; ☎ 052 800 250; **e** info@maistra.hr; **w** maistra.com. Maistra's very good family resort, opened in 2016. Big, bright rooms with floor-to-ceiling windows, surrounded by plenty of greenery & located beside a 1km-long pebble beach – & if that's not enough water for you there are 3 outdoor pools too. North of the old town towards Punta Križa. **€€€€**

Island Hotel Istra [map, page 73] (326 rooms) Otok Sv Andrija, Crveni otok; ☎ 052 800 250; **e** info@maistra.hr; **w** maistra.com. The only accommodation on the island of Sv Andrija (1 of the 2 islets forming Crveni otok), offering the complete package, including spa centre & entertainment. **€€€€**

Island Hotel Katarina [76 A4] (120 rooms) Otok Sv Katarina; ☎ 052 800 250; **e** info@maistra.com; **w** maistra.com. On Katarina island visible from the old town, this hotel is another Maistra island-takeover. Good for families wanting everything nearby. **€€€€**

✳ **Villa Tuttorotto** [80 C2] (7 rooms) Dvor Massatto 4; ☎ 052 815 181; **e** info@villatuttorotto.com; **w** villatuttorotto.com. Exquisitely decorated boutique hotel in a restored 16th-century Venetian *palazzo* filled with antique furniture – small, intimate & wonderfully hospitable. The glass floor in front of the reception desk reveals 2 stone chambers full of amphorae, discovered when the building was renovated. Tucked away in the narrow alleys of the old town, this is one of the author's favourite places to stay in Croatia. **€€€€**

Residence Dream [76 C3] (4 rooms) Joakima Rakovca 18; ☎ 052 830 613; **m** 091 579 9239; **e** dream@dream.hr; **w** dream.hr. Right in the middle of a popular alley between Carrera & the marina, this tiny hotel has an excellent restaurant serving b/fast through to dinner: linguine dishes are extremely tasty. Decorated with old-time paraphernalia, & with free Wi-Fi. **€€€**

Vila Lili [76 D6] (20 rooms) Andrije Mohorovičića 16; ☎ 052 840 940; **w** booking.com/hotel/hr/vila-lili.en-gb.html. Not far from the harbour & access to the old town, this friendly family-run boutique hotel shows lots of attention to detail & a b/fast to match – you might want to have a good swim before b/fast to make sure you make the most of it. Pets welcome. Telescope available for star-gazing. **€€€**

Villa Baron Gautsch [76 D5] (9 dbls, 2 sgls, 4 trpls) Ivana Matetića Ronjgova 7; ☎ 052 840 538; e baron.gautsch@gmx.net; **w** villabarongautsch.com. Nice, unpretentious, good-value pension a 10min walk south of the old town. Cash only. **€€€**

Pansion Romano [map, page 73] (6 dbls, 10 apts) Vukovarska 2a; ☎ 052 817 275; **e** romano@romano.hr; **w** romano.hr. Very good-value accommodation southeast of the old town. **€€–€**

APARTMENTS There are lots of gorgeous little apartments to be rented in the old town. A couple are listed here & many more can be found through **w** rovinj.info, as well as other tourist agencies around Rovinj.

Apartment Fianona [76 C3] Trg na Lokvi; **w** booking.com/hotel/hr/new-luxury-apartment-fianona-rovinj-city-center.en-gb.html. 2 bedroom apartment with kitchen. **€€€**

Casa Mulino [80 C1] Pazinska ul; **w** airbnb.co.uk/rooms/25928589; Centrally located, clean apartment with kitchen. **€€€**

CAMPING

Porton Biondi [map, page 73] Alija Porton Biondi; ☎ 052 552 552; **w** portonbiondi.com; 🕘 mid-Mar–Oct. The closest campsite to the town, only 700m north of the Balbi Arch. Can accommodate 1,200 people on 11ha of pine-wooded grounds & offers some nice beaches & views of the town. Pets allowed. Pitches from

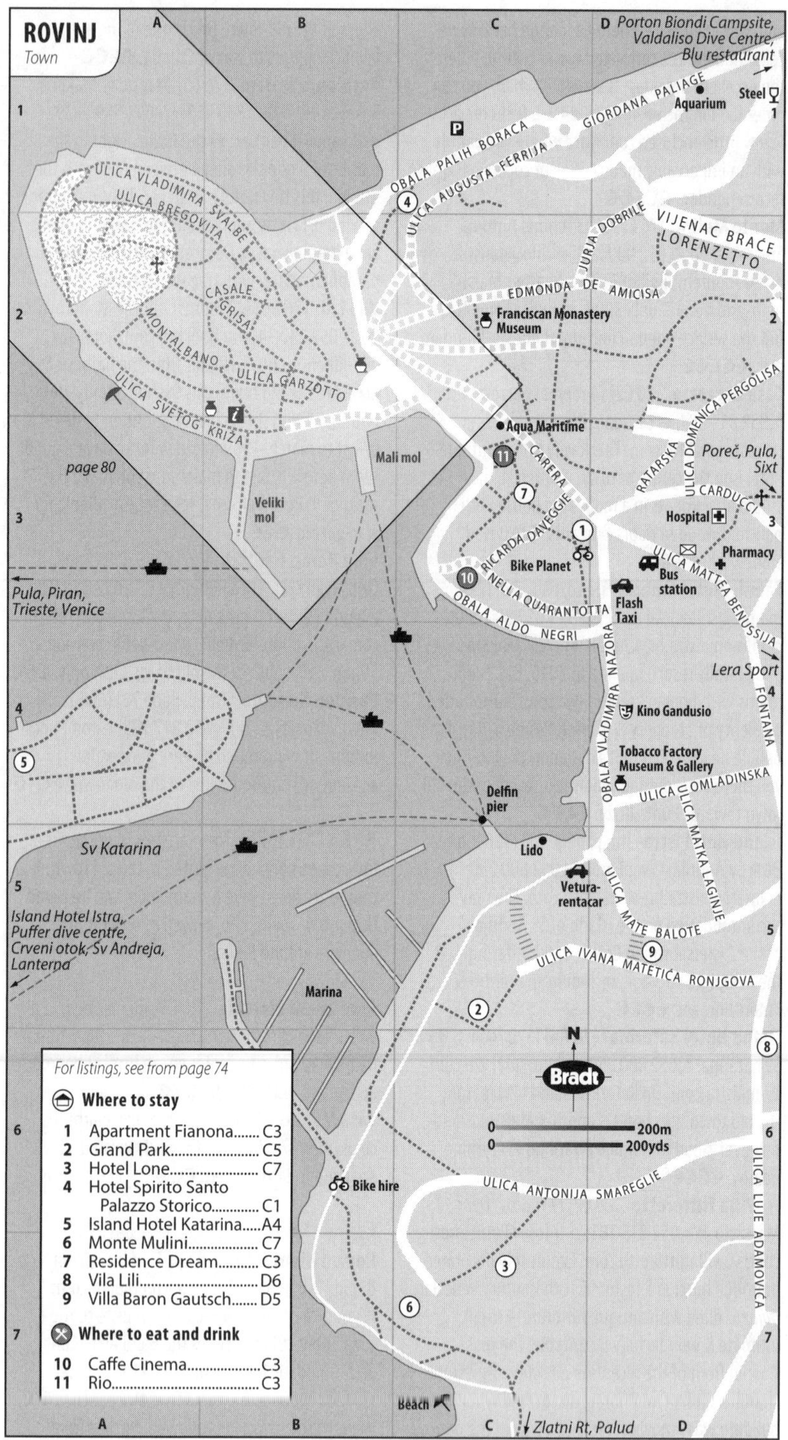

ROVINJ
Town
A
B
C
D
Porton Biondi Campsite, Valdaliso Dive Centre, Blu restaurant
Steel
Aquarium
GIORDANA PALIAGE
OBALA PALIH BORACA
ULICA AUGUSTA FERRIJA
VIJENAC BRAĆE LORENZETTO
JURJA DOBRILE
EDMONDA DE AMICISA
Franciscan Monastery Museum
ULICA VLADIMIRA SVALBE
ULICA BREGOVITA
CASALE GRISA
MONTALBANO
ULICA GARZOTTO
ULICA SVETOG KRIŽA
ULICA DOMENICA PERGOLISA
RATARSKA
Aqua Maritime
CARERA
Poreč, Pula, Sixt
CARDUCCI
Hospital
Pharmacy
page 80
Mali mol
Veliki mol
RICARDA DAVEGGIE
Bike Planet
NELLA QUARANTOTTA
ULICA MATTEA BENUSSIJA
Bus station
Flash Taxi
OBALA ALDO NEGRI
Pula, Piran, Trieste, Venice
Lera Sport
OBALA VLADIMIRA NAZORA
FONTANA
Kino Gandusio
Tobacco Factory Museum & Gallery
ULICA OMLADINSKA
ULICA MATKA LAGINJE
Delfin pier
Lido
Sv Katarina
Vetura-rentacar
ULICA MATE BALOTE
ULICA IVANA MATETIĆA RONJGOVA
Island Hotel Istra, Puffer dive centre, Crveni otok, Sv Andreja, Lanterna
Marina
N
Bradt
0 200m
0 200yds
Bike hire
ULICA ANTONIJA SMAREGLIE
ULICA LUJE ADAMOVIĆA
Beach
Zlatni Rt, Palud
For listings, see from page 74
Where to stay
1 Apartment Fianona....... C3
2 Grand Park................ C5
3 Hotel Lone................ C7
4 Hotel Spirito Santo Palazzo Storico.......... C1
5 Island Hotel Katarina.....A4
6 Monte Mulini.............. C7
7 Residence Dream........... C3
8 Vila Lili.................. D6
9 Villa Baron Gautsch....... D5
Where to eat and drink
10 Caffe Cinema.............. C3
11 Rio....................... C3

€17.50. They also have large (48m2+) modular, modern holiday homes which come with their own terrace & swimming pool. €€€€

Veštar [map, page 73] Veštar 1; 052 800 200; e info@maistra.hr; w campingrovinjvrsar.com; Apr–mid-Oct. One of 3 campsites around Rovinj owned by Maistra, with 770 pitches, some right by the beach. 5km south of Rovinj, towards Palud. Pitches from €19.50.

WHERE TO EAT AND DRINK

RESTAURANTS Rovinj has a fantastic range of places to eat, from small-scale gems like Rio & local favourites hidden away in the backstreets, to Michelin-starred Monte & Cap Aureo.

Al Gastaldo [80 C2] Iza Kasarne 14; 052 814 109; 11.00–15.00 & 18.00–23.00 daily. This little restaurant, tucked away behind the Balbi Arch, is open year-round, & being almost underground is welcomingly cool in the summer & hearteningly warm by the fire in the winter. Surrounded by wine bottles & bare stone walls, the food is equally sublime. Try their *Sv Jakov školkje* (St Jacob's scallops), which are the best I've tasted anywhere. However, it's worth pointing out that there have been a large number of reports of poor service & substandard food recently. €€€€

Lanterna [map, page 73] Sv Andreja, Crveni otok; 052 800 250; w maistra.com; mid-Apr–mid-Oct midday–23.00 daily. For those not staying on the island, the €8 return boat ride to Crveni otok does add to your bill, but if you want somewhere exclusive & quiet to eat lunch, I can't think of a better place midweek. Lanterna is set in the courtyard of the 19th-century country manor of the former owner; stone pillars, bright-red sofas & massive standing silver candelabras provide a sublime setting against the sea view. Sea bass carpaccio, warm octopus salad, & risotto with Kvarner prawns are among the fare on offer here. Reserve for the front tables on the terrace. The Captain's Club on the corner of the manor is a popular high-end bar with exceptional views. €€€€

Monte [80 B2] Montalbano 75; 052 830 203; w monte.hr; mid-Apr–mid-Oct 18.30–23.30 daily. This is the best of fine dining & fusion cuisine in Rovinj & has earned itself a place in the *Gault & Millau* – &, as of 2017, a Michelin star. Not just the fish but the lamb & suckling pig are exquisite. Although the highest restaurant in Rovinj, it does not afford views of the sea, but it is a stone's throw from the cathedral. €€€€

Puntulina [80 B3] Sv Križa 38; 052 813 186; e puntulina@gmail.com; w puntulina.eu; 13.00–22.00 Thu–Tue. Without doubt the restaurant with the best view in the whole of Rovinj. With balconies perched high on the side of the building overlooking the sea, & tables right at the water's edge, the sunset here rivals anywhere in the world. Small & cosy, it's the place for a romantic dinner, & the food's good too. Try their local speciality squid with polenta, or their house special St Jacob's scallops with brandy. Book in advance to be sure of a table. €€€€

Santa Croce [80 B2] Sv Križa 11; 052 842 240; w restoran-santacroce.hr; 17.00–23.00 daily. Set in a little square called Poljana sv Barnabe. Very popular restaurant serving fabulous seafood. €€€€

Barba Danilo [map, page 73] Polari 5; 052 830 002; w barbadanilo.com; 18.00–23.00 daily, winter 17.00–23.00 Mon–Sat, closed Nov–Mar. On the southern outskirts of town, with a cosy setting, serving traditional dishes with a modern twist. €€€

Blu [map, page 73] Val de Lesso 9; 052 811 265; w blu.hr; midday–23.00 daily, May–Oct. Located on the Rovinj side of Camp Valdaliso, the tarmac runs out just behind this restaurant. With an enviable view on to the sea & Rovinj old town, its tables also spill out on to a small veranda on the beach. Excellent food, reasonably priced. There are also 8 tastefully decorated rooms (6 dbls, 2 apts €€€€). €€€

Giannino [80 C1] Augusta Ferrija 38; 052 813 402; w restoran-giannino.com; 18.00–23.00 Mon/Wed/Thu, noon–14.00 & 18.00–midnight Fri–Sun, closed Nov–Mar. About 100m up Augusto Ferri St, Giannino's serves excellent, no-nonsense seafood dishes such as plaice with truffles, & linguine with clams. Well established & a locals' favourite with a cosy bare-stone interior. €€€

✱ **Rio** [76 C3] Aldo Rismondo 13; 052 813 564; 07.30–23.00 daily. Also called Snack Bar

Rio, this little place on the waterfront has been a popular watering hole since the late 1960s, but in 2015 expanded slightly & is now a fantastic restaurant too, under the same ownership as Puntulina (page 77). Excellent food – delicious gnocchi with scallops, polenta with cod, ravioli with black truffles are just some of the things you might find on the menu – & relaxed, friendly service. Highly recommended. €€€

Tipico [80 C2] Grisia 32; m 091 349 4006; f tipico.rovinj; ⌚ 13.00–22.00 Tue/Wed, 13.00–23.00 Thu–Mon. Excellent local dishes, including lamb, cold cuts & the usual array of fresh fish. Small & friendly. €€€

Tutto Bene [80 D1] Ul de Amicis; m 095 852 4383; f tuttobene.rovinj; ⌚ May–Oct 18.00–23.00 daily. Friendly new place with an emphasis on seafood & pasta, beautifully presented & often given a modern twist. €€€

Veli Jože [80 C2] Sv Križa 1; ☎ 052 816 337; w velijoze.net/vj.html; ⌚ 11.00–midnight daily. Easily recognisable by the old diving suit & complete head mask standing outside the front door, & its abundance of seafaring paraphernalia on the inside, this restaurant is a must-visit, even if the service is brusque & the seafood merely average. Serves better meat dishes, including a good spit-roast lamb. €€€

Balbi [80 C1] Veli trg 2; ☎ 052 817 200; ⌚ Apr–Oct 11.00–23.00 daily. Beyond the Balbi Arch is the ambitiously named little square 'Piassa Grande'. Here the popular Balbi restaurant serves a good range of seafood, meat & pasta dishes. €€

Da Sergio Pizzeria [80 C2] Grisia 11; ☎ 052 816 949; f DaSergioRv; ⌚ 11.30–22.30 daily. Da Sergio has won awards for a reason. As the newspaper articles pasted in the windows attest, the chefs here – using a traditional wood-burning oven – make some of the most authentic Italian thin-crust pizzas you'll experience outside Italy today. More than 30 different pizzas to choose from. €€

CAFÉS AND BARS

Caffe Cinema [76 C3] Trg brodogradališta bb; ⌚ summer 07.00–02.00 daily, winter 07.00–23.00 daily. Playing cool rock among old black-&-white film décor on its wide exclusive corner at the edge of the pedestrian zone, this is a great place to relax. Away from the hubbub of the centre yet still in view of the sea & islands, it's very popular with locals for large coffees, *spremutan* (freshly squeezed orange juice) & *brioches* (filled croissants) or *tost* (sandwiches) in the morning. Serves a very wide range of hot drinks, including a decent tea (although you'd still need 2 teabags for builder's strength) with milk or soy in large Dammann Frères cups.

Monte Carlo [80 C3] Sv Križa 2. A relaxing café bar overlooking the sea & a great place to have a coffee after a morning swim off the rocks.

Valentino [80 B3] Sv Križa 28; ☎ 052 830 683; e info@valentino-rovinj.com; w valentino-rovinj.com; ⌚ Apr/May midday–midnight daily, Jun–Sep 18.00–02.00 daily, closed Oct–Mar. No credit cards. This is by far the classiest & coolest cocktail bar in Istria. Your drinks are served 'on the rocks' (with ice), but literally, also, on the rocks of the seashore, with pillows & candles strewn for comfort & decoration. While the cocktails might not be expensive by world standards, they're certainly so for Croatia.

Viecia Batana [80 D1] Trg Maršala Tita bb. *The* place to drink as a local. Serves great coffee & is perfect for sitting & watching the world go by. **Al Ponto** & **Caffeteria Piazza**, also on the same square, are equally good for taking in the atmosphere.

XL Bar [80 A2] Josipa Tankovica bb; ⌚ 11.00–22.00 daily. The ideal place for sundowners after you've visited St Euphemia Church (page 81). It's a bit hidden, sitting between the front of the church & the sea. Head a bit to your right after coming down the main stairs at the front of the church. Cross the open area & go down 1 set of stairs. Angle left through the stone doorway. It's tough to find a more idyllic view.

ENTERTAINMENT AND NIGHTLIFE

The place for **clubbing and partying** in Rovinj is **Steel** [76 D1] (Ul Vijenac Braće Lorenzetto; w steelvenue.com; ⌚ 22.00–05.00 Fri, check website for events), which is located near the aquarium and has DJs and live music covering a variety of different genres and tastes.

SHOPPING

Aqua Maritime [76 C3] Carrera 55; w aquamaritime.hr; ⌚ summer 10.30–22.00, winter 10.00–16.00 Mon–Sat. This store capitalises on the navy blue & cream stripe-effect & their brand logo of a cartoon ship & a fat whale. More than just T-shirts in every size, this is a great place for souvenirs as well as something for yourself – summer dresses, hoodies, babygros, towels, thick-soled flip-flops, bags, fish soaps, & much more besides.

Rovinj market [80 C1] A small compact market, half of which is occupied by the fish hall. In addition to fruit & veg, the outdoor area has a lot of souvenir products, including Istrian liqueurs, lavender, olive oil, strings of brightly coloured peppers & garlic, honey & other local produce.

OTHER PRACTICALITIES

Hospital [76 D3] Istarska bb (entrance on Matteo Benussi); 052 813 004. This is the local accident & emergency ward.

Pharmacy [76 D3] Matteo Benussi 5; 052 813 589; ⌚ 07.00–20.00 Mon–Fri, 07.00–15.00 Sat, 09.00–noon Sun. Other pharmacies listed at w rovinj-tourism.com/en/plan-your-journey/medical-care-for-tourists/pharmacies.

Post office [76 D3] Matteo Benussi 4; ⌚ 08.00–19.00 Mon–Fri, 08.00–noon Sat

WHAT TO SEE AND DO

Rovinj has its fair share of events, festivals and concerts. For a full list of events, pick up the events brochure in the tourist information office.

Built in 1678, when Rovinj was still an island, the **Balbi Arch (Balbijev luk)** [80 D1] (Trg Maršala Tita) was the main entrance to the town. A Turk's head adorns the top of the outside of the arch as a symbol to ward off Ottoman invaders, while on the inside of the arch a Venetian's head adorns the apex as a symbol to safeguard the Venetian population on the inside of the town walls.

Almost next door to the Balbi Arch is the **Heritage Museum (Zavičajni muzej)** [80 C1] (Trg Maršala Tita 11; 052 816 720; w muzej-rovinj.hr; ⌚ 10.00–13.00 Tue–Sat; entry €2.50), which has a permanent exhibition of modern art that almost does justice to Rovinj's resident artists. Sadly, most of the 'modern' art dates from the 1990s and there isn't a nameplate or explanation anywhere in sight. The museum also houses temporary exhibitions and hosts concerts.

The **Batana House (Kuća o batani)** [80 C2] (Obala Pina Budicina 2; 052 812 593; e info@batana.org; w batana.org; ⌚ Jun–Aug 10.00–13.00 & 19.00–21.00 Tue–Sun, May/Sep 10.00–13.00 & 18.00–21.00 Tue–Sun, Mar/Apr & Oct/Nov 10.00–16.00 Tue–Sun; entry €3.30) is an ecomuseum devoted to the old wooden fishing boats you can still find in Rovinj's harbour, as well as to the fishing culture associated with them. There are recordings of Rovinj dialect, explanations of how the various nets were used for different varieties of fish, and samples of all the tools, sails and accoutrements of these old vessels. A fast-motion film of the making of a *batana* shows in 10 minutes how the boats are built from scratch in just one week. Apparently there's only one *batana*-maker left in Istria and the guide will give you his details if you're interested in owning your own. A new one sells for about €3,500. Watch for the live *batana*-making exhibition across from the entrance to the museum on Tuesdays throughout the summer. It's also a good place to buy souvenirs.

Rovinj's **St Euphemia Church (Crkva sv Eufemije)** [80 B2] (Petro Stankovica; ⌚ visitors 10.00–14.00 & 15.00–18.00; mass 08.00, 09.00 (Italian), 10.30, midday, 18.00, 19.00 Sun; 07.30, 18.00, 19.00 Mon–Sat) sits at the top of the hill on which the old town was built, and is one of the most iconic buildings in Istria. A church of St George was first on this site, and his statue remains on the central altar, but when the remains of St Euphemia came in a stone sarcophagus from Constantinople, the numbers of pilgrims quickly outgrew the small chapel. A new church bearing St Euphemia's name was built during the 10th century. Then in 1725, the townspeople rebuilt the structure into what it is today – save for the façade, which was built in the 1900s. One of its most notable features is the bell tower, modelled after that of St Mark's in Venice. For €2 you can climb the 170 steps for an unparalleled view of Rovinj and environs. On top of that St Euphemia reigns as a weathervane. Make sure to see the exquisitely restored *Last Supper* by Giovanni Contarini, originally painted in 1574.

Built in the style of the old taverns where fishermen ate and drank after their return from the sea, the **Spàcio Matika** [80 B1] (35 Vladimira Švalbe; 052 812 593; w batana.org/en/the-batana-eco-museum/spacio-matika-spacio0; late Jun–early Sep 20.00–23.00 Tue & Thu, plus Fri from 2nd week of Jul) offers a unique way to experience old Rovinj fishing culture, including traditional singing and traditional recipes for cooking the day's catch. Guests can opt for a *batana* boat ride at 20.00, taking them around Rovinj's old town to their dinner destination. Off-season, Spàcio is available for groups of 25 or more and must be booked three days in advance.

Just east of the old town is the **Franciscan Monastery Museum (Muzej franjevačkog Jamostana)** [76 C2] (De Amicis 36; m 095 871 6773; 10.00–midday

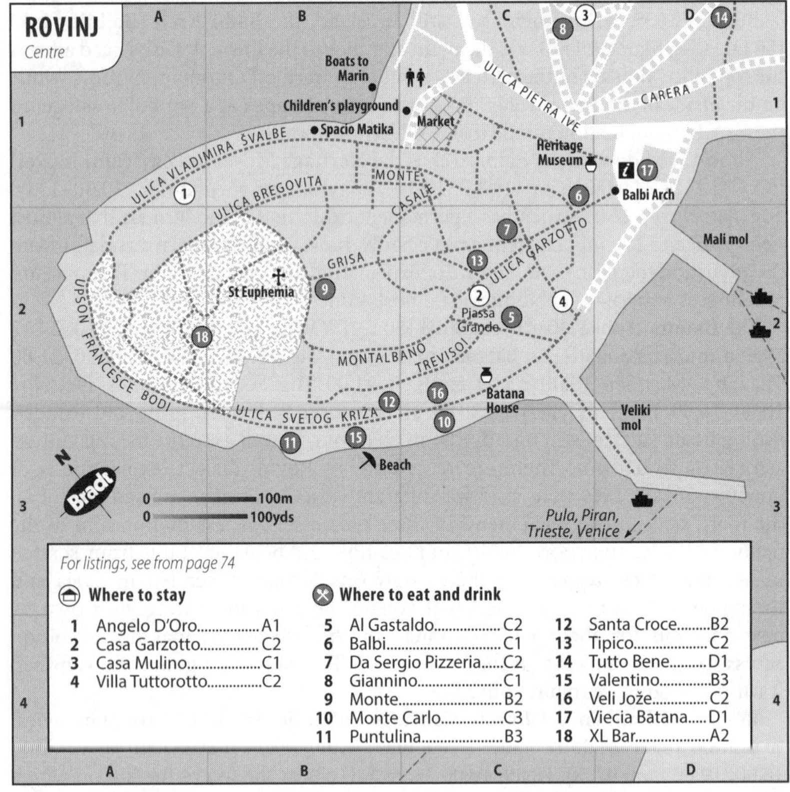

ST EUPHEMIA

Born in the village of Chalcedon near Constantinople in the 3rd century AD (Diocletian's reign), Euphemia was the daughter of a Roman senator. But her belief in the Christian God soon put her at odds with the Governor of Chalcedon, Priscus, who was demanding sacrifices to the pagan gods. Euphemia and her friends were discovered in hiding, and – for their failure to convert – were subjected to various grisly forms of torture including being broken on the wheel. It seems she survived the ordeal only to be fed to the lions (or a bear, depending on who you ask) in the arena.

As a martyr, St Euphemia's relics were later placed in a golden sarcophagus and the church built in Chalcedon to house them soon became a popular pilgrimage. So popular in fact that her relics eventually had to be moved to Constantinople to avoid their destruction by Persian invaders. Unfortunately, in the early 7th century Iconoclasts dumped St Euphemia's remains into the sea. They were allegedly rescued by two boat-owning brothers, who secreted them away on the island of Lemnos. Some 200 years later they were returned to Constantinople. However, a portion of her reliquary miraculously turned up in a large stone sarcophagus in Rovinj where they have been ever since. The rest of her can be found in the Church of St George in Istanbul.

Mon–Sat; entry €1.30). The monastery itself was completed in 1710 and is dedicated to St Francis of Assisi. The museum holds a fascinating mix of articles from old habits and reliquaries to large wall maps charting the lineage of humankind from 4004BC to AD1799, or more in-depth from 0 to AD1800. Only a minuscule number of the monastery's library of 12,000 books are on show. Sadly the exhibits could do with a lot of care, but are worth the visit nonetheless. Outside museum times, the church itself is open for services and sometimes holds concerts.

Just south of the old town heading towards the marina is **Kino Gandusio** [76 D4] (Trg Valdibora 17; w pour.hr; entry for film screenings €3.30). Here, watch current films in a classic old theatre house. There is also a venue for local theatre, burlesque, operas and operettas, political, comedy and other cultural events. Films are normally subtitled, rather than dubbed.

In a grand building opposite the main town car park, Rovinj's small **aquarium** [76 D1] (Giordano Paliaga 5; 052 804 712; 09.00–20.00 daily; entry €2.60) has only 20 tanks in all, but the fish, molluscs and plant life are a fine selection from the nearby Adriatic. Overall it's well presented, and works nicely for a quick escape from the heat.

ACTIVITIES

Hiking and **biking** along the coast are very popular activities, and large overview maps for these can be picked up at the tourist information office. Heading south of the old town takes you around **Zlatni rt nature reserve (Park Šuma Zlatni rt)** (meaning 'golden cape', and also known locally by its Italian name Punta Corrente) towards Palud bird sanctuary (page 82). Less than 1km south of the town is a large bolted **rock-climbing face** along the top section of the sea cliff, with a very wide access area. **Horseriding** is available at Farm Haber (Val de Lesso 1; m 098 368 454; e konjicki.klub@pu.t-com.hr; w farma-haber.com), and at the Horse Ranch at kilometre marker 4 just outside Rovinjsko Selo.

Palud Bird Sanctuary (Ornitološki rezervat Palud) (w inforovinj.com/eng/rovinj/znamenje/palud.asp), 8km southwest of Rovinj, is a former freshwater marsh, which was flooded with seawater when the Austro-Hungarian army based in Barbariga dug a 200m canal connecting it to the sea in 1906 in order to stop mosquitoes thriving there. Now it is Istria's only bird sanctuary, and has become an important stop for migratory birds. Some 219 species of bird have been recorded at Palud over the years. A cycle ride there along the coastline is about 13km; take care to follow the signs for the bicycle path in case you end up in the maze of nudist campers at Camping Oaza Polaris. Entrance to Palud is free, and 2-hour guided birdwatching tours are available in groups of up to eight people (adults/children €6.60/€5.30) with binoculars provided. Contact the tourist information bureau (page 74) to arrange tours.

The 19 **islands** of Rovinj's archipelago are best seen by boat. Many trips are available from Mali mol pier, but if you want to charter your own boat, then see the charter companies listed on page 44. On my last trip through the islands, I saw a solitary plastic beach lounger on a spit of rock in the middle of the sea, circled only by a pair of dolphins.

Divers might like to explore Banjole Špilja Cave, page 213.

BEACHES You don't have to go far to jump in the water or lounge around in swimwear. Around the south side of the old town there are stretches of rock that are popular with sunbathers and swimmers, and where there are ladders especially for entering and exiting the water. To bathe and tan in your birthday suit, you'll need to go a little further, and Istria's most famous gay beach is a few kilometres north of the town. For a useful list of Rovinj's beaches and their various merits, see w rovinj.com/en/beaches.

North of Rovinj from closest to furthest are the rock and pebble beaches of **Porton Biondi**, **Borik**, **Valdaliso** and **Amarin** [map, page 73]. After Amarin is **Punta Križa** nudist and gay beach [map, page 73].

For **fine gravel and/or sand beaches**, try **Kuvi Bay** – a small pebble beach, gently sloping and particularly good for young children, which stretches 1km along the coast and is 2km south of the old town. **Lone Bay** is another option, located near the five-star Hotel Lone complex, 1km south of the old town, but accessible to the public. Naturists should try **Valalta**, north of Rovinj at the Limski kanal entrance. Some 3km from the town centre by road and 7km by the coast after Kuvi Bay sport and recreation zone there is **Villas Rubin**.

Other public beaches include **Baluota**, a rock beach at the end of the old town, down from St Euphemia Church. **Cape Rusl** is less a beach than a series of large boulders, but has some spots for (careful!) jumping from height into the water. To reach **Katarina Otok** – which has rock and pebble beaches plus play areas for children – take the regular passenger boat across from Mali mol (page 72). **Škaraba Bay** is a nice beach with flat stones, but also very rocky and thus a bit less frequented by tourists. **Zlatni rt** is a really beautiful rock and pebble beach located within the nature reserve of the same name.

Poreč and the Northwest Coast

Poreč and the northwest coast is where the large majority of visitors to Istria stay, play and beach. Although there are more popular sites to visit, such as Rovinj, Pula and the hill-town retreats of Motovun and Buzet, Poreč has the copious accommodation to deal with the many summer visitors who arrive by car from nearby countries. Poreč itself has a beautiful and quite typical Croatian coastal old town centre, jutting like a small island into the sea, and is home to renowned 6th-century BC mosaics in its UNESCO-listed basilica.

POREČ

Back in Roman times Poreč was the capital of Istria. Today it retains a life of its own year-round, unlike the more highly praised Rovinj, which burgeons in the summer and is deserted in the winter. Poreč life picks up as early as the end of February, when the first of the cycling enthusiasts come to take advantage of the mild weather and light traffic on Istrian roads. And while beach facilities might close in mid-October, outdoor-sports types, especially divers, will stay into early November, when the water can retain a wonderful 18°C temperature, often warmer than the outside air.

HISTORY The Histri tribe settled in and around the area of Poreč some 6,000 years ago. By as early as 4,000 years ago, an observatory, settlement and ritual site were located at Picugi (halfway between today's Dračevac and Garbina eastsoutheast of Poreč), which may give an indication of the importance of the area at the time. When the Romans defeated the Histri in 177BC, they fortified the miniature peninsula that is now Poreč as a defensive encampment, or *castrum*. Easily accessible by ship, the encampment grew, and by AD14, Emperor Augustus had officially upgraded it to a city, known as Parentium.

By the 3rd century, Christianity was taking hold of Parentium. Mavar (later known as Maurus) of Parentium became the first bishop of the city and also its patron saint when he was martyred by Emperor Diocletian in AD304. His remains were transferred to the first basilica built in Parentium in the second half of the 4th century and remain in the current Euphrasian Basilica rebuilt there in the 6th century. The mosaics from the first basilica can still be seen today in the church gardens.

After the demise of the Roman Empire in 476, Poreč fell to the Huns and then in 493 to Theodoric the Ostrogoth. By 539 the Byzantine emperor Justinian had extended his empire to include Istria, and it was during this time of extended peace that Bishop Euphrasius built the current cathedral complex named after him. Euphrasius set a trend in building this church, by adding an additional apse (the semicircular hollow usually found at the head of the central nave of the church) at

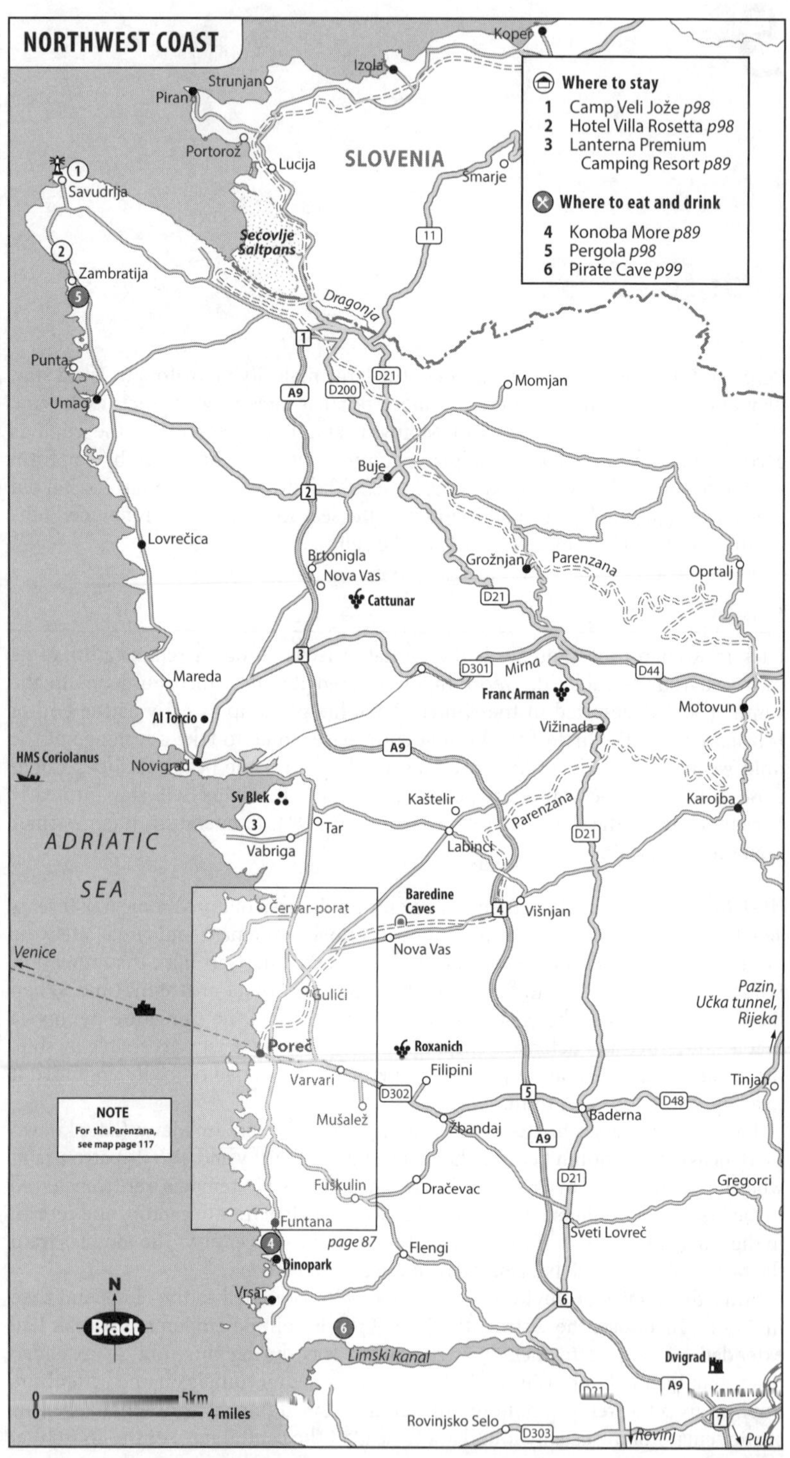
NORTHWEST COAST
Where to stay
1 Camp Veli Jože p98
2 Hotel Villa Rosetta p98
3 Lanterna Premium Camping Resort p89
Where to eat and drink
4 Konoba More p89
5 Pergola p98
6 Pirate Cave p99
SLOVENIA
ADRIATIC SEA
Koper
Izola
Strunjan
Piran
Portorož
Lucija
Šmarje
Savudrija
Sečovlje Saltpans
Dragonja
Zambratija
Punta
Umag
Momjan
Buje
Lovrečica
Brtonigla
Nova Vas
Cattunar
Grožnjan
Parenzana
Oprtalj
Mirna
Franc Arman
Motovun
Mareda
Al Torcio
Vižinada
HMS Coriolanus
Novigrad
Sv Blek
Kaštelir
Karojba
Tar
Vabriga
Labinci
Baredine Caves
Červar-porat
Višnjan
Nova Vas
Venice
Gulići
Pazin, Učka tunnel, Rijeka
Poreč
Roxanich
Varvari
Filipini
Tinjan
Mušalež
Žbandaj
Baderna
NOTE
For the Parenzana, see map page 117
Fuškulin
Dračevac
Gregorci
Funtana
Sveti Lovreč
page 87
Flengi
Dinopark
Vrsar
Limski kanal
Dvigrad
Kanfanar
Rovinjsko Selo
Rovinj
Pula
5km
4 miles
Bradt

the end of the aisles on either side of the main nave. It is thus the very first triple-apse church to be built in western Europe. For more on the history of the basilica, plus visiting arrangements, see page 93.

Byzantine rule ended for Poreč in 751, and by 788 it was part of Germanic Middle Frankia, and then fought over by Western and Eastern Frankia until in 1267, Poreč became the first Istrian city to join the Republic of Venice. Venetian rule lasted for 530 years and was marred only briefly when the Republic of Genoa invaded and destroyed large swathes of the town.

In 1797 Venice retreated from Istria and Poreč was ruled by the Habsburg monarchy. An interlude of ten years from 1805 to 1814 saw Napoleon's Kingdom of Italy and then the First French Empire rule Poreč, after which it returned to Austria-Hungary. The Austrian Empire brought with it a century of modernity and the flavour of things to come. The year 1844 saw the first steamship leave Poreč bound for Trieste, and then in 1845 Poreč's first guidebook went into print, written by Petro Kandler. In 1895 Poreč opened its first public beach and by 1902 Europeans were flocking to Poreč on the Parenzana narrow-gauge railway (page 117) that ran from Trieste.

Poreč became the capital of Istria in 1861 and thus home to the regional parliament. It also became a centre for shipbuilding. Prized by Italy, it was annexed in 1918 and remained a part of the Kingdom of Italy until 1945. The Allies air-raided Poreč 34 times in 1944 (an American Consolidated B-24 Liberator heavy bomber, shot down from outside Poreč in 1944, lies southwest of Vrsar), leaving 75% of the city in ruins. Many Italian-speakers from Poreč left with the Istrian exodus after World War II. Although many Slav-speakers from the rest of Croatia took their place, most people in Poreč, along with the entire west coast of Istria, remain bilingual.

GETTING THERE AND AWAY

By train The nearest **train station** is Sveti Petar u Šumi (local stop), or Pazin, which is on the Pula–Buzet line (page 101). For timetables, see w hzpp.hr/en.

By bus Timetables for Croatian buses serving Poreč can be found at w buscroatia.com, w arriva.com.hr or w akz.hr. There are frequent services to Rovinj and Pula, as well as services to Rijeka (at least half-a-dozen buses daily, with the fastest being those run by Arriva-Autotrans which go via Pazin and take around 90 minutes or less – taking a service which goes via the coast and Pula will take much longer), Zagreb and elsewhere, and international services to Trieste, Venice and Ljubljana. Brioni runs services from Trieste, leaving once a day at 11.00 with a journey time of around 90 minutes. Trieste bus station's timetable is at w autostazionetrieste.it. During the summer months, there is a daily bus to Piran, taking about an hour. Flixbus (w flixbus.co.uk) runs services between Poreč and Ljubljana. Poreč **bus station** [91 E4] (*Karla Huguesa 2*) is on the outskirts of town, with the taxi stand on the road right outside. It has a small café and an ATM.

By boat A great way to arrive in Istria is to take the ferry from St Basilio international ferry terminus in Venice to Poreč. Two operators ply this route during summer: **Venezia Lines** (w venezialines.com; Apr–Oct) and **Adriatic Lines** (w adriatic-lines.com; May–Oct). **Liberty Lines** (w libertylines.it/en) sails from Trieste to Poreč.

You need to be at the ferry at least 40 minutes prior to boarding, and you should allow up to an extra half an hour to disembark; outside the peak season it's possible to buy tickets at the ferry. The *Prince of Venice* (Adriatic Lines) is the (slightly) more luxurious of the ships and has an outdoor deck. Venezia Lines' ships have a first-class upper deck (indoors), access to which can be purchased once on board. Both lines include a free presentation from a tour guide on the boat in one of several languages and sell maps and guidebooks of Venice. Both lines' tour guides also arrange tours around Venice (for a fee).

Poreč ferry terminal (Obala Maršala Tita, opposite Hotel Riviera) is just a border hut on a pier, with no waiting lounge or shelter. Located in the old town, several waterside cafés and benches nearby are available to watch the boats come in. Being in the pedestrian area means that taxis can only approach to within 150m of the terminal; they usually wait by the pedestrian area barrier when the ferry arrives.

By car Poreč is a 40-minute drive from Trieste, 2 hours from Ljubljana, 2½ hours from Zagreb, 6 hours from Munich, 8 hours from Geneva and Vienna, and 10 hours from Skopje. Taxis cost around €75 per trip from Pula airport to Poreč.

GETTING AROUND Poreč is small enough to walk around, and there is no town bus service. **Taxis** (Dotto Taxi & Bus: m 098 255 245; w porec-taxi.com; & Cammeo: w cammeo.hr/hr/gradovi/porec) are available and can usually be found outside the bus station. **Bicycles** are readily available for rent and you can pick up details at the tourist information office. Try **Solis** (w solis-porec.com/rent-a-bike) or see the listings on w istra-bike.com. For bike repairs, try **Espo Bicickli** (Spadici 18; 052 434 961; e servis@espo.hr; w espo.hr) which is owned by Davor Hamaček and is perhaps more readily known by his last name. Located outside of Poreč centre, this place also services motor bikes and holds spare car parts. **Car-rental** services are listed on the tourist information office website (w myporec.com/en/travel-planning/rent-a-car) and include **Vetura-rentacar** [91 E2] (Trg J Rakovca 2; 052 434 700; w vetura-rentacar.com). Child seats and Garmin GPS are also available.

TOURIST INFORMATION **Poreč tourist information office** [91 E2] (Zargrebačka 9; 052 451 293; e info@myporec.com; w myporec.com; 15 Jun–15 Sep 08.00–22.00 daily, with gradually shorter hours towards the winter, except over the Christmas period when there are extended opening hours) is a fantastic resource for information on Poreč including accommodation listings and a calendar of events. This is where you must go to register if you are staying in private accommodation.

A number of small free **maps** are available, including basic cycling maps. For 1:30,000 topographic hiking and biking maps you'll need to buy from any number of kiosks, newsagents or supermarkets around town.

WHERE TO STAY Poreč is awash with accommodation until high season when it's booked out, and then you'll have to look a little further inland or up and down the coast (not ideal if you don't have wheels). Most of Poreč's tourism infrastructure is divided between two giant companies: Valamar and Plava Laguna. This is not great for competition, not least because smaller boutique hotels can't survive the winter

POREČ *Area*
For listings, see from page 88

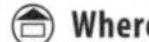

Where to stay

1 Bijela Uvala
2 Hotel Diamant
3 Isabella Castle
4 Istra Premier Camping Resort
5 Pension Gargamelo
6 Puntica
7 Sobe Daniela
8 Ulika naturist camp
9 Zelena Laguna

Off map

Hotel Filipini
Ty Istra

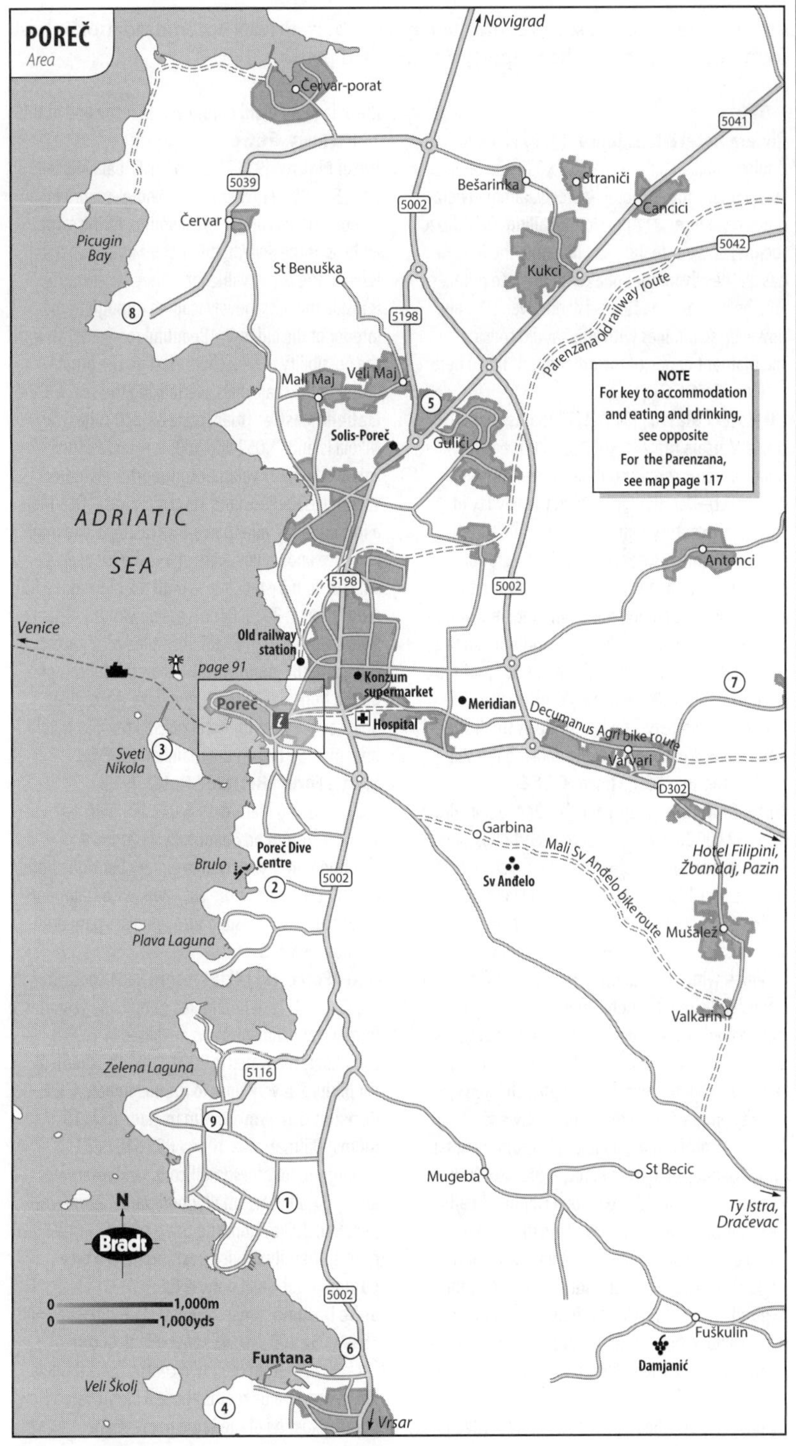

POREČ
Area
Novigrad
Červar-porat
5041
5039
Bešarinka
Straniči
Cancici
5002
Červar
Picugin Bay
5042
St Benuška
Kukci
8
5198
Parenzana old railway route
Mali Maj
Veli Maj
5
NOTE
For key to accommodation and eating and drinking, see opposite
For the Parenzana, see map page 117
Solis-Poreč
Gulići
ADRIATIC SEA
Antonci
5198
5002
Venice
Old railway station
page 91
Konzum supermarket
Meridian
7
Poreč
Hospital
Decumanus Agri bike route
Sveti Nikola
3
Varvari
D302
Garbina
Hotel Filipini, Žbandaj, Pazin
Poreč Dive Centre
Mali Sv Anđelo bike route
Brulo
Sv Anđelo
2
5002
Mušalež
Plava Laguna
Valkarin
Zelena Laguna
5116
9
Mugeba
St Becic
1
Ty Istra, Dračevac
N
Bradt
0 1,000m
0 1,000yds
5002
Fuškulin
6
Funtana
Damjanić
Veli Školj
4
Vrsar

when the summer season is controlled by a duopoly. Private accommodation is best found through one of the property agents listed below.

Hotels

Riviera Hotel & Residence [91 B2] (105 rooms, 8 suites) Obala Maršala Tita 15; 052 400 800; w valamar.com/en/hotels-porec/valamar-riviera-hotel-residence; Apr–Nov. Rivalling the Palazzo (below) & even stealing its old name, the Riviera has all the advantages of a conglomerate hotel. Free boat rides to Sv Nikola Island. Over 16s only, however, so families with kids should consider the Diamant or one of the other hotels listed here instead. **€€€€€**

BO Hotel Palazzo [91 A2] (70 rooms, 4 apts) Obala Maršala Tita 24; 052 858 800; e info@bohotel-porec.com; w bohotel-porec.com/en; Feb–Dec. Built in 1910 in the heyday of early 20th-century tourism, the original Hotel Riviera fell into disuse with the disintegration of Yugoslavia. At the turn of the 21st century it found new owners, but didn't get a complete renovation, new name & the Modernist grey additions to the ground floor until 2009. Sadly, it has not profited from its heritage & has a fairly cookie-cutter, if very nice, 4-star style on the inside. A small spa downstairs & outdoor pool overlooking the sea make it the envy of the town. **€€€€**

Hotel Diamant [map, page 87] (244 rooms) Brulo 1; 052 400 000; w valamar.com/en/hotels-porec/valamar-diamant-hotel-residence; Feb–Dec. A 4-star tower-block hotel 1km south of Poreč along the coast. Popular with tour groups, especially cycling tours in spring & autumn. Full beach facilities, with a restaurant & Poreč Diving Centre, are 5mins' walk from the hotel, which has an outdoor pool & pool fitness programme for hotel guests, as well as an indoor pool, sports hall, tennis courts, gym & spa open to non-hotel guests. Children's activity programme in the summer. **€€€€**

Hotel Filipini [map, page 87] (4 rooms, 4 apts) Near Žbandaj, 6km from Poreč; 052 463 200; e hotelfilipini@net.hr; f Hotel Filipini; all year. Despite not being in walking distance of the sea, it is worth going out of your way for this acclaimed & beautiful boutique hotel. Not quite typically Istrian in style, it is nonetheless rustic with an open fire, outdoor seating, tennis courts & plenty of space for children to play. The village of Filipini itself is quaint & hails after Captain George Filipin, whose extended family settled in the village & neighbouring Vrvari at the end of the 16th century. **€€€€**

Hotel Mauro [91 C2] (21 rooms) Obala Maršala Tita 15; 052 219 500; e info@hotel-mauro.hr; w hotelmauro.com; year-round. At the same address as the Riviera, this 4-star family-run hotel is by far the better value for money. Its entrance is inside the passageway leading through to the interior of the old town. Beautiful rooms, some with the possibility to take your b/fast on the ornate 19th-century balconies overlooking the sea. **€€€€**

Isabella Castle [map, page 87] (10 suites) Sv Nikola Island; 052 406 600; e reservations@valamar.com; w valamar.com/en/hotels-porec/valamar-isabella-island-resort; May–Oct. More a former fancy villa than a true castle, & you might not have known you were in a castle (or even a villa) in your 3-star suite – until the place got a full renovation in 2015. Rooms are now more suitably swish, the location is still unrivalled & has access to the giant 187-room Fortuna Island Hotel complex on the front side of the island. Take the regular boat service (free for hotel guests) from Sv Nikola boat pier [91 D4] on the mainland. **€€€€**

Martis Forum Heritage Hotel [91 B1] (19 rooms) Trg Marafor 9; 052 401 550; w martisforum.hr. Beautifully designed & exceptionally stylish contemporary boutique hotel, right in the heart of the old town, with fragments of Roman paving visible through glass panels in the floor. **€€€€**

Hotel Poreč [91 E4] (54 rooms) Rade Končar 1; 052 451 811; w hotelporec.com; all year. This former state-run hotel was privatised in 1997 & completely renovated in 2004. It has the charm of simplicity & is very close to the bus station. **€€€**

Pension Gargamelo [map, page 87] (16 rooms) Dalmatinska 10; m 095 518 0261; e gargamelo.info@gmail.com; w gargamelo.info; all year. Small, good-value, family-run pension, 2.5km from the town centre. Simple rooms, friendly service, restaurant, & a nice outdoor pool. Cash only. **€€€**

Sobe Daniela [map, page 87] (5 rooms) Veleniki 15a; 052 460 519; w konobadaniela.com. Located 4km from the town centre, Sobe Daniela offers good-value rooms above a highly rated & popular *konoba* of the same name. **€€€**

Ty Istra [map, page 87] (sleeps 10+) Dračevac; +33 636 093 997; w tyistra.com. A 10min drive from town is this beautifully renovated stone farmhouse with 2 additional studio apartments, complete with pool, garden & fully equipped kitchen. Full disclosure: owned by Thammy Evans, 1 of the 2 authors of this guide. **€€€–€€**

B&B and self-catering

Di-Tours [91 F3] Prvomajska 2; 052 432 100; m 091 939 8395; e di-tours@di-tours.hr; w di-tours.com. Specialising in accommodation in the Poreč area, this tourist agency is conveniently located inside town if you are on foot. Also offers excursion services.

Solis-Poreč [map, page 87] Bračka 47; m 099 221 1886; e info@solis-porec.com; w solis-porec.com; Jul/Aug 09.00–20.00 daily, rest of the year 09.00–16.00 Mon–Sat. A wide variety of self-catering property is available through this agency, & is conveniently located outside town if you're arriving by car. Also offers bike rental.

Camping There are several campsites around Poreč, some of them run by Valamar (w valamar.com), including the **Lanterna Premium Camping Resort** [map, page 84], 13km north from town (€24), & **Istra Premier Camping Resort** [map, page 87] near Funtana (€32). **Zelena Laguna** [map, page 87] (w istracamping.com/en/camping/zelena-laguna; €26) and **Bijela Uvala** [map, page 87] (w istracamping.com/en/camping/bijela-uvala; €27) are both around 5km south. **Puntica** [map, page 87] (w istracamping.com/en/camping/puntica; €26), 3km further south down the coast on the outskirts of Funtana, is the smallest of the sites & has easy access to the village & to the fisherman's festival every other Friday night. **Ulika naturist camp** [map, page 87] is 4km north of Poreč (€30).

WHERE TO EAT AND DRINK

Like most tourist towns, Poreč suffers from having an abundance of mediocre eateries in the summer. Some of the best *konoba* and fine dining are a drive away outside the town. For spit-roast pork and lamb, there are any number of roadside restaurants on the drive through Funtana, with suckling pig a speciality in Flengi. Here are some of the best restaurants in town and around.

Restaurants

Sv Nikola [91 A2] Obala Maršala Tita 23; 052 423 018; noon–23.00 daily. Michelin-recommended restaurant on the waterfront of the old town, serving top-notch seafood & other dishes. **€€€€**

Bistro Artha [91 E2] Jože Šurana 10; 052 435 495; bistroartha; noon–23.00 daily. Good-value vegetarian & vegan bistro just east of the old town. **€€€**

Istra [91 D4] Bože Milanovića 30; 052 434 636; w restaurant-istra.com; 10.00–midnight daily, closed 15 Jan–15 Mar. Genuinely good food in a traditional atmosphere at the edge of the old town. Excellent seafood & local wines. **€€€**

Konoba Aba [91 C2] Matije Vlačića 2; 052 438 669; midday–23.00 daily. Popular *konoba* with rustic stone interior. **€€€**

Konoba More [map, page 84] A Gašparini 3, Funtana; 052 445 202; morefuntana1979; midday–midnight daily. 1km or so beyond Funtana on the main road, this restaurant serves fantastic food by a beautiful fireplace, & offers freshly made *fritole* (delicious small doughnuts) for dessert. Try also their dried figs from the bowl on the counter on the way out (or in). **€€€**

Peterokutna Kula [91 C2] Decumanus 1; m 098 977 9222; w kula-porec.com.hr; noon–midnight daily. As the address suggests, this restaurant is housed in 1 of the towers of the old Roman town wall. Unrivalled views from the rooftop terrace, & not bad food & prices either. **€€€**

Bistro Nono [91 E3] Zagrebačka 4; 052 453 088; noon–23.00 daily. Many a tourist is very happy with a pizza at Nono's. Wide variety of pizzas, pastas & other dishes. **€€**

Cafés and bars

Bacchus [91 C1] Eufrazijeva 10; m 091 404 0051; w bacchus-porec.hr; summer only 11.00–02.00 daily. Atmospheric & popular *vinoteka* & bar offering Istrian wines & snacks, & some souvenirs.

Istriano [91 E2] Park Olge Ban 3; 11.00–midnight daily, closed Sun in winter. A tiny little wine bar serving a fantastic choice of Istrian wines & some from further afield. All their wines are available to drink on the premises or to take away by the bottle. They also stock *medica* (honey *rakija*) with truffles, *boškorin salami* with truffles, & serve great bruschetta & toasted sandwiches.

Torre Rotonda [91 C2] Narodni trg 3a; **m** 098 255 731; **w** torrerotonda.com; ⌚ 10.00–02.00 daily. A Venetian tower built in 1474, this café is beautifully cool in summer & offers sea views from the top of the tower.

Yesterday [91 E2] Park Olge Ban 2; ⌚ 07.30–23.00 daily. Owned by a Beatles fan from the UK & her Croatian husband, Yesterday is a must for those wanting something a little different. Beatles photos adorn the interior. Conveniently next to a small park if you need to occupy the kids. Coffee to go & ice creams available.

FESTIVALS There's so much going on in Poreč from May to Oct that it's hard to keep up. Check the Poreč tourist information office calendar of events (**w** myporec.com/en/what-to-do/events) to see what's in store. Here are a few highlights:

Ribarski fešt Every Fri along the quay in either Vrsar or Funtana is the weekly fisherman's festival, when you can truly gorge yourself on more fish than you can shake a stick at. Fresh – it's almost jumping out of the pan. For an idea of what you're eating, & what is or is not becoming endangered, see page 6.

Malvasia Wine Festival Usually the first w/end of Jun, this is a great opportunity to sample from the top-rate wineries of Istria & bag some bargains to boot.

Giostra On the 1st w/end of Sep every year, Poreč winds the clocks back to 1745. There's jousting on horseback on the beach, costumed events, music & dancing &, of course, food.

Sv Maurus As a means of celebrating a final fling before winter sets in, Poreč celebrates its patron saint's day on 21 Nov. Depending on when the w/end falls, there is usually several days of festivities surrounding the day itself, including cello concerts, polenta competitions & tastings, & a spectacular church service in the patron saint's Euphrasian Basilica (page 93). One of the nicest things about the festival is that it is so late in the season that it is predominantly a festival for locals, & thus a real treat as a visitor to be there.

SHOPPING **Supermarkets** abound in Poreč. **Konzum** [91 E2] has a small branch near Olge Ban Park and a huge store at Nikole Tesle is the closest to the centre, with Lidl, Plodine and Kaufland all on the same road but further east.

A **health food store** can also be found in the corner of the indoor market should you need one. **Zelena tržnica** [91 F2] is a local name for the **temporary market** (it only runs during the summer) over the road from the main market.

Meridian [map, page 87] Servisna zona Čimižin, Mate Vlašića 24a; ☎ 052 453 096; **e** shop@meridian.hr; **w** meridian.hr. A nautical & camping shop conveniently located by the big superstores if you're in a campervan – albeit not so convenient for sailors. The usual assortment of camping, fishing & sailing gear, & much more reasonably priced than those usually found in a Croatian marina.

Tržnica [91 F2] The **main market** is the place to get fresh locally grown produce & fish caught that morning. **Terzolo wines & olive oil** also has a shop there. Bring your own plastic or glass bottles & they can sell you Malvazija, Teran, Plavac (& early in the wine season also a fantastic Muscat) direct from their metal vats in the shop for as little as €3 per litre. In the same quadrant of the market, **Pisinium** has a small store for their local dried & cured meats, sausages & salami, including their magnificent truffle salami. Local liqueurs, *medenica* (or medica) made with honey, & *bistra* made with mistletoe are also available.

OTHER PRACTICALITIES

Accident & emergency [map, page 87] Dom zdravlja, Ul Dr Mauro Gioseffi 2, ☎ 052 451 611. The hospital reception for tourists is clearly marked at the driveway into the Poreč hospital. Also a pharmacy.

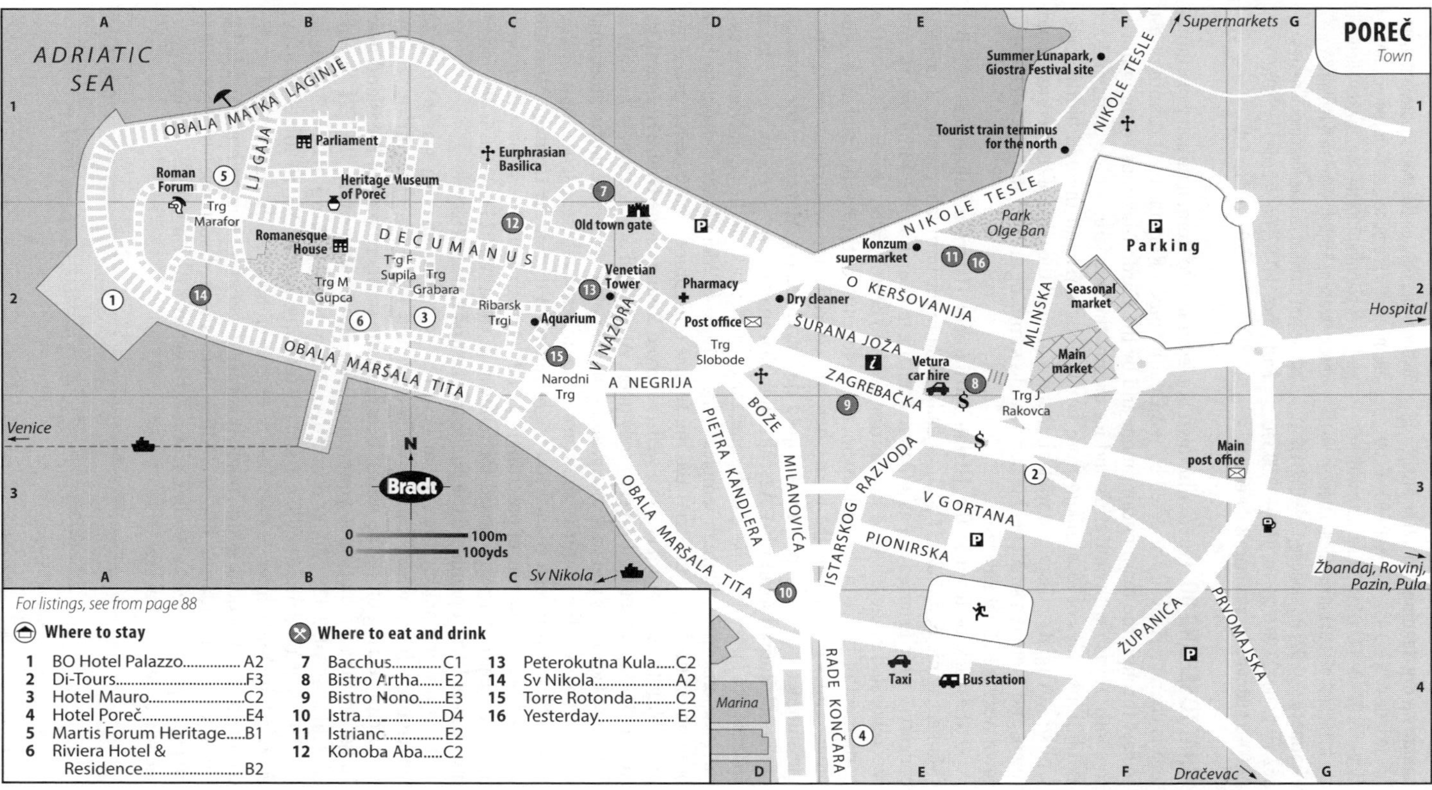

For listings, see from page 88

Where to stay

1 BO Hotel Palazzo............... A2
2 Di-Tours.................................F3
3 Hotel Mauro..........................C2
4 Hotel Poreč...........................E4
5 Martis Forum Heritage.....B1
6 Riviera Hotel & Residence.........................B2

Where to eat and drink

7 Bacchus.............C1
8 Bistro Artha...... E2
9 Bistro Nono.......E3
10 Istra....................D4
11 Istrianc...............E2
12 Konoba Aba.....C2
13 Peterokutna Kula.....C2
14 Sv Nikola....................A2
15 Torre Rotonda...........C2
16 Yesterday................... E2

Laundry & dry cleaning [91 D2] Kemiskija, Nikole Tesle 4; 052 432 910; 07.00–19.00 Mon–Fri, 07.00–14.00 Sat. A tiny place with not the friendliest of staff but excellent rates.

Pharmacy [91 D2] Trg Slobode 12; 052 432 362; 07.00–22.00 Mon–Fri, 07.00–18.00 Sat, 08.00–13.00 Sun. This pharmacy is the easiest to find being right on the main square, but there are many others around, see w myporec.com/en/travel-planning/health-care. The staff here all speak excellent English, German & Italian & can advise you on what to take for minor illnesses.

Post office [91 D2] Trg Slobode 14; 07.00–17.00 Mon–Fri, 08.00–midday Sat.

WHAT TO SEE AND DO Poreč's **old town** is a testament to Roman military planning, and is characteristically bisected by the Decumanus, a Roman street running west to east through the main encampment and by the Cardo Maximus running north to south. Awash with souvenirs and ice cream, the side streets hide crafts and art exhibitions, sales of local *rakija* from house doorways, and the odd hidden café. Unlike Rovinj, it's possible to walk all the way around the edge of the peninsula old town, and there is a small pebble beach and swimming area around the back of the town near the Hotel Palazzo.

At the back of town is the **Istrian Parliament** (**Istarska Sabornica**) [91 B1] (Matka Laginje 6; 052 431 585; daily in summer until late evening if hosting concerts), which started out as a Gothic Franciscan church in the 13th century, and was renovated in the Baroque style during the 18th century, after which it housed the parliament of Istria. In the parliament, the lapidarium of the basilica and at various other venues throughout the town, there are concerts and exhibitions throughout the summer. See w poup.hr for an up-to-date agenda. **Trg Marafor** is the location of the old **Roman forum** [91 A2], although that may not be so obvious now, for it appears as a large open space with some raised stonework on the floor. Nonetheless, the locations of two Roman temples – the Temple of Mars (later thought to have been one of the largest in Istria) and the Temple of Neptune – have been marked out there. Near the old forum is also a well-preserved **Romanesque House** (**Romanička Kuća**) [91 B2], although it is very rarely open. At this end of Decumanus, look up at the house façades as you walk along, and you will notice some amazing architectural works from over the centuries showcasing a number of different styles from Gothic to Venetian. If you get a chance you might also want to visit the **Heritage Museum of Poreč** (**Zavičajni muzej poreštine**) [91 B2] (Decumanus 9; e info@muzejporec.hr; w muzejporec.hr; still closed for renovation in early 2023), which is the oldest museum in Istria, opening to the public for the first time in 1884.

It's also worth taking the regular boat (every 20mins in high season) over to **Sv Nikola Island**, which can be walked around in a leisurely hour or so (but beware of veering off to the nudist beach, in the southern part of the island near Hotel Fortuna, if that's not your thing). The town **aquarium** [91 C2] (Franje Glavinića 4; 052 428 720; w akvarij-porec.com.hr; Jul/Aug 10.00–22.00 daily, Jun 10.00–20.00 daily, May/Sep 10.00–19.00 daily, Apr & Oct 10.00–15.00 daily; entry adult/child/under 3s €6/€3.30/free), tucked away in the eastern end of the old town, is really quite good. Small, it is easy to get around in an hour, and holds some fascinating marine life, including short-snouted seahorses (*Hippocampus hippocampus*), as well as reptiles. If you can't get to go diving, this is a good way to see what's in the local sea.

There are some super bike rides starting in Poreč, see page 196 for some suggestions.

There's lots of **hiking, biking and diving** to be done in the area (see the dedicated chapters), and there are two small electric coastal **sightseeing trains** which run from Valamar Pinia to the northern edge of the old town, and from the marina to Zelena Laguna. Southeast of Poreč, less than 1km beyond the village of Gradina, is the **megalithic hillfort site and observatory** Mordele, Picugi and Mali Sv Anđelo.

Euphrasian Basilica (Eufrazijeva bazilika) [91 C1] (Decumanus; 052 451 784; w zupaporec.com/euphrasian-basilica.html; Jul/Aug 09.00–21.00 daily, Sep–Jun 09.00–18.00 daily; €5.20) Today's Euphrasian Basilica in Poreč – the main attraction in town – was built at the behest of Bishop Euphrasius in AD553. It was built to replace the smaller 5th-century basilica that originally stood there, which in itself was built on an earlier basilica dedicated to Sv Maurus dating from AD313. The current 6th-century structure with its dazzlingly beautiful mosaics constitute one of the finest examples of early Byzantine architecture you'll find anywhere – on a par with Istanbul and Ravenna – and, along with the 5th-century floor mosaics still to be seen there, and some of the 4th-century mosaics unearthed there, it was inscribed into the UNESCO World Heritage List in 1997. Elements of the latter mosaics, including one of the fish symbol of Christ, are to be found in the garden at the far end of the basilica courtyard, along with the bishop's palace. The 5th-century mosaics can be seen under glass on either side of the main entrance into the church.

The shape of the 6th-century basilica is particularly noteworthy. At first, it looks completely normal, and that is because it is. In fact, it is the first example in western Europe of a triple-naved and triple-apsed church. Equally noteworthy are the mosaics of the basilica. In the vault above the main apse, you'll find the only early Christian depiction of Mary to be found in a western European church. To one side is the depiction of Euphrasius himself, holding a model of the church. The triumphal arch edging the top of the apse shows Christ and the 12 Apostles, and below them the Lamb of God and 12 medallion portraits of female martyrs.

While the shape of the 6th-century basilica remains intact, a number of alterations were made over the years. A bell tower was added opposite the entrance to the church in the 16th century. You can climb this for €1.60, but entry to the baptistery at the bottom of the tower is free, and usually contains a small art exhibition. Between the bell tower and the church a colonnaded atrium courtyard with several stone sculptures was later added, and then in the 17th century a clover-shaped memorial chapel.

The church is free to visit 07.00–17.30 daily, after which mass is held Monday–Saturday. Mass is held at 10.00 on Sunday. Photography inside the church is allowed. For more information on the history of the basilica, see w zupaporec.com/euphrasian-basilica.html.

Baredine Caves (Jama Baredine) (Nova Vas, 9km northeast of Poreč; m 095 421 4210 or 098 224 350; e info@baredine.com; w baredine.com; Apr/Oct 10.00–16.00 daily, May/Jun & Sep 10.00–17.00 daily, Jul/Aug 10.00–18.00 daily, individual & group tours available rest of the year with prior notice; entry adult/child €10/€6) At a cool 14°C, this is a great trip in the heat of summer. Tours take 40 minutes and depart every half an hour. With some additional on-site instruction, it's also possible to abseil to a further section of the cave. While this might not rival the best cave exhibits in the world, the adjoining museum and the tractor exhibition outside are added attractions.

BEACHES Rocky outcrops and pebble beaches abound north and south of Poreč, most with cafés, entertainment and children's play areas lining the coast. At the back of the old town is a promenade allowing entry to the sea, popular with the townspeople. Brulo, 1.5km south of Poreč, has the Poreč diving centre (page 210), and a small enclosed bathing area especially for infants, as well as big land trampolines, huge water trampolines, bumper cars and other entertainments to draw on your money. For those who prefer a less commercial feel, the bay of Červar offers wonderfully shallow, sandy access, which is ideal for young children and for playing *picugin*, the popular Dalmatian handball game played in knee-high waters.

NOVIGRAD

This miniature walled town, housed within less than 500m², is a gem of the Istrian coast. Known as Cittanova in Italian, it holds three of the top-rated restaurants in Croatia (yes, not just in Istria) as well as some unique hotels and some particularly rich naval attractions, not to mention a long stretch of beautifully preserved walls and very pleasant promenade along the waterfront. Follow it all up with a drink at Vitriol (Ribarnička 6) or one of the popular bars on Mandrač quay around the harbour, where you'll also find the tourist information office (Mandrač 29a; ☎ 052 757 075; w coloursofistria.com/en/destinations/novigrad).

GETTING THERE AND AROUND The most scenic way to get to Novigrad from Poreč is to take the coastal road past the pretty estuary of the River Mirna and the gateway of Antenal quarry. The bus station (*Epulanova bb*), which is a 10-minute walk from the centre, serves frequent buses to and from Poreč and many to further afield. The town itself is very small and easy to walk around.

WHERE TO STAY AND EAT *Map, opposite*

Hotel Nautica (38 rooms, 4 apts) Sv Antona 15; ☎ 052 600 400; e info@nauticahotels.com; w nauticahotels.com. On the marina just north of the town, this hotel gives direct access to your boat mooring. The hotel décor follows a distinctly naval theme & can seem a bit like a large ferry at times. Beautiful spa facilities & indoor pool. **€€€€**

Villa Cittar (12 rooms) Sv Anton 4; ☎ 052 758 780; e villa@cittar.hr; w cittar.hr. More recently opened & slightly smarter property under the same ownership as the Hotel Cittar (below). **€€€€**

Hotel Cittar (14 rooms) Prolaz Venecije 1; ☎ 052 757 737; e info@cittar.hr; w cittar.hr. This hotel has an impressive exterior & entrance built into the old town wall. The inside, however, is your standard hotel. **€€€**

Old Stone Guest House Santa Maria (13 rooms) Gradska Vrata 37; ☎ 052 757 444; w booking.com/hotel/hr/guest-house-santa-maria.en-gb.html. Conveniently near the old town, the exterior looks modern, but the indoor reception shows off its old stone look. Popular & pet-friendly. **€€**

Marina Sv Antona 38; ☎ 052 726 691; w marinarestaurant.eu/hr; ⌚ noon–1500 & 19.00–23.00, Wed–Mon. Another *Gault & Millau* & Michelin-listed restaurant, specialising in exquisitely prepared & presented seafood. 6- & 8-course degustation menus come in at around €90 & €110 respectively. **€€€€**

Damir i Ornela Zidine 5; ☎ 052 758 134; w damir-ornela.com; ⌚ 18.00–23.00 Tue–Sun. Listed in the *Michelin Guide* & *Gault & Millau*, this tiny restaurant is the best fine dining along this side of the Istrian coast. Excellent local fish carpaccio, fresh pastas & sinful desserts. **€€€€–€€€**

Konoba Kod Kristijan Bolnička ulica 8; m 098 420 314; f Konoba "Kod Kristijana"; ⌚ noon–15.00 & 18.00–22.00 daily. Good *konoba* with a focus on seafood – & as the sign says, no pizza, & no Ćevapčići! **€€€**

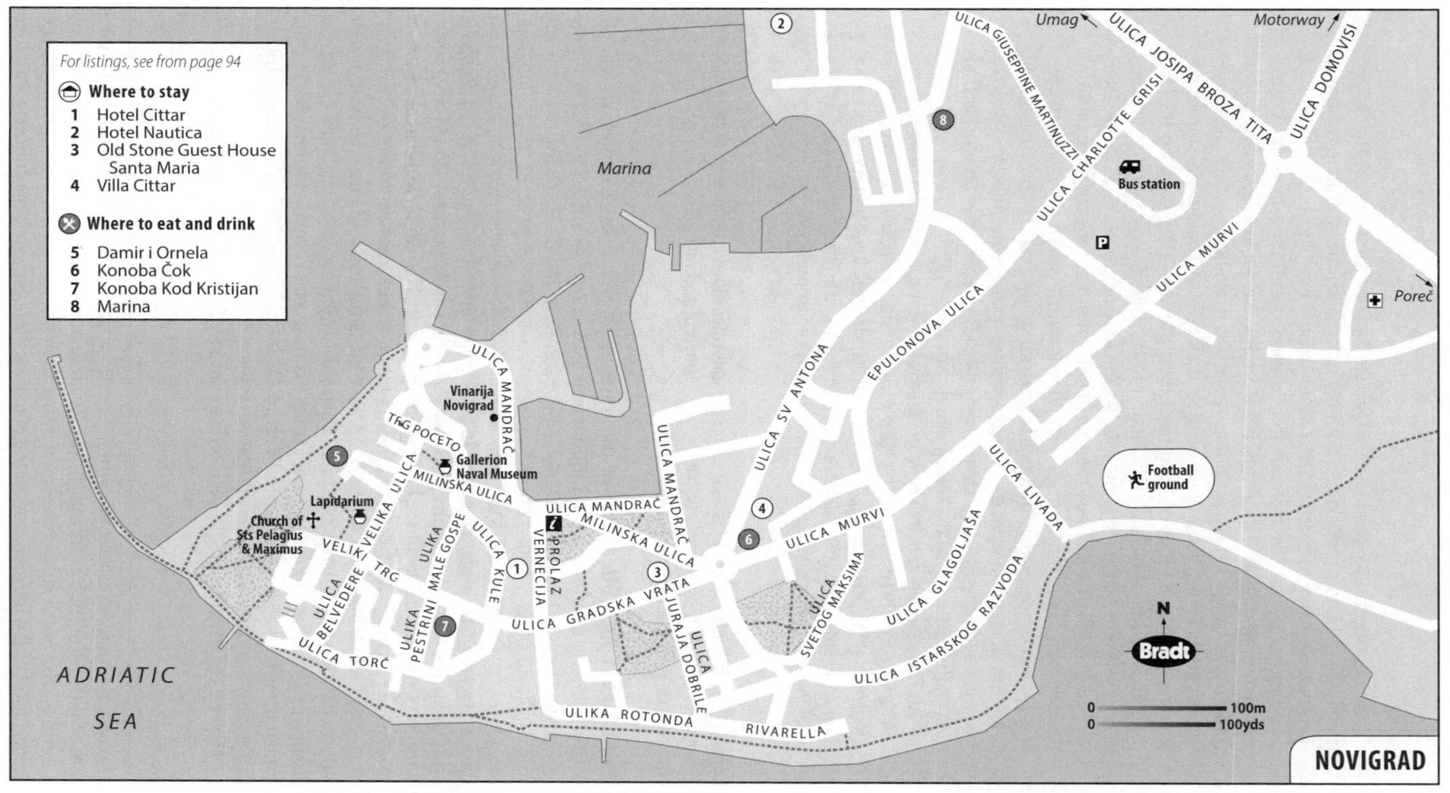
NOVIGRAD
For listings, see from page 94
Where to stay
1 Hotel Cittar
2 Hotel Nautica
3 Old Stone Guest House Santa Maria
4 Villa Cittar
Where to eat and drink
5 Damir i Ornela
6 Konoba Čok
7 Konoba Kod Kristijan
8 Marina
ADRIATIC SEA
Marina
Football ground
Bus station
Motorway
Umag
Poreč
ULICA DOMOVISI
ULICA JOSIPA BROZA TITA
ULICA CHARLOTTE GRISI
ULICA GIUSEPPINE MARTINUZZI
ULICA MURVI
EPULONOVA ULICA
ULICA SV ANTONA
ULICA LIVADA
ULICA GLAGOLJAŠA
ULICA ISTARSKOG RAZVODA
ULICA SVETOG MAKSIMA
ULICA MANDRAČ
MILINSKA ULICA
ULICA JURAJA DOBRILE
ULICA GRADSKA VRATA
RIVARELLA
ULIKA ROTONDA
PROLAZ VERNECIJA
ULICA KULE
ULIKA MALE GOSPE
ULIKA PESTRINI
ULICA TORČ
ULICA BELVEDERE
VELIKI TRG
VELIKA ULICA
TRG POCETO
Vinarija Novigrad
Gallerion Naval Museum
Lapidarium
Church of Sts Pelagius & Maximus
N
Bradt
0 100m
0 100yds

AL TORCIO

(Strada Contessa 22a, Novigrad; 052 758 093; w altorcio.hr/en) The Beletić family have been producing exquisitely good olive oils at their olive grove just outside Novigrad since 2000, when Tranquilino 'Lino' Beletić (who had previously opened the first privately owned guesthouse in Istria) started his own olive oil mill. Before this, it was impossible for local growers to take their olives to the local mill to be pressed, as it wouldn't accept quantities of less than 100kg, regardless of their quality – so Tranquilino started off by accepting quantities of 10kg from local growers. He passed on his love and knowledge of olive oil production to his wife, Đurđica, and their sons, Karmino and Kristijan, and by 2005 Al Torcio's superb olive oils were listed in *Flos Olei* (then known as *L'extravergine*) – the first time an olive oil from Croatia had appeared in the prestigious listing – where they've appeared every year since. Sadly, Tranquilino passed away in 2019, but the family tradition of creating olive oils of outstanding quality continues, and in 2019 they installed the most modern olive mill in Croatia. At the time of writing (2022) they were awaiting an organic certificate.

Al Torcio olive oils have won a whole slew of international awards, including gold medals from the New York International Olive Oil Competition (five of them in 2021 alone). They produce oils from several varieties including Bjelica, Frantoio, Ascolana, Moraiolo, Pendolino, Itrana and Rosulja, as well as a blend, and offer tastings, which are highly recommended.

Konoba Čok Sv Antona 2; 052 757 643; noon–23.00 Thu–Tue. This *konoba* with its exposed stone walls in the interior has good, well presented dishes accompanied by a very wide variety of local wines. €€

WHAT TO SEE AND DO A tour of the town takes only a few minutes, so it's well worth stopping off at **Museum Lapidarium** (Veliki trg 8a; 052 726 582; w muzej-lapidarium.hr; 1–13 Jun 09.00–15.00 Mon–Fri, 18.00–21.00 Sat, 14 Jun–end Aug 10.00–13.00 & 19.00–22.00 Mon–Sat, Sep 10.00–13.00 & 18.00–21.00 Mon–Sat, Oct–May 09.00–15.00 Mon–Fri, weekends by prior arrangement; entry €1.30, under 14s free) for a glance at the local Roman artefacts, and in the **St Pelagius and Maximus Church (Župna crkva sv Pelagija i sv Maksima)** (Veliki Trg) for its Baroque artwork inside and its 12th-century crypt. The **Gallerion Naval Museum (Muzej Gallerion)** (Mlinska 1; m 098 254 279; w kuk-marine-museum.eu; end Mar–end Oct 09.00–noon & 14.00–18.00 Wed–Sun; entry €4) has the best model-ship exhibition in all Istria, and has a prized display of artefacts from Georg von Trapp (of *The Sound of Music* fame) from his time as a U-boat commander in Pula. Finish up with a visit to **Vinarija Pevrino** (Mandrać 18; m 099 815 1266; 09.00–22.00 daily) to stock up on locally grown wine.

Divers, meanwhile, might be interested in HMS *Coriolanus*, page 211.

UMAG

Umag is best known for tennis, where the Association of Tennis Professionals holds one of its World Tour events each July (w croatiaopen.hr) at the Stella Maris Tennis Centre on the north side of the town. More than just tennis, the event has a gourmet Istrian food and wine area, and in the evenings there big open-air concerts with local and international acts. The **Jangalooz Adventure Park** (m 098 9011 194; w jangalooz.com), just up from the tennis courts, provides tree-to-tree rope bridges at heights between 1.5m and 10m and some 370m of zip lines for the adventurous (on a harness).

WHERE TO STAY AND EAT

Apartments Barbara (3 dbls, 2 apts) Vinogradska 14; 052 742 102; w apartmentsumag.com. Good-value modern rooms & apartments 2km from Umag. **€€€**

Ranch Goli Vrh (sleeps 5) Goli vrh 31; m 099 2721 820; e info@goli-vrh.com; w goli-vrh.com/en. Lovely, peaceful place to stay, a rustic wooden bungalow set in around 60ha of land. Horseriding, homemade *pršut* & delicious homemade cheese available. **€€€**

✷ **Konoba Badi** Umaška 12, Lovrečica; 052 756 293; e info@restaurant-badi.com; w restaurant-badi.com; 13.00–23.00 daily, closed Sundays in winter. The food at this outstanding Michelin- & *Gault & Millau*-listed seafood restaurant midway between Novigrad & Umag is in another league entirely. Go for the 5- or 7-course tasting menu with wine pairings, & experience some of the finest cuisine anywhere in Croatia – dishes along the lines of queen scallop tartare, giant ravioli stuffed with 'sea truffle' (a type of shellfish), & battered scorpionfish served with creamed wasabi & dehydrated olive crumbs. You can expect a selection of top-notch olive oils as well. Highly recommended. **€€€€**

✷ **Konoba Buščina** Buščina 18; 052 732 088; e info@konoba-buscina.hr; w konoba-buscina.hr; midday–midnight Wed–Mon. This superb traditional stone *konoba*, with huge garden & fireplaces, offers a great mix of coastal & inland local recipes which has earned it a well-deserved recommendation in the *Michelin Guide* & *Gault Millau*. Lovely atmosphere, very friendly & welcoming, & the food is well worth going out of your way for, with an emphasis on local, seasonal ingredients. I had scallops in cream in crisp filo pastry with truffle shavings, & strelka (an invasive fish, rather like sea bass but more sustainable) in a citrus & basil sauce – both delicious. I finished with an amazing gluten-free chocolate cake with chilli, salt & olive oil which, quite frankly, I'd travel halfway across Croatia to eat again. Highly recommended. They also have 4 beautiful Istrian villas available (6–8 people each, from €126 for 6; w buscina-villas.com/en). **€€€**

✷ **Konoba Nono** Umaška 35, Petrovija; 052 740 160; e konoba.nono@pu.t-com.hr; w konoba-nono.com; 11.00–22.00 Tue–Sun. Outstanding *konoba* just southeast of Umag on the road to Buje. Superb food, from delicious homemade ravioli stuffed with spinach to sea bass baked in salt, & a heavenly signature dessert (*torta* 'Nona'); many ingredients are from their own farm. **€€€**

Konoba Rustica Sv Marija na Krasu 41; 052 732 053; w konoba-rustica.com; midday–midnight Wed–Mon. Popular place serving grills, pizza & Istrian dishes. **€€€**

SAVUDRIJA

Tiny little Savudrija at the northwesternmost tip of Istria used to belong to the county of Piran. Its rocky outcrop has the oldest working lighthouse in the Adriatic (page 16), built in 1818. It's only possible to visit the lighthouse if accommodated in the apartment next door or on a private tour (contact Umag tourist office via w coloursofistria.com). Savudrija also offers the only golf course in all of Istria, and the coast hereabouts is good for **windsurfing**.

WHERE TO STAY AND EAT

Kempinski Hotel Adriatic (135 rooms) Alberi 300a; 052 707 000; w kempinski-adriatic.com. Sheer luxury with a price tag to match, & golf, facing Portorož. **€€€€€**

Svjetionik Savudrija (sleeps 4) Savudrija; m 099 218 8942; e turizam@plovput.hr; w lighthouses-croatia.com. This little self-catering apartment to the side of Savudrija lighthouse is relatively basic. Although in a small plot of land on its own with private boat mooring, it is surrounded by a caravan/camping site & has thus lost the idyllic charm that is seen in many of its online photos. **€€€€€**

Hotel Villa Rosetta [map, page 84] (23 rooms) Crvena Uvala 31, Zambratija; e info@hotelvillarosetta.net; w hotelvillarosetta.net/en. Small, modern hotel just south of Savudrija in the village of Zambratija, only 30m from the sea. **€€€€**

Camp Veli Jože [map, page 84] 016 426 600; w nazor.hr. Campsite near the beach with 350 pitches & 46 bungalows, plenty of sports facilities & a large terrace restaurant by the sea. **€**

Pergola [map, page 84] Sunčana Ulica 2, Zambratija; 052 759 685; w pergola.com.hr; 18.00–23.00 Thu–Sun. You'll find superb, inspired cuisine at this family-run, Michelin- & *Gault & Millau*-listed restaurant near the beach, with a focus on seafood. **€€€€**

Restaurant Toni Siparska 8; 052 759 570; noon–22.00 Thu–Tue, 18.00–22.00 Wed. Long-standing favourite, in business since 1970 & specialising in seafood. **€€€**

SOUTH TO LIMSKI KANAL

VRSAR A few kilometres south of Poreč is the small coastal town of **Vrsar**. It has a charming (and steep) old town, which is not remarkable by Istrian standards (already high). Judging by the class of the boats in the marina, however, this town is certainly a favourite place to dock for the international jet set who own a luxury yacht or cruiseboat. The marina car park is equally filled with high-end motor cars. Yet you wouldn't guess that from the town itself, which draws its main crowd on those Fridays of the month when it holds its very popular and mouth-watering **Fisherman's Festival**. During this event (which is mirrored in Funtana on alternate Fridays), local fishermen line the harbour grilling fish, and serving shellfish, *brodet* (hearty fish stew) and quaffable local wine, obscuring the stone sculptures that otherwise visibly adorn the view, courtesy of an annual stonemasonry competition at the normally abandoned Montraker quarry. There's also a **sculpture park** featuring the work of **Dušan Džamonja** (1928–2009), one of Croatia's most famous sculptors.

Boat rides to the **Limski kanal** (page 99) leave regularly during the day, and in the evening there are boat trips to see Rovinj by night for €25. Glass-bottom boats, for those who want to view underwater but can't dive, cost €10 per person. For those keen to dive, **Starfish Dive Centre** (page 210) runs dives to the *Baron Gautsch* (page 212) and *Hans Schmidt* sites.

Located on the busy road just north of Vrsar, **Funtana** has lots of restaurants and a dinosaur theme park (w dinopark.hr; Apr–Sep 10.00–18.00 daily; entry a bit steep at close to €30/€25 for an adult/child, though under 3s go free). Or, to get away from fish for a change, head into **Flengi** for suckling pig at one of the many roadside restaurants.

Just a short distance inland from Funtana, on the road between Flengi and Poreč, is one of the best wineries in Istria. The **Damjanić vineyard** (Fuškulin 50; 052 654 120; m 091 540 4315; e visit@damjanic.eu; w damjanic.eu; see page 37) has garnered a whole host of awards, and a wine tasting there should really be up at the top of your list of things to do along this stretch of the Istrian coast. Don't leave without trying the stupendously good Clemente Blanc (an oak-aged Malvazija/Chardonnay/Pinot blanc blend) and Akacija (100% Malvazija aged in acacia), and there's also a rather heavenly dessert wine, Sincerus.

 **Where to stay** The tourist office (Rade Končara 46; 052 441 746; w infovrsar.com) has a good list of private accommodation on its website.

Apartments Riva (34 apts) Obala maršala Tita 27b; 052 800 250; w maistra.com/properties/riva-apartments. Modern apartments sleeping 2–6 people, with a good, central location overlooking the waterfront. All come with balcony & small kitchenette. Free parking. **€€€€**

Hotel Pineta (95 rooms, 4 suites) Pineta 1; 052 800 250; w maistra.com/properties/hotel-pineta. One of the better value hotels in Vrsar is this 3-star on the south side of the harbour, with outdoor/indoor/kids' pools & only 100m from the beach. Bike friendly. **€€€€**

LIMSKI KANAL No trip to the Poreč area would be complete without a trip to the **Limski kanal**. The karst area here, mostly made of limestone (*lim* in Istrian comes from the Latin *limes*, plural *limites*, meaning 'channel/path/boundary', and is not related to the word limestone) sank some 10,000 years ago forming the current sea gorge. Protected from the wind and currents, it is the home of several shellfish-farming beds and is a protected natural monument, as a result of which it is illegal to swim in the eastern half of the channel.

At the eastern end of the gorge on the south bank is **Romuald's Cave** (**Romualdova pécina**), so called because St Romuald of Ravenna lived there as a hermit from 1002 to 1004. The cave, which is 105m long and several metres high, but with an entrance only 1m in height, shows evidence of Stone Age rock art on its western side (but, strangely, none on its eastern side), and the fossils of 41 different animals dating back to the Stone Age have been found there. The cave is temporarily closed to the public (early 2023), but when it reopens, visits can be arranged through Natura Histrica (w natura-histrica.hr) or the Kanfanar Tourist Office (w visitkanfanar.hr/en).

Romuald left the cave, deciding that those wanting to dedicate themselves to God should live in a community as monks, so he returned to his monastery (now no longer in existence), which he had built earlier on the north bank at Kloštar. There are legends that Sir Francis Drake left treasure there, and the whole inlet has been the backdrop for a number of films, including *The Vikings* starring Kirk Douglas (1958). There is ample parking at the road entrance to the Limski kanal on the old road between Poreč and Rovinj, where you can find information boards on the cave and local flora. It's a hike of 15–30 minutes up to the cave entrance, which becomes a difficult and exposed scramble at the top with very little railing support. Dress shoes and flip-flops are not advised.

A third of the way into the channel is the **Pirate Cave** [map, page 84] (w piratecave.net; 10.00–late daily) – a watering hole (they also sell hot snacks) and souvenir stall for the tourist boats visiting the gorge. Entry to the cave (which is more a very large hollow than a standard cave) is €1 and includes a postcard. A signposted trail from Petalon also leads down from the cliffs above, which can be reached from the end of the road going to Vrsar airport (private jets only). From the parking area at Petalon it is a 2km bike trail to the turn-off to the Pirate Cave, and a 200m hiking trail from the turn-off till you reach the cave.

Boat trips run from Poreč, Rovinj and Vrsar several times a day in the high season for around €16 per person for a 2-hour round trip, including a stop at the Pirate Cave. One of the best to take is the *Sveta Ana* small galleon replica from Vrsar leaving only once a day at 10.00. For around €25 a 6-hour trip – including lunch, 2 hours in Rovinj and a swimming stop at the Limski kanal – leaves at 10.00 and 12.30. **Diving trips** are available from Poreč diving centre (page 210) and from Starfish Dive Centre (in Vrsar; page 210).

It's possible to drive a short way into the fjord from the eastern end, where there are a few standard restaurants and lots of souvenir and local produce stalls. A couple of viewing towers adorn the north shoulder of the eastern entrance to the gorge, from where you can get the best views. The steep winding road on either side of the valley down to the water is very narrow, so be on the lookout for cyclists. Tour groups do arrive in their busloads to the eastern end of the gorge, so if you prefer a more secluded visit to the channel, then hike down from the cliff trail behind the airport.

DVIGRAD Further inland up the Lim River is the now-ruined fortress town of **Dvigrad** (meaning 'two towns'), which was decimated by the plague in 1631, and finally abandoned by the last remaining inhabitants in 1714. Its tall towers and the remains of St Sofia Church (Crkva sv Sofije) are visible from the highway over the Limski kanal, but it's best reached from Kanfanar. Now, it's slowly undergoing restoration, and you are currently free to wander the few half-cobbled little streets and open-air halls. There's sometimes a small stand selling snacks near the entrance.

SVETI LOVREČ Just off the *ipsilon* motorway north of the Limski kanal as you drive south from Poreč, Sveti Lovreč (an important military base for Venice during the 14th century) has a well-preserved medieval centre. A short walk from the main gate (Vela vrata) with its Venetian lion (and strange head, said to represent Attila the Hun, who is connected in legends to several towns in Istria) takes you past an attractive loggia to the Parish Church of St Martin (Župna crkva sv Martina) – note the triple apse from the original 11th-century construction, visible on the back exterior walls. Keep going past the church to arrive at one of the large, ruined defence towers from the old town walls, which gives a good impression of how well fortified the town once was.

6

Inland Istria

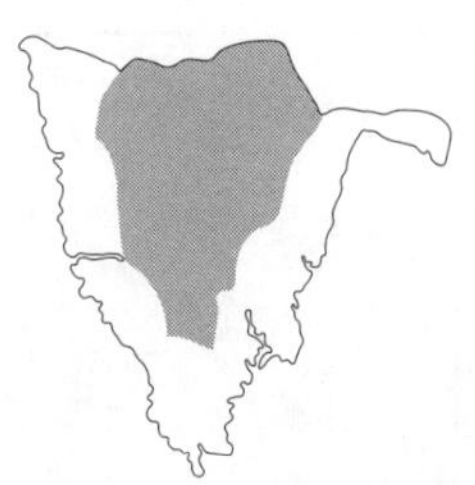

Inland Istria is, without any doubt, the least-visited part of *terra magica* (as the Romans are said to have nicknamed Istria). While tourists throng to the coast to see the iconic Rovinj, the arena at Pula or the beaches of Medulin, the Istrian interior steps down a gear or two – enter a world of perfectly preserved medieval hill towns, hidden frescoes and heavenly food.

PAZIN

Pazin (Italian Pisino, German Mitterburg), despite being the capital of the Istrian *županija* or county, is one of those places most visitors miss – which is a shame because it's an interesting little town with a cracking castle, a dramatic gorge and literary associations aplenty, which for around 1,000 years followed an entirely different historical trajectory from the rest of Istria. You can even get here easily on public transport, which is saying something for inland Istria.

HISTORY Pazin is first mentioned (as Castrum Pisinum) in a document of AD983, when its castle was given to the Bishops of Poreč by Holy Roman Emperor Otto II. In the 12th century the bishops in turn gave it to Meinhard von Schwarzenburg, after whose death it was passed to the Counts of Gorizia through the marriage of his daughter to Count Engelbert of Gorizia. Under the Counts of Gorizia, Pazin and its surroundings (including at times Tinjan, Vižinada, Žminj and other towns) were ruled as an independent state, at a time when the rest of Istria belonged either to Venice or the Bishops of Aquileia. The complicated boundaries between these were recorded in a 13th-century document known as the *Istrian Book of Boundaries* (*Istarski razvod*; page 10). In 1374 the last Count of Gorizia died without an heir, and the county of Pazin (Pazinska knežija), as it was now called, went to the Habsburgs, who leased it to various nobles. This leasing and subleasing ultimately led to increased taxes on the local peasantry, who revolted on several occasions. In 1766, Pazin Castle was bought by Count Antonio Laderchi, Marquis of Montecuccoli. Pazin County endured until the early 19th century, when along with the rest of Istria it became part of Austria (and then Italy from the end of World War I), though the castle remained in the possession of the Montecuccoli family until 1945.

GETTING THERE AND AWAY

By train Pazin lies on the railway line between Pula and Buzet, and has departures for Pula at 06.02, 07.53, 11.56, 13.56, 15.50, 18.01 and 20.51 Monday–Friday, 06.02, 11.56, 18.01 and 20.51 Saturday/Sunday. Travelling north there are trains to Lupoglav (with a bus connection to Rijeka) and Buzet (though the station's a long way from the town itself). Pazin's **railway station** (Željeznički kolodvor; Stareh Kostanji bb) is a 10-minute walk east of the old town centre, past the bus station.

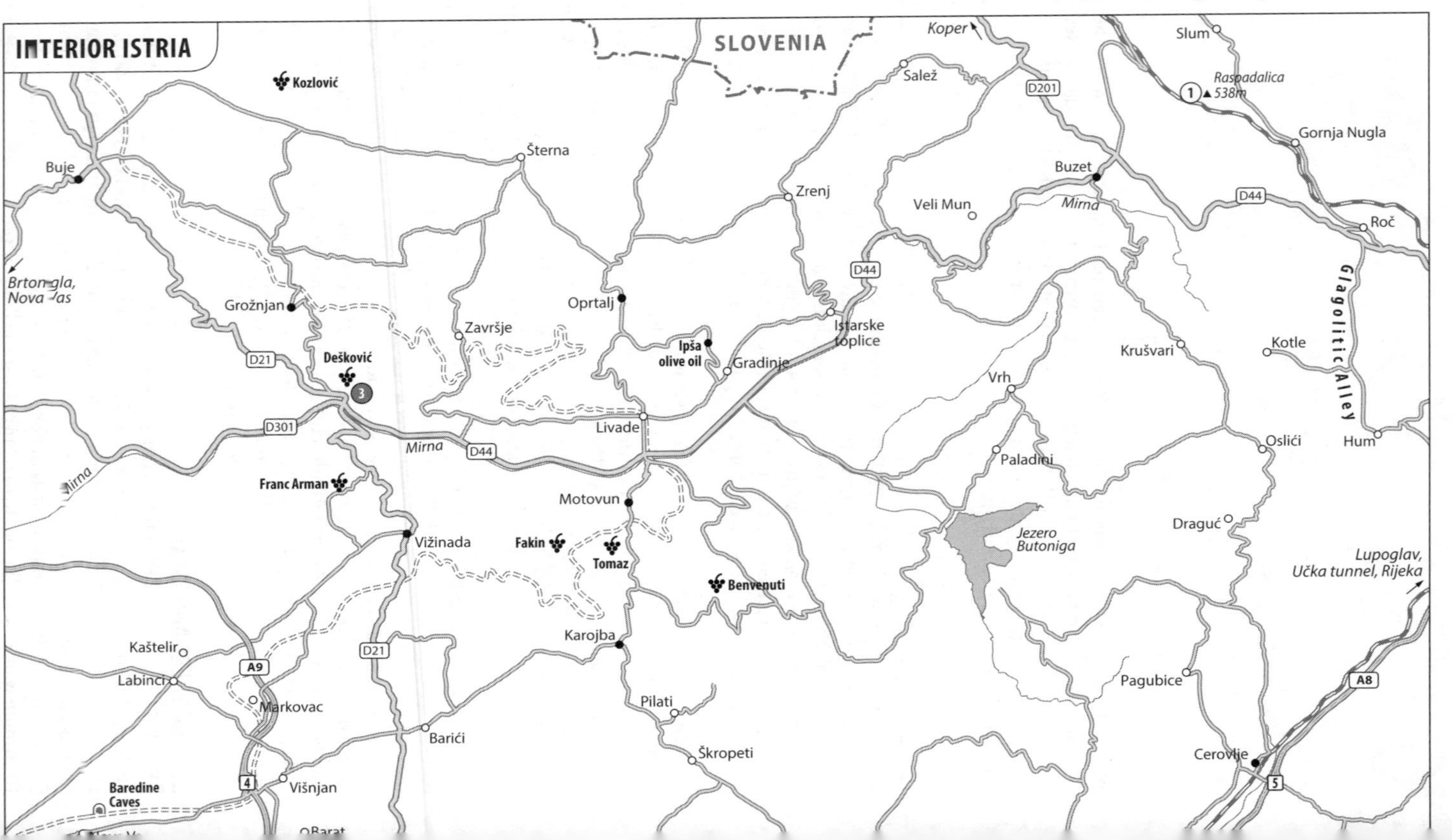
INTERIOR ISTRIA
SLOVENIA
Koper
Slum
Raspadalica
1
538m
Gornja Nugla
Kozlović
Šalež
D201
Buzet
Mirna
D44
Roč
Šterna
Zrenj
Veli Mun
Buje
Brtonigla,
Nova Vas
Grožnjan
Završje
Oprtalj
Istarske
Toplice
Glagolitic Alley
Kotle
Kruševari
Ipša
olive oil
Gradinje
Dešković
3
D21
Vrh
Livade
D301
Mirna
Paladini
Oslići
Hum
Franc Arman
Motovun
Vižinada
Fakin
Tomaz
Jezero
Butoniga
Draguć
Benvenuti
Lupoglav,
Učka tunnel, Rijeka
Karojba
Kaštelir
A9
Labinci
Markovac
Pilati
Pagubice
A8
Barići
Škropeti
Cerovlje
5
4
Višnjan
Baredine
Caves
Barat

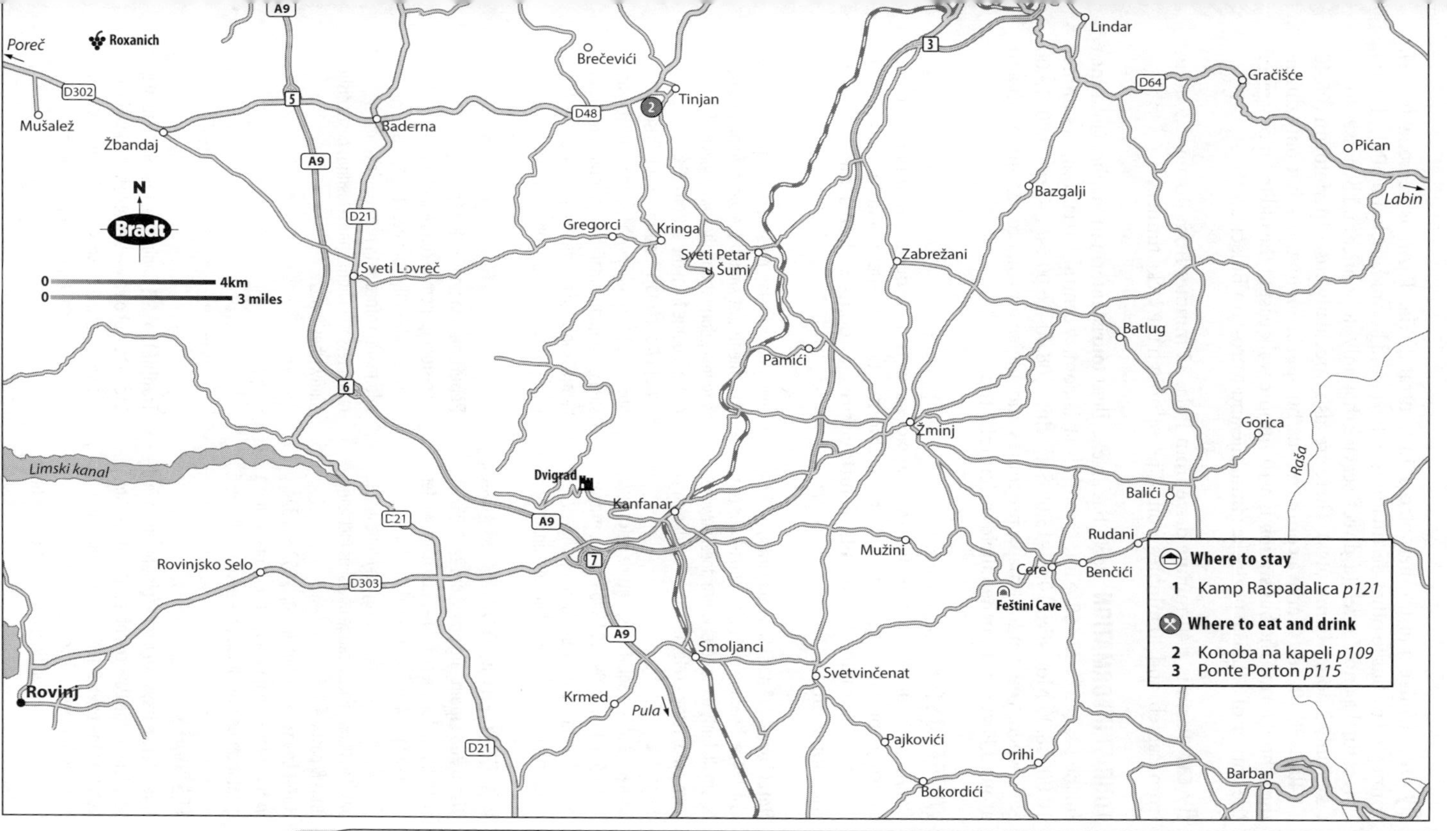
Poreč
Roxanich
Mušalež
Žbandaj
Brečevići
Tinjan
Baderna
Lindar
Gračišće
Pićan
Labin
Bazgalji
Gregorci
Kringa
Sveti Petar u Šumi
Sveti Lovreč
0 4km
0 3 miles
Zabrežani
Batlug
Pamići
Žminj
Gorica
Raša
Limski kanal
Dvigrad
Kanfanar
Balići
Rudani
Benčići
Čere
Mužini
Feštini Cave
Rovinjsko Selo
Smoljanci
Svetvinčenat
Krmed
Pula
Rovinj
Pajkovići
Orihi
Barban
Bokordići
Where to stay
1 Kamp Raspadalica p121
Where to eat and drink
2 Konoba na kapeli p109
3 Ponte Porton p115

By bus Unlike most other places in central Istria, Pazin is reasonably well connected by bus to other destinations in Istria and beyond, including Pula, Rovinj, Poreč, Rijeka and Zagreb (a 'direct' service that only stops once and bypasses Rijeka takes only 2 hours 45 minutes). There are also three daily buses to Motovun (06.40, 14.40 & 20.10; see w arriva.com.hr/en-us/bus-pazin-motovun) – but only during the school term. The **bus station** is a 10-minute walk east of the old town centre, on the corner of Šetalište pazinske gimnazije and Miroslava Bulečića.

By car Pazin is a 40-minute drive from Pula, 35 minutes from Rovinj, 2½ hours from Zagreb, and 40 minutes from Rijeka through the Učka tunnel.

TOURIST INFORMATION Pazin has an excellent **tourist information office** (Franine i Jurine 14; 052 622 460; e info@central-istria.com; w central-istria.com; summer 10.00–18.00 Mon–Fri, 10.00–13.00 Sat, winter 08.00–16.00 Mon–Fri, 10.00–13.00 Sat), where you can find maps, brochures and advice on what to see and do in and around Pazin and further afield in central Istria.

WHERE TO STAY *Map, opposite*

Pazin has one hotel, the two-star Lovac, as well as a decent number of places offering private accommodation, including the excellent Laura and Studio Apartman Amalia. For details of further private rooms and apartments, contact the tourist office.

Hotel Lovac (27 dbls) Šime Kurelića 4; 052 624 324; e tisadoo@inet.hr; w hotel-lovac.com.hr. Small, fairly basic hotel which does, however, have a nice terrace café/restaurant overlooking the gorge. €€

Laura (2 dbls, 1 sgl, 4 apts) Antuna Kalca 10/a; 052 621 312; m 099 593 9908; e apartmani-laura@hotmail.com; w booking.com/hotel/hr/apartments-and-rooms-laura.en-gb.html. Lovely place to stay, offering clean, quiet rooms & apartments just around the corner from the castle & tourist information office, with views of the castle & gorge from the balcony. €€

Studio Apartman Amalia (1 apt) Pristava bb; m 091 546 0606; w booking.com/hotel/hr/studio-aprtman-amalie.en-gb.html. Nice, clean, centrally located apartment, arranged over 2 floors with plenty of space. Good value. €€

WHERE TO EAT AND DRINK *Map, opposite*

Bistro Pod Lipom Trg pod lipom 2a; 052 622 022; summer 07.00–23.00 daily, winter 07.00–22.00 Mon/Tue & Thu–Sat, 07.00–15.00 Wed & Sun. Bistro hidden away off Muntriljska, past Sv Nikola, with a range of dishes including grills & pasta. €€€

Hotel Lovac Šime Kurelića 4; 052 624 324; w hotel-lovac.com.hr. Terrace restaurant with a great location overlooking the gorge. €€€–€€

Peperone Franine i Jurine 6; w restoranpeperone.com/en; noon–22.00 daily. Simple buffet/bar near the tourist information office with reasonable (though rather less than homemade-tasting) pasta dishes, sandwiches & pizza. €€

FESTIVALS

Jules Verne Days w istrainspirit.hr/en. In mid-Jun, Jules Verne Days celebrates the connection between the town & Jules Verne's 1888 novel *Mathius Sandorf*, with theatre performances, balloon & helicopter flights, & a fun treasure hunt for kids.

TradInEtno f tradinetno. The local TradInEtno Orchestra put on a well-established annual series of traditional music workshops & concerts in the summer months & at other times of year.

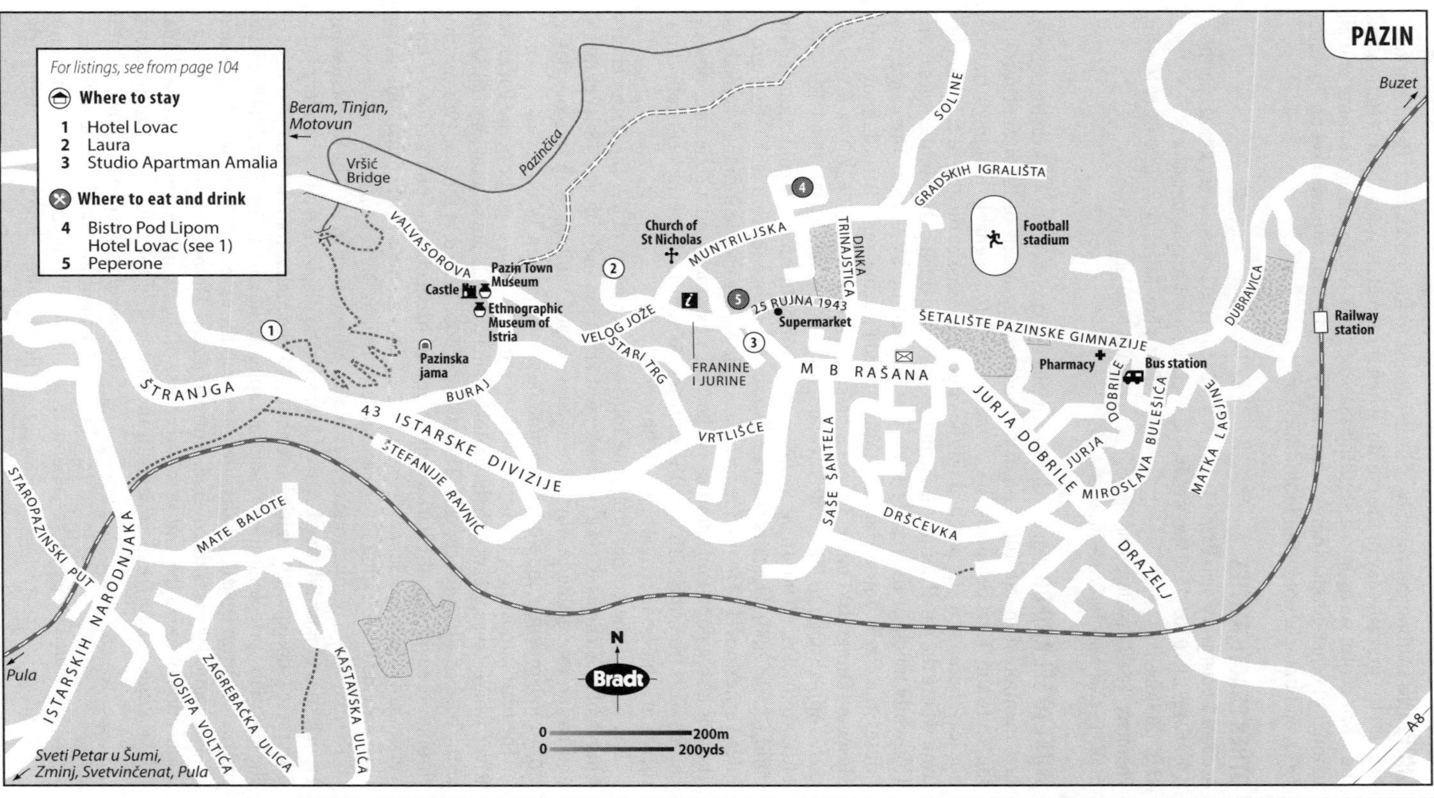
PAZIN
For listings, see from page 104
Where to stay
1 Hotel Lovac
2 Laura
3 Studio Apartman Amalia
Where to eat and drink
4 Bistro Pod Lipom
Hotel Lovac (see 1)
5 Peperone
Beram, Tinjan, Motovun
Vršić Bridge
Pazinčica
VALVASOROVA
Castle
Pazin Town Museum
Ethnographic Museum of Istria
Pazinska jama
Church of St Nicholas
MUNTRILJSKA
VELOG JOŽE
STARI TRG
FRANINE I JURINE
25 RUJNA 1943
Supermarket
DINKA TRINAJSTICA
GRADSKIH IGRALIŠTA
SOLINE
Football stadium
ŠETALIŠTE PAZINSKE GIMNAZIJE
Pharmacy
Bus station
DOBRILE
BULEŠIĆA
MIROSLAVA
MATKA LAGINJE
DUBRAVICA
Railway station
Buzet
M B RAŠANA
JURJA DOBRILE
JURJA
DRAZELJ
DRŠĆEVKA
SAŠE ŠANTELA
VRTLIŠĆE
ŠTRANJGA
BURAJ
43 ISTARSKE DIVIZIJE
ŠTEFANIJE RAVNIĆ
MATE BALOTE
STAROPAZINSKI PUT
ISTARSKIH NARODNJAKA
JOSIPA VOLTIĆA
ZAGREBAČKA ULICA
KASTAVSKA ULIĆA
Pula
Sveti Petar u Šumi, Zminj, Svetvinčenat, Pula
N
Bradt
0 200m
0 200yds
A8

SHOPPING Although probably of little interest to foreign visitors, **Pazin Market** is held on the first Tuesday of the month, when the street between the bus station and the town centre turns into a seething mass of stalls selling cheap clothing and all manner of other goods. There's a reasonably sized Diona **supermarket** on 25 Rujna 1943, and branches of both Plodine and Lidl.

OTHER PRACTICALITIES

Accident & emergency Jurja Dobrile 1; ☎052 624 393; ⏲ 07.00–14.30 Mon/Wed/Fri, 13.00–20.30 Tue/Thu

Pharmacy Šetalište pazinske gimnazije 4; ⏲ 07.00–20.00 Mon–Fri, 07.30–20.00 Sat, 09.00–13.00 Sun; see w central-istria.com/en/informacije-information/useful-info

Post office Rašana 7a; ⏲ 07.00–20.00 Mon–Fri, 07.00–14.00 Sat

WHAT TO SEE AND DO Pazin's dominant piece of architecture is its **castle** (*kaštel*), first mentioned in the 10th century though owing much of its present form to the 16th and 17th centuries. It's a massive and impregnable-looking structure, not least because it sits perched on the edge of a gorge at the top of a 100m cliff, from where the small county of Pazin was governed during the Middle Ages (page 10), while much of the rest of Istria was gobbled up by Venice. The castle now houses the **Pazin Town Museum** (**Muzej grada Pazina**) and **Istria Ethnographic Museum** (**Etnografski muzej Istre**) (Istarskog razvoda 1; ☎052 622 220; w emi.hr; ⏲ 15 Apr–15 Oct 10.00–18.00 Tue–Sun, 16 Oct–14 Apr 10.00–15.00 Tue–Thu, 11.00–16.00 Fri, 10.00–16.00 Sat/Sun; entry for both museum collections adult/child €3.50/€2.50). Upstairs you can also see the dungeon from which the hero of Jules Verne's novel *Mathius Sandorf* makes his daring escape into the Pazin abyss. There is also a good collection of Istrian folk costumes, and a collection of local church bells from the 17th to 19th centuries. As well as the permanent collections there are some good temporary exhibitions.

Just around the corner from the tourist information office, the 13th-century **Church of St Nicholas** (**Crvka sv Nikole**) was rebuilt in the 15th and 18th centuries, and has an interesting presbytery with star-shaped vaulting, with frescoes dating from 1460, probably the work of an unknown master from Tyrol.

The reason most people visit Pazin is to see the dramatic **gorge** of the Pazinčica River, where it disappears into the **Pazinska jama** or 'Pazin abyss', a cave and sinkhole at the base of a 100m sheer cliff. The cave was popularised in the late 19th century through the writings of Charles Yriarte and in particular the publication of Jules Verne's novel *Mathius Sandorf* (see opposite), though much earlier than this it may have provided inspiration for the entrance to Hell in Dante's *Inferno*.

The first serious exploration of the cave was undertaken in 1893 by the pioneering French speleologist **Édouard-Alfred Martel**, who discovered a large underground lake there (subsequently named after him). **Mirko Malez**, founder and president of the Croatian Speleological Association, explored the cave in 1967, and local caving instructor **Drago Opašić** led an expedition into the cave in 1975, in which a second underground lake was discovered, Mitrovo jezero. Despite the popularisation of a connection between the underground course of the Pazinčica and the Limski kanal à la *Mathius Sandorf*, experiments in the first half of the 20th century (including the use of marked eels) showed that it actually drains east into the River Raša.

> There are two easy hikes around Pazin, see page 191.

The Pazinčica Gorge sometimes floods after heavy rain, when the enlarged river is unable to escape

JULES VERNE AND PAZIN

Pazin's castle and gorge feature prominently in Jules Verne's 1885 novel *Mathius Sandorf*. The eponymous hero is imprisoned in the castle with his accomplices and sentenced to death after their plan to free Hungary from Austrian rule is uncovered by three villains, but he manages to escape through a window before climbing down the cliff into the gorge, and then into the cave itself. Underground rivers then carry him all the way to the Limski kanal, on the coast south of Rovinj. Though the gorge, the castle and its dungeon are all very real and can still be visited in Pazin, the hero's underground adventures are rather more fanciful. There is no evidence that the underground network of streams from Pazinska jama stretches as far as the Limski kanal (they do, however, drain into the Raša) – nor is it likely that anyone would survive such a journey – though these facts make the story no less enjoyable. Though Verne never actually visited Istria he was able to follow descriptions of the castle and cave by the French writer Charles Yriarte, who had visited Pazin, and whose *Les bords de l'Adriatique* (*Coasts of the Adriatic*) was published in 1878. Verne was also sent photographs of Pazin by its mayor.

underground down into the siphon below Martel's lake fast enough, turning the gorge into a lake – the largest recorded flood being in 1896, when the water rose to just 30m below the castle.

An easy **walking trail** leads down into the gorge from the **Vršić bridge**, and it's also possible to follow the river upstream to **Zarečki krov**, a large waterfall spilling over a rock shelf into a pool (see page 191 for a description of both these walks). To enter the cave itself, however, you must be accompanied by a guide – which is possible to arrange in July/August with an experienced member of the local speleological association (Speleološko društvo 'Istra' Pazin; **m** 091 512 1528; **e** pazincave@gmail.com; **w** central-istria.com/en/penjanje-climbing-klettern/speleoavantura; departures from the Vršić Bridge at 10.00, 13.30 & 15.30 depending on weather conditions, trips last 2hrs 30mins, prior booking essential; adults/children (minimum age 8) €30/€25; English spoken; contact the tourist information office for more information).

Alternatively, you can whizz across the gorge on a **zipline** – there are two sections, 220m and 280m long, the latter reaching speeds of up to 50km/h (**m** 091 543 7718; **f** zipline.pazin; ⌚ Jun–Aug 10.00–19.00, May/Sep 10.00–18.00; €18.60).

AROUND PAZIN

BERAM Around 3km northwest of Pazin, near the village of Beram, is an outstanding cycle of 15th-century **frescoes**, worthy of any amount of detour to see. The frescoes, which date from 1474, decorate the interior of the small **Church of St Mary of the Rocks** (**Crkva sv Marija na Škriljinah**), 1km northeast of the village itself, and are the work of a local master, Vincent of Kastav. They cover almost the entire wall space in 46 panels, mostly with scenes from the life of St Mary and the life of Christ, including a large (8m long) *Adoration of the Magi*. But it is the extraordinary ***Dance of Death***, above the main entrance, which steals the show. Figures representative of an entire cross section of medieval society are arranged in what is more of a solemn procession than a dance, all walking from left to right.

A pope, a cardinal and a bishop lead the way, followed by a king and queen, an innkeeper carrying a small cask, a small naked child, a beggar, a knight and a merchant, all interspersed with horn-blowing, scythe-bearing skeletons, and all walking into the arms of death. The frescoes are remarkably well preserved – they were covered up or painted over during the 18th century, and were only discovered beneath a layer of paint and plaster in 1913.

The church is kept locked, so you'll need to contact the local keyholder in Beram (*Ž So* Beram; 052 622 903), who'll come and open it (try to call at least half an hour in advance, preferably more). There's officially no admission fee for visiting the church at the moment, but a small offering of €2 or similar will probably be appreciated. You can walk to Beram easily enough from Pazin – there's a marked **footpath**, and a small map is available from the Pazin tourist information office (page 104) or online at w central-istria.com/en/aktivnosti-activities-aktivurlaub/pjesacenje-walking/pazin_beram_pazin. In Beram itself, the **Parochial Church of St Martin (Župna crkva sv Martina)** has some early 15th-century frescoes hidden behind the main altar.

Where to eat and drink

Konoba Vela vrata Beram 41; 052 622 801; m 091 781 4995; summer noon–23.00 Tue–Sun, winter 16.00–23.00 Tue–Sun. A good, homely tavern opposite St Martin's Church, with dishes including homemade pasta with truffles or game, sausage & pork loin with pickled cabbage. €€

TINJAN West from Pazin on the old road to Baderna and Poreč, the village of Tinjan is these days best known for its excellent ***pršut***, considered by many to be the best in Istria and celebrated with a prestigious annual *pršut* festival at the beginning of October. There are good views over the adjacent valley from a broad grassy terrace, and in the old town several houses are marked by carved symbols indicating the trade of their former inhabitants. Note the bell tower of the parish church, with its unusual top.

ISTRIAN *PRŠUT*

Though *pršut* (dry-cured ham, similar to Italian prosciutto) is produced widely in Dalmatia, many would argue (the authors included) that Istrian *pršut* is superior.

The village of Tinjan and its surroundings, elevated and exposed to a cool northeasterly wind, are considered to produce the finest Istrian *pršut*, which is still made using traditional methods in this area.

The pig's hindleg is cleaned, lightly salted and left in a wooden press (*kasela*) for about a week, weighted by stones to drain off any blood. It is then rubbed with a mixture of salt, herbs (bay leaves and rosemary) and pepper, before being hung to 'dry' for the winter in the loft or upper storey of a building – and with the arrival of spring and warmer weather, in a cool stone cellar. The entire curing process lasts for 12–18 months. When the ham has finally matured there can be an enormous difference in taste and colour between hams of different ages and from different producers, even within a small area.

The slightly less muscular foreleg is also cured in a similar manner, and is known as *špaleta*.

THE VAMPIRE OF KRINGA

Just west of Sveti Petar u Šumi, the tiny village of Kringa is notable mainly for the legends attached to one of its 17th-century inhabitants, one Jure Grando – claimed to be Europe's earliest recorded vampire. The 17th-century Slovenian writer Johann Weikhard Valvasor wrote an account of the happenings in the village, which he claimed to base on conversations with local inhabitants in Kringa. Valvasor wrote that following Grando's death and burial, he rose from his grave every night for 16 years, going about the village and knocking on people's doors (which would soon be followed by the death of some member of the house), and jumping into bed with his own (horrified, one can only assume) widow. When locals had finally decided enough was enough, a group of nine men were sent into the cemetery to open Grando's grave where they found his body perfectly preserved. Failing to finish off the sleeping fiend with a willow stake, they lopped off his head instead, after which his nocturnal wanderings finally ceased.

Where to eat and drink

Konoba na kapeli [map, page 102] Milinki 146; 052 626 318; midday–22.00 daily. This is a great *konoba* & *kušaona pršuta* – meaning 'a place to taste *pršut*'. There will usually be *pršut* from around 4 different local producers available – best ordered as a platter with local cheeses & other nibbles, & savoured with a jug of wine. It lies just outside Tinjan itself at the junction with the road from Pazin to Baderna & Poreč. €€

SVETI PETAR U ŠUMI The small village of Sveti Petar u Šumi, around halfway between Tinjan and Žminj, grew up around the Benedictine monastery of the same name, rather than the other way round. The **Monastery of St Peter in the Woods (Pavlinski samostan Sveti Petar u Šumi)** is first mentioned in 1174, as having already existed for 50 years before that, and there was probably a monastery here even earlier. In the 15th century the Paulines took over, restoring the monastery and cloister, which is one of the more beautiful in Istria – note the Renaissance columns on the lower level, added at this time, and the earlier Romanesque columns above. Part of the monastery and the adjacent **Church of St Peter and St Paul (Crkva sv Petra i Pavla)** were burnt down in the 17th century, and it was during subsequent rebuilding in the early 18th century that the church gained its Baroque façade, and elaborately decorated interior, the work of the painter Leopold Keckheisen and sculptor Pavao Riedl, both of whom were members of the Pauline brethren. The ruined building beside the monastery was probably used for livestock. The Paulines were suspended by order of the Austrian Emperor Joseph II in 1783, but returned to Sveti Petar u Šumi in 1993.

Legend connects Sv Petar u Šumi with the 11th-century Hungarian king Solomon, who some say spent some years at Sveti Petar u Šumi before continuing to Pula, where he ended his life as a monk (page 61). Others say he was slain on the battlefield near Edirne.

SOUTH TO PULA

ŽMINJ If you're driving south on the old road from Pazin or Sveti Petar u Šumi to Svetvinčenat (page 110), you'll pass through **Žminj** (Italian Gimino), where it's worth stopping to have a quick look at the massive ***kula*** or tower, which once would have formed part of a 15th-century castle. Just down the road past two old wells (and a bust of Istrian poet Mate Balota) is the main square and the **Parish Church of St Michael Archangel (Župna crkva sv Mihovila Arkanđela)**, with its Baroque façade. There is a large annual village fair in Žminj on St Bartholomew's Day (at the end of August), known as **Bartulja.**

Žminj also has a particularly good guesthouse, **Casa Matiki** (Matiki 14, Žminj; m 098 299 040; e sonja@matiki.com; w matiki.com; **€€€**, b/kfast €10 extra) – a traditional Istrian stone house, tastefully decorated, which has three beautiful apartments, each with its own kitchen and set among beautiful gardens, alongside a swimming pool.

FEŠTINSKO KRALJEVSTVO Some 8km southeast from Žminj on the road to Barban, in a field near the village of Feštini, is **Feštini Cave or Feštinsko kraljevstvo** – literally 'the Feštini Kingdom' (m 091 561 6327; w sige.hr; ⌚ Jun–Sep 10.00–18.00 daily, Apr, May & Oct 10.00–18.00 Sat/Sun; entry adults/children €5.50/€3.50), a 67m-long cave slung with stalactites and stalagmites. The cave was apparently only discovered accidentally in the 1930s while a local farmer was digging in the field and his hoe disappeared into the ground. During the Italian occupation of Istria in World War II the entire adult male population of Feštini was killed, save one survivor who was hiding in the cave.

SVETVINČENAT A few kilometres south of Žminj, the beautiful village of **Svetvinčenat** is best known for its castle, **Kaštel Grimani**, which is one of the largest and best preserved in Istria. Built in the 13th century but owing its present appearance very much to the 16th century and Venetian influence, the castle originally belonged to the Bishops of Poreč, then the Morosini family, and in the 16th century became the property of the **Grimani di San Luca**, a powerful Venetian patrician family (their Palazzo Grimani is a familiar landmark in Venice).

The castle stands on the north side of the remarkably large square or ***placa***, at the centre of which is a **well** dating from 1808. On the east side of the square is the early 16th-century **Parish Church of the Annunciation (Župna crkva Navještenja)** with its distinctive Renaissance trefoil façade, and there's a **loggia** on its southwest corner. The helpful **tourist information office** (Svetvinčenat 20; 052 560 349; e info@tz-svetvincenat.hr; w tz-svetvincenat.hr; ⌚ summer 08.00–16.00 Mon & Wed–Fri, 09.00–17.00 Tue, 10.00–14.00 Sat/Sun) is on the west side of the square.

A 200m walk southeast of the *placa* will bring you to the small 14th-century **Church of St Catherine (Crkvica sv Katerine)**, the interior of which is decorated with a cycle of frescoes from the early 15th century (the church is kept locked, but someone from the tourist information office should be able to come and open it). The small 12th-century **Church of St Vincent (Crkva sv Vicenija)**, in the cemetery on the northeast side of the village, is decorated with three layers of frescoes, the oldest (of which only fragments now remain) dating from the late 13th century and showing clear Byzantine influence, the others from the late the 14th and early 15th centuries (again, the church will be locked, so ask at the tourist information office first).

Where to stay and eat Svetvinčenat has a good number of **cafés** for a place of its size, mostly scattered along the road northwest of the castle. Note the block of stone with an inscription built into the corner of one, with the date 1714 – almost certainly from a nearby church or other building, though no-one's quite sure which.

Apartman Enna (1 apt, sleeps 4) Svetvinčenat 17; 052 560 301; m 098 169 1701; e mladen.doblanovic@pu.t-com.hr; w booking.com/hotel/hr/apartment-enna.en-gb.html. A ground-floor apartment in a gorgeous renovated stone house just off the *placa*, with its own terrace & garden. **€€€**

Foscari – The Fine B&B (8 dbls) Svetvinčenat; m 099 354 2200; e office@foscari-thefinebb.com/; w foscari-thefinebb.com. Opened in 2019 by a pair of Swiss owners (one of whom is an interior decorator – & it shows), this is a lovely boutique B&B in 2 beautifully restored old houses on the main square, with modern art hanging on the exposed stone walls. **€€€**

Konoba Klarići Klarići 83a; 052 579 137; 16.00–23.00 Mon–Sat, 13.00–23.00 Sun. Located out of town on the road south towards Vodnjan, this serves traditional Istrian dishes. **€€€**

Pizzeria Grimani Svetvinčenat 71; 052 560 395; summer 07.00–midnight Tue–Sun, winter 11.00–22.30 Tue–Sun. Enjoy well-priced pizzas on the northeast side of the *placa*, with tables outside on the square below the castle walls. **€€–€**

MOTOVUN

Motovun (Italian Montona), without any doubt the best known and most photographed of central Istria's hill towns, sits atop a 277m flat-topped hill on one side of the Mirna Valley.

HISTORY Once the site of a prehistoric hillfort, and a Roman settlement from at least the late 2nd century AD, when clay was extracted from the surrounding area for the production of amphorae, Motovun is first mentioned in a historical document from 804, at which time it belonged to the Bishops of Poreč. From the 13th century it came under the sphere of Venice (when the town walls were built), before passing to Austria with the rest of Istria at the beginning of the 19th century, and to Italy after World War I, before becoming a part of Yugoslavia and then the Republic of Croatia.

GETTING THERE AND AWAY Apart from a very limited local **bus** service (departing Pazin at 06.40, 14.40 and 20.10; see w arriva.com.hr/en-us/bus-pazin-motovun, during school term only), the only way to get to Motovun is with your own wheels, either by car or by bicycle – which is more than a little mind-boggling, given that it's the most visited place in central Istria.

By car it's a 15-minute drive to Pazin or Buzet, 30 minutes to Poreč, and 1 hour to Pula. Note that traffic is highly regulated in Motovun, and you can't take a car all the way up to the top of the hill and the old town (you'll see why when you get there on foot – the streets are tiny – and it makes it a much nicer place to wander around anyway). You can drive to within about 250m from the top, where there's a small parking area (€3 per day), from where it's only a short walk up to the main square (if you're staying at Hotel Kaštel they can send someone down to help with your luggage, as long as you let them know in advance). Otherwise, or if the parking area closer to the upper town is full, there's a large parking area at the bottom of the hill. If you're **cycling**, the **Parenzana** (page 117) passes close to Motovun.

TOURIST INFORMATION The small **tourist information office** has local information and accommodation details (Trg Andrea Antico 1; % 052 681 726; e info@tz-motovun.hr; w tz-motovun.hr; Jun–Aug 10.00–17.00 daily, Apr/May & Sep/Oct 10.00–17.00 Sat/Sun).

WHERE TO STAY, EAT AND DRINK *Map, page 112*

The tourist information office can supply information on **private accommodation** in Motovun (though you are advised to have booked in advance) – see w tz-motovun.

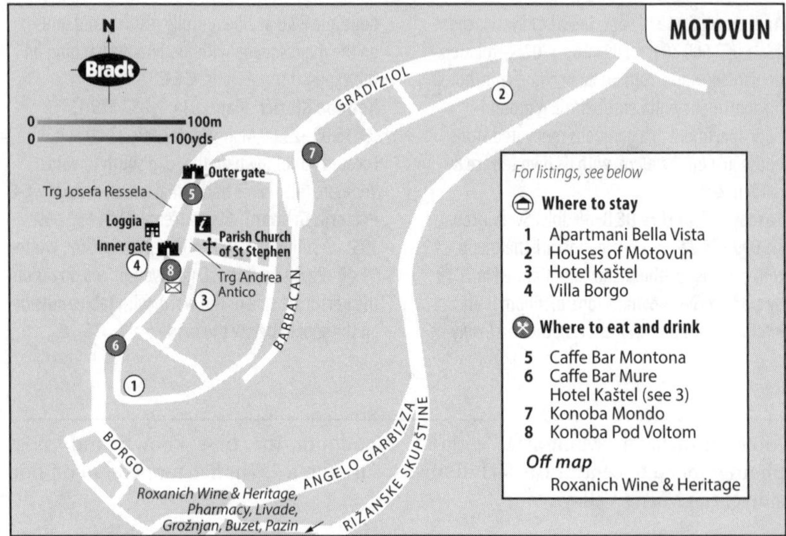

hr/en/accommodation/rooms-and-apartments. Try **Houses of Motovun** (Gradiziol 46; 098 955 7978; **e** livio.lanca@pu.t-com.hr; **w** booking.com/hotel/hr/house-of-gold.en-gb.html), which offers four rooms and an apartment.

Roxanich Wine & Heritage Hotel (38 dbls and suites) Kanal 30; 052 205 700; **e** reservations@roxanich.com; **w** roxanich.com; all year. Supremely luxurious & extremely stylish boutique hotel, owned by maverick winemaker Mladen Rožanić. Its upscale restaurant (€€€€) serves the likes of octopus, mackerel & trout caviar as a cold entrée, & dry-aged Boškarin T-bone steak as a main. Also offers wine tastings, which include cheeses & other nibbles & a tour of the winery (90mins; €43, bookings required). Located just outside town, where the Parenzana crosses the road leading south. **€€€€€**

✱ **Hotel Kaštel** (33 rooms & suites) Trg Andrea Antico 7; 052 681 607; **e** info@hotel-kastel-motovun.hr; **w** hotel-kastel-motovun.hr; all year. Lovely boutique hotel occupying a former palace, with the most enviable location in Motovun – right on the square, at the top of the old town. Go for a room with a balcony overlooking the square if you can. There's a wonderful spa with an indoor pool, sauna & massage rooms, & a peaceful, leafy garden with deckchairs & hammocks. The hotel has an excellent restaurant (€€€€), with plenty of Istrian specialities including homemade pasta & various truffle dishes, *boškarin* beef & some vegetarian options & a lovely broad terrace in front of the hotel at one end of the main square, where you can sit & eat dinner or sip coffee in the shade of ancient chestnut trees. Half board is only €16 extra, so is well worth considering. **€€€€**

Apartmani Bella Vista (4 apts) Gradiziol 1; 052 681 724; **m** 098 219 607; **e** info@apartmani-motovun.com; **w** apartmani-motovun.com; all year. Apartments in a renovated 19th-century villa, 3 of them with balconies overlooking the Mirna Valley. **€€€**

Villa Borgo (6 dbls, 1 apt) Borgo 4; 052 681 708; **m** 098 434 797; **e** info@villaborgo.com; **w** villaborgo.com; all year. Nicely renovated place just outside the town's inner gate, by the loggia, with clean rooms, friendly staff & lovely views of the Mirna Valley from its terrace. **€€€**

✱ **Konoba Mondo** Barbacan 1; 052 681 791; **w** konoba-mondo.com; summer noon–22.00 Wed–Mon. Lovely little *konoba* with a focus on Istrian specialities & in particular, truffle dishes, including wonderful homemade pasta (in particular the giant ravioli stuffed with cheese), beef carpaccio & delicious polenta. Consistently good, over several years of visiting. Can get quite busy so worth reserving a table. **€€€**

Konoba Pod Voltom Trg Josefa Ressela 6; 052 681 923; podvoltom; midday–22.00 daily.

Low-key, homely *konoba* hidden beneath the arch of the main town gate. €€€

Caffe Bar Montona Trg Josefa Ressela 2; ⌚ 08.00–22.00 daily. Bar & ice-cream café with an unbeatable view of the Mirna Valley, from tables along this square between the inner & outer town gates.

Caffe Bar Mure Mure 7; f CaffeBarmureMotovun; ⌚ 09.00–18.00 daily. Down below the Hotel Kaštel terrace is this nice, unpretentious little café, with good coffee, fair prices & tables along the cobbled street overlooking the Mirna Valley.

FESTIVALS

Motovun Film Festival w motovunfilmfestival.com. This film festival runs for 5 days in Jul & has rapidly grown into one of Croatia's most important film festivals. Launched in 1999 in response to the ongoing closure of many small & repertory cinemas in Croatia at that time, it tends to focus on low-budget films & world cinema, with screenings on the main square, &, appropriately enough, in a renovated old cinema which had been closed down.

SHOPPING Motovun has plenty of boutique shops selling truffles, wine, olive oil, art, jewellery and souvenirs, especially along Gradiziol, the street leading up to the city gate. But for a wine tasting to really knock your socks off (after which you can stock up on an armful of bottles), head down to the small tasting room of the multi-award-winning **Fakin winery** (e fakin.marko@gmail.com; w fakinwines.com/our-winery; ⌚ daily), located a short way outside town. The Malvazija is wonderful, obviously, the Muškat divine, and the rosé is one of these authors' particular Istrian favourites. Great atmosphere and, as the ever so clever moniker goes, Fakin good wines.

OTHER PRACTICALITIES

Pharmacy Istarske ljekarne Kanal 4; ⌚ 12.00–20.00 Mon/Tue, 07.00–15.00 Wed–Fri, 08.00–13.00 every other Sun

Post office Mure 2; ⌚ 08.00–17.00 Mon, 08.00–14.30 Tue–Fri

WHAT TO SEE AND DO The main thing to see in Motovun is the town itself – a walled Gothic and Renaissance citadel draped across the top of a flat-topped hill. Walking uphill from the upper car-parking area along Gradiziol, a narrow street lined with boutique souvenir and truffle shops, you pass through the first of the two Gothic town **gate towers**, and on to **Trg Josefa Ressela**, from one side of which there are breathtaking views out over the **Mirna Valley**, and at the far end of which is a **loggia**, first mentioned in 1331. The second **town gate** leads you up under a vaulted ceiling into the citadel and on to the cobbled main square, **Trg Andrea Antico**, which is named after the 16th-century Renaissance music printer, who was born in Motovun. On the far side of the square is the 17th-century **Parish Church of St Stephen (Župna crvka sv Stjepana)**, possibly designed by the great Venetian architect Palladio, with its Baroque façade. The interior has a large *Last Supper* by an unknown Venetian painter. The Romanesque-Gothic **bell tower** dates from the 13th century, and its crenellated top, visible for miles around protruding above the citadel, is one of the more iconic images of central Istria. On the opposite side of the square, the large **town hall** was built in the 13th century, though most of it dates from the Renaissance, and is one of the largest such buildings in Istria. You can **walk** along the 13th-century Venetian walls from the far end of the square. The 18th-century Polesini Palace, now the **Hotel Kaštel**, sits on one side of a terrace shaded by giant chestnut trees.

Some of the best views of Motovun are when approaching from the west, and from near the village of Zamask.

AROUND MOTOVUN

LIVADE There's not much to see in Livade (which means 'meadows'), apart from the small **Parenzana Museum (Muzej Parenzane)** (052 644 150; w parenzana.net; Jul/Aug 10.00–16.00 Tue–Fri, 10.00–18.00 Sat–Sun, otherwise try asking at Konoba Dorjana across the road). Truffle aficionados, however, will want to come here for the **Tuberfest** (white truffle fair) on the first weekend in October (11.00–19.00), and for Giancarlo Zigante's restaurant, where the focus is very much on *tartufi*.

Where to eat and drink

Restaurant Zigante Livade 7; 052 664 302; w restaurantzigante.com; noon–22.00 daily. Opulent & very formal dining experience at the centre of the Zigante empire, with a price tag to match. €€€€€–€€€€

✷ **Konoba Dolina** Gradinje 59, Gradinje; m 099 893 2847; f konobadolina; midday–21.00 Wed–Mon. Outstanding *konoba* halfway along the backroad between Livade & Istarske toplice, serving exquisite truffle & homemade pasta dishes in a relaxed, low-key setting. Don't miss the *fuži* with truffles in a cream sauce. €€€

Konoba Dorjana Livade 4a; 052 664 093; 11.00–22.00 Thu–Tue. Simple *konoba* with a nice leafy terrace across the road from the Parenzana Museum, with homemade pasta dishes, *maneštra* & other Istrian staples, as well as pizza. €€

OPRTALJ Almost directly opposite Motovun across the Mirna Valley, the village of **Oprtalj** (Italian Portole) receives much less attention – and infinitely fewer visitors – than its more famous neighbour. Perched on a hillside around 7km uphill from Livade, Oprtalj's medieval fortifications have now almost all but disappeared beneath a veneer of brightly painted houses.

IPŠA OLIVE OIL

About 1.5km east from Livade on the backroad to Istraske toplice, a minor road turns north towards Oprtalj, passing above a terraced hillside planted with olive trees, where **Klaudio Ipša** is now widely regarded as producing some of the finest olive oils anywhere in Croatia. Ipša grows three Istrian varieties of olive – *istarska bjelica*, *bugla* and *črnica* – and the Italian varieties *frantoio* and *leccino*. Olives are hand-picked at optimum ripeness, and cold-pressed within 4 hours, ensuring maximum freshness and resulting in some wonderfully rich and aromatic extra virgin olive oils, with a slightly piquant taste. In 2005 along with Al Torcio, Ipša's olive oils became the first Croatian olive oils to be included in *L'extravergine*, the prestigious Italian guide to the world's best olive oils. They have been included every year since and have also garnered awards from the Slow Food Association and at Vinistra and elsewhere.

You can purchase olive oil here and arrange tastings (Ipši 10; 052 664 010; m 091 206 0538; e info@ipsa.com.hr; w ipsa-maslinovaulja.hr; summer 10.00–18.00 daily, winter 11.00–16.00 daily), though not usually during harvest time (second half of October). Choose between Selection (2 olive oils & 2 wines; 1hr; €21.50) and Expert (3 olive oils & 3 wines, 90mins; €28.50), both accompanied by locally sourced cheeses and other nibbles – more in the case of the Expert tasting, with vegetarian/vegan options available if you let them know ahead of time. The Ipša family also offers accommodation in nearby Oprtalj.

The Rijeka Carnival is the largest in Croatia. Expect all manner of eccentric entertainments, including the *zvončari* (pictured) PAGE 147 above (RA)

At the Giostra festival in Poreč you can see jousting on horseback and people in colourful period dress, and sample the usual offering of great Istrian food PAGE 90 below left (TBP)

Istria's humble but beautifully constructed *kažuni* stone shelters have become emblematic of the region PAGE 17 below right (PK/S)

The Sečovlje saltpans on the Slovenian coast are an ornithologist's paradise PAGE 169 bottom (A/S)

left (RA) Built between 2BC and AD14, Pula's enchanting Temple of Augustus was used as a theatre by the Venetians and is now a lapidarium PAGE 61

below (RA) The population of the now-ruined fortress town of Dvigrad was decimated by the plague in 1631 and the town was abandoned in 1714 PAGE 100

bottom (RA) Brijuni's oldest Roman settlement is Kastrum, where both olive oil and wine were once produced PAGE 68

15th-century frescoes, including the *Dance of Death*, decorate the interior of St Mary of the Rocks Church in Beram PAGE 107 — above (RK/TBCI)

Glagolitic script, on the town gates at Hum, which lies on the so-called Glagolitic Alley PAGE 123 — right (P/D)

One of the few surviving instances of a 'pillar of shame' in Istria, where those who had committed minor offences were bound and subjected to humiliation during the medieval period PAGE 122 — below left (RA)

A dinosaur footprint on Brijuni, formed when these large reptiles walked across tidal and mud flats some 100 to 115 million years ago PAGE 70 — below right (IK/S)

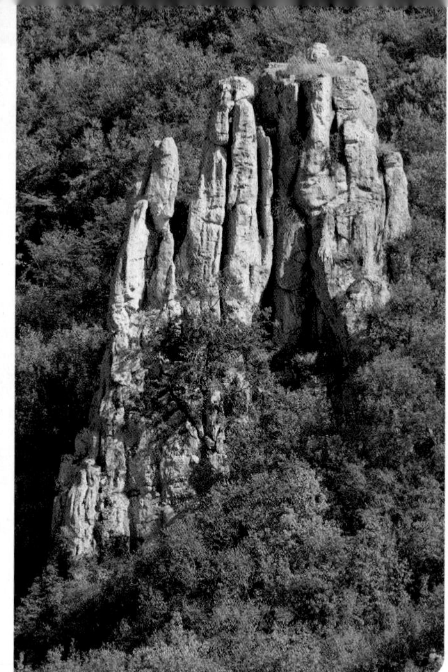

above left (JG/STB) The vast Škocjan Caves in Slovenia are a UNESCO World Heritage Site PAGE 170

above right (RA) A prominent limestone outcrop near Dvigrad, typical of karst scenery in the region PAGE 4

below (AM/S) The Limski kanal, just north of Rovinj, is a protected national monument rich with caves and marine life PAGE 99

Rt Kamenjak – a slender, highly indented peninsula at the southern tip of Istria, with remote coves and spectacular flora and butterflies PAGE 65

above (IK/S)

Boškarin cattle are native to Istria and said to be one of the oldest breeds in Europe PAGE 5

right (RY/ITB)

Zarečki krov, a waterfall near Pazin, which can be reached along an easy hiking trail PAGE 107

below (M/S)

top left (RA) *Fuži* (traditional Istrian pasta) with wild boar, Buzet PAGE 34

above left (RA) Truffle hunts with Karlić tartufi in Paladini, near Buzet PAGE 38

above right (RA) Saturday morning at the fish market in Rijeka PAGE 146

below left (m/P) Celebrating the annual Asparagus Festival in Lovran PAGE 39

below right (RA) Cheese-maker David Ličen (Golden Ring Cheese) in the Vipava Valley, Slovenia PAGE 181

bottom left (GS/ITB) Istria produces some of Croatia's finest olive oils PAGE 41

bottom right (RA) Award-winning beekeeper Dario Vežnaver has a small shop in Oprtalj PAGE 115

Stone tower on Vojak, the highest point of Učka Nature Park, which has views across the Istrian hinterland and makes for a rewarding hike from Lovran on the coast, or from the Poklon Visitor Centre PAGE 187

above (SS)

Diving at the *Baron Gautsch* wreck – one of the many excellent dive sites around the Istrian coast PAGE 212

right (aq/S)

Cycling on the Parenzana, a former narrow-gauge railway line between Trieste and Poreč PAGE 117

below (GS/ITB)

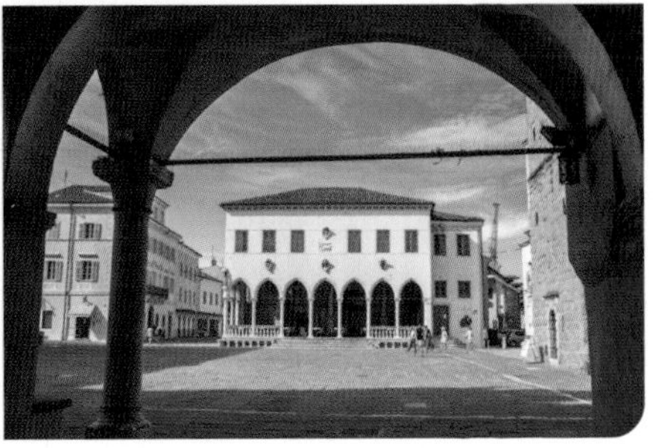

top (K/S) Slovenia's Predjama Castle sits massive and impregnable-looking within a 123m-high cave in an overhanging cliff PAGE 178

above left (RA) Horses being released into paddocks in the morning at Lipica Stud Farm, Slovenia PAGE 173

above right (SS) Titov trg – Koper's main square – is a good starting point for a tour of the historic town PAGE 158

below (NJ/S) With its beautiful architecture and setting on a slender peninsula, Piran is considered by many to be the jewel in the Slovenian Adriatic crown PAGE 162

At the entrance to the village there is a large Venetian **loggia**, and a lovely **terrace** overlooking the Osoje Valley, which runs southwest to the Mirna, from beneath ancient chestnut trees. There's not a great deal to see within the walls – entering the village through the main **gate** leads you past a medley of renovated and abandoned houses, to the 16th-century **Parish Church of St George** (**Župna crkva sv Jurja**) and its square-topped bell tower. Award-winning local beekeeper and **honey** producer **Dario Vežnaver** (Pčelarstvo Vežnaver; 052 644 052; m 092 114 2423; w api-veznaver.eu) has a small shop just inside the main gate (alternatively you can buy honey and other products from the Vežnaver beekeeping farm at Škofi 34, about 5km northeast of Oprtalj).

Just to the south of the terrace and loggia, the small **Church of St Rok** (Crkva sv Roka) has some 16th-century **frescoes** by Antun of Padova (that's not the Padova in Italy, but a village near Butoniga jezero in Istria – and no, that's not called Padova either; it's called Kašćerga); and downhill from the village on the road to Livade is the 15th-century **Church of St Mary (Crkva sv Marije)**, with frescoes by several different painters including Clerigino, a master from Kopar. Both churches are locked, so ask at the **tourist information office** if you want to look inside (Matka Laginje 21; 052 644 150; w oprtalj.hr/index.php (Croatian and Italian only); f visit.oprtalj). Private accommodation can also be found through the tourist information office, and Klaudio Ipša and family (of Ipša olive oil; page 114) have a three-room house and a suite in Oprtalj which can be rented to guests. Though it is the centre of a large municipality, the village of Oprtalj has only some 100 inhabitants.

Where to eat and drink

Konoba Oprtalj Matka Laginje 17; m 092 299 0516; midday–22.00 daily. A nice, low-key *konoba* by the parking area & loggia with tables outside on the terrace beneath the chestnut trees. Dishes include truffles with polenta, & pizzas. Also sometimes called Taverna Portole. €€

VIŽINADA It's worth stopping in Vižinada to look at the large square with its well-preserved Venetian wells and loggia. The Knights Templar established a church here in the 12th century, and Vižinada was also the birthplace of the celebrated 19th-century ballet dancer **Carlotta Grisi**, famous for the title role in *Giselle*. It also lies on the route of the **Parenzana** (page 117).

Just to the northwest of Vižinada (between the villages of Bajkini and Vrbani) are the **Franc Arman Vineyards and Winery** (Narduči 5; m 091 446 2266; e info@francarman.hr; w francarman.hr; summer 08.00–20.00 Mon–Sat, winter 08.00–16.00 Mon–Sat), where you can buy wine or arrange a tasting in the old wine cellar or *konoba*. The vineyards have been here since 1850, and Franc and his son Oliver make some very, very drinkable (and award-winning) wines – including a crisp Malvazija and a robust Teran, and a rather lovely oak-aged Malvazija Classic. North of Vižinada just across the Mirna you'll find a good restaurant, **Ponte Porton** [map, page 102] (Ponte Porton 76; 052 208 435; w ponteporton.com; €€€€–€€€).

GROŽNJAN

Grožnjan (Italian Grisignana) is, like Motovun, one of the more popular of the Istrian hill towns, helped no doubt by its relative proximity to the northwest coast. It is a pretty little town, with a well-preserved old medieval centre and fine views over the Mirna Valley. Despite having been left largely deserted after the Italian exodus that followed World War II (page 11), the municipality of Grožnjan today has a higher proportion of people describing Italian as their first language than anywhere else in Istria. Artists in particular were encouraged to move to the largely depopulated town from the late 1960s onwards, and today the self-styled 'Town of Artists' is full of little galleries and boutique shops selling art, handmade jewellery, wine, olive oil, etc. Full being a relative term, of course – Grožnjan, like other Istrian hill towns, is still a fairly sleepy place, and has fewer than 100 inhabitants.

Cycle from Grožnjan to either Livade (page 197) or Koper (page 202) on the Parenzana.

Grožnjan puts on an international **jazz festival** in July, 'Jazz is Back' (w jazzisbackbp.com), with local and international acts which in past years have included the likes of Georgie Fame. The festival was founded by Croatian jazz musician Boško Petrović in 1999, and was voted Europe's best boutique jazz festival in 2008. It also has an art festival in September (**Extempore**), and during the summer is the venue for the Croatian branch of **Jeunesses Musicales International**, with a summer school for young musicians and various concerts. Grožnjan is around 8km northwest of Motovun, the last section on an unsealed road, or further if you take the sealed road via Buje, and is also on the route of the **Parenzana** (see opposite).

WHERE TO STAY, EAT AND DRINK The **tourist information office** (Gorjana 3; 052 776 131; w tz-groznjan.hr – look under 'Smještaj') should be able to help with details of **private accommodation**, otherwise you could try **Villa San Vito** (Park Spinotti Morteani 2; m 099 7552 837; e villasanvito-info@gmail.com; w villasanvitoinfo.wixsite.com/sanvito; **€€**) and, about 1km out of town towards Buje, **Casa Margherita** (Peroj 13a; m 091 506 0197; e lorena.oplanic@gmail.com; w casa-margherita-istra.com; **€€**).

Konoba Pintur (4 dbls) Mate Gorijana 9; 052 776 397; Mar–Sep 08.00–22.00 Tue–Sun. Small, friendly *konoba* (€€) & guesthouse in the centre of town, housed in an old stone building, with tables outside under an old tree. **€€**

BUJE

From the northwest of Istria, Buje is the gateway to the interior, and the first of a series of hilltop towns in the north. At 222m above sea level this 'Sentry over Istria', as the town is known, has retained many of its former fortress features, including several fortified towers, the old cathedral and some of its stone paved interior. In the surrounding hills are several excellent vineyards, olive groves, the old Parenzana railway route (page 117) and some beautiful private accommodation.

Make sure you visit the excellent Cattunar winery, while another treat not worth missing is the aptly named Casa Romantica La Parenzana – and San Rocco in nearby Brtonigla is one of the loveliest places you could hope to stay (and eat) anywhere in Croatia. Some other very good restaurants await the intrepid in the hills.

WHERE TO STAY AND EAT The **Buje Tourist** Office (1 Svibnja 2; 052 773 353; w coloursofistria.com/en/destinations/buje; Jan–May 08.00–15:00 Mon–Fri, 09.00–14.00 Sat, Jun–Sep 08.00–20.00 daily & Oct–Dec 08.00 15.00 Mon–Fri, 09.00–13.00 Sat) can help you with finding private accommodation.

THE PARENZANA

The Parenzana was a 123km-long narrow-gauge railway line between Trieste and Poreč, which ran from 1902 to 1935 and connected some 35 stations in Istria, and spanned what is now Italy, Slovenia and Croatia. It was used to carry both passengers and freight – olive oil, flour, vegetables, wine, hides, salt from Piran, lime and stone – navigating the hilly karst landscape between remote villages via a series of tunnels, bridges and viaducts.

In 2002, on the 100th anniversary of its opening, the old Parenzana line was developed into a cycling and hiking route, beginning with sections in Croatia and Slovenia and later the whole line. By far the longest section of the Parenzana is in Croatia (78km, compared with 32km in Slovenia and 13km in Italy), and among the towns and villages it connects between Poreč and the Slovenian border are Buje, Grožnjan, Oprtalj, Motovun, Vižinada and Nova Vas.

Over its history the Parenzana has had several names – to its Austrian builders it was the Parenzaner Bahn, to the Italians it was the Parenzana, and to the local population it was the Istrijanka or Istranka (or sometimes Poreška or Porečanka – after the town of Poreč, known as Parenzo in Italian).

See page 197 for a description of the route between Grožnjan and Livade, and page 202 for a description of the route from Grožnjan to Koper.

ISTRIAN TERROIR

Brtonigla near Buje stands at the intersection of the four very different soil types which, among other things, each add a distinctive character to Istrian wines: terra rossa, the typical 'red' soil of Istria; so-called 'black' soil, fertile and rich in humus, on a bed of marl; 'grey' soil, a dusty soil with plenty of flysch and limestone; and finally 'white' soil, similar to grey but with a higher limestone component. To really see (or more specifically, taste) some of the different characteristics of wines produced on these four distinctive terroirs, head to **Cattunar Winery** (Nova Vas 94, Brtonigla; 052 720 496; e info@vina-cattunar.hr; w vina-cattunar.hr) for a tasting – their '4 TERRE' range includes a Malvazija from each.

San Canzian Village & Hotel (24 rooms & suites) Mužolini Donji 72; 052 853 897; e reception@san-canzian.hr; w san-canzian.hr. A luxury hotel village consisting of a cluster of beautifully restored stone houses, set among lovely terraced gardens, with its own pool & spa, fine-dining restaurant (Luciano €€€€), wine bar & an impressively well-stocked wine cellar. Located just off the road between Buje & Grožnjan. **€€€€€**

✱ **San Rocco** (12 rooms) Srednja ulica 2, Brtonigla; 052 725 000; e info@san-rocco.hr; w san-rocco.hr. Awarded best boutique hotel in Croatia for 5 years in a row, the San Rocco has set a standard in Istria, which many can only hope to aspire to. It is spacious, with full spa facilities & fabulous rooms with plenty of heritage features, & an excellent Michelin-listed restaurant (€€€€) offering seasonal degustation menus, including the likes of langoustines with ricotta, handmade *boškarin* tortellini with wild asparagus sauce, or scallops with white truffle – all paired with exceptionally fine local wines. This is slow food at its best, prepared with local, seasonal ingredients. Infinity pool overlooking olive groves at the bottom of the peaceful garden. Located in the village of Brtonigla, just 5km from the coast. They also produce their own olive oil, which is delicious & is available for sale. What a wonderful place – highly recommended. **€€€€€**

✱ **Casa Romantica La Parenzana** (16 rooms) Volpia 3; 052 777 458 (guesthouse), 052 777 460 (restaurant); e info@laparenzana.com; w laparenzana.com. A mere 2km north of Buje in the village of Kaldanija, & just off the old railway line (& modern cycle route), the beautifully restored Istrian farmhouse & *konoba* are dedicated to the memory of the Parenzana. Austrian Guido & his Croatian wife Maruška are true enthusiasts, which shows through in everything they do from the boutique nature of the rooms to the Istrian cooking classes they offer. The food (€€€) is outstanding, the lavender-filled garden setting for the outdoor tables is lovely, & it's all a wonderful change from some of the mediocrity on the touristy coast. Highly recommended & extremely good value. **€€€**

Cattunar Wine Residence (11 dbls) Nova Vas 94, Brtonigla; 052 720 496; e info@vina-cattunar.hr; w cattunar.hr. Stylish, newly built & very spacious rooms with a spa & pool, at the excellent Cattunar winery. There's no restaurant – but, in this part of Istria, you're spoilt for choice in that respect anyway, & there's no shortage of amazing places to choose from nearby. **€€€**

✱ **Konoba Malo Selo** Fratrije 1, Buje; 052 777 332; f konoba.selo; noon–22.00 Thu–Tue. Small, friendly tavern with cosy, unassuming décor – think chequered tablecloths & a roaring fire where the chef comes out to throw things on the grill & outstandingly good food, including the best *fuži* with truffles I have ever eaten. Michelin-recommended, & hands down one of my favourite restaurants anywhere in Croatia. **€€€**

Konoba Rino Dolinja Vas 23, Momjan; 052 779 170; w prelac.hr/konoba; midday–22.00 daily. About 5km north of Buje in the village of Momjan is this homely & popular (as you can probably tell by the number of 4x4s with Italian number plates outside) konoba, owned by the local Prelac vineyard. The vineyard also offers accommodation in the form of the small B&B Tinka (**€€€€–€€€**). **€€€**

Morgan Bračanija 1; ☎ 052 774 520; e konoba.morgan@gmail.com; w morgan.hr; ⌚ noon–22.00 Wed–Mon. About 2km from Brtonigla, off the road towards Buje, is a true *konoba* with not a fish in sight. For meat lovers you'll find here *boškarin* tagliata, fiorentina porterhouse steak, seasonal game & a host of other finger-licking good grills, sausages, pastas & soups. €€€

Primizia Bunarska 2, Brtonigla; ☎ 052 774 704; w primizia.hr; ⌚ 13.00–23.00 daily. Under the same ownership as San Rocco, this small, welcoming *konoba* located in the centre of Brtonigla is great value & serves delicious, traditional Istrian dishes made from locally sourced, seasonal ingredients. €€€–€€

BUZET

Perched on a hill and overlooking the truffle-rich Mirna Valley on one side and the forested slopes of the Ćićarija Mountains on the other, Buzet (Italian Pinguente) is, for one of the authors at least, the most rewarding of the Istrian hill towns – with colourful festivals, great hiking and biking opportunities in the surrounding hills and valleys, and a wealth of cultural interest in nearby towns and villages. There's even a good bus service to Rijeka and Zagreb. Nevertheless, Buzet receives much less attention and fewer visitors than Motovun and Grožnjan further west. Often called the 'City of Truffles', there are two big truffle events in its annual calendar, and Istria's favourite local beer, known appropriately enough as Favorit, is brewed here.

HISTORY Like many surrounding hilltop settlements, Buzet was inhabited by Illyrian tribes during the Bronze Age, and was under Rome (Roman Pinquentum) from AD177–476, though unlike many other towns in the region it escaped the devastating plague of the 2nd century AD. It was under Frankish rule from the 8th century, and under the Patriarchs of Aquila until 1497, when it fell to Venice. During this period it became an important regional centre of Venetian power, in particular after becoming the seat of the De Raspo Captaincy (whose coat of arms you'll encounter in the old town) in 1511, when its fortifications were strengthened and several palaces built. After the fall of Venice in 1797 and a brief spell under Napoleon, Buzet passed to Austrian rule until the close of World War I.

GETTING THERE AND AWAY

By train Buzet is on the railway line from Pazin (50 minutes) and Pula (2 hours) – but the **railway station** is around 3.5km northeast and uphill from the bus station (follow the road up through Sveti Martin).

By bus Buzet's **bus station** (*Riječka ulica*) is a 10–15-minute walk from the old town – from the bus station follow the main road (Riječka ulica) towards the old town, then turn left over the bridge and left up a long flight of steps leading to the main gate, Vela vrata. There's also a short cut from opposite the bus station (though unsuitable for navigation with suitcases, being steep, unsealed and often rather dusty) – follow the unsealed road uphill from beside the small supermarket, which brings you to the Mala vrata (small gate) on the northeast side of the old town. There are direct, fast buses to Rijeka (50 minutes) and Zagreb (3½ hours), departing Buzet at 10.15 daily.

By car Buzet is a 50-minute drive from both Rijeka (through the Učka tunnel) and Rovinj, and 1 hour from Pula.

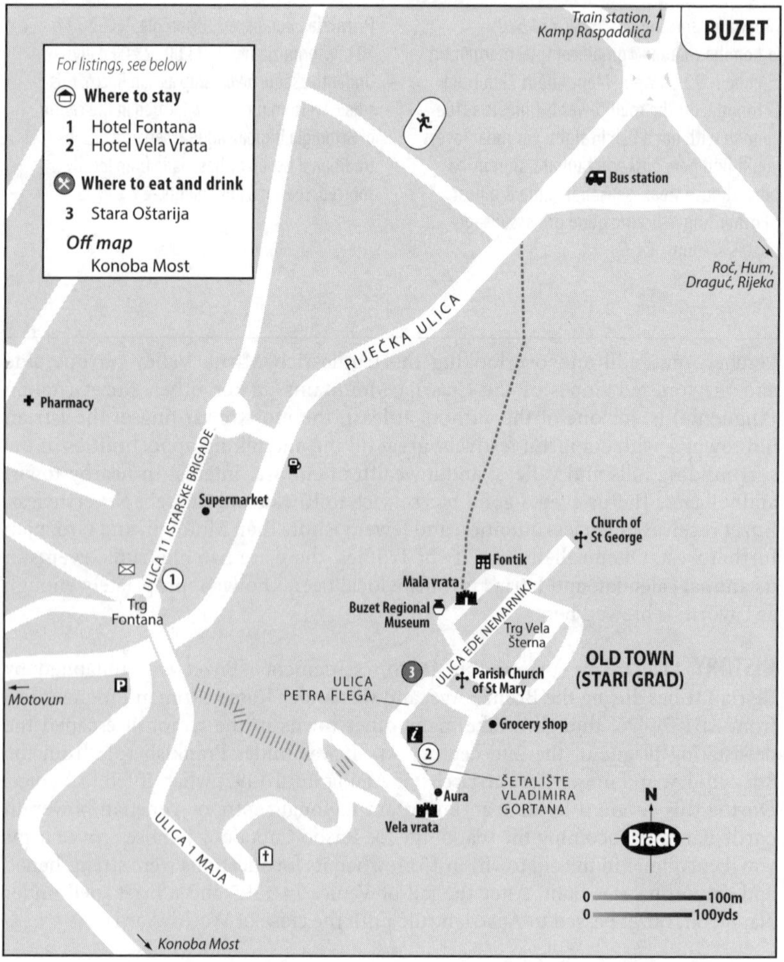

TOURIST INFORMATION Buzet's helpful **tourist information office** (Šetalište Vladimira Gortana 9; 052 662 343; w tz-buzet.hr; 08.00–15.00 Mon–Fri) is located in the old town, next door to Hotel Vela Vrata.

WHERE TO STAY AND EAT *Map, above*

✷ **Hotel Vela Vrata** (18 dbls) Šetalište Vladimira Gortana 7; 052 494 750; e booking@velavrata.net; w velavrata.net; all year. Lovely boutique hotel in Buzet's old town, with stylish rooms & impeccable service. The hotel has its own restaurant (€€€€–€€€), with tables outside & on the medieval walls themselves, & the food is excellent – from pasta with truffles to tender beef in cranberry sauce, & homemade truffle ice cream. €€€€

Hotel Fontana (57 dbls) Trg Fontana 1; 052 662 615; e info@hotelfontanabuzet.com; w hotelfontanabuzet.com; all year. In the lower town, conveniently close to the bus station. Popular with walking/cycling groups. €€€

Stara Oštarija Petra Flega 5; 052 694 003; midday–22.00 Wed–Mon. Excellent restaurant with an emphasis on truffles, from gnocchi with truffles to brown trout with truffles, as well as *fuži* with game & some vegetarian options, & a wonderful view. €€€

Konoba Most Most 18; 052 662 867; w konobamost.hr; noon–22.00 daily. Good-value *konoba* in the lower town. €€

Camping If you want to get away from it all, there's a nice little campsite up at **Raspadalica** [map, page 102] in the foothills of the Ćićarija Mountains (Kamp Raspadalica; m 098 924 7300; e raspadalica@gmail.com; w raspadalica.com), about a 1½-hour hike from Buzet (page 189), with space for around 30 people (showers but no hot water or electricity, though they're usually able to charge your phone for you, €8 per person). The location (around 550m above sea level) means nights can be refreshing, so take a cardigan or fleece. The altitude offers one particular advantage, however: Raspadalica is also a renowned paragliding club (tandem flight €95).

FESTIVALS

KIK Fest w poubuzet.hr & click on 'Manifestacije' at the bottom. A festival of Istrian *klapa* (a form of traditional a cappella singing in Croatia) is held in Buzet in Mar.

Istra Open Croatia's top paragliding championship takes off – literally – from Raspadalica, on the cliffs northeast of Buzet in Jul.

Subotina subotinabuzet. Held in Buzet on the 2nd w/end of Sep, this is one of Istria's most colourful festivals, with people dressed in traditional & period costumes, music, & stalls selling locally made traditional crafts, food & produce from freshly milled cornflour to *fritule*. On the previous night, to celebrate the opening of the **truffle season**, an enormous **omelette** is prepared in the lower town (on the small square opposite Hotel Fontana, on Ulica Istarske Brigade, in front of one of Zigante's shops) from some 2,000 eggs – 2,023 in 2023, to be precise – & 10kg of truffles. Yes, you get to eat it, too (€5 a portion with a big chunk of bread, which you can wash down with a glass of Favorit or local wine from a stall nearby – how often do you get to eat truffles off a paper plate?).

Weekend of truffles Buzet's premier truffle festival takes place over the 1st w/end in Nov.

SHOPPING There's a large Diona **supermarket** behind the Hotel Fontana (Trg Fontana 8/2) and a smaller grocery shop in the old town (Trg Josipa Fabrijančića 4). For **souvenirs**, there's a nice little shop just inside the entrance to a house on the old town's main square, **Trg Vela Šterna**, selling handmade jewellery and ceramics, and a branch of **Aura** by the main gate (2 Istarske brigade 1/2; 052 694 250; w aura.hr) selling local wines, olive oils, *rakija* and other produce.

OTHER PRACTICALITIES

Pharmacy Naselje Gorčica 1; 052 662 832; summer 07.00–20.00 Mon–Fri, 08.00–15.00 Sat, winter 08.00–20.00 Mon–Fri, 08.00–14.00 Sat

Post office Trg Fontana 3; 07.00–20.00 Mon–Fri, 08.00–noon Sat

WHAT TO SEE AND DO Buzet's **old town (Stari grad)** is tiny and it only takes a few minutes to walk from one side to the other. Unlike Motovun's old town, it is accessible by car – though you might prefer to park in the large car park below and walk up the steps into town. From the 16th-century **Main Gate (Vela vrata)** with its relief sculpture of St George, Buzet's patron saint, turn left past **Hotel Vela Vrata** and the **tourist information office**, with views southwest across the Mirna Valley to the green hills around Vrh from the ramparts on the left. Continue uphill past **Stara Oštarija** restaurant to the 18th-century **Parish Church of St Mary (Župna crkva bl Djevice Marije)**, with its late 19th-century **bell tower** (though the bell itself is inscribed in Glagolitic with the date 1541). On your left there's a 16th-century **Venetian storehouse** (with one of the many coats of arms you'll see around the old town). Continue past this on Ulica Ede Nemarnika, then turn left to the Regional Museum. Buzet's **Regional Museum** (Zavičajni muzej; Trg rašporskih kapetana 5; 052 662 792; w poubuzet.hr;

⌚ 10.00–15.00 Mon–Fri; entry €2) is housed in the 17th-century **Bigatto Palace (Palača Bigatto)**. Its archaeological collection includes various pieces of Roman stonework and tombstones (including an interesting marble relief with a faun, found in the old town itself), and Iron and Bronze Age objects from nearby caves. There's also a small ethnographic collection and an exhibit of Glagolitic inscriptions, including copies of famous pieces like the Plomin inscription.

Hike from Buzet to the rock outcrops of Raspadalica and Kuk (page 189).

From the museum continue to the **Small Gate (Mala vrata)**, completed in 1592, next to which is a stout tower (known as the **Fontik**) which in the 16th century was used by the Venetians as a storehouse for wheat. From here walk up Ulica Mala vrata to reach the main square, **Trg Vela Šterna**, with its 18th-century **wellhead**. At the far (northern) end of the old town is the 17th-century **Church of St George (Crkva sv Jurja)**.

There are several **hiking trails** leading up over the western slopes of the Ćićarija Mountains and Učka – see page 189 for a description of the short walk up to Raspadalica from Buzet's old town – and there are potential **cycle routes** leading in all directions, both along roads and off them. A visit to the 'pillar of shame' at Salež (see below) via the Bračana Valley is one possibility, or continuing from Salež to Oprtalj (page 114). Another popular road route is to bike to Roč and Hum, then over to Draguć (page 124) via Kotle and back to Buzet.

Truffle hunts and tastings can be arranged with **Karlić tartufi**, in the village of Paladini, near Butoniga jezero (Paladini 4; ☎ 052 667 304; **m** 095 198 6068; **e** info@karlictartufi.hr; **w** karlictartufi.hr).

AROUND BUZET

SALEŽ A few kilometres northwest of Buzet and really only accessible by car or bike (with a fair bit of pedalling uphill), the tiny rural settlement of Salež is remarkable for being one of the few places where a so-called **pillar of shame (Stup srama)** has survived intact, this one from the 18th century. It's a particularly interesting one, too – shaped as a human figure wearing a fez, and carved from a block of stone not found locally. One of the figure's hands is on his chest, and would once have had shackles attached to it; his other hand is between his legs, covering his groin. Pillars of shame performed a similar function to the stocks – offenders and petty criminals were tied or chained to them, and subjected to public torment and humiliation. Locals call it the *berlin*.

To get to Salež from Buzet, head towards Motovun then turn right after passing turnings to both Veli Mlun and Mali Mlun, where the road ducks under the aqueduct. Keep an eye out for the ruins of **Pietrapelosa Castle (Kaštel Pietrapelosa)** on a crag on your left, and turn left just before reaching Abramci. Follow the winding road uphill then turn left on to the road to Salež (continuing straight ahead would take you to Zrenj and Oprtalj). The pillar is near the cemetery, which is on the left before the village itself. Whether you are cycling or driving, you can vary your return to Buzet by continuing north from Abramci to the main road (at which point you're less than 5km from the Slovenian border), then turning right and back into Buzet.

ROČ Roč (Italian Rozzo), an ancient settlement with a well-preserved, walled medieval core, lies around 8km southeast of Buzet on the road to Lupoglav and

Rijeka. Entering the town through the **Main Gate (Vela vrata)** you find the first of the town's three churches, **St Roch (Crkva sv Roka)**, a Romanesque chapel with frescoes from the 14th and 15th centuries. The **Parish Church of St Bartholomew (Župna crkva sv Bartola)** dates from the 15th century, while the **Church of St Anthony (Crkva sv Antuna)** dates from the 12th century and has 14th-century frescoes and a votive cross bearing a Glagolitic inscription from the 12th century. The churches are locked – ask at the tourist information centre (⏲ Jun–Sep 10.00–17.00 daily) on the square or contact the tourist office in Buzet (☎ 052 662 343). Roč was an important centre of **Glagolitic** learning during the medieval period, and it was here that the **first Croatian printed book**, the so-called *Roč Missal*, was prepared in 1483 (that's only around 30 years after the famous Gutenberg Bible). There's a copy of the Gutenberg printing press in the tourist information office, and Roč hosts a Glagolitic script workshop for Croatian schoolchildren in July. Roč also holds an **Accordion Festival** in May.

Getting there and away **Buses** travelling between Buzet and Rijeka or Zagreb will go past Roč, which is also on the Buzet–Pazin railway line – though the station is around 1km northwest from the village.

Where to stay and eat For **private accommodation** in Roč, try **Apartman Pod Lipom** (Roč 44; ☎ 098 425 276; w booking.com/hotel/hr/pod-lipom.en-gb.html; €€). For somewhere to eat, the homely **Ročka konoba** (Roč 14; m 091 575 8947; f rockakonoba; ⏲ noon–22.00 Thu–Sun; €€) serves local Istrian dishes.

GLAGOLITIC ALLEY The 7km of road between Roč and Hum is known as the '**Glagolitic Alley**' (**Aleja glagoljaša**), and is marked at various points by 11 sculptures or monuments relating to the Glagolitic alphabet. The sculptures are the work of Croatian sculptor Želimir Janeš and Croatian philologist Joseph Bratulić, and date from 1977. The series begins with the *Pillar of the Chakavian Parliament* just outside Roč, and finishes with the elaborate door knockers on the town gate at Hum.

HUM The tiny, walled hilltop settlement of **Hum** – which loudly proclaims itself to be the 'smallest town in the world' – has a grand total of around 20 inhabitants, and consists of little more than a church, a few houses and two streets. The small **Church of St Jerome** (**Crkva sv Jeronima**) has frescoes from the 12th century, along with various bits of Glagolitic 'graffiti' dating from between the 12th and the 15th centuries. The 16th-century altarpiece by Antun of Padova (page 115) which once stood in the church is now in a museum in Poreč. The church is kept locked – ask at Humska *konoba* (see below) for the key.

While in Hum, make a point of sampling **Humska biska**, a local type of *rakija* with white mistletoe and four kinds of grasses (unless of course you're driving, in which case it will put you straight over the limit). Hum holds a ***rakija* festival** at the end of October.

Where to stay and eat For **private accommodation** in Hum – there are a couple of rooms and apartments available – try **Apartment Delores** (Hum 9; m 091 566 6661; f app.rooms.doresHum; **€€**), or ask at the *konoba*. If you're hungry, the only place to eat is **Humska konoba** (☎ 091 600 3456; w humskakonoba.hum.hr; ⏲ mid-Mar–mid-Nov noon–18.00 Tue–Thu & noon–20.00 Fri–Sun, mid-Nov–mid-Mar noon–20.00 Sat/Sun; €€). This is a nice little *konoba* with a small terrace serving *fuži* with goulash, pork loin with pickled cabbage and other dishes. Like the town, it's small, so the idea is to time your visit not to coincide with the arrival of a tour bus.

KOTLE Turning west at Brnobići on the Roč–Hum road takes you to **Kotle**, where the River Mirna pours over a cascade, and there's a restored **watermill**. Notice how the limestone riverbed has been gouged out into deep hollows (*kotle* is derived from the Croatian word for 'cauldron'). There's a *konoba* by the river. A path from Kotle also provides a convenient short cut (either on foot or by bike) to the Buzet–Cerovlje road, which it meets just north of Draguć.

DRAGUĆ A little over halfway from Buzet on the road to Cerovlje, a turn-off to the right (west) leads down to what must be counted one of the most beautiful villages in Istria. Sighted on top of a slight bump in the hillside overlooking Butoniga jezero, it was once an important centre for the cultivation of silkworms, though it's now a quiet settlement with a population of fewer than 100. Draguć is a popular film location and has appeared in Croatian as well as international productions (including *La Femme Musketeer* with Gérard Depardieu and Nastassja Kinski).

On the right before entering the village itself you pass a small cemetery and the 13th-century **Church of St Elijah** (**Crkva sv Elizeja**) – the oldest church in the village – with fragmentary 13th-century frescoes and a Roman stele for an altar. Much more impressive, however, is the little **Church of St Roch** (**Crkva sv Roka**), built during the early years of the 16th century as a votive offering to ward off plague, and standing just beyond the far end of the village overlooking a hillside planted with vines. The interior is decorated with an extensive cycle of frescoes, the work of **Antun of Padova**, the same local master who painted the frescoes at Oprtalj (page 114) and Hum (page 123), and are signed by him in both Latin and Glagolitic. Rather confusingly he was actually from the nearby village of Kašćerga – which, as it happens, is visible across the far side of Butoniga jezero from in front of the church – not Padova in Italy. The frescoes were painted in two phases, in 1529 and 1537, and, unlike most other medieval frescoes in Istria, were not later covered up with paint. The scenes include an *Adoration of the Magi*, a *Baptism of Christ* and *Temptation into the Wilderness*. Both buildings are kept locked. The local keyholder is Zora Paćelat (Draguć 21; 052 665 186 or contact the tourist office in Buzet). The medieval **castle** which once stood in Draguć has now almost entirely vanished, though you can see some traces of it supporting one of the walls of the 15th-century **Church of the Cross** (**Crkva Svetog Križa**).

Where to eat and drink

Zora Draguć 35; 052 665 105; summer 13.00–20.00 Tue–Sun. A small, friendly café buffet on the square, where you can get a coffee or jug of wine, as well as local *pršut* & cheese. They also have a couple of apartments (**€€€**). €€

Festivals

Bajs festival End Jun. Draguć holds a *bajs* festival with performances in the town square. The *bajs*, also known as the *gunjac*, is a traditional 2-stringed instrument which looks like a cello.

7

The East Coast and Opatija

The east coast of the Istrian Peninsula is much less frequented than its western equivalent. This in itself makes much of it an attraction in the summer in particular, when the hordes have amassed on the western beaches. Rocky beaches here can still be found with hardly a soul in sight.

Historically, the east coast has had much less influence culturally from Italy, although it remained under Venetian, Aquilian or Italian rule for much the same period as the west coast. However, the population here had a higher percentage of Slavic-speakers during those times. So while the fascist Italian dictator Mussolini did leave his mark culturally in the construction of the towns of Raša and Podlabin (page 134), some might argue that these were an aberration rather than evidence of the symbiotic relationship which Italian culture has had with the west coast.

Two main centres stand out on the east coast of the Istrian Peninsula: Labin and Opatija, the latter technically in the **Kvarner** region and part of the Primorje-Gorski Kotar County rather than Istria itself, but included in this guide along with Rijeka (page 139) due to their interest and proximity.

Labin is a **medieval, hilltop town**, once a centre of mining and now a focus for art. Opatija is the **riviera** of Kvarner Bay, and it's only a short bus ride east from here to Rijeka. Other hilltop forts of note are Plomin and Barban, where the annual **ring-tilting festival** takes place. If you're arriving in Istria *from* Rijeka, it's worth taking the coastal road through Opatija and Lovran into Istria, as the backdrop of the Učka Mountains against the vista of the Kvarner Bay islands is sublime.

OPATIJA

A mere fishing village 200 years ago, Opatija became the first spa resort on the entire Croatian coast. Largely only for the rich, privileged and noble 150 years ago, it still has, as a result, what must be the highest concentration of high-end spa hotels in Croatia, especially for its size. These hotels and villas alone are worth a stroll along the 12km **promenade**, and many think there is only this to see and do in Opatija. Yet Opatija hides a few more gems, including its **botanical gardens (botanički vrt)**, **Benedictine abbey of St James (Opatija sv Jakova)**, the **medieval fort** at Veprinac and – just a short stroll along the coast at one end of that lovely promenade – the pre-eminent gastro-enclave anywhere in Croatia, at the sleepy little fishing village of **Volosko**.

HISTORY Opatija derives its name from the Slavic word for abbey, and hence it grew originally from the mid 15th century as a hamlet around the Benedictine abbey of St James, which still stands on the seafront south of the Hotel Kvarner. The abbey stood in contrast to the hillfort of Veprinac situated above the hamlet at 519m above sea level. Then in 1844, a fabulously wealthy industrialist from Rijeka, Iginio Scarpa,

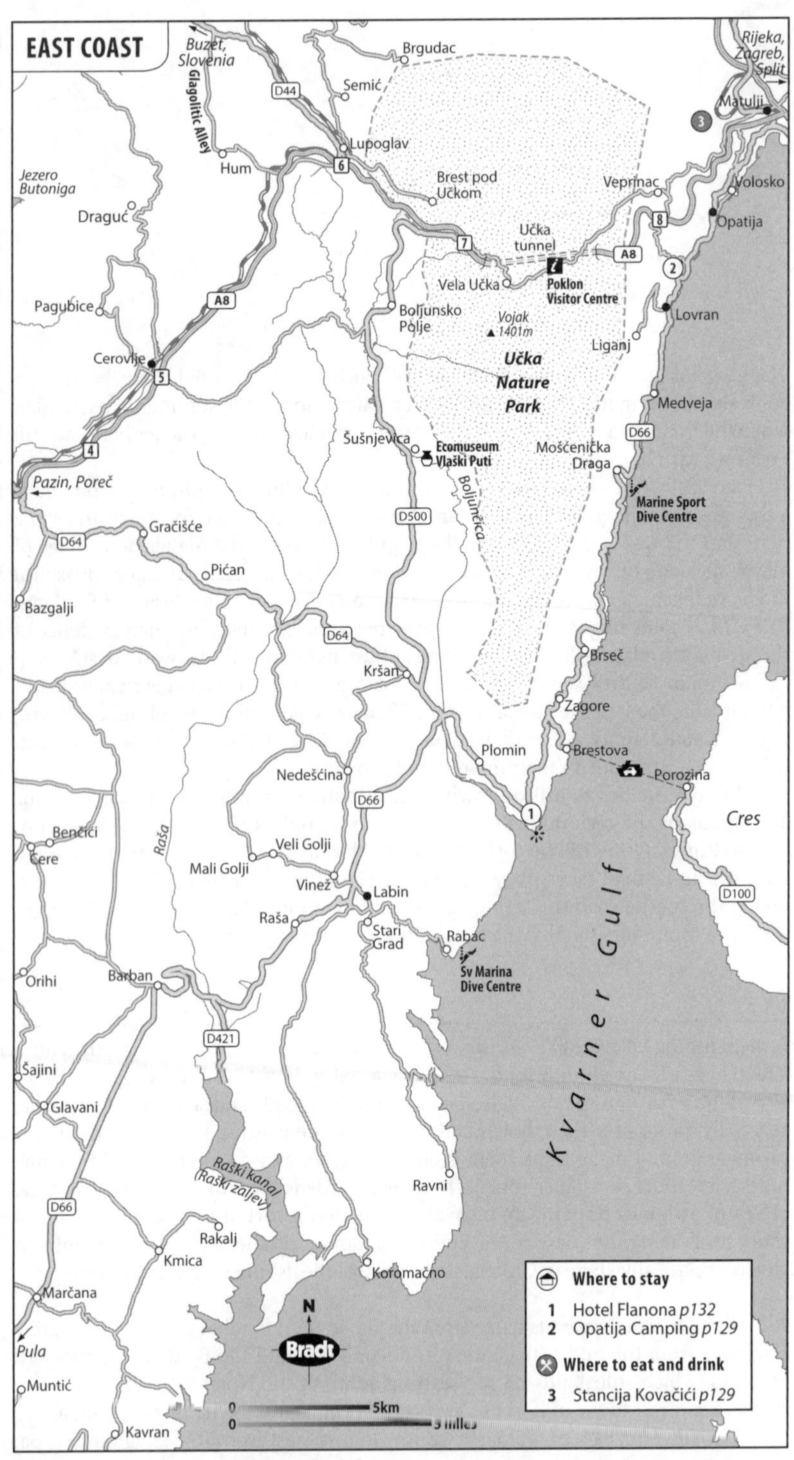
EAST COAST
Buzet, Slovenia
Glagolitic Alley
Brgudac
D44
Semić
Lupoglav
6
Hum
Jezero Butoniga
Brest pod Učkom
Veprinac
Volosko
Rijeka, Zagreb, Split
Matulji
3
Opatija
8
Dragué
Učka tunnel
7
A8
2
Vela Učka
Poklon Visitor Centre
Lovran
Pagubice
A8
Boljunsko Polje
Vojak 1401m
Liganj
Cerovlje
5
Učka Nature Park
Medveja
D66
Šušnjevica
Ecomuseum Vlaški Puti
Mošćenička Draga
4
Pazin, Poreč
Boljunčica
Marine Sport Dive Centre
D500
Gračišće
D64
Pićan
Bazgalji
D64
Brseč
Kršan
Zagore
Plomin
Brestova
Porozina
Nedešćina
Cres
D66
1
Benčići
Cere
Raša
Veli Golji
Mali Golji
Vinež
Labin
Kvarner Gulf
D100
Raša
Stari Grad
Rabac
Sv Marina Dive Centre
Orihi
Barban
D421
Šajini
Glavani
Raški kanal (Raški zaljev)
Ravni
D66
Rakalj
Kmica
Koromačno
Marčana
N
Bradt
Pula
Muntić
0 5km
Kavran
Where to stay
1 Hotel Flanona p132
2 Opatija Camping p129
Where to eat and drink
3 Stancija Kovačići p129

built the Villa Angiolina with its botanical gardens as a retreat for himself and his guests, naming it after his deceased wife. The rich, famous, influential and royal all stopped to stay, and soon the mild winter climate and pleasant summer showers were heralded as a tonic for the stressed elite of the Austro-Hungarian Empire and beyond. Opatija's renown as a spa resort doubled after 1873, when the Rijeka to Pest railway was completed, and in 1884 the first hotel on the Croatian Adriatic, the Hotel Quarnero (today's Hotel Kvarner), was opened, followed by the Hotel Imperial and the Palace Bellevue. Opatija has never looked back.

GETTING THERE AND AROUND

By bus The **bus station** (Trg Vladmira; w arriva.com.hr) is lively as buses are the only public transport available in Opatija. As a result it is fairly well served by even long-distance buses to elsewhere in Croatia and to Trieste (four per day). Information on buses to and from Dubrovnik, Split, Zagreb, Rovinj, Poreč and Pula can be found at w akz.hr, w buscroatia.com or w autobusni-kolodvor.com. Local and city buses also run regularly, from as early as 04.30 to just gone midnight. A minibus service, Opatija's **City bus,** runs a loop from Slatina Beach around a dozen times a day on weekdays, at intervals of 45 minutes between 06.00 and 16.30 – for the current timetable go to w opatija.hr and search for 'city bus', then click on *vozni red* (timetable).

Local bus #32 runs between Rijeka bus and train stations via Volosko and Opatija all the way down the coast to Lovran and Mošćenička Draga; **bus #35** plies a shorter route between Opatija, Volosko Ičići and Veprinac; while **bus #36** runs from Lovran up to Lovranska draga. For timetables see the Autotrolej website (w autotrolej.hr/linije) – scroll down to 'Prigradske linije' and click on the appropriate service, or check the route map (*shema linija*). Single tickets can be bought on board, although cheaper return tickets can be bought from local kiosks. Long-distance buses with local stops also ply these routes, but may be full. Bus transfers to **Rijeka airport** (on the island of Krk) usually run to Rijeka itself rather than Opatija – see w rijeka-airport.hr/en/bus. You can find more information on bus services on the Kvaner Tourist Office website w kvarner.hr/en/tourism/plan_a_trip/move_around_the_kvarner_region/public_transportation.

By car **Parking** is almost impossible during the peak season, although there are five public **car parks** between Opatija harbour next to Park Angiolina and Volosko. In summer you may be better off parking in Lovran and walking the Lungomare seaside promenade or taking the bus into the centre and back.

By taxi **Taxis** can be found at the stand outside the Hotel Milenij, or call **Hallo Taxi** (Matka Laginje 14; ☎051 704 100; m 091 270 4100; e taxi@opatija.net; w hallotaxi.opatija.net).

TOURIST INFORMATION Opatija comes under the regional tourism board of Kvarner, whose head office is here (Nikole Tesle 2; ☎051 272 988; e kvarner@kvarner.hr; w kvarner.hr; ⏲ 09.00–17.00 Mon–Sat). This is where you can find out about the whole county of Primorje-Gorski Kotar (and the website is generally much more useful than that of the Opatija City Tourist Office). Accommodation registrations take place in local branches.

Opatija town tourist information office (Vladimira Nazora 3; ☎051 271 310; e tic@visitopatija.com; w visitopatija.com; ⏲ 15 Jun–15 Sep 08.00–21.00 daily, otherwise 09.00–16.00 Mon–Sat, closed Sun in winter) is located one street further

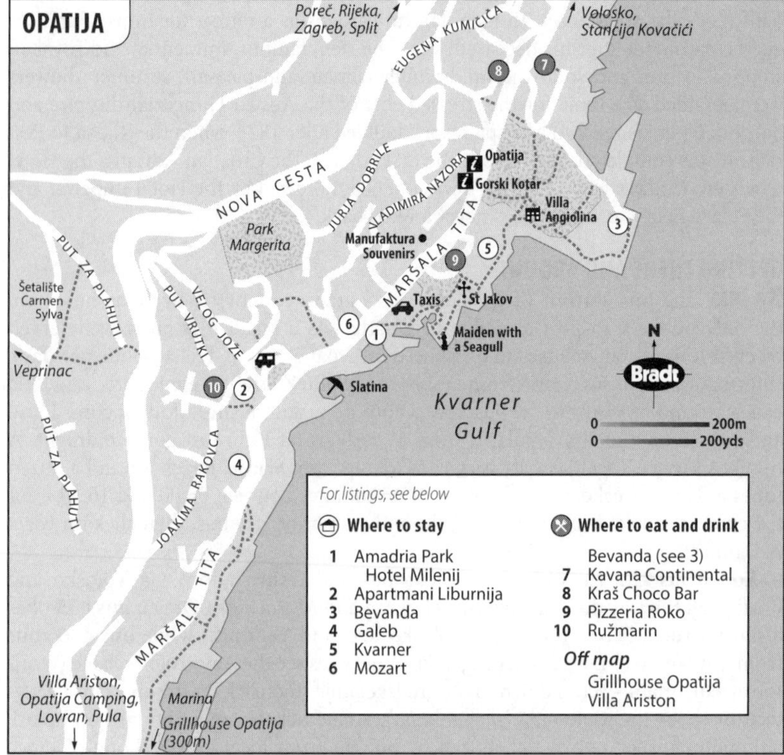

north than the county office, and also covers Volosko. It has plenty of useful information, including city maps.

WHERE TO STAY *Map, above, unless otherwise stated*

There's no end of ultra-upmarket hotels, such as the Admiral, Ambassador, Opatija and Amadria Park Hotel Milenij. Here we list some of the earlier high-end hotels for historical value, as well as the less well-advertised mid-range options. Budget hotels, in Opatija itself, are largely non-existent (though there is a hostel in nearby Lovran; page 132). Some **private accommodation** can be found through the Opatija tourist office, and, particularly in Volosko, at **w** opatija-apartments.com.hr.

Amadria Park Hotel Milenij (102 rooms) Maršala Tita 109; 051 278 016; **w** amadriapark.com. 5-star luxury on the waterfront next to Park Angiolina, complete with original 1920s frescoes in the former ballroom, & a fabulous terrace & spa. **€€€€€**

✷ **Bevanda** (10 rooms) Zert 8; 051 493 888; **w** bevanda.hr/en. Supremely stylish boutique design hotel right on the waterfront, with fabulously luxurious rooms which are, frankly, a cut far, far above the rest of the places you could stay in the centre of town. The rooms are named after some of Opatija's most celebrated visitors over the years, including James Joyce & Isabella Duncan, & the bespoke furniture is the work of local designers. The restaurant is excellent – perhaps not surprisingly, given that the hotel took on the mantle of the highly regarded restaurant of the same name which opened in Volosko in the 1970s – & the service impeccable. Highly recommended. **€€€€€**

Kvarner (87 rooms) Pave Tomašića 2; 051 271 233; **e** reservations@liburnia.hr; **w** liburnia.hr. The original spa resort hotel opened in 1884, but has since been updated with a crystal ballroom which opened in 1913 – & all other mod cons since. You can't get more central than this, surrounded by parks Angiolina & Jakov, with the harbour close by. €€€€

Mozart (29 rooms) Maršala Tita 138; 051 718 260; e info@hotel-mozart.hr; w hotel-mozart.hr. Opened in 1984, this beautiful family-run boutique hotel has had a tumultuous history, including as an army HQ & a children's home, & as many names to match. Attention to every detail best describes the service & furnishings of this completely renovated establishment, which retains some beautiful examples of antique furniture & has its own small spa. €€€€

Apartmani Liburnija (2 rooms, 4 apts) Joakima Rakovca 7; m 099 536 0800; w apartmaniliburnija.hr. Clean, well-appointed apartments & rooms. €€€

Galeb (25 rooms) Maršala Tita 160; 051 271 177; e info@hotel-galeb.hr; w hotel-galeb.hr. Run by the Brko family, this neat hotel has a small wellness spa & swimming pool, & a lovely glasshouse restaurant. Spillover accommodation is also available at the nearby Hotel Savoy. €€€

Opatija Camping [map, page 126] Liburnijska 46; 051 704 836; e opatijacamping@gmail.com; w rivijera-opatija.hr. Situated closer to Lovran than Opatija, between Ika & Ičići, Opatija Camping applies the usual complicated scheme of tariffs which depend on the number of people, type of pitch & length of stay, starting at around €12 for 1 person with a tent for the 1st night.

WHERE TO EAT AND DRINK *Map, opposite, unless otherwise stated*

Opatija is filled with a mix of exclusive high-end restaurants and less-expensive pizzeria-grills. Something in the middle is more difficult to find, unless you go out of town. The fishing village of **Volosko** (page 131), just north of Opatija, is the preferred place for many, where the tiny quay overlooking all the local fishing boats houses some excellent restaurants (the restaurant at Hotel Navis, a little further along the coast, is one of the best in Croatia). **Viennese-style coffee houses** (despite the incongruence with landlocked Austria) are in abundance along Maršala Tita, including the popular cafés Palma, Paris and Stephanie.

Bevanda Zert 8; 051 493 888; w bevanda.hr/en; 11.00–23.00 daily. The excellent restaurant at Hotel Bevanda offers top-notch fine dining overlooking the sea. Seafood is a central focus, with an Asian twist – think along the lines of sashimi & fish carpaccio along with a Kvarner shrimp tartare & fresh oysters for an entrée, & grilled premium white fish with kale cake parmigiana for a main. €€€€€

Villa Ariston Maršala Tita 179; 051 271 379; w villa-ariston.hr; 18.00–midnight daily. At the hotel of the same name, this Michelin- & JRE-listed restaurant is now one of the supreme fine-dining spots on the Opatija Riviera. €€€€€

Pizzeria Roko Maršala Tita 114; 051 711 500; 11.00–23.00 daily. Opatija's most popular pizzeria. €€€

Ružmarin Veprinački put 2; 051 712 673; w restaurant-ruzmarin.com; 11.00–midnight daily. This great little grillhouse not far from the bus station is a little more caring & generous than the seafront restaurants tend to be, & its reputation is much more local than tourist. €€€

Stancija Kovačići [map, page 126] Rukavac 51, Matulj; 051 272 106; w stancija-kovacici.hr; noon–23.00 Wed–Sat, noon–19.00 Sun. Highly regarded, family-run restaurant 4km north of Opatija, near Matulj. They also have 5 well-appointed rooms (€€€). €€€

Grillhouse Opatija Maršala Tita 220; m 098 952 4669; f grillhouse.opatija; midday–23.30 Tue–Sun. Located on the edge of town, this family-run restaurant is reasonably priced & has nice outdoor seating. €€

✷ **Kavana Continental** Maršala Tita 85; 07.00–23.00 daily. Opatija's ultimate destination for exquisite cakes is this landmark café on the ground floor of the Hotel Continental – don't miss the excellent *sacher torta*.

Kraš Choco Bar Maršala Tita 94; 051 603 562; w kraschocobar.com; 07.00–22.30 Mon–Fri, 07.00–23.30 Sat/Sun. Run by Croatia's best-known manufacturer Kraš. If you like very sweet chocolate this is without a doubt the place for you, with a mouth-watering array of truffles as well as a variety of hot & cold chocolate drinks, coffees, cocktails & ice creams.

SHOPPING Manufaktura Souvenirs (Maršala Tita 112; ⌚ 09.00–13.00 Mon–Wed, Fri, 09.00–20.00 Thu/Sat; f ManufakturaSouvenirsCroatia). A good place to shop for local wine and *rakija*, honey and cosmetics.

WHAT TO SEE AND DO Located in the centre of Opatija is the beautiful **Villa Angiolina** and **botanical garden** (Park Angiolina 1; ☎ 051 603 636; e info@hrmt.hr; w hrmt.hr; ⌚ Jul–Sep 09.00–13.00 and 17.00–21.00 Tue–Sun; entry €2.60, 1st Sun of each month free). The villa has become the **Museum of Croatian Tourism (Hrvatski muzej turizma)** and is filled with informative, well-presented displays including some fantastic old photos. The garden itself is home to over 150 species of flora including Japanese camellia. The grounds were originally bought by the wealthy industrialist Iginio Scarpa for 700 florins, who sold them in 1910 for the princely sum of 2.5 million crowns. Sadly, the original grounds have been divided between the Park Angiolina and Sv Jakov Park by the church and old abbey, and only a total of 3.6ha remain. Look out for the large murals in the gardens by Croatian street artist Anja Ferenčić, with portraits of some of Opatija's famous visitors, including Gustav Mahler and Albert Einstein.

The impressive **St James Church (Crkva sv Jakova)** dates back to 1420, when it is believed to have been built as part of a monastery for Benedictine monks. Little remains of the original church, which saw major renovation and expansion in 1506, over the course of the end of the 18th century and lastly in 1930. During the 19th century the church housed Opatija's first school. Today it remains a fully working church and occasionally holds chamber concerts.

On the waterfront itself you'll find one of Opatija's most photographed landmarks – the '*Maiden with a Seagull*' (*Djevojka s galebom*), a sculpture by Zvonko Car dating from 1956 which replaced an earlier statue of the Madonna del Mare. There are other works by well-known Croatian sculptors nearby.

The **coastal road** from Opatija down to Plomin is peppered with little fishing villages. The road is idyllic for most of the year, but can get jammed with day trippers and those wanting to take the ferry from Brestova to the island of Cres. Our advice to enjoy the road at its best once the boardwalk from Rijeka stops at Lovran, is to bike or drive the road very early in the morning: sunrise from the bay is spectacular, and usually the privilege of only fishermen in the summer.

Carmen Sylva Forest Path This 5km path in the woods above Opatija was created with funding from King Carol of Romania after he got lost horseriding in the woods there on a visit in 1896. It was completed in 1901, but only named Carmen Sylva – after the pen name of his wife Elizabeth, a literary and musical artist – from 1998. To get on to the path, follow the narrow road straight uphill from the end of Nikole Tesle Street. Once up on to the well-signposted path, the gradient remains gently undulating and offers great shaded views of the bay. The path is popular in early spring (March/April) for gathering wild asparagus, and in autumn for sweet chestnuts.

The Lungomare from Volosko to Lovran The 12km promenade from Volosko in Preluk Bay to Lovran is known as the Lungomare. It was started in 1888 and finished in 1911, and was designed (along with the Carmen Sylva) to place Opatija as the leader in health tourism. It boasts 39 separate points of interest along its route, all of which are described at w opatija.net/en/sights/lungomare-the-seaside-promenade. The path ends at the minute old town of Lovran (from the Roman Lauriana, meaning 'laurel'). For those who still have the energy a marked trail leads from the old town up to the Učka Mountains.

In the hills between Lovran and Medveja is the Michelin-starred **Draga di Lovrana restaurant** (Lovranksa Draga 1; 051 294 166; e info@dragadilovrana.hr; w dragadilovrana.hr; 13.00–midnight daily; €€€€), which is well worth the hike or drive for its impressive views and excellent food. Originally opened in 1910, but then dormant from 1923 when it was consumed by fire, **Draga di Lovrana** was reopened in 2005, and in addition to its reputation as a restaurant, it offers four lovingly renovated double rooms and a large suite with jacuzzi and fireplace (**€€€€**).

You'll find yet another gastro highlight a little further along the coast at Mošćenička Draga – Michelin-listed **Johnson** (Sv Petar bb; 051 737 578; €€€€), which is named after US president Lyndon B Johnson and dishes up some truly excellent seafood.

BEACHES There are three public beaches in Opatija. The main one with extensive facilities is Kupalište Slatina, which is the southernmost in town. The smaller, central and original Lido is accessed from Park Angiolina. Northernmost is Kupalište Tomaševac next to the Hotel Ambassador.

Further down the coast, Kupalište Medveja, south of Lovran, is renowned as one of the best beaches in Istria. It has a modern funky feel, with trendy café bars and music, which you can enjoy on rented four-poster bed-loungers. A bit further on, but still on the #32 bus route, there's a nice beach at Mošćenička Draga.

VOLOSKO

At the northern end of the Lungomare, the sleepy little fishing village of Volosko developed several years ago into one of the finest gastro-enclaves in Croatia, boasting some of the country's top tables without ever really losing its fairly quiet, low-key charm. Volosko makes a good place to stay while exploring the Opatija Riviera, whether or not you have your eye on its highly regarded restaurants, with at least two small family-run boutique hotels that are genuinely outstanding.

Volosko is just a 30-minute stroll along the waterfront from Opatija, and buses running between Opatija and Rijeka (such as the #32) stop here. For private accommodation in Volosko, see w opatija-apartments.com.hr. Booking should be considered mandatory for most restaurants in Volosko.

WHERE TO STAY, EAT AND DRINK

Hotel Laurus (24 rooms, 3 suites) Nova cesta 12A; 051 741 355; w liburnia.hr/en/hotel-laurus. This boutique hotel is perched a few hundred metres above the main Opatija–Rijeka road, just a 10min walk up from the waterfront in Volosko. Go for the sea-facing rooms, the balconies of which have spectacular, panoramic views of the Kvarner Gulf & islands. The terrace restaurant (Laurus) has long held a reputation as a superb place to eat. Until recently, when it was bought by Liburnia, the hotel was owned & run by Kruno Kapetanović, who also opened the superb Navis down by the waterfront. **€€€€**

✷ **Hotel Navis** (44 rooms) Ivana Matetića Ronjgova 10; 051 444 600; w hotel-navis.hr. Opened in 2015 by the owners of the former Villa Kapetanović, this über-stylish design hotel with a nautical theme is located right on the waterfront on the edge of Volosko. All rooms have sea views, & the hotel has its own restaurant (€€€€–€€€) – which is phenomenally good; the 4-course *degustation* menu is excellent – & spa. Don't miss the poached eggs with truffles at b/fast. One of my favourite hotels in Croatia. Highly recommended. **€€€€**

Plavi Podrum Frana Supila 4; 051 701 223; w plavipodrum.com; midday–23.30 daily. This restaurant, called the Blue Basement, is another for the gourmand. As a result popular seats on the terrace are always packed, but it is possible to reserve. True to its name, it specialises in all things blue, using squid ink as a colouring, including for bread & coffee! Tasty & novel. €€€€

✷ **Trattoria Mandrać** Frana Supila 10; 051 322 601; w trattoriamandrac.hr/en; 11.30–23.30 daily. Fine-dining fusion overlooking the working boats, this has to be one of my favourite locations for a restaurant in all of Istria, with a glass-fronted terrace allowing for an outdoor feel even in the (mild) winters. The bijou servings are worth every lipa, & you can't help but feel indulgent here. The gourmet who misses this restaurant, does her or himself a disservice. €€€€

Laurus Nova cesta 12a; 051 741 355; 051 710 444; w liburnia.hr/en/hotel-laurus; 11.30–23.00 daily. Laurus, the restaurant at the former Villa Kapetanović, has built a reputation for outstanding cuisine, with an emphasis on fresh, seasonal local ingredients. €€€€–€€€

Pizzeria Moho Obala Franja Subila 8; m 099 256 2289; f p.MOHO; 11.00–23.00 daily. Good pizzas at reasonable prices, nestled on the waterfront beside more upmarket options like Trattoria Mandrać. €€€

Valle Losca Andrija Štangera 2; m 095 580 3757; midday–23.00 daily. Highly regarded little *konoba*, slightly uphill from (& also cheaper & more low-key than) most places on the waterfront. €€€

LOVRAN

Named after the bay tree, or laurel, Lovran is the first main town on the western coast of Kvarner Bay. In Roman times it was called Lauriana. Lovran had been a main shipbuilding town until the late Middle Ages, when Venetian expansion of Trieste and Pula, and later Rijeka's rise on the shipbuilding scene, dwarfed the town's further development. The expansion of Opatija as a spa resort of the Austro-Hungarians in the 19th century brought renewed life to Lovran. As the end destination of Opatija's 12km Lungomare its medieval architecture, surrounded by early 20th-century villas and parks, makes for a fitting rest to a healthy walk, or a scenic start to a **hike** up from sea level to the 1,401m **Mount Vojak** (page 187). The Lovran tourist office (w tz-lovran.hr) has details of private accommodation.

WHERE TO STAY, EAT AND DRINK

Ikador Luxury Boutique Hotel & Spa (16 rooms & suites) Ul Svetog Nikole 2, Ika; 051 207 020; e info@ikador.com; w ikador.com. Opened in 2019, this boutique hotel & spa offers the height of luxury on the waterfront just north of Lovran. €€€€€

Villa Astra (6 suites) Viktora Cara Emina 11; 051 294 400; e sales@hotelvillaastra.com; w hotelvillaastra.com. This is almost as exclusive as it gets. A neo-Gothic early 20th-century castle-like villa, offering its own bar, vitality restaurant, an outdoor pool (heated in winter), & a small exclusive beachfront. €€€€€

Hotel Flanona [map, page 126] (10 rooms) Plomin bb; 052 864 426; e info@hotel-flanona.com.hr; w hotel-flanona.com.hr. Located at the southern apex of the coastal road, known in Roman times as Capo Pax Tecum ('the cape of peace be with you'), this ostentatiously modern 3-star hotel has an enviable restaurant & terrace with a 180° view of Kvarner Bay. The food is standard & a little pricey, but worth the view. €€€€

Lovran (12 rooms) Maršala Tita 19; 051 291 222; e office@hotel-lovran.hr; w hotel-lovran.hr. This hotel offers excellent service, value for money, sea views & a small wellness spa. €€€€–€€€

Link Hostel (114 rooms) Maršala Tita 9; 051 202 090; e info@linkhostel.com; w linkhostel.com. Opened in 2014, this is a welcome addition to accommodation choices on the Opatija Riviera. Clean rooms in a renovated building right on the waterfront. All rooms are dbl or trpl. €€

Lovranska Vrata Stari grad 94; 051 291 050; Apr–Oct 11.00–23.00 daily. In the quaint stretch of the old town, this family-run restaurant retreats to Konoba Bellavista at Stari grad 22 in winter. Great seafood & a very good grill at the *konoba* in winter. €€€

WHAT TO SEE AND DO Lovran does not take long to get to know, and it is more a base (quieter and cheaper than Opatija) for striking out to nearby activities. Trg sv Juraj, the town square, has a 12th-century Romanesque church dedicated to St George. Opposite is the town hall, upon which is carved a relief of St George himself, and one of the few in the region in which he is actually slaying a dragon. One of the more famous reliefs in the square though is the *mustačon*, a face with a curly blue moustache above the door of a Venetian red villa that is meant to ward off evil. Built in 1722, back then we might have been more scared of what lay inside.

Hike from Lovran to Učka's highest point, Vojak. (page 187).

FERRY FROM BRESTOVA TO CRES ISLAND For those wanting to visit the island of Cres (and Lošinj, which used to be connected to it at Osor until the islands were divided by a seaway and reconnected by an opening road bridge) there is a regular car ferry, which operates from Brestova to the town of Porozina on Cres. The journey takes 20 minutes and ferries run in the high season approximately every 90 minutes. Queues in the summer can be long. Timetables are at w jadrolinija.hr. Cres is not as well visited as many of Croatia's other islands, which makes it attractive in its own right. The village of Porozina (whose name is derived from the Latin *pharum insulae*, meaning 'island light' from the lighthouse that used to be atop the hill there) is home to the well-preserved ruins of St Nicholas Franciscan Monastery and a 15th-century Gothic church with Glagolitic wall inscriptions. See pages 31 and 141 for more information on visiting the Kvarner Islands from Istria.

PLOMIN Plomin signals the end of your view of the sea, but affords much to see of its own. Dating back to Roman times, this fortified village on a prominent hill has retained its Roman foundations, upon which current buildings were erected in medieval times. Originally the town was named Flanona after the bay plunging below it. Its narrow, cobbled steep streets hide two churches to the patron saint of the town, St George. The outside wall of the Church of St George the Elder (the second church is to St George the Younger) contains the Plomin tablet. Most historians agree that this is an 11th-century religious text dedicated to St George (before he was known as a dragon-slayer during the Crusades), but there is some dispute as to whether it might be an earlier carving of the Roman god Silvanus (god of flora and fauna) with the Glagolitic text graffitied on later, unfinished and reading 'This is written S…'.

Abandoned by its largely Italian population after World War II, the village now has a population of only 130. Catering facilities here are slight to say the least, but other places to dine and sup are not far away.

If you head up behind the Učka massif on a backroad past the village of Kožljak, you'll find the so-called **'drunken tracks'** (Pijana pruga) – the undulating, wonky and much-photographed stretch of railway tracks that used to carry trains up to Lupoglav. Further north, in the village of Šušnjevica, is the small **Ecomuseum Vlaški Puti** (052 743 662; w vlaskiputi.com/en/about-us/ecomuseum), dedicated to the highly endangered language and culture of the Vlachs who lived in this area from the 15th century.

LABIN AND RABAC

Perched on a hill 320m above the sea, **Labin** has a proud history, in which it has often asserted an independent spirit. Once a mining town, and renowned for staging the first anti-fascist revolution, it's now better known within its medieval walls for its flourishing art.

Labin saw human settlement as early as 2,000 years ago, when a Bronze Age fort was founded under the name Kunci. Illyrian Celts later named the settlement Alvona, meaning 'town on a hill'. More recently it became the centre of Istrian coal mining (below) by the beginning of the 20th century.

Rabac lies around 3km from Labin, down on the coast, and grew from a tiny fishing village into a popular seaside resort in the late 19th century. One of its more celebrated early visitors was the British traveller Sir Richard Francis Burton (he of the original English translation of the *Arabian Nights*, not the more famous film star), who was posted as consul in Trieste and wrote a pamphlet entitled *Notes on the Castellieri or Prehistoric Ruins of the Istrian Peninsula*.

GETTING THERE AND AROUND **Labin bus station** (Trg 2 ožujka, Podlabin) is well served by buses to Pula and Rijeka, and also has buses to Rovinj and Split. A local bus also runs regularly between Labin and Rabac (for timetables, see w rabac-labin.com/en/8-local-bus-time-table). It's very easy to walk around the old town of Labin, and thus there is no public transport. **Taxis** can be called on m 098 916 1863.

TOURIST INFORMATION The main **tourist information office** (Aldo Negri 20; 052 855 560; e tzg.labin@pu.htnet.hr; w rabac-labin.com; 15 Jun–15 Sep 08.00–21.00 daily, 09.00–16.00 out of season, closed Sun in winter) lies on the main road between the old town and Podlabin. This is where to register for all accommodation on the east coast of the county of Istria from Brestova south. There is also a small information office in the old town (Titov trg 2/1; 052 852 399; e info@rabac-labin.com; same opening hours as the main office).

BLACK GOLD: THE FADS OF ECONOMIC DEMAND

Coal mining started in Istria in the 1600s, when coal resin used for the impregnation of wooden boat hulls was ordered en masse by the Venetian governors of Istria. This saw the rise of Labin as an important commercial centre. Although anthracite (hard coal) was discovered in the Labin area in the 18th century, it was almost another century before coal mining here was undertaken in earnest. Thus, shortly after Venice was taken over by the French in 1805, Napoleon ordered further coal mining in Istria. By 1881 a railway connected the mines of Raša to Raša Bay at Bršica, and thus to the rest of the industrialised world.

THE REPUBLIC OF LABIN Ever the hazardous occupation, miners in the Labin area went on strike in 1921 protesting against the working conditions imposed under Italian rule. The strikes lasted for five weeks – during which time the strikers declared the town's independence as the Republic of Labin – and evolved into one of Europe's earliest anti-fascist protests. This prompted military intervention, at which point the strike was quickly quelled.

COAL TOWNS In response to the coal miners' strikes of the previous decade and the need for yet more coal, Mussolini ordered that a village be built for the miners of Istria. Thus was born Istria's youngest village, **Raša** (named after a local river, even though the village itself sits on a tributary), which was completed in 547 days and opened on 4 November 1937. Designed to be the perfect village, Raša has a church and other public amenities built around a village square.

WHERE TO STAY AND EAT There are several small B&Bs in Labin and nearby villages, as well as a lovely four-star hotel within the town itself. Rabac on the coast has plenty of large hotels and self-catering apartments jammed against the hillside. Accommodation in Labin and Rabac is listed on the Labin tourist information website (w rabac-labin.com/en/18-accommodation). Rabac offers a string of restaurants and entertainment along the bay, all much of a muchness with the notable exception of Lino (page 136).

Labin *Map, page 136*

✷ **Hotel Pateani** (11 dbls, 3 sgls) Aldo Negri 9; 052 863 404; e info@hotel-peteani.hr; w hotel-peteani.hr. Opened in 2016 in a renovated modern villa, this is a wonderfully welcoming little hotel with stylish rooms & its own outstanding restaurant (€€€), which is a destination in its own right. Free use of mountain bikes. Highly recommended. **€€€€**

Villa Calussovo (10 dbls, 2 sgls) Kras 18, Ripenda; 052 851 188; e villacalussovo@aol.com; w villacalussovo.com. Around 4km from Labin in the village of Ripenda, this old farmhouse has been lovingly restored & offers stone-exposed bedrooms, a fireplace for winter, & an excellent restaurant (€€€). **€€€€**

Due Fratelli Montozi 6; 052 853 577; w restaurantduefratelli.com; 11.00–23.00, closed Mon in winter. As you might guess, this restaurant on the road down to Rabac is run by 2 brothers, who catch & then cook the fish themselves. A popular venue among shady trees, not least because of the memorable boat lurching out of the wall in the main dining hall. Reserve in the summer. €€€

Kvarner Šetalište San Marco bb; 052 852 336; w kvarnerlabin.com; 09.00–23.00 Mon–Sat, midday–23.00 Sun. On the south side of Labin town, on the edge of the town wall, the views from this restaurant over Kvarner Bay are magnificent. The food matches the view. Try their hot sampler plate of local pastas with meat & game. They also offer private accommodation (**€€€**). €€€

The church, dedicated to St Barbara, the patron saint of miners, is notable for being built in the shape of an upturned miner's barrow with a miner's lantern shape for the bell tower. More a strip than a village, the residential areas were divided firmly by class with lower Raša to the southwest housing ordinary miners, upper Raša to the northeast housing senior miners, and larger gated villas close to the village centre assigned to the mines' managers. A few years later **Podlabin** (or Pozzo Littorio as it was known then) was also further developed along functionalist lines for the miners.

DEATH KNELL At its heyday during World War II, the mining of black gold in Istria employed over 10,000 workers, extracting 1.158 million tonnes of anthracite in the record year of 1942. Coal remained important in the post-World War II reconstruction of Yugoslavia, but the advent of cheaper imports from Poland and the former Soviet Union, as well as the switch to oil as the fuel of choice, sounded the death knell for Istria's mines. By the mid 1960s Istria's coal was largely exhausted under the mining practices of those days, and in 1989 the mines of Raša were closed down. Istria's last mine, with 300 miners at Tupljak at the start of the Raša River, was closed in 1999.

Today Raša is a mere ghost of its former functionalist fervour. It remains nonetheless a mesmerising spyglass on the past and the **Raša Kavana** (year-round 07.00–11.00 daily; €) on the main square provides a welcome coffee, *rakija* or simple grill.

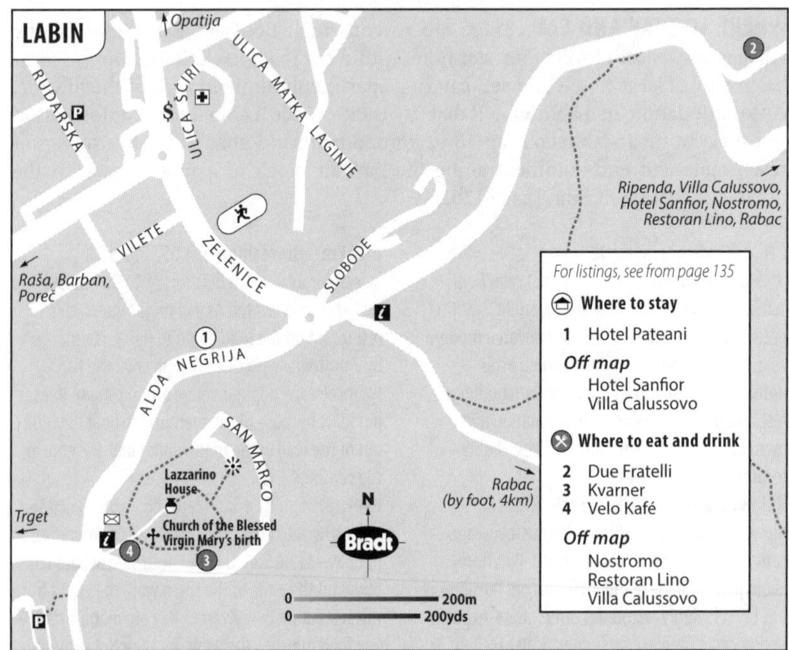

Velo Kafé Titov trg 12; 052 852 745; velokafe; 11.00–23.00 daily. Popular restaurant/café on the main square of the old town, with good food at a very affordable price. €€€

Rabac

Hotel Sanfior (242 rooms) Lanterna 2; 052 465 000; w valamar.com. Large modern hotel with prime waterfront location in Rabac, popular with families, right next to the beach, with indoor & outdoor pools & wellness centre. €€€€

Nostromo Obala Maršal Tito 7; 052 872 601; w nostromo.hr; 15 Apr–15 Oct noon–22.00 daily. Family-run restaurant in Rabac, at the small hotel of the same name. €€€€

Restoran Lino Obala Maršal Tito 57; m 091 799 4279; 15 Apr–15 Oct midday–22.00 daily. Serves all the usual suspects with additional signature dishes of Fra Davalo spicy lobster & Cres lamb for those who have had enough fish. €€€€

WHAT TO SEE AND DO **Porta Sanfior** are the main doors of the town wall, dating from 1589 with the Labin coat of arms and the Serenissima lion above. The cannon at the doors dates from Austrian times, and was reinstated there in 1995 after a long period in storage.

The Labin City Museum (**Narodni muzej Labin**) (1 Maja 6; 052 852 477; w uciliste-labin.hr/muzej; muzej.labin; 10.00–15.00 Tue–Sat; entry adult/child €4.50/€2.60) was formerly a Baroque palace belonging to the Battiala-Lazzarini family. The last resident, Count Guiseppe Lazzarini, sold up his several properties in the Labin area and left just before World War II, portending what was to come.

The three-nave **Church of the Blessed Virgin Mary's Birth** (**Župna crkva Rođenja Balžene Djevice Marije**) in the centre was built in 1336 on the foundations of a smaller church from the 11th century. It was reconstructed several times, most recently in 1993. The church has six marble altars, one of which holds the relics of St Justin, which were brought to Labin from Rome in 1664. A Venetian lion with a sphere in his mouth – a symbol of Labin recognising the Venetian government – was put on the front façade in 1604. By the end of that century, in 1688, a Baroque statue of Senator Antonio Bollani, a combatant against the Turks, was put on the same façade. The bust is one of the most beautiful examples of the secular sculptural art of Istria in the 17th century. On the right from the church is a palace that belonged to the Schampicchio family.

Merania is a good place to shop for local pottery (1 Maja bb; m 091 544 4918 ; w merania.hr; by request).

SOUTH TO PULA

BARBAN This well-preserved hillfort 12km southwest of Labin has shown some sort of human settlement since the Bronze Age over 3,500 years ago. It suffered the plague in 1312, but was resettled by Finodol Dalmatians (people, not the dogs) shortly afterwards. During the Republic of Venice, it was bought in 1535 from the Counts of Pazin by the Loredan family (of the Venetian nobility). They rebuilt the entire fort, giving it its current palace and the Church of St Nicholas inside the town walls, and leaving the tiny Church of St Anthony with its 15th-century frescoes still standing outside the town gates.

Barban is most often visited now in August (in particular the third weekend in the month) for its annual **ring-tilting tournament** – Trka na prstenac – when jousting knights compete on a charging horse to spear a hanging ring. Another festival of Barban worth a visit is the annual **fig festival**, which takes place every second weekend in September. During the festivals, live music gigs are played in the evenings at the popular **Caffe Bar Roy** (Barban 10; caffebar.roybarban; 06.00–noon Sun–Thu, 07.00–02.00 Fri & Sat), and the place to eat is at Restoran Prstenac (Barban 10; 099 3030232; Restoran Prstenac ; 07.00–22.00 Wed–Sat; €), both on the village square. The restaurant is über-lively during the festival and sleepy the rest of the year, but in all events offers very good value for money for its spit roasts, grills (fish and meat), game pastas and fish soup. The Barban tourist office has more information on local history and culture (Barban 69; 052 567 420; w tz-barban.hr; 08.00–16.00 Mon–Fri).

RAŠKI KANAL The Raša River (Arsa in Latin; also known locally as Raški zaljev) has been a natural and political boundary for centuries, because of the steep sides of the valley in which it lies, and its relatively straight if short course. It is only 23km in length, at the end of which is the Raški kanal deep sea-channel of just ten nautical miles. The old mining railway and a footpath run the river's entire course.

A good place to eat down on this waterway is in the tiny deep-water harbour of Trget at **Martin Pescador** (Trget 20; 052 544 976; noon–22.00 Tue–Sun; €€€). It's very popular with the locals, who come even from afar to eat on this working quay overlooking the shipments of timber and marble. Decorated with fishing paraphernalia, it's hard not to want to eat the fresh fish here caught that morning, but offerings of the four-legged variety are also tempting. Entry to the restaurant goes past the timber and marble holds, and into the gated harbour, where the restaurant will suddenly appear, with ample parking.

UČKA NATURE PARK

Učka Nature Park or Park prirode Učka (Main office at Liganj 42, Lovran; 51 293 753; w pp-ucka.hr; free entry) stretches southwest from Opatija, parallel with and just inland from the coast, and covers an area of around 160km^2. It is one of 11 nature parks in Croatia – the only one in Istria – and includes the Učka massif as well as part of neighbouring Ćićarija. Fauna ranges from wild boar and roe deer to endemic subterranean cave beetles and endemic land snails, and around 250 species of butterflies and moths.

The highest point on Učka, Vojak (also known as Vrh Učka), rises to just over 1,400m above sea level, and is crowned by a stout stone tower (*kula*), as well as a paragliding ramp just below this – not to mention a gigantic telecommunications aerial, but don't let that put you off. The surrounding slopes are lushly forested, punctuated by the occasional meadow as well as some stark areas of limestone scenery, including the knobbly fingers of rock protruding from Vranjska draga, close to the inland entrance to the Učka tunnel. The *kula* was built as an enhanced viewpoint in 1911 (and it is quite a view from up here), and was renovated in 2004.

A road leads up over a saddle below Vojak, passing the Poklon Visitor Centre, and a bus comes up here from Rijeka and Opatija but only on Sundays (page 189). There are plenty of **hiking trails** on Učka, the best of which is the route from Lovran on the coast up to Vojak (see page 187 for a route description).

Don't miss the excellent new **Poklon Visitor Centre** (Poklon 8; 051 770 100; w pp-ucka.hr/en/poklon-visitor-centre; 09.00–19.00 daily; entry adult/child €9.50/€4.65, less in winter), which opened in 2021. Set on the pass and built on the site of an abandoned poultry farm, it has genuinely fascinating, interactive displays covering the flora, fauna, history, heritage and folklore of this wonderful sprawl of mountains. A hiking trail to the summit sets off almost directly opposite the visitor centre.

8

Rijeka

Although like neighbouring Opatija it is located just outside Istria proper in the Kvarner region, at the head of the Kvarner Gulf, Rijeka is a place that many visitors to Istria will pass through, whether they arrive by train, bus or ferry, and it is certainly worthy of a stopover of one or two nights. Croatia's third-largest city and its busiest port, Rijeka has plenty of grand Secessionist architecture, broad pedestrian streets strewn with cafés, some excellent restaurants, a major pilgrimage site up on the hill at Trsat, and one of the largest, most vibrant carnivals to be found anywhere in Europe. In January 2020, Rijeka also became European Capital of Culture (ECOC) – the first Croatian city to be awarded this prestigious title, having successfully won its bid against better-known heavyweights including Dubrovnik – ushering in a huge new regeneration programme for Rijeka.

Like many other towns and cities in the region, Rijeka was once an Illyrian and then a Roman settlement – though unlike much of the rest of the Croatian coast, it has the distinction of never quite having fallen under the rule of Venice. Backed by the great arc of mountains that form the Gorski kotar range, Rijeka has a mild climate, and is a living city all year round, not somewhere that closes up over the winter when the tourists leave. The town centre is divided from the residential area of Sušak by the River Rječina, and gets its name (in both Croatian and Italian) from the word for river, *rijeka* (*fiume* in Italian). Along the coast to the east is the suburb of Pećine, while up on the hill above Rijeka at 138m above sea level is the suburb of Trsat. There are beaches along the coast to the west and southeast of the city.

HISTORY

There was a hillfort at Trsat, the hill behind Rijeka, from at least the 4th century BC, inhabited by the Illyrian Japodes tribe, while the Illyrian Liburni controlled the coast below. Following their defeat of the Illyrians the Romans built a town (Tarsatica) on an area just north of what is now the Korzo, while the hillfort became a Roman signalling station. Tarsatica developed into a walled city, controlled after the departure of the Romans by Ostrogoths, Byzantines, Avars, the medieval Kingdom of Croatia, and then Hungary.

A period under the local Frankopans of Krk was followed by Habsburg rule from the 15th to the 18th centuries, during which it successfully repelled several attacks by Venice (in particular in 1508), and was granted the charter of a free port in 1719. The city thrived – despite much of it being razed by an earthquake in 1750 – receiving heavy Hungarian investment in the 19th century (it was Hungary's only port on the Mediterranean), and gaining rail connections with Budapest and other centres in the Habsburg realm. During this period it was the site of the Austro-Hungarian Naval Academy. Prototypes of a torpedo were tested here in the 1860s, and the world's first torpedo factory, the Robert Whitehead Torpedo Co, was

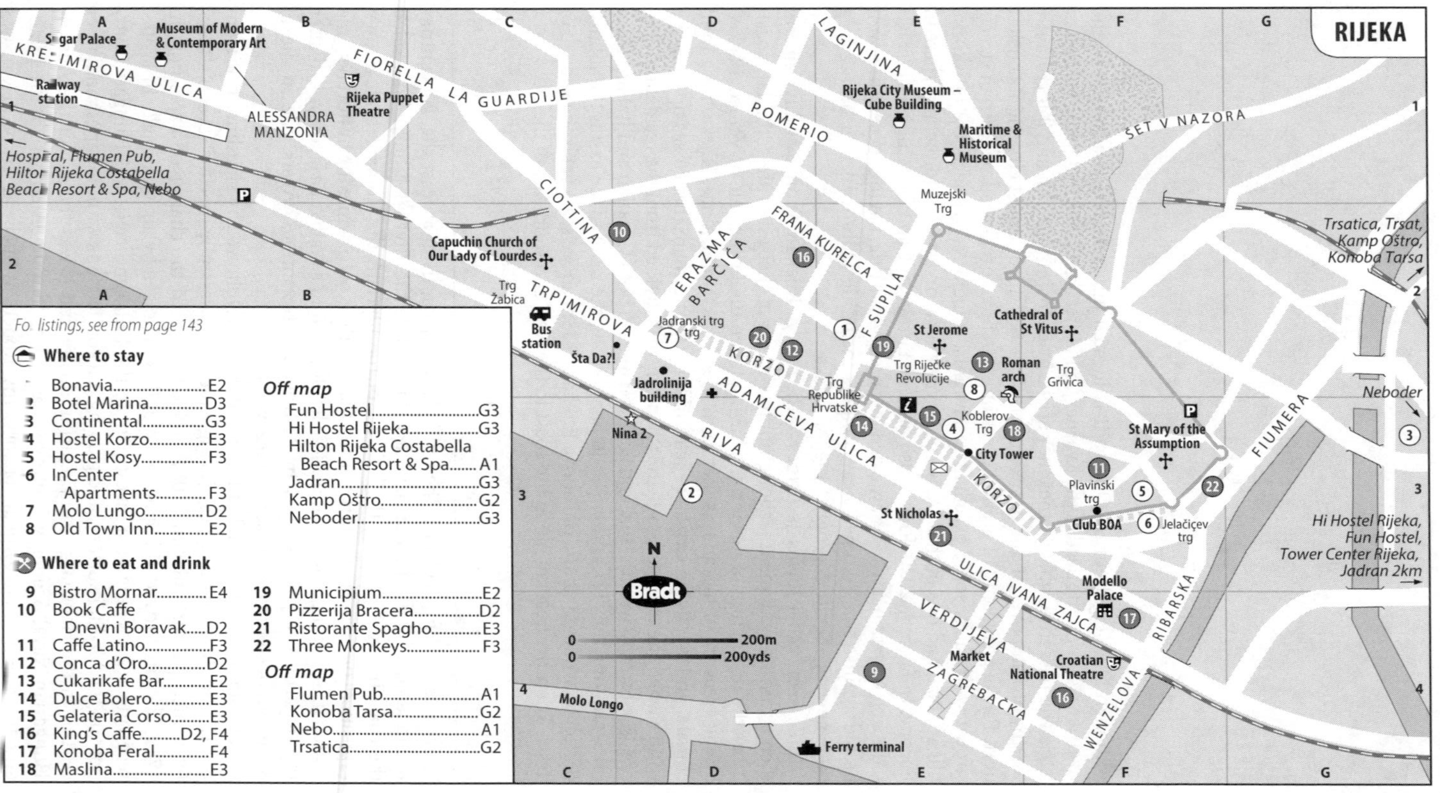
RIJEKA
Sugar Palace
Museum of Modern & Contemporary Art
KREŠIMIROVA ULICA
Railway station
FIORELLA LA GUARDIJE
Rijeka Puppet Theatre
ALESSANDRA MANZONIA
Hospital, Flumen Pub, Hilton Rijeka Costabella Beach Resort & Spa, Nebo
LAGINJINA
Rijeka City Museum – Cube Building
POMERIO
Maritime & Historical Museum
ŠET V NAZORA
Muzejski Trg
CIOTTINA
Capuchin Church of Our Lady of Lourdes
FRANA KURELCA
ERAZMA BARČIĆA
F SUPILA
Trg Žabica
TRPIMIROVA
Bus station
Šta Da?!
Jadranski trg
KORZO
Jadrolinija building
ADAMIĆEVA ULICA
Trg Republike Hrvatske
St Jerome
Trg Riječke Revolucije
Cathedral of St Vitus
Roman arch
Trg Grivica
Koblerov Trg
City Tower
St Mary of the Assumption
Plavinski trg
Club BOA
Jelačićev trg
FIUMERA
Neboder
Trsatica, Trsat, Kamp Oštro, Konoba Tarsa
Hi Hostel Rijeka, Fun Hostel, Tower Center Rijeka, Jadran 2km
Nina 2
RIVA
St Nicholas
ULICA IVANA ZAJCA
Modello Palace
RIBARSKA
VERDIJEVA
Market
ZAGREBAČKA
Croatian National Theatre
WENZELOVA
Molo Longo
Ferry terminal
0 200m
0 200yds
Bradt
For listings, see from page 143
Where to stay
1 Bonavia E2
2 Botel Marina D3
3 Continental G3
4 Hostel Korzo E3
5 Hostel Kosy F3
6 InCenter Apartments F3
7 Molo Lungo D2
8 Old Town Inn E2
Off map
Fun Hostel G3
Hi Hostel Rijeka G3
Hilton Rijeka Costabella Beach Resort & Spa A1
Jadran G3
Kamp Oštro G2
Neboder G3
Where to eat and drink
9 Bistro Mornar E4
10 Book Caffe Dnevni Boravak D2
11 Caffe Latino F3
12 Conca d'Oro D2
13 Cukarikafe Bar E2
14 Dulce Bolero E3
15 Gelateria Corso E3
16 King's Caffe D2, F4
17 Konoba Feral F4
18 Maslina E3
19 Municipium E2
20 Pizzerija Bracera D2
21 Ristorante Spagho E3
22 Three Monkeys F3
Off map
Flumen Pub A1
Konoba Tarsa G2
Nebo A1
Trsatica G2

founded in Rijeka in 1875. Rijeka also became the site of the first oil refinery in Europe in 1882.

After World War I the Italian poet Gabriele D'Annunzio marched into town and, despite having no support from Italy, set up his own, short-lived regency here, from 1919 to 1921. Rijeka (Italian Fiume) became part of Mussolini's Italy in 1924, with the border running down the River Rječina, and the eastern suburb of Sušak lying across the border in what was then Yugoslavia. Following the end of World War II Rijeka became part of Yugoslavia, until Croatian independence in 1991.

GETTING THERE AND AWAY

BY AIR **Rijeka airport** (w rijeka-airport.hr), located on the island of Krk which is connected to the mainland by road bridge, has direct flights to the UK with Ryanair (w ryanair.com) and easyJet (w easyjet.com), via Zagreb with Croatia Airlines (w croatiaairlines.com), as well as other flights within Europe. A **shuttle bus** operated by Autotrolej connects the airport with Rijeka and Opatija (for timetables, see w visitrijeka.hr).

BY TRAIN Rijeka's **railway station** [140 A1] (Krešimirova 5) is a 5-minute walk west of the bus station. There are four trains a day to Zagreb (4–5 hours), with connections to Budapest and Venice, and two to Ljubljana (3 hours). For trains to Pazin there is a connecting bus service between Rijeka and Lupoglav. For timetables, see w hzpp.hr/en. There are plenty of city buses going from the centre to the railway station, including #1, #8 and #32.

BY BUS Rijeka is a major transport centre with regular buses from the rest of Croatia, including Zagreb (2½–3 hours; services almost every hour), Pula (90 minutes; at least 14 services daily), Pazin (1 hour; at least 6 services daily) and Poreč (90 minutes; at least 6 services daily). Timetables for Croatian buses serving Rijeka can be found at w akz.hr, w buscroatia.com or w autobusni-kolodvor.com. International services include Trieste, Ljubljana and Munich.

Rijeka's **bus station** [140 C2] (Trg Žabica 1; 060 302 010) is a 2-minute walk west from the Korzo, or 5 minutes' walk east of the railway station. It has several small shops and kiosks for emergency, last-minute snack-buying, including a bakery.

BY BOAT Rijeka is Croatia's largest port, and the main headquarters for the state-run ferry company, Jadrolinija (housed in a rather magnificent building on the waterfront at Riva 16; page 150) – so hardly surprisingly, it is very well served by ferry and catamaran. Jadrolinija has daily catamaran services to Cres and Mali Lošinj (3 hours) and to Rab and Novalja on the island of Pag (2½ hours). The **ferry terminal** [140 D4] (Riječki lukobran bb; 051 211 444) is located out on the jetty (allow a 5-min walk from the marina), and you can buy tickets here (buy catamaran tickets in advance if you can, as they tend to fill up) or online (w jadrolinija.hr).

BY CAR Rijeka is a 90-minute drive from Pula, 40 minutes from Pazin, 2½ hours from Zagreb, 4½ hours from Split and 90 minutes from Trieste.

GETTING AROUND

Rijeka's town centre is fairly compact and can easily be explored on foot, including getting to the bus and train stations and up the hill to Trsat. Local **buses** also ply

RIJEKA 2020

Rijeka's successful bid to become European Capital of Culture 2020 was a hugely impressive coup for this often much underrated city, given that it is the first Croatian city to gain this title, and that it was up against some stiff competition for the title, running against Dubrovnik, Osijek and Pula.

One of the founding principles of the European Capital of Culture (ECOC) initiative, when it was first launched in 1985, was (to quote from its own manifesto) 'to highlight the richness and diversity of cultures in Europe', and at the same time to encourage the long-term regeneration of a city, fostering the contribution of culture to its development. When the ECOC Commission awarded Rijeka the title for 2020, it acknowledged that other candidate cities satisfied the necessary criteria, but awarded the title to Rijeka based not only on the programmes the city had proposed for 2020, but also on 'all the things [Rijeka] is planning to realise in the years after it becomes ECOC 2020.' Among the key projects of Rijeka 2020 are the Sugar Palace (a beautifully renovated 18th-century mansion, part of the former sugar refinery and now the new home of the Museum of Rijeka) and the so-called 'Children's House', part of the former Rikard Benčić factory buildings which had remained derelict for years but now stand at the core of the city's new art quarter.

The Rijeka 2020 programme kicked off spectacularly, magnificently and unforgettably, with its opening performances on 1 February, culminating in the breathtaking *Opera Industriale*, with its genuinely amazing (and completely unexpected) rendition of the old anti-fascist song, *Bella Ciao* – which must count as one of the most moving musical performances I've ever been lucky enough to attend. Yes, I cried – as did most people I've spoken to since who attended the opening. Owing to the Covid-19 pandemic however, all performances and events from a couple of months after that were cancelled, with some, though not all, being rescheduled once Covid restrictions were lifted.

For more, see w rijeka2020.eu.

the centre as well as up to Trsat (#1B, 2 and #8) and west to Opatija (#32) and east to Pećine (#1). For more information on local buses in Rijeka, see w autotrolej.hr/en/routes. There are **taxi** stands at the bus station, railway station and on Matije Gupca, and several operators including Cammeo, which offers some of the best fares (☎ 051 313 313; w cammeo.hr/en/cities/rijeka), and Taxi Rijeka (m 091 500 3355; w taxirijeka.com). **Car-hire** services in Rijeka include Sixt (w sixt.co.uk/car-hire/croatia/rijeka/rijeka-railway-station) at Prolaz M Krucifikse Kozulic 3. Note that car-hire offices at Rijeka airport will be on the island of Krk! Rijeka's **TouRIst Bus** (w autotrolej.hr) offers tours of the city (as well as Trsat and Opatija) in eight languages between June and September. Tickets are valid 24 hours and cost €6.50 for adults, €4.50 for children (under fours free), which include entry to Trsat Castle. **Cycle** routes in the Rijeka area are listed at w bikerijeka.com/en. Download the app, which has maps and trail details for the 63km Rijeka Area Cycle Route together with information about accommodation and other services.

TOURIST INFORMATION

Rijeka's helpful and friendly **tourist information office** [140 E3] (Korzo 14; ☎ 051 335 882; e info@visitrijeka.hr; w visitrijeka.eu; ⏰ mid-Sep–mid Jun 08.00–19.30

Mon–Fri, 08.00–13.30 Sat, mid-Jun–mid-Sep 08.00–20.00 Mon–Sat, 09.00–14.00 Sun, with reduced hours on holidays) is conveniently located on the Korzo, amid myriad cafés and ice-cream vendors. Make sure you pick up a copy of the useful city map available here, which includes the centre as well as Trsat and Pećine. There are also two information points (*info punkt*) on the Riva and one at Trsat Castle.

WHERE TO STAY

Rijeka has several large hotels in the centre and out at Pećine, certainly enough to cater for the moderate number of visitors who stay here; most of them are owned by Jadran (w jadran-hoteli.hr). Several hostels have also opened in the city centre in recent years, and there are some fabulous places to stay between Rijeka and Opatija. Private rooms in the city centre are fewer than in more heavily touristed areas, though there are several; a good place to start looking for private accommodation is on the Rijeka Tourist Board website (w visitrijeka.eu).

HOTELS

✷ **Hilton Rijeka Costabella Beach Resort & Spa** [140 A1] (132 rooms, 62 suites & villas) Opatijska ulica 9; 051 600 100; e costabella.info@hilton.com; w hilton.com/en/hotels/rjkochi-hilton-rijeka-costabella-beach-resort-and-spa; all year. The big new recent opening in Rijeka is the Hilton Costabella, overlooking the sea on the road out to Volosko & Opatija (bus #32), which instantly outclasses anything this side of Volosko. Very stylish & modern, with spacious, luxurious rooms, all of which come with a balcony & suitably fabulous views across the head of the Kvarner Gulf. It has its own beach access, spa & swimming pools, restaurants including The Kitchen by Miljenko €€€€–€€€ &, for fine dining, the Michelin-starred Nebo €€€€€ (page 144), along with a lounge bar where you can sip cocktails & watch the sunset. **€€€€€**

Bonavia [140 E2] (87 dbls, 20 sgls, 7 suites) Dolac 4; 051 357 980; e bonavia@plavalaguna.com ; w plavalaguna.com/en/hotels/bonavia; all year. The 4-star Bonavia is centrally located just off the Korzo & is the most upmarket place to stay in the town centre, with its own wellness centre & highly rated restaurant, & prices to match. **€€€€€–€€€€**

Jadran [140 G3] (66 dbls, 3 apts) Šetalište XIII divizije 46, Pećine; 051 494 000; e jadran@jadran-hoteli.hr; w jadran-hoteli.hr; all year. The 4-star Jadran, which opened its doors in 1914, is along the coast at Pećine (a 20min walk into the centre of Rijeka, or a short ride on the #1 bus), right on the waterfront. Most rooms have sea views & balconies. **€€€€**

Continental [140 G3] (65 rooms, 4 suites) Šetalište Andrije Kačića-Miošića 1; 051 372 008; e continental@jadran-hoteli.hr; w jadran-hoteli.hr; all year. Partly renovated in 2008, with enough old-world charm & friendly staff (even under pressure upon the arrival of a tour bus), a broad terrace shaded by old trees where you can enjoy coffee or drinks & watch the world go by. On the east side of the Rječina & only 5mins' walk from the Korzo, the 3-star Continental was built in 1888 & is the oldest hotel in Rijeka still running. **€€€**

Neboder [140 G3] (54 dbls) Strossmayerova 1; 051 373 538; e neboder@jadran-hoteli.hr; w jadran-hoteli.hr; all year. While it may not be the most attractive building from the outside, the 14-floor Neboder can certainly claim some of the finest views in Rijeka from its upper rooms. The Neboder has friendly & helpful staff & is just around the corner from the Continental. **€€€**

✷ **Botel Marina** [140 D3] (35 rooms) Adamićev gat; 051 410 162; e info@botel-marina.com; w botel-marina.com/en; all year. Friendly, good value, fun & very central, Botel Marina is as its name implies – a renovated 1930s steamship, moored permanently on the waterfront. It has sgls, dbls, trpls & quads, & there's a bar & restaurant. **€€**

HOSTELS

There are more hostels listed at w visitrijeka.hr/hostel.

Fun Hostel [140 G3] (29 beds) Šetalište 13; m 091 121 9111; f funhostelrijeka; all year. Popular, colourful hostel by the beach, out towards Hotel Jadran. **€**

Hostel Korzo [140 E3] (8 beds) Korzo 18; 051 334 608; w hostel-korzo.com; all year. Central location right on the Korzo. Beds are arranged in a 6-bed dorm & a dbl with balcony. Clean & friendly. €
Hostel Kosy [140 F3] (22 beds) Užarska 1; m 091 222 3550; w booking.com/hotel/hr/hostel-kosy.en-gb.html; all year. Near the theatre, with clean, colourful rooms. Dorm beds & some dbls. Friendly staff. €
Hi Hostel Rijeka [140 G3] (61 beds) Šetalište XIII divizije 23, Pećine; 051 406 420; e rijeka@hicroatia.com; w hicroatia.com/en/hostel/hi-hostel-rijeka; all year. In a lovely 19th-century villa at Pećine, & only around a 15min walk into town (or a short hop on the #1 bus), this must be counted as one of the nicest youth hostels anywhere in Croatia. €

GUESTHOUSES AND PRIVATE ROOMS

InCenter Apartments [140 F3] (2 apts) Jelačićev trg 10; m 091 727 2596; w incenter.com.hr; all year. Clean & spacious, with a good location at the eastern end of the Korzo. €€
Old Town Inn [140 E2] (4 rooms) 13 Ul pod Voltun; m 095 910 6363; w oldtown.rest/; e info@oldtown.rest; all year. Smart, clean rooms in a renovated 19th-century building bang in the heart of the city centre. €€
Molo Lungo [140 D2] (6 rooms & apts) 1a Ul Trpimirova; w mololongoaccommodation.com/en or w booking.com/hotel/hr/integrated-molo-longo-central-apartments.en-gb.html; all year. Nice rooms & apartments with several locations across the city centre. €

CAMPING

Kamp Oštro [140 G2] Oštro 16, Kraljevića; 051 281 218; e ostro@jadran-hoteli.hr; w jadran-hoteli.hr; Apr–Oct. Around 24km southeast of Rijeka, this has 298 pitches (from €16pp for a pitch) & 20 apartments. €

WHERE TO EAT AND DRINK

Rijeka has several excellent restaurants, the majority of them not on the Korzo itself (which instead abounds in cafés and ice-cream shops) but in surrounding streets.

RESTAURANTS

Nebo [140 A1] 9 Ul Opatijska; 051 600 119; w neborijeka.com; all year. Michelin-starred Nebo is a top-notch fine-dining restaurant at the new Hilton Rijeka Costabella Beach Resort & Spa, where head chef Deni Serdoč creates impeccably prepared & presented 7- & 11-course degustation menus. €€€€€
Conca d'Oro (also known as Zlatna školjka) [140 D2] Kružna 12a; 051 213 782; concadorori; 11.00–23.00 daily. One of the best (& oldest – there's been a tavern here since 1885) restaurants in Rijeka, Conca d'Oro (the Golden Shell) serves a wide range of seafood, including traditional staples as well as inventive numbers such as Swiss chard parcels filled with warm-smoked fish terrine, in a mildly spicy bonito dashi with samphire. €€€€
Municipium [140 E2] Trg Riječke revolucije 5; 051 213 000; 11.00–23.00 Mon–Sat. Upmarket & fairly formal restaurant next to the Dominican monastery. €€€€
✷ **Konoba Feral** [140 F4] Matije Gupca 5b; 051 212 274; e info@konoba-feral.com; w konoba-feral.com; 08.00–midnight Mon–Sat, midday–18.00 Sun. Excellent & very reasonably priced seafood in a low-key, friendly & wholeheartedly traditional setting – this is the place to come for succulent grilled squid (*lignje na žaru*), mussels simmered in wine & garlic (*dagnje na buzaru*), seafood stew (*brodet*) & premium fish by the kilo. A local favourite, & not in the slightest bit stuffy. €€€
Konoba Tarsa [140 G2] J. Kulfaneka 10, Strmica, Trsat; 051 452 089; w tarsa-konoba.com; 08.00–22.00 daily. On the way up to Trsat you'll find this local favourite, serving hearty traditional dishes from ravioli with snails & bacon, to monkfish in white wine & capers served with gnocchi, or pork loin stuffed with mozzarella & prosciutto, sautéed with vegetables & potatoes (for 2). €€€
Pizzerija Bracera [140 D2] Kružna 12; 051 213 782; concadorori; 11.00–23.00 daily. Set in an atmospheric passageway off the Korzo, opposite (& under the same ownership as) Conca d'Oro, Bracera turns out good pizzas as well as other dishes – although based on my last couple of visits it's not as good as it used to be, & is perhaps resting

on its laurels somewhat. The brightly painted interior is decked out with artwork by Croatian painter Vjekoslav Vojo Radojčić, sports a traditional local fishing boat (*bracera*, whence its name), & there are tables in the passageway outside (where, if you're lucky, you might still get served). €€€

✷ **Ristorante Spagho** [140 E3] I Zajca 24a; 051 311 122; w ristorante-spagho.com; 11.30–22.30 Mon–Thu, 11.30–23.00 Fri/Sat, 12.00–22.30 Sun. Lovely, stylish little spaghetteria-pizzeria on the corner of I Zajca & I Henckea, with very friendly staff & a good wine list (including several types of Malvazija, & others, by the glass), serving what is without any doubt one of the best risottos with scampi I have ever tasted. €€€

Trsatica [140 G2] Šetalište J Rakovca 33; 051 452 716; w restaurant-trsatica.com; 10.00–23.00 daily. If you're up in Trsat for the afternoon or evening then this is the place to come for massive steaks & grills, or a whole hock on the large, breezy terrace with a view. They also have some vegetarian dishes such as stuffed courgettes & large salads. €€€

Bistro Mornar [140 E4] Riva Boduli 5a; 051 312 222; bistromornar; 08.00–22.00 daily. Well-priced bistro near the waterfront. €€

Maslina [140 E3] Koblerov trg bb; 051 563 563; w mnzt.hr; 11.00–23.00 Mon–Sat. Plenty of atmosphere on one of the nicest squares in the city centre, with a variety of dishes including several vegetarian & vegan options, & good pizzas which perhaps knock those of Bracera off their pedestal. €€€–€€

CAFÉS AND BARS In Rijeka you'll find a huge number of cafés & bars to choose from both on & off the Korzo, whether it's coffee, ice cream or cakes you're after. A few favourites are listed here, & the terrace in front of the Hotel Continental (page 143) is another good spot.

Book Caffe Dnevni Boravak [140 D2] Ciottina 12a; BookCaffeDB; 07.00–midnight Mon–Fri, 09.00–midnight Sat, 16.00–midnight Sun. Popular little café with live music some evenings.

✷ **Caffe Latino** [140 F3] Pavlinski trg 4a; 06.30–22.00 Mon–Fri, 07.00–14.00 Sun. One of my favourite cafés in Rijeka, on a square hidden away between the Korzo & Ante Starčevica, serving impeccable coffee at good prices.

Cukarikafe Bar [140 E2] Trg Jurja Klovića 4; cukarikafe; 08.00–midnight Mon–Thu, 08.00–02.00 Fri/Sat, 10.00–22.00 Sun. Popular little café near Sv Vida, with good coffee, a nice terrace & a cosy interior with painted wooden panelling.

Dulce Bolero [140 E3] Krešimirova 60; 07.00–22.00 Mon–Sat, 08.00–22.00 Sun. Popular ice-cream café with a wide range of flavours, just off the Korzo.

Flumen Pub [140 A1] Krešimirova 16a; 08.00–23.00 daily. Good local draft beers, between the bus & the railway stations.

Gelateria Corso [140 E3] Korzo 20; 07.00–23.00 Mon–Sat, 08.00–22.00 Sun. The most popular ice-cream café on the Korzo, with plenty of flavours to choose from.

King's Caffe [140 D2] Frana Kurelca 3a; w kings-caffe.com; 07.00–02.00 Mon–Fri, noon–02.00 Sat–Sun. A good place to go for craft beers (including from its own brewery). Can be smoky inside, in which case the King's Caffe [140 F4] at Verdieva 7b (which also serves food) might be a better bet.

Three Monkeys [140 F3] Fiumara 5; threemonkeysri; 07.00–midnight Mon/Wed, 07.00–02.00 Tue, 07.00–01.00 Thu, 07.00–03.00 Fri–Sat, 10.00–22.00 Sun. Hugely popular place whether for coffee or cocktails, with DJs some weekends.

ENTERTAINMENT AND NIGHTLIFE

Club BOA [140 F3] Ante Starčevica 8; 091 210 055; ClubBoaMalinskaRijekaRovinj; 06.00–02.00 Mon–Thu, 06.00–05.00 Fri–Sun. Club-bar just off one end of the Korzo, with live DJs, a lounge-bar-style interior & 2 terraces.

Croatian National Theatre [140 F4] Uljarska 1; 051 337 114; w hnk-zajc.hr. Theatre, opera & ballet performed in a magnificent late 19th-century building. Performances are often excellent, & ticket prices are much, much lower than in western Europe.

Rijeka Puppet Theatre [140 B1] Blaža Polića 6; 051 325 690; w gkl-rijeka.hr. Great for grown-ups as well as kids.

FESTIVALS

Riječki Karneval (Rijeka International Carnival) w visitrijeka.hr/rijecki-karneval. The main event on Rijeka's annual calendar (see opposite). Usually held in Feb.
Fiumare (Kvarner Sea & Maritime Tradition Festival) f Fiumare; Held late May/early Jun, on & around the Mrtvi kanal (once a centre of commerce in the city), with traditional boats & stands showcasing traditional crafts & local produce.
St Vitus Days On 15 Jun there is a series of events centred on Rijeka's patron saint, St Vitus (Sv Vida).
Fiumanka (International Sailing Regatta) w fiumanka.eu. Large sailing regatta held in the 2nd week of Jun.
Riječke Ljetne Noći (Rijeka Summer Nights) w hnk-zajc.hr/rljn. Music, theatre, opera, ballet & other performances throughout the city in Jun/Jul, from public squares to disused factory buildings to local beaches.
Jazz Time f jazztimeri. Long-running jazz festival, held in Nov.
Revija Lutkarskih Kazališta Rijeka (Rijeka Review of Puppet Theatres) w gkl-rijeka.hr. Rijeka has a long history of puppetry stretching back to the years following World War II, & the work of local & international puppet theatres is showcased in a series of performances at this annual event. Held in the first half of Nov.
Ri Rock w rirock.hr. Held in Dec, this is a long-running festival featuring new local bands, the central event of Rijeka's alternative music scene.

SHOPPING

Several supermarket chains have branches in the centre, including a Konzum on Vatroslava Lisinskog by the market, and there's a large Konzum at the Tower Centre.

Main Market (Velika Tržnica) [140 E4] ⌚ 06.00–14.00 Mon–Sat, 06.00–noon Sun. Rijeka's bustling main market occupies 3 attractive Art Deco buildings opposite the Modello Palace & near the National Theatre – 1 for fish, 1 for fresh & cured meats, 1 for cheese & dairy produce – with stalls selling vegetables, fruit & flowers spilling out along the streets surrounding these. The buildings date from 1880 and the early 1900s. Often just called the '*placa*' by locals, it is particularly busy on Fri & Sat mornings, & is well worth visiting whether you're self-catering or just want a vibrant glimpse of daily life here, with endless temptations to get sidetracked by coffee & freshly made *burek*.
Šta Da?! [140 D2] Užarska 14; ⌚ 08.00–20.00 Mon–Fri, 08.00–13.00 Sat. Named after the popular Rijeka catchphrase (meaning 'Really?!'), with locally made souvenirs.
Tower Center Rijeka [140 G3] Janka Polića Kamova 81a, Pećine; w tower-center-rijeka.hr; ⌚ 09.00–21.00 Mon–Sat, 10.00–21.00 Sun. Rijeka's largest shopping complex, outside the centre at Pećine, with around 150 shops on 5 floors as well as a cinema & an enormous car park.

OTHER PRACTICALITIES

Accident & emergency [140 A1] Krešimirova 42; ☎ 051 658 111; w kbc-rijeka.hr. Rijeka hospital has another site at Sušak, & there's a children's hospital at Kantrida (Istarska 43; ☎ 051 659 111).
Pharmacy [140 D2] Jadranski trg 1; ☎ 051 213 101; ⌚ 24hrs. At the western end of the Korzo & a 2min walk from the bus station. There's another 24hr pharmacy at Riva 18.
Post office [140 E3] Korzo 39; ⌚ 08.00–20.00 Mon–Fri, 08.00–13.00 Sat. The main post office is conveniently located at one end of the Korzo.

WHAT TO SEE AND DO

Rijeka has several sites worth visiting, and there's certainly enough to keep you busy for a day or two. Much of what you see of Rijeka today dates from the second half

RIJEKA CARNIVAL

Held on the last Sunday before Lent (usually February), the Rijeka Carnival (w visitrijeka.hr/rijecki-karneval) is now the second largest in Europe after Venice, attracting over 600,000 spectators from Croatia and overseas. Events are spread over several days, culminating in the International Carnival Parade – an enormous event with well over 10,000 participants, which sees a procession of floats and cavorting Croatians in outrageous costumes make their way through the streets of Rijeka. Expect dancing bees, prancing chimney sweeps and all manner of other entertainments, including the increasingly intoxicated, sheepskin-wearing *zvončari* or bell ringers (see page 148).

The parade sets off from the corner of the Riva and Riva Boduli, travelling east along Ivana Zajca to the Mrtvi kanal, then turns north and back along the Korzo, before returning to the Riva for ongoing festivities. Most people tend to watch from the Korzo, in which case you need to arrive early enough to get a decent view, but a better, 'insider' tip is to watch the parade from Ivana Zajca, where there are far fewer spectators – you can then cross to the Korzo later to catch some of the participants a second time around. It can take around 7 hours between the start of the parade and the last float arriving back on the Korzo, after which the party lasts well into the night.

Don't expect to be able to park in central Rijeka on the day of the parade, and if you're leaving Rijeka by bus or train the same evening, book your seat early in the day as a few thousand other people will also be leaving at the same time, and buses in particular fill up fast.

If you see only one carnival in Croatia, make sure it's this one – and if you're anywhere even remotely near Rijeka at this time of year, you'd be mad to miss it. This is the day (and night) when the city well and truly lets down its hair, and is without question one of the most wildly enjoyable events I've attended anywhere in the world.

of the 18th century and later: a massive earthquake flattened most of the city's older buildings in 1750.

At the heart of Rijeka's daily life is the **Korzo**, a broad pedestrian artery running from east to west through the city centre, lined with cafés. Partway along the Korzo (between Jadranski trg and Trg Republike Hrvatske) you'll find *The Walker*, a 2010 **sculpture** by Ivan Kožarić, one of Croatia's greatest modern artists, who died in 2020 and is perhaps most famous for his sculpture of the poet Antun Gustav Matoš sitting on a bench in Zagreb. Other sculptures in the centre include the Croatian avant-garde writer and satirist Janko Polić Kamov near Hotel Continental (he was born just round the corner in the suburb of Sušak in 1886).

The **City Tower** or **Clock Tower** (**Gradski toranj**) [140 E3] on the Korzo dates back to the medieval period and marks the site of one of the old city gates, though what you see now is Baroque. Note the imperial coat of arms above the arch, and the relief of the Austrian emperors Leopold and Charles VI.

Rijeka's **old town** occupied the area north of the Korzo, between the Korzo, Muzejski trg and Jelačićev trg, though little evidence of it remains today. The square beyond the City Tower, Trg Ivana Koblera, would once have been the site of the medieval town market. There's a **Roman arch** (**Stara vrata**) [140 E2] just off to the left as you walk from the City Tower to the cathedral, which probably gave access to a central compound in the old Roman town. The **Cathedral of St Vitus** (**Katedrala Sv vida**) [140 F2], the patron

ZVONČARI

The *zvončari* or 'bell ringers' – men dressed in sheepskins with elaborate, horned masks and headgear, stylised maces and with huge cowbells tied to their backsides – are among the most striking (and these days, best known) participants of the Rijeka Carnival. You will find references to them all over Rijeka, from tourist souvenirs and trinkets sold on the Korzo to a large mural near the Church of the Assumption. They come from the villages of the Kastav region (the mountainous area inland from Rijeka), and continue an old pagan tradition in which masked, bell-wearing figures would go from house to house in the village before Lent, driving out evil spirits which might have settled there during the preceding winter. There are several groups of *zvončari* from Kastav, including the Halubajski (w halubajski-zvoncari.com). They form part of a wider tradition which includes the *kurenti* of Slovenia, which feature prominently at the Ptuj Carnival. The *zvončari* were inscribed on the UNESCO List of Intangible Cultural Heritage in 2009.

saint of Rijeka, lies just uphill from the City Tower. Its unusual design is more or less unique in Croatia – a large rotunda, modelled on Santa Maria della Salute in Venice. It was built in the late 17th century on the remains of an earlier church (also dedicated to St Vitus) by the local Jesuits. Inside there's a 13th-century wooden crucifix from the earlier church with an interesting cult attached to it. It is said to have bled when a certain ne'er-do-well named Petar Lončarić threw a rock at it, after losing at gambling (and before he was immediately swallowed up by the earth).

Rijeka's must-see museum is the beautifully renovated **Sugar Palace** [140 A1] (Krešimirova 28; 051 336 711; w muzej-rijeka.hr/en/home; ⌚ 11.00–18.00 Tue–Sun; entry adult/child €8/€4), opposite the railway station and part of the Rijeka City Museum (Muzej Grada Rijeka) which is spread across three locations (see below). One of the key projects of Rijeka 2020, the Sugar Palace (part of a former sugar refinery) now houses a series of excellent displays covering the city's history, including fascinating sections on its industrial past, World War II, the development of the torpedo, the years under Communism and Rijeka's wonderfully vibrant music scene, from the birth of punk to bands like the legendary Let 3 (see opposite).

Next door to the Sugar Palace is Rijeka's **Museum of Modern and Contemporary Art (Muzej moderne i suvremene umjetnosti or MMSU**; Krešimirova 26c; 051 492 611; w mmsu.hr; ⌚ summer 11.00–20.00 Tue–Fri, 11.00–14.00 & 18.00–21.00 Sat/Sun, winter midday–19.00 Tue–Fri, midday–17.00 Sat/Sun; entry adult/child €4/€1.30) [140 A1], which has a major collection of works by modern and contemporary Croatian artists.

West from the cathedral on Žrtava fašizma (note the air-raid shelters on the opposite side, marked *sklonište*, and the massive masonry of the Palace of Justice) is Muzejski trg, which is where you'll find Rijeka's Maritime and Historical Museum and the old building of the Rijeka City Museum.

The old premises of the **Rijeka City Museum** (**Muzej Grada Rijeke**) [140 E1], now also called the 'Cube building' (Muzejski trg 1/1; 051 336 711; w muzej-rijeka.hr; ⌚ noon–18.00 Tue–Sat; entry adult/child €4/€2.50) is on Muzejski trg, just west of the cathedral on Žrtava fašizma (note the air-raid shelters on the opposite side, marked *sklonište*, and the massive masonry of the Palace of Justice). The Cube building has a variety of exhibits from the city's history, from ethnography to numismatics. There's a lapidarium, and the gardens are filled with old torpedoes (the modern torpedo was invented in Rijeka, and the world's first torpedo factory, the Robert Whitehead Torpedo Co, was founded in Rijeka in 1875). You can visit the **Rijeka Torpedo** exhibition, part of the City Museum, though it's only open by prior arrangement (Žabica 4; w muzej-rijeka.hr/en). It's possible to **buy a combined ticket** covering the different collections of the City Museum, including some of its temporary exhibitions – see w muzej-rijeka.hr/en/contact/#tickets.

Next door, the **Maritime and Historical Museum** [140 E1] (quite a mouthful in Croatian, **Pomorski povijesni muzej Hrvatskog primorja**) (Trg Riccarda Zanelle 1; 051 213 578; w ppmhp.hr; 09.00–18.00 Mon, 09.00–20.00 Tue–Sat, 09.00–16.00 Sun; entry adult/child €4/€2) has exhibits drawn from Rijeka's extensive maritime tradition, and is housed in the former **Governor's Palace (Guvernerova Palača)**, which dates from 1892. The Governor's Palace was built by one of the leading Hungarian architects of the time, Alajos Hauszmann, whose other works include the Parliament building in Budapest, though the exterior and grounds these days exude a rather sad air of neglect.

Two of Rijeka's larger **parks and gardens** are just to the northeast of the Governor's Palace: Mlaka Park and Nikola Host Park, both of which were laid out in the 19th century. For those who want a longer stroll, **Učka Nature Park** (page 137) along the coast above Lovran has miles of well-marked footpaths (page 187), as does the Gorski kotar region further inland and northeast of Rijeka, including Risnjak National Park (w np-risnjak.hr).

On **Revolution Square (Trg Riječke revolucije)** you'll find the **Dominican monastery and Church of St Jerome (Samostan i crkva sv Jeronima)** [140 E2], both of which, despite their Baroque appearance, formed part of an Augustinian monastic complex founded in the early 14th century. The church has the (rather faint) remains of frescoes on the vault of one of its chapels. To one side of the square is a stone pillar known as the **Stendarac**. This is where a flag was raised by the emperor Maximilian in memory of the city's loyalty during the (brief) Venetian occupation of 1508. Or rather, this is one of the places it was raised – the Stendarac originally stood in front of the old town hall, and changed its location several times after that. The relief at the top shows St Vitus holding a model of the city of Rijeka, and there are inscriptions from 1509, 1515 and 1766.

Over towards the Mrtvi kanal, near Pavlinski trg, is the **Church of St Mary of the Assumption (Crkva Unesenja Blažene Djevice Marije)** [140 F3], some of which dates back to the 15th century, though most of what you see now is 18th-century work, when

SOUNDS OF THE CITY

Rijeka has long held a reputation as the spearhead of the alternative music scene in Croatia. It was here in Rijeka that Paraf, the country's first punk band, was formed in late 1976. In their wake came Termiti, whose best-known song was 'Vjeran pas' (Faithful dog), and whose bass player Damir 'Mrle' Martinović went on to form Let 3, infamous for their wildly irreverent song lyrics and frenetic live performances (including performing naked with the exception of strategically placed dog muzzles). They're still around, with lead singer Zoran 'Prlja' Prodanović performing at the opening concert of Rijeka 2020, and Mrle having produced a pair of quite beautiful children's albums with his wife, singer Ivanka Mazurkijević (the duo are known, rather cleverly, as MrLee and IvaneSky). Let 3 were Croatia's entry into the Eurovision Song Contest in 2023. Don't miss the sound booth at the Sugar Palace (see opposite), where you can listen to some of Rijeka's flamboyant musical heritage.

a group of master craftsmen from Ljubljana were brought here to work on the church. The bell tower leans rather precariously, and has the date 1377 inscribed above the doorway. This was the location of the **forum** during Roman times – mosaics have been uncovered here, as well as evidence of a Roman bath – part of which became a focal point or meeting place for an early Christian cult during the 5th and 6th centuries.

Much of the area south of the Korzo is built on land reclaimed from the sea. The **Croatian National Theatre** (**Hrvatsko Narodno Kazalište**, or **HNK** for short) [140 F4] occupies a suitably lavish building near the Mrtvi kanal. There has been a theatre here since the mid 18th century, though this was rebuilt in 1806. The current building dates from 1885 (most of Croatia's National Theatre buildings are of a similar date and style), and was designed by specialised theatre architects Herman Gottlieb Helmer and Ferdinand Fellner of Vienna.

West of the National Theatre across a well-manicured square is the city's **main market** or *tržnica* (page 146). On the opposite side of Ivana Zajca are the richly decorated façades of the **Modello Palace** (**Palača Modello**) [140 F4], built at the same time (and by the same architects) as the National Theatre. The Serbian Orthodox **Church of St Nicholas** (**Crkva sv Nikole**) [140 E3], around the corner on Ivana Henckea, dates from 1790, and has some beautiful icons on the altar. The church was built by local Serbian families, who controlled much of the trade in Turkish goods brought to Rijeka by the late 18th century. Towards the western end of the Riva is the **Jadrolinija** building – one of the most beautiful in Rijeka – built in 1882, and known as the 'Adria Palace'. Its opulent yellow façades and sheer grandeur are perhaps the finest reflection of the city's pre-eminent maritime history. Just beyond the bus station you'll find the **Capuchin Church of Our Lady of Lourdes** (**Kapucinska crkva Gospe Lurdske**) [140 C2], built between 1904 and 1929, with its striking neo-Gothic striped masonry, atop a grandiose double staircase.

TRSAT Up behind the town centre to the northwest is the suburb of **Trsat** [140 G2], once the site of an Illyrian hillfort, later of Roman defences against barbarian incursions, and Austro-Hungarian defences against the Ottomans.

The 13th-century **castle** here, once a stronghold of the Frankopans, was purchased by Field Marshal Laval Nugent of Austria in 1826, and renovated in its current, Romantic style complete with a small temple (the Nugent family mausoleum) and boisterous-looking bronze dragon. Apparently George Bernard Shaw's aunt was also buried here, though the whereabouts of her and other tombs are now something of a mystery. There are wonderful views of the coast and the city below, and a small café on the breezy terrace where you can unwind.

What brings people up here in their thousands, however, is the nearby **Sanctuary of Our Lady of Trsat** (**Crkva Gospe Trsatske**), one of the largest pilgrimage sites in Croatia, which according to popular belief was the site where the wood from the Virgin Mary's house remained between 1291 and 1294, on its journey from Nazareth to Loreto in Italy. Following the departure of these holy relics, a miraculous icon (the Image of Our Lady of Trsat) was given to the population by Pope Urban V in 1367, and the local Frankopans built a small church to house it in (though the icon you see now is a copy). The current church and Franciscan monastery date from the late 17th century. Pope John Paul II joined the pilgrimage to Trsat in July 2003, and a larger-than-life-sized sculpture of him can be found in front of the church, his bronze hand now worn smooth by tens of thousands of passing faithful.

You can walk up to Trsat, following Stube Petra Kružića (also known as 'Trsatske stube'), a long flight of over 500 steps leading uphill from the corner of Titov trg, the route followed by pilgrims – otherwise take bus #55 or #8 from the Riva.

9

The Slovenian Adriatic

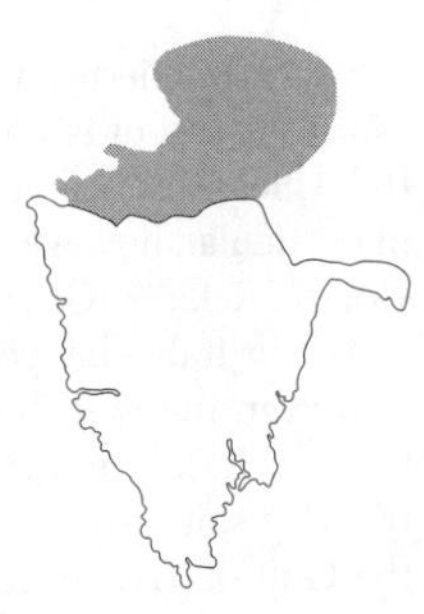

Country code +386

Geographically and culturally, Istria extends into Slovenia, in fact beyond the coastal municipalities into some of the fabulous landscape of the Karst region. The coastal towns of the Slovenian Adriatic – Koper, Izola, Piran and Portorož – are each little gems and a walk, cycle or drive along them reveals a lush and rich panorama of seaside activity. The main town of **Koper** has a rich architectural history and is an important port where luxury cruise liners are known to dock. At the other end of this set of coastal towns, **Portorož** holds natural hot-spring facilities and spas, and the whole coastline entered another league of sophistication when the Kempinski Palace opened in Portorož in 2008. However, for many, Piran is the jewel in the Slovenian Adriatic crown.

Because of the ease and proximity of visiting the impressive **Postojna Cave** (**Postojuska jama**) and UNESCO-listed **Škocjan Caves** (**Škocjanske jame**), as well as the world-famous Lipizzaner stud farm at **Lipica** and the beautiful Vipava Valley with its excellent wines and hikes, these are also included in this chapter and can be visited either as day trips or over several days.

HISTORY

The history of the Slovenian Adriatic followed a very similar course to the northwest coastal area of the rest of Istria, and was essentially ruled by Venice or its predecessors until the fall of the Serenissima Republic in 1797. At this point the whole of geographical Istria became part of the Holy Roman Empire and became known as the Austrian Littoral (*Küstenland*). With the fall of the Holy Roman Empire, rule of the *Küstenland* passed briefly to the Napoleonic Kingdom of Italy from 1806 to 1813, before the reconstituted Austrian Empire wrested the *Küstenland* back again for just over a century from 1814 to 1918.

SLOVENIA AT A GLANCE

Country name	Republic of Slovenia (Republika Slovenija)
Official language	Slovene
Population	1,964,036 (2022 census)
Area	20,273km^2
Capital	Ljubljana
Time	CET (Central European Time, GMT+1/BST+1)
Currency	Euro (€)
International dialling code	+386
Electricity	220V AC (standard European round two-pin plug)

By 1918, Trieste had already won autonomy from the *Küstenland*, and after World War I the rest of Istria was also given to Italy in recognition of the latter siding with the Allies. Fascist Italianisation of the region was vehemently opposed by Slovenes in particular, however, and thus was born the first anti-fascist organisation, Trst Istra Gorizia Reka (TIGR, standing for Trieste, Istria, Gorizia and Rijeka).

When Italy changed sides in World War II, most of Istria went to Yugoslavia. However, the Free Territory of Trieste established under United Nations Security Council Resolution 16 on 10 February 1947 created an internationally administered free city-state around Trieste. In the shape of a bottom-heavy crescent moon around the Gulf of Trieste from Duino in the north to the Mirna River in the south, the area was divided into Zone A (now in Italy) and Zone B. Zone A was administered by British and American forces, while Zone B was administered by Yugoslavia. In 1954, the Free Territory was officially dissolved in the London Memorandum, and Italy formally took over the rule of Zone A, with the exception of a few villages on the border with Zone B.

After Slovenia and Croatia both declared independence from Yugoslavia in 1991, they disputed claims by the other over the division of the border and sea in the Piran Gulf, with Slovenia insisting that it had policed the gulf up to Savudrija during Yugoslav times. This dispute initially blocked the entry of Croatia into the EU, until after the resignation of Croatia's prime minister Ivo Sanader in July 2009, when both countries agreed to have the dispute arbitrated internationally. Croatia subsequently withdrew from the arbitration process in 2015 following allegations that Slovenia had breached the rules of the arbitration tribunal.

GETTING THERE AND AROUND

From further afield, Koper is the main gateway to the Slovenian Adriatic, with trains to Ljubljana and buses along the coast including Izola and Piran. From Croatian Istria many will drive in and out of the area via the smaller Sečovlje border crossing connection with Portorož rather than take the main border crossing at Dragonia, where queues at the border can take longer. **Trieste airport** (w triesteairport.it/en) is a 40-minute drive from Koper; that from Ljubljana and Pula airports is each around 1 hour 20 minutes. **Portorož international airport** (w portoroz-airport.si) is used mainly for panoramic flights and flight training, and some charter flights. **Venezia Lines** (w venezialines.com) runs fast **hydrofoil** services between Venice and Rovinj, calling at Piran. Or, best of all, hire bikes and **cycle** along the **Parenzana** which runs from Grožnjan and beyond in Croatian Istria to Piran, Izola and Koper (page 117).

AIRPORT TRANSFERS Taxis are expensive, and public buses to the airports are non-existent (except for Trieste airport to Trieste central station on bus #51; w triestetrasporti.it). An economical option is to book a transfer through **Goopti** (w goopti.com), whose online booking system allows them to combine requests and usually offer a minibus service to and from the airport.

BY TRAIN Five trains a day run in each direction between Ljubljana and the end of the railway line in Koper (Kolodvorska 11; w potniski.sz.si/en), with a journey time of around 2½ hours. Trains run via Divača (the jumping-off point for Škocjan Caves, or for the train to Sežana, the nearest station to Lipica) and Postojna (for Postojna Cave and Predjama Castle). Over the past few years the section of the journey between Koper and Divača has been replaced with a bus service on some,

ARRIVING FROM LJUBLJANA OR TRIESTE

Istria, and in particular the Slovenian Adriatic coast, are easily reached from Trieste in Italy and the Slovenian capital, Ljubljana – both of which have direct flights to the UK and are fascinating destinations in themselves. With this in mind, here are a few travel essentials for these two gateway cities.

LJUBLJANA A regular bus service links **Ljubljana Airport** (Ljubljana Jože Pučnik Airport; w lju-airport.si) with Ljubljana railway/bus station (w arriva.si or w ap-ljubljana.si/en). The **Ljubljana Tourist Office** (w visitljubljana.com) is near the Triple Bridge (Adamič-Lundrovo nabrežje 2; +3861 306 1215). A **Ljubljana Card** gets you free entry into 15 attractions, as well as free travel on city buses. There are direct **rail** (w potniski.sz.si/en) and **bus** (w ap-ljubljana.si) services to the Slovenian coast. **Hotel Cubo** (Slovenska cesta 15; +3861 425 6000; w hotelcubo.com; **€€€€**) is a fabulous boutique hotel; **B&B Slamič** (Kersnikova ulica 1; +3861 433 8233; w slamic.si/en; **€€€**) is a good mid-range choice.

TRIESTE There's a regular bus service (w aptgorizia.it) between **Trieste Airport** (Trieste – Friuli-Venezia Giulia Airport; w triesteairport.it/en) and Trieste. The **Trieste Tourist Office** (w discover-trieste.it & w turismofvg.it) is on the corner of Piazza Unità d'Italia (Via dell'Orologio 1; +39 335 742 9440). An **FVG Card** gives free access and discounts at attractions all over Friuli-Venezia Giulia. From Trieste there are **buses** to Koper and Pula (w flixbus.co.uk). **Duchi d'Aosta** (Piazza Unità d'Italia 2; +39 40 760 0011; w duchi.eu; **€€€€€**) is a grand old hotel on the main square; **L'Albero Nascosto** (Via Felice Venezian 18; +39 40 300 188; w alberonascosto.it; **€€€**) is an exceptionally beautiful and welcoming little B&B.

though not all journeys (there are usually a couple of direct intercity journeys a day), an arrangement that seems set to continue for the foreseeable future. The intercity trains have a dedicated bicycle and luggage wagon.

BY BUS There is a regular bus service (w arriva.si) that runs the entire length of the coastal road every 15–25 minutes between Koper and Portorož via Izola and Piran.

Koper **bus station** (Dantejeva ulica 4) is co-located with the train station. Buses to regional destinations run frequently (at least four services a day to Postojna), with buses also going to Trieste and to towns in Croatian Istria (twice daily to Pula for example). Sunday buses run less frequently than during the rest of the week. For timetables, see w ap-ljubljana.si or w arriva.si.

BY BOAT A myriad options are available from **Venice and Trieste** into the region in high season, especially at weekends. **Venezia Lines** (w venezialines.com) operates a service to Piran in summer, with a journey time of around 2 hours 30 minutes. Boat-taxis between ports (but not internationally) are also popular, and can easily be picked up from the ports.

BY CAR Getting to the Slovenian Adriatic is easy by motorway, but beware that all the towns are pedestrianised, although well served also by frequent bus services and by park and ride. Note that the use of Slovenian motorways requires an e-vignette

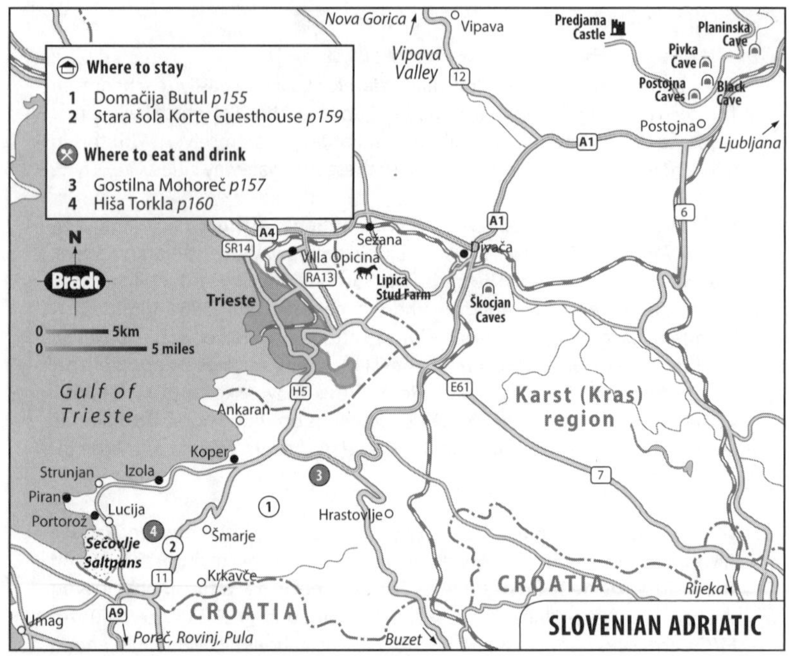

(**w** evinjeta.dars.si/en), a stickerless toll payment which can be bought online and costs €15 for a weekly pass for a class 2A vehicle (which will include most cars). For car hire see under *Tourist information*, below.

BY BICYCLE It's perfectly possible to cycle around most of the Slovenian Adriatic, and it's by far the best way to enjoy the coast, the whole length of which lies on the Parenzana cycle route. To hire bicycles, see under individual towns.

TOURIST INFORMATION

The official tourist information (**w** slovenia.info) bureaux for Slovenian towns are very helpful, with heaps of free useful brochures and friendly knowledgeable staff. They also have lots of free maps, including for local hiking and biking routes, as well as small general maps. Individual bureaux are listed under each town.

For tour operator services including **car hire**, try **Topline** (Obala 114, 6320 Portorož; ☎056 747 161; **e** info@topline.si; **w** topline.si) for tourism services within Slovenia, or **Kompas** (Pristaniška 17, 6000 Koper; ☎05 6630 584; **e** vednozvami@kompas.si; **w** kompas.si) for onward travel.

KOPER

The tightly packed old town of Koper is a real gem, with its impressive Praetorian Palace, campanile and loggia dominating the main square Titov trg. Its narrow cobbled streets hide exquisite little shops selling Slovenian brands at very reasonable prices, including a chocolate shop, the Salt Museum shop and a handmade shoe shop. This is Slovenia's major port and as a result has a busy dock life only a few steps from the heart of the town.

HISTORY Koper was an island until the 1930s. The ancient Greek name for Koper was Aegida. Then under the Romans it became known by its local name Capraria, 'goat island', and the surrounding shallow waters were used to harvest salt. In 1278, Koper joined the Republic of Venice, after which the town walls were slowly demolished and the local saltworks were enlarged. As Koper grew in significance, it became the capital of Venetian Istria, and was known as Caput Histriae, the 'head of Istria'. Today's Italian name, Capodistria, is rooted in this.

Koper's economic standing in the larger Piran Bay was seriously dampened in 1719 when Trieste became a free port of the Holy Roman Empire. During the 19th century, the salt pans gradually fell into disuse as the price of salt dropped. Under Italian rule after World War I, the area around Koper was drained and reclaimed and Koper ceased to be an island. As a result, the local bay of Škocjan behind Koper became a lagoon and is now an important reserve for marine and wetland wildlife.

In the census of 1900, 92% of Koper was Italian. Today, Slovenes make up over 70% of the town after the majority of the Italian population voluntarily left when Zone B was handed to Yugoslavia in 1954. The Roman Catholic diocese of Koper, which had been merged with that of Trieste in 1828, did not separate again from Trieste until 1977.

GETTING AROUND The old town is pedestrianised. **Buses** #1 and #55 (for timetables see w arriva.si/en/passenger-transport/city-bus-transport/city-transport-koper) leave from the train and bus station 156 G3] in the southeastern quarter of the town. It's a 20-minute walk from the station to the old town. Tickets need to be bought in advance, as it is no longer possible to buy them on the bus. Several **taxi** companies operate from the station, around the edge of the town, along the coast and to Trieste airport, eg: Taxi Srečko (m 040 386 000; w taxisrecko.si); and **Taxi Morje** (041 222 111; w taxi-koper.si).

Bicycle hire is available at **Istranka Tours** [156 A3] (Ulica XV Maja 10; 056 272 140; w istrankatours.com) and there's a list of bike rental outfits on the tourist office website (w visitkoper.si/en) – go to 'Schedule visit' and then 'Frequently asked questions'.

TOURIST INFORMATION **Tourist information** [156 B3] (Titov trg 3; 056 646 403; e tic@visitkoper.si; w visitkoper.si/en; summer 09.00–20.00 Mon–Sat, 09.00–13.00 Sun, winter 09.00–17.00 Mon–Sat) is grandly located in the Praetorian Palace. It is very well stocked with free information and maps, and its website is a good place to find lots of local accommodation, especially self-catering and rural farms.

WHERE TO STAY

Hotel Grand Koper [156 B4] (60 rooms) Pristaniška ulica 3; 056 100 500; e hotel@grandkoper.com; w grandkoper.com. Opened in 2021, this supremely stylish design hotel right on the waterfront has immediately shot to the top of the list of places to stay in Koper. It has also a very good restaurant, Capra (page 157). **€€€€**

Domačija Butul [map, opposite] (3 dbls, 2 apts) Manžan 10d; m 041 718 219; e info@butul.net; w butul.net. Smart rooms & very highly rated home-cooked food, 5mins outside town. **€€€**

Hostel Histria [156 C4] (34 beds in 6- & 8-bed dorms) Ulica pri velikih vratih 17; w hihostels.com/hostels/koper-youth-hostel-histria. Very nice dorms in a renovated stone house above the Lord Byron pub. **€€**

Hostel Museum [156 B3] (38 beds in sgl/dbl/trpl rooms & 8-bed dorm) Muzejski trg 6; 041 504 466; w hostel-museum.com. Central location, close to beach, with terrace & BBQ facilities. **€€**

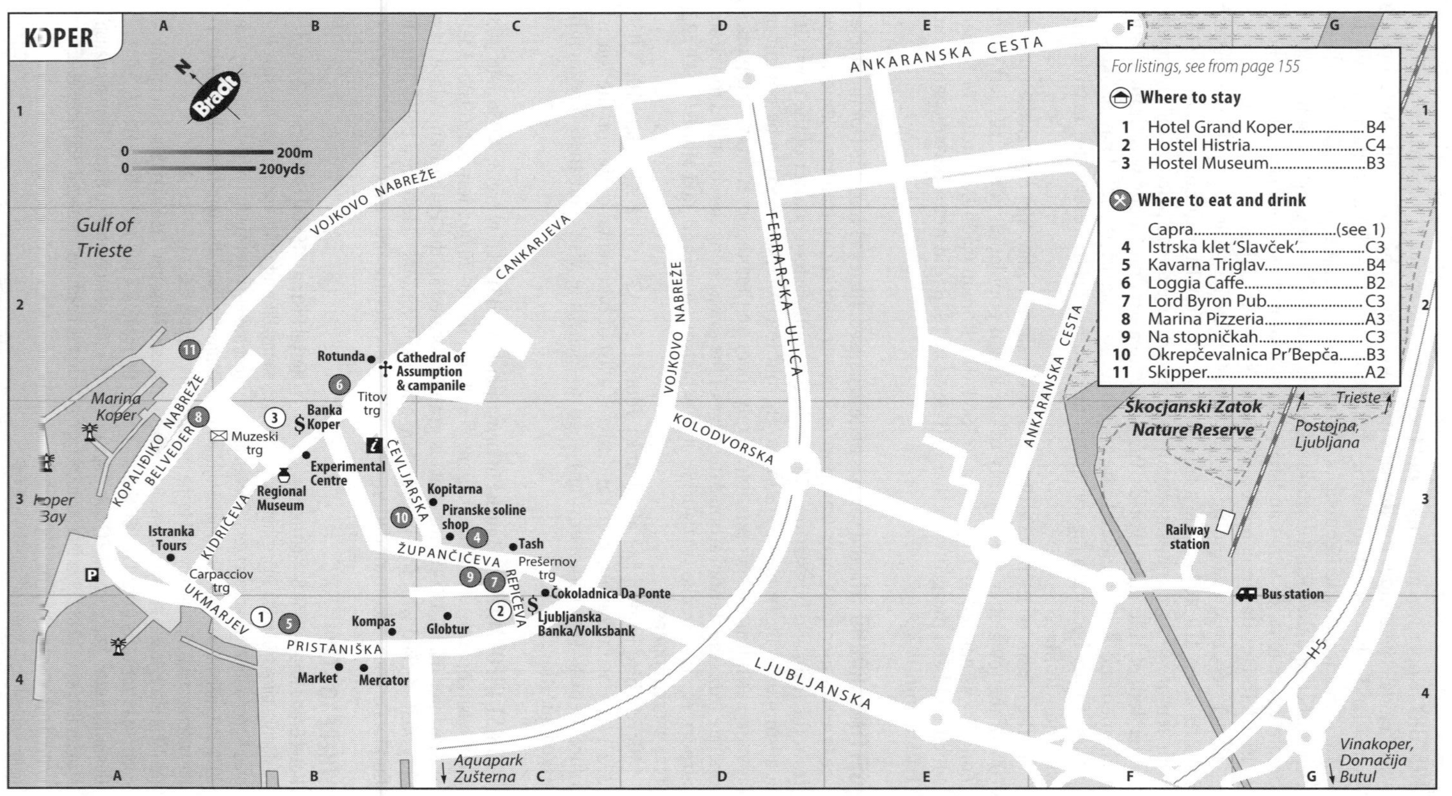
KOPER
Bradt
0 200m
0 200yds
Gulf of Trieste
Koper Bay
Marina Koper
VOJKOVO NABREŽE
CANKARJEVA
KOPALIĐIKO NABREŽE
BELVEDER
KIDRIČEVA
UKMARJEV
PRISTANIŠKA
ČEVLJARSKA
ŽUPANČIČEVA
REPIČEVA
FERRARSKA ULICA
KOLODVORSKA
LJUBLJANSKA
ANKARANSKA CESTA
H5
Rotunda
Cathedral of Assumption & campanile
Titov trg
Banka Koper
Muzeski trg
Experimental Centre
Regional Museum
Kopitarna
Piranske soline shop
Tash
Prešernov trg
Čokoladnica Da Ponte
Ljubljanska Banka/Volksbank
Istranka Tours
Carpacciov trg
Kompas
Globtur
Market
Mercator
Aquapark Žusterna
Railway station
Bus station
Škocjanski Zatok Nature Reserve
Trieste
Postojna, Ljubljana
Vinakoper, Domačija Butul
For listings, see from page 155
Where to stay
1 Hotel Grand Koper....B4
2 Hostel Histria....C4
3 Hostel Museum....B3
Where to eat and drink
Capra....(see 1)
4 Istrska klet 'Slavček'....C3
5 Kavarna Triglav....B4
6 Loggia Caffe....B2
7 Lord Byron Pub....C3
8 Marina Pizzeria....A3
9 Na stopničkah....C3
10 Okrepčevalnica Pr'Bepča....B3
11 Skipper....A2

WHERE TO EAT AND DRINK

Capra [156 B4] Pristaniška ulica 3; 056 100 500; e hotel@grandkoper.com; w grandkoper.com; 07.00–22.00 Sun–Fri. 'Jazz fusion' is how this top-notch restaurant at the new Grand Hotel Koper describes itself, where head chef Marja Černe works with locally sourced seasonal ingredients, & seafood takes pride of place. €€€

Gostilna Mohoreč [map, page 154] Kubed 66a, Gračišče; 056 532 114; w mohorec.si; midday–22.00, Thu–Sun. For those who fancy heading out of town on 2 wheels or 4 (or if you're driving towards Postojna or Škocjan Caves, it would be a short detour off the main road), this well-regarded *gostilna* in the village of Kubed is a good place to stop for lunch – it's around 11km from Koper, heading towards the village of Gračišče. Good traditional Slovenian dishes prepared from local, seasonal produce, a warm welcome & a nice terrace. €€€

Istrska klet 'Slavček' [156 C3] Župančičeva 39; 056 276 729; istrskakletslavcek; 07.00–22.00 Sun–Fri. A small local place offering grilled meat & Slovenian stews. €€€

Marina Pizzeria [156 A3] Kopališko nabrežje 2; 056 271 982; w pizzeriamarina.business.site; midday–22.00 Tue–Sun. A wide variety of pizzas & seafood in this busy restaurant above the dock. €€€

Skipper [156 A2] Kopališko nabrežje 3; 056 261 810; restarvracija.skipper; 10.00–22.00 daily. In a modern building above the working docks, this is a popular place with dock staff. Good solid food, & some interesting twists including scampi soup. €€€

Na stopničkah [156 C3] Gortanov trg 12; 031 680 075; nastopnickahkoper; 11.00–23.00 daily. Nice vegetarian & vegan place – a rare find in these parts. Friendly owners, good food & coffee, colourful décor (bright-blue walls & red chairs) & very good value. €€

Okrepčevalnica Pr'Bepča [156 B3] Čevljarska 36; 09.00–22.00 Mon–Fri. A tiny welcoming place with a big window opening on to the street. Fast-food-style Italian eatery, under new management since 2020. €€

Kavarna Triglav [156 B4] Pristaniška 5; w kavarnatriglav.si; 07.00–midnight daily. Formerly Caffe Oro, this place next to the Hotel Grand Koper does the most amazing array of cakes, including to order (& even gluten, egg or sugar free).

Loggia Caffe [156 B2] Titov trg 1; w loggia-koper.com; 08.30–10.30 Mon–Fri, 09.00–23.00 Sat–Sun. There is nowhere better than the Loggia to view & enjoy the architectural delights of this Gothic square. Great range of drinks & ice creams, & I ate the scrummiest apple buns here with cream fondant icing.

Lord Byron Pub [156 C3] Repičeva 2; Lord Byron Pub; 07.00–midnight Mon–Thu, 07.00–01.00 Fri, 08.00–01.00 Sat, 09.00–midnight Sun. Inside, this looks just like an English pub, except that there's waiter service.

SHOPPING Koper is a great place to shop for interesting gifts. Čevljarska and Župančičeva streets hide a myriad little shops mostly sporting very good-quality Slovenian clothes and shoe brands that are sold worldwide. L'Occitane toiletries is about as international as it gets in the old town, and there's even an old-fashioned haberdashery at Čevljarska 43.

Čokoladnica Da Ponte [156 C3] Župančičeva 38; m 040 981 152/041 504 863; w cokoladnicadaponte.si; 07.30–19.00 Mon–Fri, 08.00–noon Sat. This is Koper's 1st chocolate shop. A bewildering array of pralines fill the small shop's counter, & they sell their own brand of teas & coffee beans. The milk chocolate with lavender, & the dark chocolate with salt flower are local specialities.

Kopitarna [156 C3] Cnr of Ulica Osvobodilne fronte & Čevljarska ulica; 056 279 088; w kopitarna.com; 08.00–19.00 Mon–Fri, 08.00–13.00 Sat. If you can't afford Tash in time or money, then Kopitarna does very reasonable Slovenian-made shoes.

Piranske soline [156 C3] Župančičeva 40; w soline.si/en/shops/koper; 09.00–17.00 Mon–Sat. A branch of the Sečovlje Salt Museum shop. Here you can get candles, body scrubs & lotions, bath salts & soaps, salt grinders, kitchen utensils, recipe books &, of course, salt. Fascinating.

Tash [156 C3] Župančičeva 43; m 040 599 344; e info@tash.si; w tash.si; 09.00–17.00 Mon–Fri. If you want a truly amazing pair of handmade leather shoes, this is the place to come.

OTHER PRACTICALITIES

Pharmacy Obalne Lekarne, Kidričeva 2; 056 110 000; w obalne-lekarne.si; 07.30–19.00 Mon–Fri, 07.30–13.00 Sat, 08.00–noon Sun. This is the head branch of a chain of pharmacies along the Slovenian coast, with online ordering available. Well-informed English-speaking staff.

Post office [156 B3] Muzeski trg 3; 08.00–19.00 Mon–Fri, 08.00–noon Sat

WHAT TO SEE AND DO **Titov trg** [156 B2] is the place to start your look around the historic old town. On the north side is the 15th-century loggia, now a prestigious café downstairs (page 157) and a small art gallery upstairs, **Loža Gallery** (**Galerija Loža**) (Tartinijev trg 3; 056 712 080; w obalne-galerije.si; mid-Jun–mid-Sep 09.00–noon & 18.00–22.00 Tue–Sun, mid-Sep–mid-Jun 10.00–17.00 Tue–Sun; entry €3). On the eastern flank is the 12th-century **Cathedral of the Assumption** (**Stolnica Marijinega vnebovzetja**) [156 B2] containing a Vittore Carpaccio Renaissance painting of 1516, the *Sacra Conservatione*. The cathedral's **campanile** (09.30–13.30 & 16.00–18.00 daily; entry €5) holds one of Slovenia's oldest bells, dating from 1333. At 36m high, the campanile is another miniature of St Mark's in Venice, and gives the best view of the tightly woven streets of the town, as well as of the working docks and the whole bay of Piran. To the north of the cathedral is the **Rotunda of John the Baptist** (**Rutunda Janeza Krstnika**) [156 B2]. On the southern side of the square is the entrance to the **Praetorian Palace (Pretorska palača)**, which used to be the seat of the Venetian-era mayor and is now the tourist information bureau. The remainder of the palace takes up the entire flank of the western side of the square.

Koper Regional Museum (Pokrajinski muzej Koper)

[156 B3] (Kidričeva 19; m 041 556 644; w pokrajinskimuzejkoper.si; May–Aug 08.00–16.00 Tue–Fri, 09.00–17.00 Sat–Sun; entry €5 for Belgramoni Palace, or €6 covering all venues inc Belgramoni Palace & the Ethnographic Collection on Bramsci trg, & valid for 2 days) The museum is located in Belgramoni Palace on what is now known as Muzeski trg. Among the usual everyday items preserved as a record of life in the past, the museum also holds a copy of the 12th-century painting of the ***Dance of Death***, the original of which lies in Trinity Church in Hrastovlje (there is also another *Dance of Death* in Beram; page 107). Next door is the **Experimental Centre** (**Center eksperimentov**) [156 B3] (Kidričeva 17; 056 272 077; w centereksperimentov.si; 09.00–13.00 & 16.00–19.00 Mon–Fri, 09.00–13.00 & 15.00–18.00 Sat; entry free), which those with children might find a lot more fun than the museum. All ages can find out how machines work, explore gravity and take part in creativity workshops.

Towards the far end of Kidričeva are the **churches** of St Nicholas (dating from the late 16th century, and formerly the seat of the Brotherhood of Sailors and Fishermen) and of the Holy Trinity (18th century), as well as the Totto Palace (note the Venetian lion on the façade), and two timber medieval houses at Nos 31 and 33. **Carpacciov trg** [156 B3] at the end of the street holds more Venetian buildings, cafés and the nearby Hotel Koper, all looking out on the sea. From here a long **walkway** lined with benches stretches out towards Izola, and eventually becomes a cycle path along the edge of the sea. St Anne's monastery on Destradijev trg, on the eastern side of the old town, has a nice cloister.

ACTIVITIES

Aquapark Zušterna

[156 C4] (Istarska 67; 056 100 304; w terme-catez.si/en/slovenian-coast/aquapark-zusterna; 09.00–21.00 daily; 3hrs' entry €12 adults/€8 children aged 4–14 Mon–Fri, €16.50/€11 Sat/Sun, under 4 years free; tickets for 2hrs & day tickets also available) An extensive water park, but with limited restaurant facilities (considering you are not meant to bring your own food). The **public lido and beach** opposite Zušterna, on the sea-side of the main road, is better value for money (entry €3).

Škocjanski Zatok Nature Reserve [156 F3] (Bertoški bonifika; ☎ 056 260 370; e info@skocjanske-zatok.org; w skocjanski-zatok.org; ⏲ Jan–Jun 07.00–21.00 daily, Jul–Dec 09.00–16.00 daily; visitor centre open shorter hours & closed Mon; entry free) A birdwatcher's paradise as well as for all nature aficionados. Paths criss-cross the reserve and the Parenzana cycle trail (page 117) skirts part of its edge. Guided tours for groups are available during the week (09.00–14.00; limited numbers so booking up to 2 weeks in advance recommended; €50 for up to 15 people).

IZOLA

Originally an island, and caught between its larger neighbours Koper and Piran, Izola has a history of struggling for autonomy and independence. The Roman town and port of Haliaetum was just southwest of the current town from at least 2BC, but the island of Izola itself only saw settlement with the arrival of refugees from Aquileia during the constant conflicts there in the 7th century. Known for harbouring pirates and rebels, in 1253 it declared independence, but by 1267 it joined the Republic of Venice at the same time as Poreč, 16 years before Piran and 20 years before Koper.

Thermal springs were found in Izola in 1820, thus starting its life as a **spa and wellness destination**. The town walls were demolished and used to fill the narrow stretch of sea separating the island from the mainland, which until then had only been connected by a stone bridge. From 1902 to 1935 it was connected to Trieste and Poreč by the Parenzana railway line. Today it thrives as the **arts, film and music capital** of the Slovenian coast.

GETTING AROUND Izola is small enough to walk around. To go further afield, **bicycle hire** is available at **Rentabike Izola** (Prešernova cesta 4a; ☎ 070 714 748; e rentabikeizola@gmail.com; w en.rentabikeizola.com; €20 for 10hrs). Izola's main **bus** stop is outside the main post office on Cankarjev Drevored.

Taxis are available at **Taxi Izola** (m 040 602 602) and there are more operators listed at w visitizola.com/en/info/basic-info. For those arriving by private boat, **Marina Izola** (Tomžiceva 4a; ☎ 056 625 400; e izola@marinaup.com; w marinaup.com/en) has 700 berths and 24-hour landing assistance.

TOURIST INFORMATION Izola **tourist information centre** (Ljubljanska 17; ☎ 056 401 050; e tic.izola@izola.si; w visitizola.com/en; ⏲ Jul/Aug 09.00–21.00 Mon–Sat, 09.00–noon Sun, Sep–Jun 09.00–18.00 Mon–Fri, 09.00–noon Sat) is very helpful and offers listings of local accommodation as well as all the other tourist attractions in the area, plus good local maps.

WHERE TO STAY *Map, page 161, unless otherwise stated*

Hotel Marina (52 rooms) Veliki trg 11; ☎ 056 604 100; e recepcija@hotelmarina.si; w hotelmarina.si. Right next to the centrally located harbour, with views on to the sea, friendly & welcoming staff, a large terrace restaurant, & a small wellness centre where you can hire the massage pool just for private use. **€€€€**

Stara šola Korte Guesthouse [map, page 154] (17 rooms, 2 apts) Korte 74; ☎ 056 421 114; e info@starasolakorte.com; w oleander.si/starasola. As its name in Slovene says, this is literally an old school. Beautifully refurbished, it is bright & cheerful with fantastic surroundings, lovely terrace, grand old stairs, a canteen, & a small library in the old principal's office. Very bicycle friendly. Rooms have 1–4 beds (& 1 has a jacuzzi). While not by the sea, it is worth going out of your way for. Under 6 years free, 7–14 years 50% discount. **€€€€–€€€**

Lighthouse Izola (6 apts) Gramscijeva ul 9; w booking.com/hotel/si/lighthouse-izola.en-gb.html. Beautifully decorated & right on the waterfront. **€€€**

Hostel Alieti (25 beds in 4/5/6-bed dorms) Dvoriščna 24; 051 670 680; e info@hostel-alieti.si; w hostel-alieti.si. Hostel in the centre of the old town, near Trg Manzioli. **€€**

WHERE TO EAT AND DRINK *Map, opposite, unless otherwise stated*

Gostilna Sidro Sončno nabrežje 24; 056 414 711; f RESTAVRACIJASIDRO; 09.00–22.00 daily, except Thu in winter. Upmarket restaurant with indoor & outdoor seating, the house speciality is sea snails with polenta. €€€€

Hiša Torkla [map, page 154] Korte 44b, Korte; 056 209 657; w hisa-torkla.si; noon–22.00 Wed–Sun. Michelin-listed restaurant serving traditional local dishes with an emphasis on grilled meat, in an old 19th-century mill house in the village of Korte. Private accommodation (1 dbl; **€€€€**) also available. €€€€

Gostilnica Gušt Drevored 1, Maja 5; 031 606 040; f gostilnica.gust; 11.00–22.00 daily. Popular restaurant with a nice terrace, though service has received some mixed reviews. €€€

Gostilna I Picerija Istra Trg republike 1; f picerijaistra; 07.00–22.00 Mon–Sat, 08.00–22.00 Sun. Tavern-style restaurant with a fireplace. Plenty of seafood, of course, as well as a pizza oven for really good pizzas. Excellent cakes & coffee too. €€€

✷ **Morski Val** Veliki trg 10; 031 618 196; w morski-val.si; 11.00–23.00 daily. This is a great spaghetteria/pizzeria on the waterfront with a large terrace, a wide range of good pasta dishes & other meals, cheerful service & vast portions. Best meal in Izola. €€€

Manzioli Wine Bar Manziolijev trg 5; f manzioli; 08.00–midnight daily. On the ground floor of Manzioli Palace is a relaxed bar, where you can sample local Slovenian wines, including those of the Zaro family, the managers. The Zaros are one of the two oldest families in Izola, tracing back to 1348. Their vineyard (Polje 12a, Pivol; m 041 218 547; w vinozaro.com) growing Malvazija, Refošk, & endemic strains Istska Belina, Maločrn & Muškat, is 1km outside Izola & open for visits & tastings.

ENTERTAINMENT AND NIGHTLIFE

Ambasada Gavioli Industrijska cesta 10; m 070 374 470; w ambasadagavioli.net; 23.00–03.00 or later. Besides the attraction of famous DJs from around the world, the fascination of Gavioli is its architecture. Italian architect Gianni Gavioli used themes from Alice's Wonderland, Romeo & Juliet's balcony, & Jean Baudelaire's evil flowers. Opened in 1995, Ambasada Gavioli's musical choice was initially based in strong ideological grounds following the neuropolitan teachings (that's the practice of communicating with the dead – I had to look it up too) of Chiron Morpheus. Since 2005, the venue has smelled the money & become much more earthly, but the architecture will still blow your mind (& your wallet – entry on some nights is upwards of €25).

FESTIVALS

Izola Cinema International Film Festival w isolacinema.org. Takes place at the beginning of Jun. Showcasing a great range of films, mostly from outside western Europe & North America, it's a true exploration of world cinema. Many of the festival's films are screened outdoors, including at Manzioli trg, & on the beach at Cape Petelin. Workshops also take place where people can learn some of the secrets of cinematography from the many film directors attending.

OTHER PRACTICALITIES

Pharmacy Oktobrske revolucije 11; 056 400 300; e lekarna.izola@obalne-lekarne.si; 07.30–19.00 Mon–Fri (also 15 Jun–31 Aug 07.30–20.00), 07.30–13.00 Sat. See Koper head branch (page 158) for 24/7 service & contact details.

Post office Cankarjev drevored 1; 08.00–19.00 Mon–Fri, 08.00–noon Sat

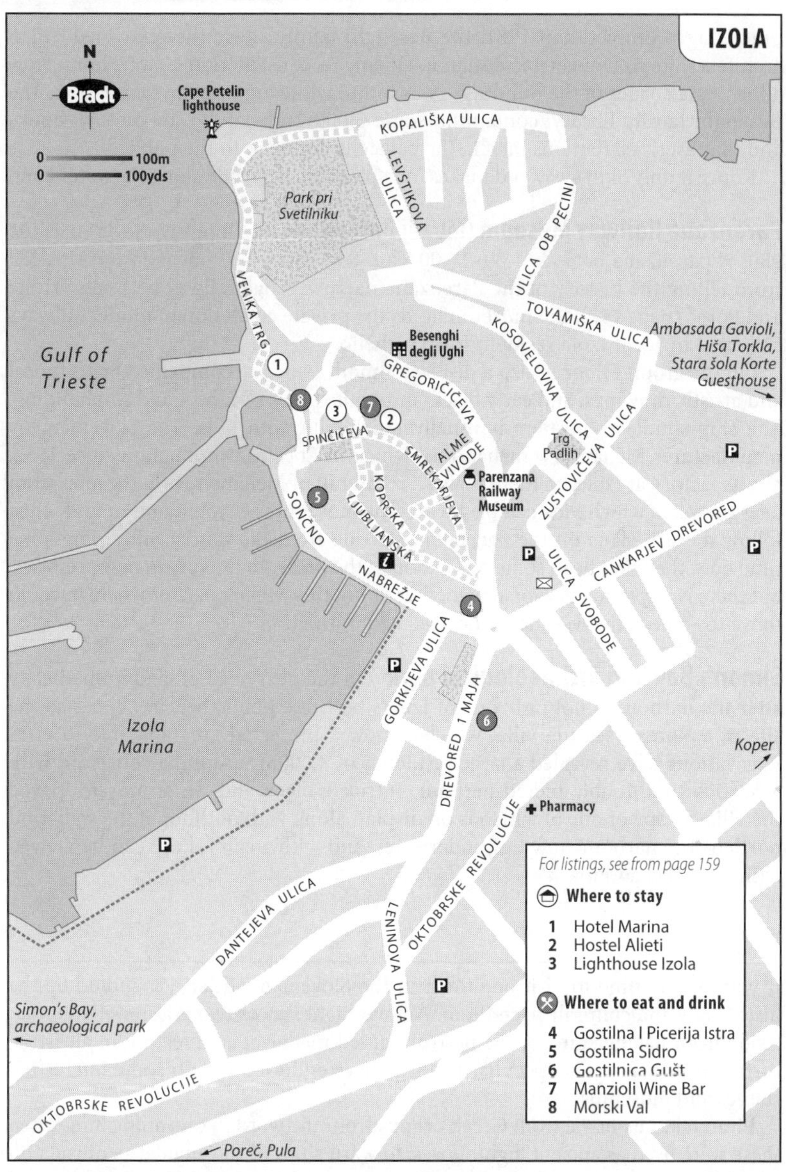

WHAT TO SEE AND DO Izola is delightful to walk around. The **park** in the northwest corner, with its minute **lighthouse** (more like a large lamp post really) at Cape Petelin is a favourite destination, including for swimming. The town's winding little backstreets host a multitude of **private galleries and art workshops**. Some are housed in the town's many old palaces, but Koprska and Ljubljanska streets have been turned into something of a **street museum** showcasing old crafts and trades.

The most revered palace of all Izola is the **Besenghi degli Ughi** (Gregoričičeva 76), which is now a music school, from which you can hear high-quality student practising. Completed in 1781, the Besenghi family chose the renowned Milan architect Filippo Dongetti to design it. During its construction, a stone lion – now adorning a corner of the building – was found while digging the foundation. The Besenghi family library, containing some 3,000 16th- and 17th-century books and manuscripts, remains intact. The palace is not open to the public.

Koper is only 8km away and makes for a pleasant cycle ride along the waterfront.

Parenzana Railway Museum (Muzej Parenzana) (Alme Vivode 3; 056 401 050; w parenzana.net; 11.00–17.00 Thu–Sat; entry €3, concessions €2) Aside from telling the history of the Parenzana narrow-gauge railway between Trieste and Poreč (page 117), the museum holds the private collection of model railways collected by local Izola resident Josip Mihelič.

On the ground floor is also a display of model ships, accompanied by technical and artistic drawings, and early black-and-white photos of ships and shipbuilding. The ship-simulator upstairs is usually quite a hit with kids. The Slovenian toy manufacturer Mehano (w mehano.si), which has been in production since 1952, has its factory at Izola, so there is also a room full of Mehano toys and games from over the years which kids can play with. The museum is easy enough to find – just follow the fish signs on the pavement, starting from the tourist office. For some time now, there has been some discussion of the museum moving to new premises, but there is as yet no decision on whether or not this will happen, or where it would move to – check the website for up-to-date information.

Simon's Bay and archaeological park On the next head of land immediately after the harbour is not only one of Izola's best free public beaches, but also the site of a Roman seaside villa, which is now a protected area and free to visit. Excavations have revealed a large residence of 3,000m^2 around a courtyard with a portico to a double-piered harbour. Intricate black-and-white mosaics paved the villa, a copy of one of which is on display, along with outlines of the walls and portico. The harbour now lies underwater, and with a careful eye can be viewed with a snorkel and mask.

PIRAN

If you've only time to visit one town in the Slovenian Adriatic, it should be the historically and culturally rich Piran. An overnight stay or two is also well in order. Aside from having some of the best-preserved medieval architecture in all Istria, certain historical events peculiar to Piran have endowed it with some interesting statues and museums.

Piran takes its name from Greek origins from the word *pyr* meaning 'fire', when these were used as ancient 'lighthouses' to warn ships of the angular peninsula on which the old town lies. By 1283 it had joined the Republic of Venice, following the local lead of Izola. In 1692 Piran was the birthplace of composer and violinist Guiseppe Tartini, whose statue – erected to celebrate the 200th anniversary of his birth in 1892 – dominates the main square named after him, Tartinijev trg. Tartini's house, now a museum, dates from at least 1384. In 1812 the Battle of Pirano took place between the British HMS *Victorious* and the Napoleonic *Rivoli* in the waters just off Piran. It is the only naval battle to take place in what are now Slovenian waters, and more can be read about it in the naval museum at the Gabrielli Palace.

Although never an island, the old town is surrounded by the sea on three sides and by the considerable remains of its thick town wall on the other. A mere 500m across at the town wall end, tapering gradually to a point less than 1km to the northwest, it is very easy to walk around. Always a completely pedestrianised town, a vehicular service was first introduced to Piran in 1909, when the first trolleybus in the Balkans started in Piran and ran the coastal routes to neighbouring towns. The trolleybus was replaced by an electric tram in 1912 and then by the current bus service in 1953.

On 12 November 2010, when Ghanaian-born Peter Bossman became mayor of Piran, he was the first black mayor to be elected anywhere in Slovenia or more widely in eastern Europe. Bossman was born to a politically active family in 1955 in what was then British Togoland. The Bossman family was forced to leave the country following the 1966 coup in Ghana, and Peter subsequently chose to take up medical studies in Yugoslavia. He was sent to Ljubljana and quickly fell in love, first with 'clean and green' Slovenia, as he describes it, and then with his now wife, a Croatian fellow student. Following their studies, Bossman and his wife moved to Piran to practise medicine, where they have remained ever since and now run their own private medical clinic. A member of the Social Democrat Party, Bossman was re-elected in October 2014, remaining in office until 2018, following which he returned to his medical practice.

GETTING AROUND Piran's **bus station** [164 C4] is in fact just a bus stop on the southwest edge of the town and the harbour. It's a 10-minute walk from there to the central square, and only 5 minutes from there to the park and ride further south on the coast at Fornače. A free shuttle bus (a small white bus with a blue-and-white stripe down the side) runs every 15 minutes from near the bottom of the multi-storey car park at Fornače to Tartinijev trg (show your parking ticket). You can also catch the regular service (plain white bus) between the coastal towns, which also goes into Tartinijev trg, but this will cost you €1.50 (card payments only on bus).

Taxi Piran (✆ 056 730 700; e info@bevk.si; w bevk.si) can be found near the bus station and the southern end of the harbour, and also between Tartinijev trg and the harbour.

Cycle hire is available from the excellent **Luma Šport** [164 C4] (Dantejeva 3; m 041 781 414; e luma.sport@hotmail.com; w lumasport.com), opposite the bus station, which has good mountain bikes for €25/day, including kids' bikes. They also have information on cycle routes in the area. We hired adult and kids' bikes from Luma for several days while cycling the Parenzana, and they were definitely up to the job.

TOURIST INFORMATION Piran **tourist information office** [164 D2] (Tartinjev trg 2; ✆ 056 734 440; e ticpi@portoroz.si; w portoroz.si) is a sub-branch of that in Portorož.

WHERE TO STAY

Art Hotel Tartini [164 D3] (46 rooms) Tartinjev trg 15; ✆ 056 711 000; e welcome@arthoteltartini.com; w arthoteltartini.com. Small, very friendly & welcoming hotel in a prime location right on the main square. There's a nice café & a good restaurant downstairs (salads are great), though the latter wasn't operating in 2022, & excellent cycle facilities (secure storage room). Great for people-watching on the main square. **€€€€**

Hotel Piran [164 C3] (80 rooms, 27 apts) Stjenkova 1; ✆ 056 667 100; e piran@eh.si; w hotel-piran.si/en. Fantastic sea views, standard 3-star facilities in a refurbished 1960s building, & a small beach across the road in front of the hotel. **€€€€**

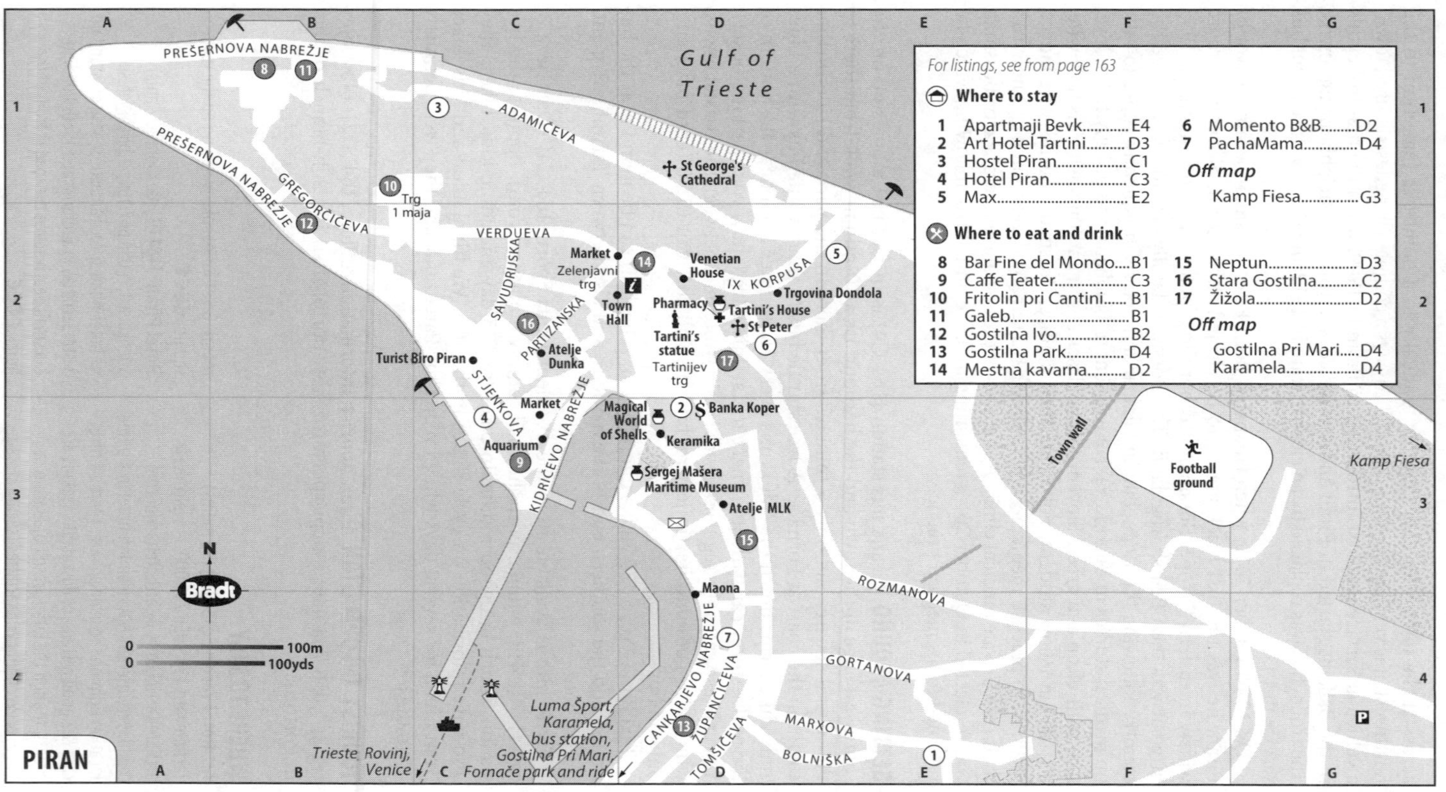

PIRAN
Gulf of Trieste
For listings, see from page 163
Where to stay
1 Apartmaji Bevk.......E4
2 Art Hotel Tartini.......D3
3 Hostel Piran.......C1
4 Hotel Piran.......C3
5 Max.......E2
6 Momento B&B.......D2
7 PachaMama.......D4
Off map
Kamp Fiesa.......G3
Where to eat and drink
8 Bar Fine del Mondo....B1
9 Caffe Teater.......C3
10 Fritolin pri Cantini......B1
11 Galeb.......B1
12 Gostilna Ivo.......B2
13 Gostilna Park.......D4
14 Mestna kavarna.......D2
15 Neptun.......D3
16 Stara Gostilna.......C2
17 Žižola.......D2
Off map
Gostilna Pri Mari.....D4
Karamela.......D4
PREŠERNOVA NABREŽJE
ADAMIČEVA
GREGORČIČEVA
St George's Cathedral
Trg 1 maja
VERDUEVA
SAVUDRIJSKA
PARTIZANSKA
Market
Zelenjavni trg
Town Hall
Venetian House
IX KORPUSA
Trgovina Dondola
Pharmacy
Tartini's House
St Peter
Tartini's statue
Tartinijev trg
Atelje Dunka
Turist Biro Piran
STJENKOVA
Market
Aquarium
KIDRIČEVO NABREŽJE
Magical World of Shells
Banka Koper
Keramika
Sergej Mašera Maritime Museum
Atelje MLK
Maona
ROZMANOVA
GORTANOVA
MARXOVA
BOLNIŠKA
CANKARJEVO NABREŽJE
ŽUPANČIČEVA
TOMŠIČEVA
Town wall
Football ground
Kamp Fiesa
N
Bradt
0 100m
0 100yds
Luma Šport, Karamela, bus station, Gostilna Pri Mari, Fornače park and ride
Trieste, Rovinj, Venice

Max [164 E2] (6 rooms) IX korpusa 26; 041 692 928; e info@maxpiran.com; w maxpiran.com. In a beautifully refurbished 1700 building with stone-exposed b/fast room downstairs, this little family-run hotel is hard to beat. A heartfelt b/fast & service is delivered by Max & his staff. Really excellent value. **€€€**

Memento B&B [164 D2] (11 rooms) Bolniška ul 8; 051 394 432; facebook.com/mementopiran. Beautifully kept small B&B set just off Tartini Sq. **€€€**

PachaMama [164 D4] (12 rooms) Župančičeva 18 (reception at Trubarjeva 8); 051 214 518; e info@pachamama.si; w pachamama.si. Bright, clean rooms & central location near the main square. **€€€**

Apartmaji Bevk [164 E4] (6 apts) Marxova 13; 059 022 111; m 051 623 682; e info@bevk.si; w bevk.si. Very nice self-catering apartments in 2 renovated buildings not far apart. Small fitness centre & roof terrace, & nicer furnishings in the 3 apartments on Prežihova. Larger apartments with a roof terrace on Marxova. **€€€–€€**

Hostel Piran [164 C1] (8 rooms) Vodopivčeva ulica 9; 031 627 647; e hostelpiran@gmail.com; w hostelpiran.com. Bright, friendly hostel just 100m from the main square, with beds in dbls, trpls & quads. 1 of 2 hostels under the same ownership in the centre of Piran, the other being the nearby Pirano. **€€€–€€**

Camping

Kamp Fiesa [164 G3] Fiesa 57b; 056 746 230; e kamp.fiesa@gmail.com; w portoroz.si/en/plan-your-stay/accommodation/camping-places; 1 May–30 Sep. Just over 1km east of the old town. Cheap hotel accommodation, & cabins for 4 also available. **€**

WHERE TO EAT AND DRINK

Gostilna Ivo [164 B2] Gregoričičeva 31; 056 732 233; w gostilna-ivo.com; 11.00–23.00 daily. Ivo distinguishes itself from the rest of the seafront restaurants by its simple & consistently good dishes, which, for the same price as other places, are much better value. €€€€

Neptun [164 D3] Županičičeva 7; 056 734 111; 11.00–23.00 daily. In the old bus station, this restaurant with fishing nets hanging from the ceiling is very popular with locals, & in part because without sea views & a terrace it is less popular with tourists. €€€€

Stara Gostilna [164 C2] Gregoričičeva 31; 041 439 008; e info@stara-gostilna.com w stara-gostilna.com; 18.00–midnight Mon–Sat. Michelin-listed restaurant serving traditional dishes with a modern twist – think *fuži* with smoked sea bream, or pasta with scampi & prunes. Small & elegant, with an extensive wine list, and an 8- or 10-course degustation menu as well as à la carte options. €€€€€

Fritolin pri Cantini [164 B1] Prvomajski trg 6; m 041 873 872; noon–midnight daily. Small, homely seafood restaurant serving good grilled squid & other dishes at decent prices. €€€

Galeb [164 B1] Pusterla 5; 056 733 225; 11.00–16.00 & 18.00–midnight daily. Equally popular with locals & tourists on the northern seafront. €€€

Gostilna Park [164 D4] Župančičeva 21; 11.00–22.00 daily. Popular place serving seafood, pasta, grills & other dishes. €€€

Gostilna Pri Mari [164 D4] Dantejeva 17; 056 734 735; w primari-piran.com; 17.00–22.00 Tue–Thu, noon–22.00 Fri–Sun; Nov–Mar midday–16.00 & 18.00–22.00 Tue–Sat, noon–16.00 Sun; closed Jan. On the main road leading south, just past the bus station, serving good, traditional Slovenian fare in a friendly, welcoming setting. €€€

Bar Fine del Mondo [164 B1] 24 Prešernovo nabrežje; facebook.com/bar.finedelmondo; 09:00–23:00. Simple bar on the waterfront with cocktails, wicker chairs & sunset views to die for.

Caffe Teater [164 C3] Kidričevo Nabrežje bb; w caffeteater.com/en; 08.00–midnight daily. This place is like it's been lifted straight out of Vienna – high Art Deco ceilings, tall arched windows, plush chairs & an enviable view of the sea & the dock. Live music, including a Jazz Festival in the first week of Jul.

Karamela [164 C4] Obala 18; 08.00–22.00 daily. Heavenly ice cream, the best in Piran. By the bus station.

Mestna kavarna [164 D2] Tartinjev trg 3; 08.00–23.00 daily. Good coffee, cakes & ice cream, on the main square.

Žižola [164 D2] Tartinjev trg 10; 09.00–23.30 daily. This tiniest of café/bars looks like it is stuck in time. Often only standing room on popular summer evenings. The name, in case you're wondering, comes from the jujube or red date, *žižola* in Slovene, which is grown locally & is used to make a spirit – also called *žižola*. Order a *žižola* & you may find one of the small fruit lurking at the bottom of your glass.

OTHER PRACTICALITIES

Pharmacy [164 D2] Obalne Lekarne, Tartinjev trg 4; ☎ 056 730 150; ⌚ 07.30–19.00 Mon–Fri (also 15 Jun–31 Aug 07.30–20.00), 07.30–13.00 Sat/Sun. See Koper head branch (page 158) for 24/7 service & contact details.

Post office [164 D3] Leninova 1; ⌚ 08.00–19.00 Mon–Fri, 08.00–noon Sat

WHAT TO SEE AND DO **Tartinijev trg** is the central place to head for in Piran. For a tiny town it is uncharacteristically large, and this is because it was in fact an inner harbour until it was filled in to form the current piazza in 1884. Shortly thereafter, **Tartini's statue** [164 D2] was erected there in 1892. The square was renovated in 1987–89 by the leading Slovenian post-Modernist architect Boris Podrecca, whose other works include the renovation of Piazza XXIV Maggio in Cormons, Italy, and the Millennium Tower in Vienna. The renovated square's prominent white stone ellipse is a reference to the old tram service that used to run along the coast from Piran to Portorož (thus linking Piran with the Parenzana railway line), which used to turn around on the square.

Venetian House (Benečanka) [164 D2] At the north end of Tartinijev trg is the characteristically deep rustic red Venetian house, with its inscription '*lassa pur dir*' (let them talk). Legend has it that a Venetian merchant had built the house for his local sweetheart, and had the inscription written in defiance of local gossip about their love. On the ground floor is the popular museum shop of the Piran saltpans.

Maritime Museum Sergej Mašera (Pomorski muzej Sergej Mašera) [164 D3] (Cankarejevo nabrežje 3; ☎ 056 710 040; e muzej@pommuz-pi.si; w pomorskimuzej.si/en/museum; ⌚ Sep–Jun 09.00–17.00 Tue–Sun, Jul/Aug 09.00–midday & 17.00–21.00 Tue–Sun; entry adult/child €5/€3) The museum houses a variety of local seafaring and coastal-life exhibits in the 19th-century Gabrielli Palace, which was only partially finished and then turned into a museum in 1954. Also run by the Maritime Museum is the **Museum of Salt Making** (page 169). Look out for the Galeb cutter sail boat, donated in 1994 by the ballet choreographers Pia and Pino Mlaker, in the harbour nearby.

Town Hall (Mestna hiša) [164 D2] The town hall is a relatively young building in Piran dating back only to 1877, when it was built over the site of the old municipal palace with its Venetian loggia – though you can still see a Venetian lion on the façade. The new town hall is the seat of the mayor and town council and also holds the town archives.

Piran Aquarium [164 C3] (Kidričevo Nabrežje 4; ☎ 05 673 2572; ⌚ Feb/Mar & Nov/Dec 09.00–17.00 Tue–Sun, Apr–mid-Jun & Sep/Oct 09.00–19.00 daily, 15 Jun–31 Aug 09.00–20.00 daily; entry adult/child €5/€3) A small fish collection.

Magical World of Shells (Čarobni Svet Školjk) [164 D3] (Tartinijev trg 15; m 40 700 053; w svet-skoljk.si; ⌚ 1 Mar–end May & 1 Oct–end Nov 11.00–17.00 Tue–Sun, 1 Jun–end Sep 10.00–18.00 daily, 1 Dec–end Feb 11.00–17.00 Sat/Sun;

entry adult/child €4/€3) Opened in 2011 on one corner of the main square, Piran's shell museum comprises the personal collection of local shell collector Jan Simič. The museum now holds around 4,000 shells from all over the world – many of them spectacularly colourful, and ranging in size from tiny molluscs to an enormous giant clam. The collection is well displayed and clearly labelled, with interactive and educational displays making it great for kids. Fascinating.

St George's Cathedral (Cerkev Sv Jurija) [164 D1] The cathedral dominates the town and Tartinijev trg from the north. The view from here is definitely worth the trek. Originally built in the 12th century, its current structure dates from its expansion in the early 14th century, and its subsequent Baroque facelift in 1637. The belfry (entry €2), completed in 1608, sports a magnificent view of the bay, and when the cold northeast *bora* wind blows the skies clear, it's possible to see as far as the Italian Alps and the Dolomites. Inside are two statues of St George, the patron saint of Piran, on his horse (no dragon in sight). There's another great view in Piran – walk east from the cathedral then turn left and follow the old city walls, which lead to higher ground from where you can look down on to the cathedral and old town – the quintessential picture-postcard view of the city.

St Peter's Church (Cerkev sv Petra) [164 D2] The church can be found in the piazza. It dates back to 1272 when it stood outside the original 7th-century town walls. As the town expanded, the **town walls** were rebuilt between 1470 and 1534 further out in their current location. Seven town gates are still intact.

Tartini's House (Tartinjeva hiša) [164 D2] (Kajuhova 12; ☎ 056 633 570; f casatartini; ⏲ 09.00–14.00 Tue–Fri, 09.00–14.00 & 15.00–18.00 Sat; entry €4/€3) Tartini's House – the composer's birthplace – is on the northeast corner of the square. It is one of the oldest buildings in the town, having been mentioned in town documents dating back to 1384. This museum is worth visiting just to see the exquisite frescoes that were uncovered and beautifully restored in the late 1980s. The first-floor memorial room houses some of Tartini's original musical score sheets, one of his many violins, letters from the composer, and his death mask. Other floors, all part of the Italian Community main office, also often hold cultural events and exhibitions.

PORTOROŽ

A miniature riviera (smaller than Opatija's 12km seafront stretch), Portorož is the **spa kingdom** of the Slovenian Adriatic. Thermal waters have been known and used here since Roman times but it was not an area developed during Venetian rule (as were the other towns along the coast), largely due to the lack of a suitable port. Nonetheless, with the rise of spa tourism during the 19th century, the 'Port of Roses' with its thermal waters was a prime location for development. Its first hotel, the Hotel Palace (now the Kempinski Palace) with its grand façade, was opened in 1910. Since then a slew of large hotels have been built along the coast here such that it is hard to find space to even get into the sea in the high season. Piran's picturesque Venetian-style old town is only 3km along the coastal path.

GETTING AROUND In true health and spa style, just as the doctor prescribes, **walking** is the order of the day. **Bicycle hire** is available through your hotel or from GoPortorož (w goportoroz.si; €25/day, €20/5hrs; page 168), or – best of all in terms of price, quality of bike and knowledge of local cycling trails – from Luma Šport in Piran (page

163). Portorož's main **bus** stop is outside the small indoor market opposite Kempinski Palace. **Taxi Piran** (☎ 059 022 111; **w** bevk.si) serves Portorož, or see **w** portoroz.si/en/plan-your-stay/be-mobile-around-the-town/taxis, .

Marina Portorož (Cesta solinarjev 8; ☎ 056 761 100; **w** marinap.si) is 1km south at Lucija and is Slovenia's first purpose-built yacht marina. Built on the old saltpans, it has over 1,000 berths and a full repair service, with the capacity to lift 60 tonnes. The marina also has two restaurants, and a recreational centre with minigolf, table tennis, a variety of other sport pitches, a tennis school with 19 courts, and an outdoor Olympic-size pool – though not all of this is open to non-yachters.

Confusingly, the street numbering of the esplanade Obala goes 1–27 on the shore side going west to east, and then starts again at the west end of the land side with 28–144. Numbers are not opposite each other, and between the Life Class complex and the Kempinski Palace, numbers 34–44 no longer exist.

TOURIST INFORMATION The **tourist information bureau** (Obala 16; ☎ 056 742 220; **e** ticpo@portoroz.si; **w** portoroz.si; ⌚ 09.00–17.00 daily) has a very useful website. A friendly tourist agency in Portorož is **GoPortorož** (Obala 14; **m** 040 461 000; **e** info@goportoroz.si; **w** goportoroz.si), located in a geodome on the main street.

WHERE TO STAY AND SPA Private accommodation in Portorož is possible through the tourist agencies, but really people come here to stay at the big spa hotels with full access to the hot springs, and in the hope of catching a glimpse of the rich and famous at the five-stars.

Kempinski Palace (181 rooms) Obala 45; ☎ 056 927 000; **e** reservations.portoroz@kempinski.com; **w** kempinski.com/en/istria/palace-portoroz. A 5-star deluxe Kempinski has standards, & you'll find these here as in any other Kempinski. The only thing that's unique about this Kempinski is its façade, which is exactly that. Originally built in 1910, the building was declared a cultural heritage monument in 1983. As a result, when Istrabenz bought & renovated the building in conjunction with Kempinski, only the façade was kept & the rest was demolished. The Rose Spa is pure luxury & open to outside guests at €45 for a day pass. Massage & treatments extra. **€€€€€**

Life Class Hotels & Spa (791 rooms) Obala 33; ☎ 056 929 001; **e** booking@lifeclass.net; **w** lifeclass.net. With 6 hotels to choose from, crammed into the entire complex at Obala 33, you should be able to find a room. The Grand Hotel is 5-star, the remainder (Slovenia, Riviera, Neptune, Mirna & Apollo) are 4-star. A 5-star beach & a 4-star beach across the road are for the exclusive use of guests. Full spa treatments, including Wai Thai, Ayurveda & Thalasso are available, as well as fitness & pilates centres, & an ice-cave in their sauna park, offering 7 different types of sauna & using salt from nearby Sečovlje. Physiotherapy & a host of other treatments can be booked. Non-guests can use the spa facilities (€40 for 4hrs) & the thermal spring seawater pools year-round. **€€€€€**

Marko (48 rooms) Obala 28; ☎ 056 174 000; **e** info@hotel-marko.si; **w** hotel-marko.si. A family-run hotel in its own grounds at the western end of the esplanade. Considerably more privacy than the conglomerates. **€€€€**

WHERE TO EAT AND DRINK For a place with such high-end hotels there was something of a lack of high-end restaurants until recently – however, these days it has a rather more impressive list of fine-dining establishments.

COB Letoviška 1; ☎ 056 745 074; **w** cob.si; ⌚ 11.00–23.00 daily. At the Michelin-starred COB (an acronym for 'Cooking Outside the Box'), head chef Filip Matjaž (Gault & Millau Slovenian Chef of the Future in 2022) leads guests on an interactive journey through traditional Slovenian gastronomy, with 8- & 15-course degustation menus priced at €95 & €150. **€€€€**

Rizibizi Obala 20; 059 935 320; e info@rizibizi.si; w rizibizi.si; noon–23.00 daily. Rizibizi means rice with peas, a simple dish known widely across the former Yugoslavia, though you can expect something rather more refined & elaborate at this friendly, Michelin-recommended place which is right by the beach. Their tasting menus are good value at €50 & €80 (5 & 8 courses respectively), while signature dishes include prawns & pumpkin with truffles, & sea bass carpaccio with truffles. Good wine list. €€€€

Sophia Obala 45; 056 927 000; e reservations.portoroz@kempinski.com; w kempinski.com/en/istria/palace-portoroz/dining; 18.00–23.00 daily. Michelin-recommended fine-dining restaurant at the Kempinski Palace, named after actress Sophia Loren, with a focus on Istrian cuisine. The signature dish, *linguini a la buzara*, is doubtless one the screen goddess would have adored. €€€€

Fritolin Obala 53; 056 740 210; 11.00–23.00 daily. Popular, good-value seafood restaurant decorated with a nautical theme. €€

Cacau Obala 14; w cacao.si; 08.00–23.00 daily. Good for cakes, coffee, juices & ice cream in a comfortable lounge-bar-style setting with plenty of tables outside.

OTHER PRACTICALITIES

Dentist Top Dent, Grand Hotel Metropol, Obala 77; 041 638 967; e topdent.it@gmail.com; w topdent.si; 09.00–19.00 Mon–Fri, 09.00–13.00 Sat. More expensive than some dentists, in part due to its location, but still excellent prices compared with private treatment costs in the UK or US.

Pharmacy Cesta solinajev 1; 056 778 250; e lekarna.lucija@obalne-lekarne.si; w obalne-lekarne.si/poslovalnice; 07.30–19.00 Mon–Fri (15 Jun–31 Aug till 20.00 Mon–Fri), 07.30–13.00 Sat, 08.00–midday Sun & public holidays (except 1 Jan, 1 May & 25 Dec). See Koper head branch (page 158) for 24/7 service & contact details.

Post office K Stari 1; 08.00–19.00 Mon–Fri, 08.00–midday Sat

WHAT TO SEE AND DO The coastal path spanning from the saltpans (see below) and **Forma Viva sculpture park** in the east along the entire coast to Koper is almost 30km, which you can do in 3–4 hours on a **bicycle** (don't forget to double it to return). A **spa** treatment or massage afterwards (see opposite) will be well earned.

The Obala is lined with cafés, bars and pubs, perfect for whiling away the time and relaxing over an ice cream or cake. Many head to Izola for evening cultural events and the fabled Ambasada Gavioli nightclub. Portorož's **open-air auditorium** (Senčna pot 10; 056 766 777; w avditorij.si) holds regular live events too. The whole coastline is available for a **swim** in the sea. For information about the sports facilities at Portorož Marina recreational centre, see opposite.

If you're visiting Sečovlje Salina it's worth heading inland to the village of **Krkavče**, right next to the border with Croatia. Around 400m south of the village cemetery there's a single standing stone, known as the **Krkavče stone (Krkavški kamen)** protruding about 1.6m high and dating from…well, no-one's quite sure of that, though the 12th century seems probable. It probably functioned as a pillory pole or 'pillar of shame' (there's another good example at Salež near Buzet; page 122). The stone has a human figure carved on each side near the top, the head of each surrounded by what looks like wild spiky hair but is meant to represent the rays of the sun. According to local tradition, there was once an annual procession hereabouts shortly before Ascension Day, and people would gather by the stone while the local priest gave a blessing.

Sečovlje Salina Nature Park and Museum of Salt Making (Krajinski park Sečoveljske Soline & Muzej Solinarstva)

(Seča 115; 056 721 330; e info@soline.si; w kpss.si and w soline.si; Jan–Mar & Nov/Dec 08.00–17.00 daily, Apr/

May & Sep/Oct 07.00–19.00 daily, Jun–Aug 07.00–21.00 daily; the museum itself is open Apr/May & Sep/Oct 09.00–17.00 daily, Jun–Aug 09.00–20.00 daily; entry €7 in summer, €6 in winter, concessions for children, students & over 65s) The Sečovlje saltpans were first noted in court documents from AD804. The *soline*, as they are known in Slovene, are made up of working saltpans in the northern half (Lera), and a nature park in the now disused saltpans to the south (Fontanigge). The museum, which is a renovated local worker's house, looks remarkably plain, and lies in the south side. Both sides are open to the public – so you can see how salt is harvested in Lera, and see the wide array of halophytes (salt-loving vegetation) and accompanying fauna in Fontanigge.

The area is an ornithologist's paradise, with over 270 different bird species recorded, including a very high number of wintering birds that migrate from colder climates. Little egret, yellow-legged gull and pygmy cormorant are just some of the many species you're likely to see here. Other wildlife is also abundant, not least because the park harbours four different ecosystems – land, fresh water, brackish water and seawater – in a remarkably small area. In 1993 it became the first site in Slovenia to be declared a Ramsar site (Wetland of International Importance).

The two sides have different entrances. To enter Lera working area, turn off at the village of Seča. To enter the nature park, you'll need to take the road to Fontanigge which lies in no-man's-land between the Croatian and the Slovenian border posts. Fontanigge and Lera are divided by the Drinica dyke, over which there is no crossing inside the park. The park can be explored on foot or bicycle, but take care on both sides not to disturb the saltpans. This would destroy the purity of the salt harvested in Lera and disturb the habitat of the many nesting birds in Fontanigge. Sunsets here are spectacular, so bringing a good camera and a sturdy tripod is recommended.

Guided tours are available and should be booked through the website (**w** kpss.si/en/visiting/guided-tours).

In the summer, the ***Solinarka*** (**m** 031 653 682; **w** solinarka.com) sails to the Sečovlje salt pans and runs picnic excursions of various lengths along the coast. If you miss the boat back from the saltpans or want longer there, then try Taxi Piran (☎ 059 022 111; **w** bevk.si).

ŠKOCJAN CAVES (ŠKOCJANSKE JAME)

While it is Postojna Cave (page 176) that sees the bulk of visitors, it is Škocjan Caves (Škocjanske jame) (Matavun 12, Divača; ☎ 057 082 110; **w** park-skocjanske-jame.si; ⏰ daily Jun–Sep 09.30–19.00, Apr & May/Oct 09.30–16.00, Nov–Mar 09.30–15.00; pricing options opposite) that is inscribed a UNESCO World Heritage Site. Škocjan and Postojna are quite different as visitor experiences – the former involves a walk in, the latter a train ride; Postojna is more extensive while Škocjan stands within a wider protected area – but both are hugely impressive and neither should be missed.

Unlike most other UNESCO-listed cave systems (eg: Lascaux and others in the Vézère Valley, France), Škocjan's UNESCO listing is as a natural, as opposed to a cultural, site – a designation only shared by the Aggtelek Caves on the border between Hungary and Slovakia, the Carlsbad Caves in New Mexico and the Mammoth Caves in Kentucky. The cave was formed in the Pleistocene Era by the River Reka, which disappears underground here and has carved out a vast underground river canyon, over 140m high in places. Despite its huge size, the underground canyon is drained by a comparatively small siphon – meaning that after heavy rainfall, the cave can flood dramatically, with water levels rising by around 100m, as a marker in the cave shows. It's a wonderful, magical place, set within a protected landscape covering an area of some 413ha.

GETTING THERE AND AWAY The nearest railway station to the caves is Divača, on the line between Koper and Postojna (and continuing to Ljubljana) – check timetables at w potniski.sz.si/en, as some services have been replaced by bus transfers on parts of the route. From the station, a free shuttle bus runs at 10.00, 11.00, 14.00 and 15.00, returning at 10.07, 11.22, 14.05 and 15.05. If your train (or the rail-replacement bus from Koper) arrives late, the shuttle bus should wait for it (ours did). It's also possible to walk to the caves from the railway station – it's around 3km and a map showing the route can be found at the railway station (allow 35 minutes each way). If you miss the last shuttle bus back to Divača from the caves and you don't fancy walking, a taxi will cost around €12 (ask at the souvenir shop or ticket office and they'll point out where the taxi is waiting).

WHERE TO STAY AND EAT If you want to stay overnight near the caves or at Divača, there's a useful list of private accommodation at w park-skocjanske-jame.si/en then, under 'Tourist Information' click 'Other Tourist Facilities'. Accommodation at Matavun, the village next to the entrance to the caves and included in the protected area of the nature park, includes **Rooms Pr Vncki** (Matavun 10; ☎ 057 633 073; w slovenia holidays.com/eng/rooms-pr-vncki-divaca.html; **€€€**), which offers two rooms in a traditional village house, with breakfast included. There's also the **Hostel & Bistro Škrla** (Matavun 10; 040 848 859 6215; info@hostelskrla.com; w hostelskrla.com; **€€€**) with simple, clean rooms and a small restaurant in a traditional house, and a restaurant, **Pivovarna & Gostilna Mahnič** (Matavun 12; ☎ 056 800 100; w mahnic.si; ⏲ 10.00–23.00 daily; **€€€**).

You can also stay at nearby Bretanja, just east from the caves – try **Tourist Farm Pr´Betanci** (Betanja 2; ☎ 057 633 006; w sloveniaholidays.com/eng/tourist-farm-prbetanci-divaca.html; **€€**), which offers three rooms and traditional local cuisine. And definitely not to be missed is the little **ice-cream** stall towards the top of the path as you climb up from the funicular to the entrance and ticket office, which has half-a-dozen flavours of some of the most delicious homemade ice cream I have ever tasted.

WHAT TO SEE AND DO There are two tours offered through the caves. The first (with a guide) goes through the underground canyon – the most famous part of the cave system – at the end of which a short walk uphill leads to a funicular that whisks you back up to the entrance and ticket office. The second continues along the River Reka without taking the funicular (you walk this part yourself, without a guide), and ascends to the entrance on foot. It's well worth continuing along the second part of the trail, which meanders along the course of the river and through two huge collapsed dolines, Velika dolina and Mala dolina (165m and 120m deep respectively), these having once been part of the cave system as well before their roofs collapsed several thousand years ago.

Tours depart hourly from 10.00 to 16.00 (with another at 11.30) daily in July/August, hourly from 10.00 to 15.00 in May/June and September/October, daily at 10.00, noon, 13.00 and 15.00 in April, and daily at 10.00 and 13.00, with an additional tour at 15.00 on Sundays, from November to March. Tickets for the first ('underground canyon') part of the cave complex cost €24/€12.50 for adults/children in July/August, dropping to €22/€10 in May/June/September, and

€16/€7.50 in the winter months; to continue along the River Reka, tickets cost an additional €6/€3.50 (on top of the 'underground canyon' route).

There's also a guided tour of the Hanke Channel, more difficult and lasting 4 hours (minimum age 15), with full caving gear provided and departing at 09.00 (prior booking required, and places tend to fill up; €100). Bags can be left in lockers beside the ticket office (ask at the ticket office for a key).

LIPICA

While you're exploring the Slovenian Adriatic coast and the Karst region, don't miss the opportunity to visit the historic Lipica Stud Farm. Lipica is the original stud farm of the Lipizzaner horse breed, and today maintains a tradition stretching back more than 435 years.

HISTORY Lipica Stud Farm was established in 1580 as the royal stud for Lipizzaner horses by the Austrian Archduke Charles II (1540–90) – who among other things also founded the university at Graz, and was a suitor to England's Queen Elizabeth I – at a time when this area, along with a vast tract of other territories, formed part of the Habsburg Empire. Built from the abandoned summer residence of the Bishop of Trieste, it is the original stud farm for this breed, and remains the oldest European stud farm breeding Lipizzaner horses. Lipizzaner horses were bred from Spanish, Italian, Arabian and local Karst stock, with Lipica being chosen as a location for the stud farm since the climate and the surrounding karst landscape gave it certain similarities with those of Spain. Horses had been bred in the surrounding area since long before the stud farm was established, and local horses had a reputation for their strength, speed and endurance. Adult Lipizzaners are usually a pale, dappled grey colour (their skin is dark, under a white coat), although the foals are born dark (bay or black), and lighten gradually as they grow.

The story of the Lipizzaners is closely linked to the history of classical dressage, which developed at the Spanish Riding School in Vienna – so called because it originally used horses from Spain, though these were soon replaced by Lipizzaners from Lipica Stud Farm.

Breeding began in 1581 when two-dozen mares and six stallions were brought to Lipica from Spain, and new buildings (including the Velbanca stable, the oldest now surviving) were constructed in the early 1700s. The 300-strong herd had to be evacuated to Hungary three times during the Napoleonic occupation in the late 18th and early 19th centuries, and following their return stables had to be rebuilt and the surrounding landscape restored.

The horses at Lipica today are descended from six lines of stallions of Andalusian, Italian, Danish and Arabian stock that were introduced in the second half of the 18th and early 19th centuries – Pluto (b 1765), Conversano (b 1767), Maestoso (b 1773), Favory (b 1779), Neapolitano (b 1790), and finally an Arab stallion called Siglavy (b 1810), which arrived in 1816. The Lipizzaner blood line can also be traced through 17 families of mares. The studbooks go back to 1810 (when Siglavy was born) – the earlier ones were lost during the Napoleonic occupation.

There are over 350 horses at the stud farm today. Reading the history of Lipica during the 20th century, however, it sometimes seems remarkable that any of its horses survived at all. During World War I the herd was again evacuated, this time to Laxenburg near Vienna and Kladrub in what is now the Czech Republic. After the war, part of the herd was returned from Laxenburg (but not from Kladrub) to Lipica, which was then under Italian occupation. Following the capitulation of Italy, Lipica came under German occupation, and the Germans sent the herd to Hostau in the Czech Republic, with more horses being added from the German cavalry. At the close of World War II, following a proposal from Colonel Reed (head of US cavalry intelligence), General Patton undertook a military operation to rescue the herd and transfer it to territory under the control of Allied Forces. Most of the horses went to Italy – only 11 horses from the herd removed by the Germans actually returned to Lipica. Following several periods of financial loss and varying fortunes under Yugoslavia, the Lipica Stud Farm became a public institution owned by the Republic of Slovenia in 1996.

GETTING THERE AND AWAY The nearest railway station and bus stop to Lipica is Sežana, on the Italian border around 4km north of the stud farm. Trains run to Sežana from Divača, which is on the line from Koper to Postojna (and on to Ljubljana). A taxi from Sežana station to the stud farm will cost around €15. Sežana is only around 5km from Villa Opicina in Italy, from where local buses or the historic Villa Opicina tram line (out of operation for several years but due to reopen in 2023) runs down to Trieste on the coast.

WHERE TO STAY AND EAT

Hotel Maestoso (139 rooms & suites) Lipica 5, Sežana; 057 391 790; w lipica.org/en/new-hotel-maestoso. You can't really get much closer or more convenient for visiting the stud farm than this. The Maestoso is a large hotel within the grounds at Lipica, right by the entrance to the stud which is just a 2min walk away. There's a restaurant & terrace downstairs. Bikes are available for guests, so you can cycle off around some of the bridle paths. **€€€€**

WHAT TO SEE AND DO At **Lipica Stud Farm** (Lipica 5, Sežana; w lipica.org; Apr–Oct 10.00–18.00 daily, Nov–Mar 10.00–16.00 daily; entry adult/child inc guided tour €18/€9, under 6s free, family tickets available; ticket prices drop to €15/€7.50 out of season), you can both explore the grounds of the estate via a network of avenues, which enables you to see the horses as they graze, and visit the historic core including its stables. If you want to see the 'classical riding presentation' or book a pony/carriage ride (see below), pay for these when you buy your admission ticket to avoid incurring an additional fee. **Guided tours** of the stud farm run from April to October, and last around 50 minutes (10.00, noon, 14.00 & 16.00). If you miss (or don't fancy) one of the tours, you can download a smartphone app that will take you through the history and highlights of the stud farm. The skill of the Lipizzaners is showcased at the **classical riding presentation** by the Lipica Classical Riding School (Jun–Sep 15.00 Tue, Fri & Sun, May & Oct 15.00 Fri/Sun, Apr 15.00 Sun; adult/child €25/€12 inc general admission), which lasts 45 minutes and includes complex dressage manoeuvres set to music. On days when there is no Classical Riding Presentation, visitors can see the Lipizzaners having their training sessions (Jun–Sep 11.00 Wed/Thu/Sat, May/Oct 11.00, Sat; €22 inc general admission).

Perhaps the highlight of any visit, however, is seeing the herd of Lipizzaners being released from the stables into the paddocks (at 09.00), or brought back from the paddocks (at 18.00 in summer and earlier in winter), often charging along the broad avenue in a cloud of dust and flying white manes (visitors watch safely from the other side of a fence).

Lipica is a great place for children. There are interactive pony workshops (45mins; €15 per child) – and it really is so much nicer to see kids with ponies that are well cared for, as these very clearly are, as opposed to some of the unfortunate, scrawny and undernourished animals that so often get used for children's horse and pony rides at resorts and elsewhere. Children can also feed them handfuls of grass through the fence of their enclosure (horses and ponies should be fed from the palm of your hand, keeping fingers straight out and away from the mouth to avoid them getting nipped. There is also a playground.

POSTOJNA

Though it's the nearby Škocjanske jame that has UNESCO World Heritage Site status, it's undoubtedly **Postojna Cave (Postojnska jama)** that you'll hear about more often. One of the most popular tourist attractions anywhere in Slovenia, Postojna Cave receives over half a million visitors a year – but whatever you've seen or know about the cave, prepare to be genuinely awe-struck when you actually get inside. The other reason to come here is **Predjama Castle** (**Predjamski grad**), perched fairy-tale-like within a sheer cliff.

HISTORY Unlike other, smaller caves in the area, in which evidence has been discovered of human habitation dating back some 150,000 years to the late Stone Age, there is no evidence of prehistoric habitation in Postojna Cave. Perhaps it was simply too large to feel safe, and certainly the constant air movement would have made it a cold dwelling place. Graffiti in Postojna Cave shows that it was visited at least as early as the 13th century, and from the late 18th century this area became the focus for early studies into karst geomorphology and hydrology (page 4). It was opened to the public in 1819, its first official visitor being Austria's Archduke Ferdinand I (as you sit on the train when entering the cave, spare a thought for the workers whose job it was back in those early days to push visitors around in carriages by hand).

GETTING THERE Numerous agencies and hotels in Istria and elsewhere in Croatia – Elim (w elim.hr/excursions.html) and Planet Rovinj (w planetrovinj.com/index.php), both in Rovinj, and Hotel Park Plaza Histria in Pula, to name just three examples – as well as in Ljubljana and towns on the Slovenian Adriatic, run tours and day trips to Postojna Cave and Predjama Castle.

By bus From Postojna there are around five buses a day to Koper, a couple of which continue to Piran and Portorož, and more than ten to Ljubljana (around 80 & 70 mins respectively). Postojna's **bus station** (Titova cesta 2) is less than 5 minutes' walk from Titov trg, and there's also a bus stop near the cave entrance.

By train Postojna's **railway station** (Kolodvorske cesta 25) is 15 minutes' walk southeast of Titov trg. There are four trains daily to Koper (1½ hours, with a replacement bus service running between Divača and Koper), and around ten to Ljubljana (1 hour).

By car Postojna is a 1-hour drive from Ljubljana, 1 hour from the Slovenian coast, 3 hours from Poreč and 1 hour from Rijeka.

GETTING AROUND **Postojna Cave** is less than 1km northwest of Postojna's town centre along Jamska cesta, so you can easily walk there (10 minutes on foot from Titov trg, 25 minutes from the train station). For a **taxi**, call m 031 777 974. **Predjama**

Castle is 9km northwest of Postojna town centre, past Postojna Cave. A return trip by taxi with waiting time shouldn't set you back more than around €25.

TOURIST INFORMATION The **tourist office** (Trg padlih borcev 5; 040 122 318; w visit-postojna.si; 08.00–16.00 Mon–Fri, 10.00–15.00 Sat) is located near the main square and has maps and information on accommodation, or there's **Kompas Postojna** (Titov trg 2a; 057 211 480; w kompas-postojna.si; 08.00–18.00 Mon–Fri, 09.00–13.00 Sat), conveniently located on the main square, which has maps, brochures and other information and can book accommodation and arrange tours.

WHERE TO STAY, EAT AND DRINK

Hotel Jama (80 dbls) Jamska cesta 30; 057 000 200; e hotel.jama@postojnska-jama.eu; w postojnska-jama.eu. Refurbished hotel right next to the cave entrance. Reopened in 2016 after a complete makeover, & now boasts swish, spacious rooms with big balconies from which to watch the sunset, & an excellent restaurant. Packages include room plus entrance to the cave, Predjama Castle, etc. **€€€€**

Restavracija & Apartmaji Proteus (2 dbls, 1 quad, 6 apts) Titov trg 1a; 052 700 0103; w postojnska-jama.eu; f restavracijaproteus. Conveniently located on the main square & serves good, hearty fare such as gnocchi with goulash, & also has a self-service salad bar. Above the restaurant (€€€) are several smart rooms & apartments at reasonable prices. €€€

Nona B&B (6 rooms) 4 Studeno; 064 169 165; w nonabb.si. Nice B&B in a renovated farmhouse with a garden, around 5km north of Postojna & 6km from Predjama. **€€**

Vila Lemič (8 rooms) Rakitnik 30, Prestranek; 031 560 119; w lemic.si/en/home. Another nice B&B, this one located just south of Postojna, with clean, modern rooms. **€€**

Youth Hostel Proteus (90 beds in 3-bed dorms, rising to 240 beds in Jul/Aug) Tržaška cesta 36; 058 501 020; e recepcija.sgls@guest.arnes.si; w proteus.sgls.si. Opened in 2013 in a renovated 1980s building (the hostel won a design award for the renovation project), which in turn stands on the foundations of the once rather fashionable Grand Hotel Adelsberg, whose fortunes took a downturn when it became a World War I barracks & later a boarding school. Very clean with bargain-priced beds, along with kitchen, cinema, internet lounge & bike hire. **€€–€**

Modrian Homestead Jamska cesta; w postojnska-jama.eu; Apr–Sep 10.00–20.00 daily. On the slope just below the souvenir shops running up to the cave entrance, near a restored mill. Grills & other hearty fare on a nice terrace. €€€

Štorja pod Stopnicami Ulica 1, Maja 1; 059 927 898; w bistrostorja.si; noon–22.00 Mon–Sat. Highly rated restaurant serving traditional Slovenian dishes. €€€

Briljant Jamska cesta; opening hours vary according to how long the cave is open – in the summer months, 09.00–20.00 daily. Decent buffet-style place for lunch near the cave entrance, below Hotel Jama, with reasonably priced pasta & other dishes. €€

SHOPPING If it's souvenirs of Postojna Cave you're after, you'll find a plethora of official shops and kiosks around the entrance to the cave itself, as well as stalls selling local honey, liqueurs and other products. Inside Predjama Castle there's a nice little shop with wine, honey, liqueurs and other delicacies.

OTHER PRACTICALITIES

Pharmacy Prečna ulica 2; 057 211 700; w kraske-lekarne.si/pharmacy/lekarna-postojna; 07.30–19.00 Mon–Fri, 07.30–13.00 Sat

Post office 1 Maja 2a; 08.00–18.00 Mon–Fri, 08.00–midday Sat

WHAT TO SEE AND DO On Titov trg you'll find the **Karst Research Institute** (**Inštitut za raziskovanje krasa**), with a sculpture of an enormous olm (page 177) at the bottom of the front steps, and behind Restavracija Proteus, the **Parish Church of St Stephen (Župnijska cerkev sv Štefana)**. However, the main reason most visitors make their way to Postojna is to see the sublimely beautiful Postojna Cave and nearby Predjama Castle.

Postojna Cave (Postojnska jama) (Jamska cesta 30; ☎ 057 000 100; e info@postojnska-jama.eu; w postojnska-jama.eu; ⏲ daily, guided tours last 1½hrs & run to the following timetable: Jul/Aug 09.00–18.00 hourly plus 14.30, Apr–Jun 10.00–16.00 hourly except 13.00, Sep 09.00–17.00 hourly, Oct 10.00–16.00 hourly except 14.00, Nov–Mar 10.00, noon & 15.00; entry adult/child/under 5s €27.90/€16.70/€1; adult/child €40.30/€24.20 inc Predjama Castle; €46.60/€25.80 for Postojna Cave, Predjama Castle, plus Proteus Vivarium & EXPO Postojna Cave Karst; a combined ticket also gets you a ride on the free shuttle bus between Postojna Cave & Predjama Castle) Postojna Cave is an amazing place. As you walk through the cave, vast galleries open out, bristling with stalactites and stalagmites of all imaginable shapes and sizes, and ranging in colour from 'pure' milky white limestone to pink and red (the latter due to the presence of iron oxide). Some ceilings are festooned with thin, 'spaghetti' stalactites, while in other places massive columns protrude from floor and ceiling, and elsewhere 'curtain' formations extend down the walls, like some extended sheets of translucent fruit peel.

Postojna Jama was formed more than a million years ago by the underground course of the River Pivka, which disappears underground at the cave entrance and still flows through its lower sections, below the part now open to the public. The river once flowed through the upper parts of the cave, now open to visitors – but as it enlarged the cracks, galleries and channels in the limestone rock by mechanical and chemical erosion, its course shifted ever deeper (see page 4 for more information on karst).

Postojna Cave is some 11km long (11,235m to be precise) and forms part of a much larger cave system with two other caves: **Black Cave (Črna jama)** and **Pivka Cave (Pivka jama)**, which, respectively, are 3,294m and 794m long. Together they add up to a cave system over 24km in length, the second longest in Slovenia – an even longer cave system (over 24km) was discovered in 2012 beneath a mountain called Tolminski Migovec in Triglav National Park.

Postojna Cave is remarkably accessible, being horizontal rather than vertical, and the whole length of Postojna Cave open to normal visits has no steps at all, just an easy, well-maintained path and a few inclines. Visitors are transported from the entrance into the heart of the cave system on small trains, after which the 'standard' walking route is around 1.8km. The cave remains at a constant temperature of around 9°C – so you'll probably want to wear a pullover or fleece, whatever the temperature outside. Black Cave – so called because of the black colouring of the stalagmites and stalactites, which is due to the presence of ash from a massive forest fire in the area several thousand years ago – is even cooler, at around 5°C.

Postojna Cave and Black Cave are linked by an artificial tunnel, dug secretly by the Italians during the 1930s, for strategic military purposes rather than in the name of exploration (Postojna lay on the border between Italy and the Kingdom of Yugoslavia). It is said that the Italians used workers from Sicily rather than northern Italy to dig the tunnel, so that locals would not be able to understand them or find out about the tunnel or exactly where it led. In any case the tunnel was never used by the Italians, and was later bricked up at its halfway point. However, during World War II (when Slovenia was occupied by Germany) the Partisans (page 11) used the tunnel to enter Postojna Cave from Black Cave, and blow up the fuel depot established by the Germans at the main entrance to the cave. The damage from the huge explosion, combined no doubt with souvenir hunting in the early years of the cave's history, is one of the reasons there aren't many stalactites and stalagmites in the initial galleries on the train route.

If you're planning to visit Predjama Castle (page 178) as well, it's cheaper to buy an all-inclusive ticket for both, or a bumper ticket including the Proteus Vivarium (see below) and EXPO Postojna Cave Karst if you're planning to visit those (and you should).

Highly recommended is one of the **special tours** of all three caves, starting from Pivka Cave, crossing to Black Cave through one of the artificial tunnels, then continuing to Postojna Cave itself through another artificial tunnel (adult/child €60/€30). The entrance to Black Cave is far more atmospheric than the main entrance to Postojna Cave, involving a steep walk down steps from the forest into the cave entrance, followed by a path alongside the underground course of the River Pivka (sometimes roaring, at other times magically silent), as patches of gold and silver algae glitter on the roof of the cave overhead. Note the different-coloured rock indicating the high-water level on the cave walls. It's possible to walk out from Postojna Cave rather than take the train, passing through some nice galleries on the way. Other special 'adventure' tours are available, some much more physically challenging and requiring rubber boots and body suits (supplied), in small groups and costing €80/€40 per adult/child.

Don't forget to visit the **Proteus Vivarium** (best included in combined tickets, otherwise entry adult/child €10.90/€6.50), beside the entrance to Postojna Cave, where you can see and learn more about the **olm** (see below) – you can also see graffiti from early visitors, mostly from the 19th century (though there's also some from as early as the 13th century elsewhere, ie: several hundred years before the

THE HUMAN FISH

Postojna's most famous resident is the **olm** or **cave salamander** (*Proteus anguinus*), known in Slovene as *človeška ribica (čovječja ribica* in Croatian), which translates as 'human fish'. One look at the pale, pinkish skin, the embryonic red gills and the tiny, fingered 'hands' and feet will make the comparison seem immediately appropriate. These amphibians can grow to a length of up to 30cm (large enough for locals during medieval times to believe they were baby dragons), and their geographical distribution is limited to the karst caves and subterranean rivers of Slovenia and Croatia, as well as parts of northeast Italy and Bosnia (ie: they lead a solely subterranean existence). The animal has become a popular symbol of Postojna, decorating T-shirts and fridge magnets galore, not to mention (in the form of a large sculpture) the wall of the Karst Research Institute in Postojna itself.

You can see olms in the Vivarium Proteus, as well as a tank in the cave itself (your chances of actually seeing an olm in the wild are slim indeed) – but please *do not* use flash to photograph these creatures, in the vivarium or anywhere else. Although blind (sight not being a prerequisite for living in pitch blackness), the olm is extremely sensitive to light, and will try to swim away from bright light sources or bury itself under pebbles or small rocks. Excessive exposure to light damages its sensitive skin, which turns a reddish colour as if sunburnt, and can lead to the animal's death.

cave was officially 'discovered'). It's also really worth seeing the **EXPO Postojna Cave Karst** which has fascinating and informative displays explaining the karst underworld of Postojna and its surroundings, with plenty of interactive and well-thought-out displays for kids. Hats off to parents who can get past the old locomotive from the cave train, which kids can sit in and toot the whistle, without stopping there for quite a length of time! Entry costs the same as the Proteus Vivarium. For opening hours for the Proteus Vivarium and EXPO Postojna Cave Karst, see w postojnska-jama.eu/en/timetables.

Predjama Castle (Predjamski grad) ☏ 057 000 100; e info@postojnska-jama.eu; w postojnska-jama.eu; ⏲ daily Apr–Jun & Oct 10.00–17.00, Jul/Aug 09.00–19.00, Sep 09.00–18.00, Nov–Mar 10.00–16.00; entry adult/child aged 6–15/under 5s €16.90/€10.10/€1; or adult/child €40.30/24.20 inc Postojna Cave, inc use of a shuttle bus running between the 2 attractions early Jul–mid Sep) Just over 8km northwest of Postojna Cave, Predjama Castle sits massive and impregnable-looking within a 123m-high cave in an overhanging cliff. Built in the 12th or 13th century, it owes much of its present form to a 16th-century development.

The castle's most famous (or infamous, depending on your point of view) resident was Erazem, a 15th-century knight. Following a quarrel in which he killed a friend of the Austrian Emperor Frederick III, he was besieged in his castle for a year, taunting his would-be captors by offering them fresh cherries while they sat miserably in the valley below, until he was betrayed (while on the toilet, to be precise) by a servant. He is said to be buried beneath the enormous linden tree by the church, which you pass just before reaching the castle by road.

A secret passage from the castle leads up to the top of the cliff, emerging through a sinkhole. Part of the cave below the castle can also be visited between May and September – at 13km long, it is the third-largest cave system in Slovenia.

VIPAVA VALLEY

The Vipava Valley runs in a line across the southwest corner of Slovenia, a truly lovely area sandwiched between the contrasting landscapes of the Karst, the Adriatic and the crumpled foothills of the Julian Alps. Its broad floor follows the meandering ribbon of the Vipava River, below the steep slopes of the Trnovo Forest Plateau and the Nanos hills. The Vipava Valley is one of Slovenia's top wine regions, and has plenty of wonderful places to eat, as well as some beautiful little towns – best explored on two wheels, stopping at a vineyard or two for wine tastings – and exhilarating walks on the hills which surround it.

GETTING THERE AND AROUND Solkan and Nova Gorica lie at one end of the railway line which runs to Jesenice (direct trains several times a day via Bled; timetables w potniski.sz.si/en). From Jesenice there are rail connections to Ljubljana and to Villach in Austria; from Gorizia (just across the border in Italy) there are trains and buses to Trieste, Venice and elsewhere in Italy. The motorway through the Vipava Valley branches off the E61 between Divača and Postojna, although despite the short distance from here to Ajdovščina this route is less well served by public transport than you might have hoped. There is however a bus service between Ljubljana and Nova Gorica, which runs through Postojna, Hruševje, Vipava and Ajdovščina (around 5 services per day, journey time Postojna to Vipava around 35 minutes, 10 minutes more to Ajdovščina; for timetables see w arriva.si). Otherwise, there are several shuttle and transfer services operating in the area (see w vipavskadolina.si/

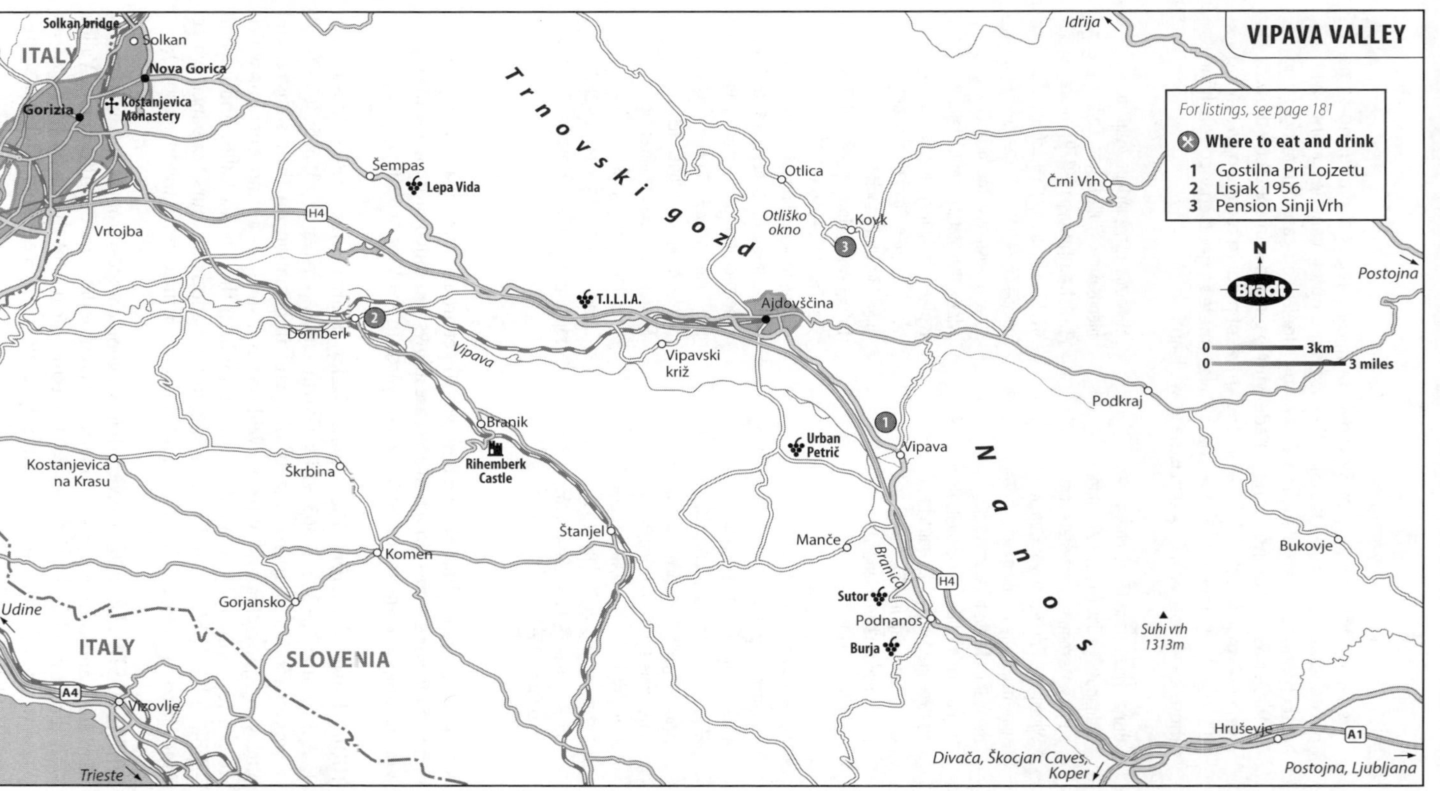
VIPAVA VALLEY
For listings, see page 181
Where to eat and drink
1 Gostilna Pri Lojzetu
2 Lisjak 1956
3 Pension Sinji Vrh
N
Bradt
0 3km
0 3 miles
Solkan bridge
Solkan
ITALY
Nova Gorica
Gorizia
Kostanjevica Monastery
T r n o v s k i g o z d
Šempas
Lepa Vida
H4
Vrtojba
Otlica
Otliško okno
Kovk
Črni Vrh
Idrija
Postojna
T.I.L.I.A.
Ajdovščina
Dornberk
Vipava
Vipavski križ
Podkraj
Branik
Rihemberk Castle
Urban Petrič
Vipava
N a n o s
Kostanjevica na Krasu
Škrbina
Štanjel
Komen
Manče
Branica
Bukovje
Udine
Gorjansko
Sutor
Podnanos
Burja
Suhi vrh 1313m
ITALY
SLOVENIA
A4
Vizovlje
Trieste
Hruševje
A1
Divača, Škocjan Caves, Koper
Postojna, Ljubljana

VIPAVA VALLEY WINES

The Vipava Valley is one of Slovenia's best wine regions, producing some outstanding Malvazija, Rebula, Refosco and other varieties along with autochthonous grapes such as Zelen and Pinela. You can increasingly find field blends, and orange wines, made with extended skin contact – the way wine was made in the area before the arrival of modern technology. Among the standout vineyards of the Vipava Valley (there's a good chance you'll find these on wine lists in Croatian Istria as well) are:

Burja [map, page 179] Orehovica 46, Podnanos; +386 041 363 272; info@burjaestate.com; w burjaestate.com. Winemaker Primož Lavrenčič produces some genuinely stunning wines below the soaring Nanos hills. Standouts include Burja White (a field blend from his two oldest vineyards, which has won gold medals from Decanter) and Burja Reddo (a barrel- and barrique-aged Pinot Noir).

Lepa Vida [map, page 179] Osek 4b, Šempas; +386 41 211 778; e contact@lepavida.si; w lepavida.wine. Along with Pinot Sivi and Malvazija they make a Malvazija/Sauvignon blend called Mi (named after owners Matija & Irena), & oOo, an orange wine (Malvazija/Rebula blend).

Sutor [map, page 179] Podraga 30, Podnanos; +386 05 366 9367; w sutor.si. Along with an excellent Malvazija, wines include 2 superb blends, Sutor While & Sutor Red.

T.I.L.I.A. [map, page 179] Potoče 41, 5263 Dobravlje; +386 05 364 66 84; info@tiliaestate.si; w tiliaestate.si. The focus of winemaker Matjaž Lemut's talents is pinots, including some very good smoky brambly Pinot Noirs under the 'black' & 'white' labels.

Urban Petrič [map, page 179] Slap 53a, Vipava; +386 41 991 210; vino.petric@gmail.com; w vino-petric.com/en. Urban Petrič is an 8th generation wine producer across the river from Vipava. Along with Pinela & Zelen his wines include a Yellow Muscat, & Bela Natura (an orange wine from a Malvasia/Rebula/Zelen blend. They also have 5 rooms & an apartment in nearby Dobravlje.

en/ostani/transfer--shuttle). The best way to get around the Vipava Valley itself is to hire a bike or e-bike – which in any case allows you much more scope to stop for wine tastings at some of the fantastic vineyards in the Vipava Valley.

TOURIST INFORMATION The **Vipava Valley Tourist Office** (Prešernova ulica 9, Ajdovščina; +386 5 365 9140; Glavni trg 8, Vipava; +386 5 368 70 40; w vipavskadolina.si/en) has plenty of useful information on their website, and offices in Ajdovščina and Vipava. **Wajdušna** is a small local tour operator which we can recommend very highly, running tours in the Vipava Valley and beyond – from e-bikes, hiking and paragliding, to food and wine tours (Župančičeva 1c, Ajdovščina; +386 41 232 548; e wajdusna@wajdusna.com; w wajdusna.com).

WHERE TO STAY, EAT AND DRINK There's a good choice of rooms and apartments, farm stays and some vineyards offering accommodation along the Vipava Valley, with the tiny village of Vipavski Križ making for one of the nicest bases. As for places to eat and drink, you are genuinely spoilt for choice – from Michelin-starred fine dining to homely taverns.

Villa Irena (1 apt) Vipavski Križ 50; +386 41 370 622; w villairena.net; all year. Beautifully renovated house in Vipavski Križ, spread over 2 floors with kitchen & dining area downstairs & dbl bedroom upstairs, exposed wooden beams & a small terrace. **€€€€**

* **Vipavski Križ 54** (3 rooms) Vipavski Križ 54; +386 41 728 518; e info@vk54.si; w vk54.si; all year. Big, spacious rooms each sleeping up to 4 people, in a renovated stone house in the heart of the old town, with a kitchen/dining area downstairs. Very friendly & welcoming, good value, & the room with a mezzanine accessed by ladder (Zelen) is great for families. Highly recommended. **€€€**

Youth Hostel Ajdovščina (Hiša Mladih Ajdovščina) (50 beds) Cesta IV. Prekomorske 61a, Ajdovščina; +386 5 368 9383; e info@hostel-ajdovscina.si; w hostel-ajdovscina.si/en; all year. Hostel on the northern edge of town, with dorm beds from €19pp. They also have bike rental. **€**

* **Gostilna Pri Lojzetu (Dvorec Zemono)** [map, page 179] Dvorec Zemono, Vipava; +386 5 368 70 07; w prilojzetu.si; 17.00–22.00 Wed/Thu, midday–22.00 Fri/Sat, midday–18.00 Sun. Also known as Gostilna Pri Lojzetu (locally it's usually called Dvorec Zemono), this is an outstanding, Michelin-starred restaurant housed in a beautifully restored 17th century manor house, where chef Tomaž Kavčič creates amazing & imaginative dishes from locally sourced, seasonal ingredients. Order à la carte, or better still go for the superb tasting menu (available in 4-, 5- or 6-courses; €75–95). And on no account should you miss the signature dessert, a lemon, lime, juniper & gin sorbet (TK makes has his own gin label, Monologue, which frankly knocks the socks off any other gin I've ever tasted). Quite possibly the author's favourite restaurant in Slovenia (& the competition for this title is pretty fierce). Highly recommended. **€€€€**

Faladur Ulica Ivana Ščeka 6, Vipava; +386 40 232 987; w faladur.si; noon–22.00 Mon & Wed–Sat. Boutique modern wine bar & restaurant just a hop & a skip from the main square in Vipava. **€€€**

Lisjak 1956 [map, page 179] Zalošče 40, Dornberk; +386 31 390 901; w vinalisjak.si; all year. Excellent farm-to-table style food – think platters of local cheeses & charcuterie, heritage beetroot carpaccio & more substantial dishes like gnocchi with game – all accompanied by some lovely wines from their award-winning vineyard (their Malvazija is outstanding). **€€€**

Arkade Cigoj (also known as Kmetija Cigoj) Črniče 91, Črniče.; +386 5 366 6000; e arkade.cigoj@siol.net; w arkade-cigoj.com; by reservation, noon–midnight Fri/Sat, midday –17.00 Sun. Well-known farm producing their own prosciutto, sausages & other charcuterie, with a good restaurant – think hearty traditional fare, huge portions & a warm welcome in a tavern-like setting. They also have 6 simple but clean rooms (**€€€**). **€€€–€€**

Pension Sinji Vrh [map, page 179] (12 rooms) Kovk 10a, Col; +386 31 836 813; e info@sinji-vrh.si; w sinji-vrh.si; all year. Absolutely wonderful restaurant overlooking the Vipava Valley from the edge of the Trnovo Forest Plateau, with traditional local dishes based on seasonal produce from their own organic farm & good wine, served at big wooden tables surrounded by local artworks (they run an annual art competition), with a few rooms (min 2 nights; **€€€**). Don't miss the local superstar cheeses from Golden Ring Cheese (w goldenringcheese.com/products). Sinji Vrh makes a perfect base for hikes on the Trnovo Forest Plateau, & they also have e-bikes for hire. If you're up here it's well worth getting full or at least half board (only €25/€15pp on top of the price of a room). **€€**

Caffe-bar Jolly Glavni trg 12, Vipava; w jollyvipava.si. Nice little café on the corner of the main square in Vipava, with good coffee & drinks, cakes, burgers & other snacks. **€**

SHOPPING The Vipava Valley produces some particularly good **wines**, and there are plenty of vineyards in the valley where you can buy bottles, perhaps following a tasting (see opposite). If you want to buy some excellent local cheeses, have a look at what's available from **Golden Ring Cheese** (w goldenringcheese.com/products) – fabulously rich, and matured in the damp concrete tunnels of a former reservoir beneath the hillside at Sinji Vrh, built by the Italian army before World War I. Local craft brewery **Pelicon** has a store next to their brewery in Ajdovščina (IV. Prekomorske 61, Ajdovščina; w pelicon.beer).

WHAT TO SEE AND DO **Vipava**, the valley's small capital, sits below the Nanos hills, at the headwaters of the River Vipava – which has the distinction of being the only **delta-shaped riverhead** in Europe. Water comes gushing up from karst springs near the town centre, rushing along multiple streams between old stone houses, and spanned by some 25 bridges. The centre of the town is the large main square, Glavni trg, surrounded by old trees with the **Lanthieri Mansion** (Dvorec Lanthieri) at one end – a rather handsome building, which dates from the mid 17th century and in its heyday hosted the likes of Venetian playwright Carlo Goldoni. It's been beautifully restored and can be visited by appointment (contact the tourist office). Just outside the northwest edge of town is a small cemetery, which – rather unexpectedly – contains two massive **Ancient Egyptian sarcophagi** dating from the Fifth Dynasty (2494–2345 BC). Only six of this type of sarcophagi are known in the world today – two in the Cairo Museum in Egypt, one in the British Museum in London, another in the Pelizaeus Museum in Hildesheim – and these two among the vineyards of the Vipava Valley. They were sent back to Slovenia by Anton Lavrin, the Habsburg Consul in Egypt, who was born into a wealthy landowning family in Vipava in the late 18th century, and educated in Vienna. Lavrin became an avid collector during his time in Egypt, sending finds back to Vienna, and selling some of his collection to decorate Miramare Castle near Trieste. Inside the sarcophagi are the remains of Lavrin's father and mother, and his son who died while still a child. **Dvorec Zomono**, a beautifully restored 17th century manor house which sits on a low hill just outside Vipava, is home to one of the finest restaurants anywhere in Slovenia, the Michelin-starred **Gostilna Pri Lojzetu** (page 181).

Northwest from Vipava, **Ajdovščina** is larger than its neighbour, and was the site of a Roman military fort Castrum Ad Fluvium Frigidum, built on the Roman road and trade route which ran through the Vipava Valley to Emona (Ljubljana), close to the source of the Hubelj river. Some 14 of the old towers which once formed part of the Roman defensive walls remain intact (many of the town's other Roman remains can be seen in the Goriški muzej in Nova Gorica). Later, a medieval town grew up within the Roman walls, and in the 16th century ironworks were built on the Hubelj at the order of Emperor Ferdinand I, which were to bring huge prosperity to the town, and remained in operation until the early years of the 20th century.

There's an absolute gem of a small art collection in Ajdovščina – this is the **Pilon Gallery**, where you can see an extensive collection of works by one of the greatest Slovenian artists of the 20th century, Veno Pilon (Prešernova ulica 3; ☎ +386 05 368 9177; w venopilon.com; ⌚ 09.00–18.00 Tue–Fri, 15.00–18.00 Sat–Sun; closed for renovation until summer 2023). Pilon was born in Ajdovščina in 1896, and was the first Slovenian artist to exhibit graphic prints at the Venice Biennale, in 1924. Later he moved to Paris, where he fell under the spell of photography, returning to Ajdovščina in the late 1960s, where he died in 1970. The gallery occupies two buildings – the bakery where his father worked, and the studio Pilon later set up next door. It's a lovely space, and his richly coloured paintings, drawings and etchings are beautifully presented, with a separate area dedicated to his photography.

Across the river from Ajdovščina, the tiny village of **Vipavski Križ** is perhaps the most charming of the Vipava Valley's settlements – a cluster of beautifully preserved stone houses, and narrow cobbled streets. Despite its diminutive appearance, the village was once of considerable importance, with a castle being built here in the late 1400s to repel the Ottomans who had by then captured Gorizia, and the town (walled by this time) going on to be granted market rights in the 16th century. A Capuchin monastery was built in the 17th century, and the small parish church houses an enormous Baroque painting on canvas. There's a **Festival of Zelen** dedicated to the local Zelen grape, held in Vipavski Križ in June.

The impressive **Rihemberk Castle** (+386 05 1201 910; w rihemberk.com; Jul–Sep 10.00–13.00 Mon–Fri & 10.00–19.00 Sat–Sun; Apr–Jun & Oct–11 Nov 10.00–18.00 Sat–Sun; entry adult/child €5/€3) overlooks the valley from steep slopes above the village of Branik. Built in the late 12th century, it was later owned by the Lanthieri family, and was severely damaged during World War II. It was partially restored in 2017.

Running along the northern edge of the Vipava Valley, the **Trnovo Forest Plateau** (Trnovski gozd) is a fantastic area for hiking. The best-known feature on the plateau is **Otliško okno**, a natural rock arch framing a view of the valley floor far, far below. A well-marked hiking trail leads up from the edge of Ajdovščina (it starts from near the Ajdovščina Youth Hostel) to Otliško okno – about a 90-minute walk with 750m of ascent. You can return the same way or follow a trail to Sinji Vrh which makes for an unbeatable spot for lunch (page 181), then descend towards Stara Baba and from there meet the outward trail near the source of the River Hubelj. Another popular area for hiking is **Nanos**, at the eastern end of the valley. It can get quite windy up here – the Vipava Valley receives the full force of the *burja* wind when it's blowing, a northeasterly with gusts reaching over 200km/h. However, unless the wind gets up beyond 50km/h or so, most locals probably wouldn't consider it worth mentioning – a local joke goes that when it reaches around 80km/h, people send their children out for a bit of fresh air.

The Vipava Valley comes to an end at **Solkan** and **Nova Gorica** (the latter was only built after World War II, when the town of Gorizia became part of Italy) in the northwest, where the River Soča marks the border with Italy. The **Solkan Bridge** is quite a marvel of engineering, built in the early 1900s as part of the Neue Alpenbahnen which linked Austria with the then Habsburg-controlled port of Trieste. At 85m it's the longest stone arch bridge in the world, constructed from over 5,000 tonnes of precisely cut stone blocks with a 12mm layer of cement between them. It was built in a staggeringly short amount of time, just 18 days (something which should make most modern engineering projects hang their head in shame), and when the mass of wooden scaffolding was removed the whole structure sank by only 6mm, so accurate was the design. It was blown up by the retreating Austrians in World War I, and rebuilt in the late 1920s (the only difference being that the original bridge had five arches in each spandrel, as opposed to the present four, and the main arch was a smidgen wider).

In 2025, **Nova Gorica** will be a European Capital of Culture (a title it will share with Gorizia, in a rather fitting gesture for a population once divided, now reunited) – so expect plenty of events and new projects to spring up in the two cities, which you can keep track of at w go2025.eu/en. A plaque on the pavement just outside the railway station, marking the border, shows just how closely bound the two cities are.

While you're in Nova Gorica, don't miss the **Kostanjevica Monastery** (+386 05 330 7750; w samostan-kostanjevica.si/en; 09:00–midday & 15:00–17:00 Mon–Sat, 15:00–17:00 Sun; free), which sits on a hill on the edge of town. It's here that you'll find the tomb of Charles X – the last king of France, who fled the country following the outbreak of the French Revolution, taking refuge in Edinburgh then Prague, where he contracted cholera, and finally died in Nova Gorica in 1836. **Madonca** (Erjavčeva Ulica 43; +386 64 222 206; w madonca.si; €€€€–€€€) is a great place to eat – the *Idrijski žlikrofi* are delicious – and they also have some nice rooms (**€€€**). For more of a splurge, head for the Michelin-starred **DAM** (Ulica

Vinka Vodopivca 24; +386 05 333 1147; €€€€€). Information on the area's **World War I** history and heritage can be found on the website of The Walk of Peace (w thewalkofpeace.com).

Part Three

ACTIVITIES

10

Hiking in Istria

Istria, like much of Croatia, is covered in an extensive network of hiking trails. The five walks described here can each be done in a day, ranging from one to several hours, and from a simple stroll on the coast to a 1,400m ascent from near sea level. None requires any technical or climbing skills, though a reasonable level of fitness is advisable on the longer routes, and all are on clearly marked paths or tracks. None requires camping equipment. There is of course scope for more walks, including multi-day routes through Učka and Ćićarija (before setting out on one of these routes, see the note on fire hazards on page 3).

It has to be said there is a certain allure in being able to hike through beautiful scenery and at the end of your walk find yourself back by the sea or in a medieval hill town, where you can put your feet up with a crisp glass of Malvazija and dine on freshly caught seafood or truffles. Oh, the hardship.

MAPS

The most detailed and accurate hiking maps available for Croatia are those produced by **SMAND** (w smand.hr), and the ones produced by the **HGSS** (Hrvatska gorska služba spašavanja, Croatian Mountain Rescue Service; w gss.hr/hgss/kartografija), in both cases at a scale of around 1:25,000 with 25m contour lines. Hiking trails, huts, springs and other features are all clearly marked. The HGSS produces up-to-date sheets covering Učka (#38) and Ćićarija (#19) at 1:25,000. There are SMAND sheets being prepared for Učka and Ćićarija, though at the time of writing they were not yet available. HGSS and SMAND maps are available in the UK through The Map Shop (w themapshop.co.uk), and at bookshops in Croatia (you may have less luck finding them in Istria itself, so try in Rijeka or Zagreb if you're travelling through either of these cities first).

A series of maps published by Mateus covers the whole of Istria in seven large sheets at 1:30,000; these are quite accurate, though harder to get in Croatia (again, The Map Shop stocks them in the UK), and those from HGSS and SMAND are preferable for hiking. A detailed (1:30,000) map of Učka Nature Park is available from tourist information offices and bookshops in Rijeka, Opatija, Lovran, etc. Some local tourist offices have produced quite detailed maps with cycling or hiking routes marked – the Istria Bike map for Buzet, available from the tourist office in Buzet (page 120), covers the terrain for walks east of Buzet. **Pazin tourist office** (w central-istria.com) has some route maps and descriptions of walks around Pazin. You're unlikely to need a map for Rt Kamenjak, but there's one available in Premantura (page 65), though it doesn't show much detail. For information on hiking guidebooks, see page 231.

There's now a really good range of trails online at w istria-trails.com/en/trails, including maps and route details as well as GPS tracks.

FOOTWEAR AND CLOTHING

Despite the balmy Istrian sunshine, the weather in the mountains can change with very little warning, and you should always carry a waterproof jacket and warm clothing when hiking on Učka and Ćićarija. Hiking in trainers or sandals is not advised in the mountains, particularly on longer routes – you are more likely to sprain your ankle than if you're wearing decent hiking shoes or boots, and sandals are poor protection from snakebite – though for walking along the coast or down Rt Kamenjak, they're ideal.

TRAIL MARKINGS

Hiking trails in Istria, and Croatia and Slovenia as a whole, are almost always extremely well marked with an easily identifiable series of markings (*markacije*), which are maintained or repainted by local hiking clubs. A white dot surrounded by a red circle is what you'll be looking for, or a stripe or arrow (also in red and white) indicating a turn or change in direction, painted on a rock or tree trunk beside the trail. Around Buzet you may sometimes see blue and red trail markings instead, a local peculiarity – in the rest of Croatia blue trail markings would indicate a hydrological feature, but not here. Forestry markings – a series of bars with a number, stencilled or spray-painted on to a tree trunk – have nothing to do with hiking trails and should be ignored.

HUTS AND CAMPING

Although there are only a few mountain huts in Istria, it's worth knowing that those in Croatia fall into three different types. A *planinarski dom* (often abbreviated PD before the name of the hut) is the most useful, open during the summer or sometimes all year, and often (at least in the main hiking areas and national parks) staffed. There will be beds in dorms with mattresses (though you'll usually need to bring your own sleeping bag); kitchen facilities; toilets; and sometimes, showers. A *planinarska kuća* is similar but is locked, the key being available from a keyholder in a nearby town, so is much less useful. Most of those in Istria are of this type. A *skloništa* is a small, basic, unstaffed shelter, usually open all year.

WATER

Istria is karst country (page 4), and as such most rainwater disappears rapidly into the ground, with streams and even freshwater springs likely to dry up by the middle of the summer. This means that you generally need to carry sufficient drinking water to last for an entire walk (or day, on a multi-stage walk).

1. LOVRAN TO VOJAK (UČKA)

A long but rewarding hike, beginning just above sea level in the small town of Lovran, and climbing to the highest point of Učka, known as Vojak or sometimes Vrh Učka. Almost 1,400m of ascent on clearly marked trails, mostly through forest and sometimes open meadows, are rewarded by spectacular views from the summit, over the Adriatic and the islands of the Kvarner Gulf, and far across the undulating hills of the Istrian interior. Plenty of people drive up to the top of Učka from Rijeka and Opatija, but the path from Lovran is by far the nicest way to approach this mountain, with the road and the huge telecommunications tower just

Start/finish point	Lovran (Trg Slobode); page 132
Distance	8km
Grade	Medium–hard
Approximate time	4½ hours (ascent only; if you're hiking back down to Lovran allow an additional 2½ hours)
Highest altitude	1,401m
Lowest altitude	5m
Total height climbed	1,400m
Map	Učka park prirode (available at tourist information offices and bookshops in Rijeka, Opatija, Lovran, etc); HGSS PP Učka (#38)
Eating and drinking	Lovran
Best season	Spring, summer or autumn
Water	None between Lovran and Poklon Visitor Centre (40 minutes from Vojak)
Further information	w pp-ucka.hr

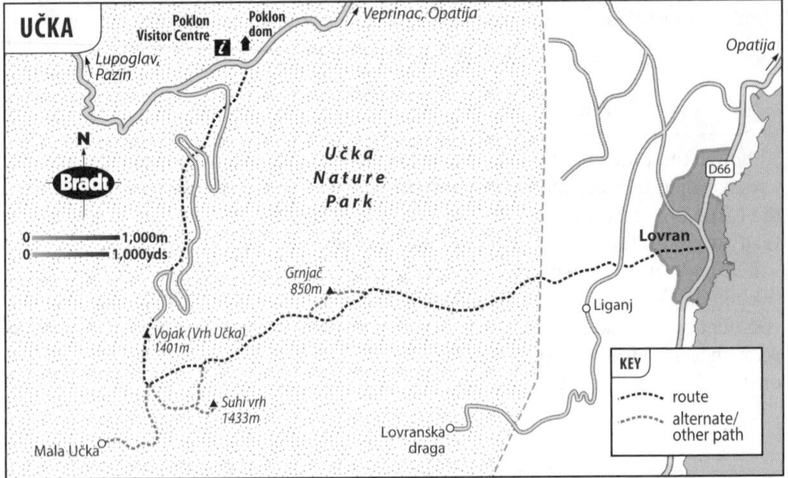

below the summit remaining completely hidden until the final moment. A bus runs between Rijeka and Poklon dom, the mountain hut on the saddle below Vojak, also stopping in Opatija – but it only runs on Sundays (bus #34 departs Opatija at 09.30 and 17.10; returns from Poklon dom at 10.30 and 18.00).

From Lovran's Trg Slobode, walk to the junction and the beginning of the trail markings. Turn right, passing a small votive shrine then following the road around to the left. From here a series of several flights of steep, walled steps lead up past the houses of **Liganj** to a junction, about an hour from Lovran. Keep straight ahead following the signs to Vojak and Grnjac, first on a rocky path and (briefly) a sealed road, then a rocky trail again and a forest track. After crossing a low ridge, the path follows the side of a valley, with wonderful views out over steep pine slopes to the sea from occasional clearings and rock outcrops.

After passing trails to Grnjac, the village of Mala Učka and Lovranska Draga, you reach a series of three clearings with low trees, wild roses and nettles, from where you get a brief glimpse of the red-and-white antenna on Vojak, and pass a small hunting lodge on the left. After the third clearing the path ascends through the trees on a brutally steep set of switchbacks, and passes a trail to **Suhi vrh** ('dry peak'; 1,332m) on the left. If you want some additional exercise (and some super views) you can hike over Suhi vrh as a detour and rejoin the main route later; otherwise keep straight ahead, crossing the forest road twice to emerge on an open saddle (where a path from Suhi vrh meets the main trail from your left), with the imposing limestone bulk of Vojak towering on your right. A final, steep ascent leads to the summit of **Vojak** (1,401m) with its stone lookout tower and spectacular views in all directions.

On a clear day you can clearly see the mountains of Gorski kotar to the northeast, and the islands of Cres, Lošinj and Krk to the southeast, with the Velebit Mountains beyond, and the rolling Istrian interior to the west, dotted with medieval hill towns. Keep an eye out for paragliders to the northwest – the slopes of Ćićarija are one of the best paragliding spots in Croatia.

If you're planning to return by bus, you'll need to descend from Vojak to the Poklon pass, 40 minutes downhill on a clearly marked path, crossing the road at several points. The **bus stop** is near the excellent new **Poklon Visitor Centre** (which is definitely worth visiting; ☎051 770 100; **w** pp-ucka.hr/en/poklon-visitor-centre) and the old mountain hut, **Poklon dom** (meant to be open at weekends, but often closed). Otherwise, the hike from Vojak back down to **Lovran**, following the same route as the ascent, requires around 2½ hours.

2. RASPADALICA AND KUK

Start/finish points	Buzet (Mala Vrata); page 119
Distance	9km
Grade	Medium
Approximate time	3 hours
Highest altitude	556m
Lowest altitude	210m
Total height climbed	420m
Map	Istria Bike (Buzet)
Eating and drinking	Buzet
Best season	Spring, summer or autumn; the Istria Open Paragliding Championship at Raspadalica takes place during July; winter is also possible for those suitably dressed, as there will be snow on Raspadalica

A short but fairly steep walk from the gates of Buzet's old town, mostly on paths and tracks through forest, to the rocky outcrops of Raspadalica and Kuk, from where you are rewarded with stupendous views back over the old town, the Mirna Valley and Butoniga jezero. The route involves crossing the tracks of the railway line at two points – caution required. You can extend the walk considerably by continuing from Raspadalica to Gomila (1,029m), one of the many knobbly peaks that make up the Ćićarija Mountains, a route which entails over 600m of additional ascent – making it a very long day from Buzet.

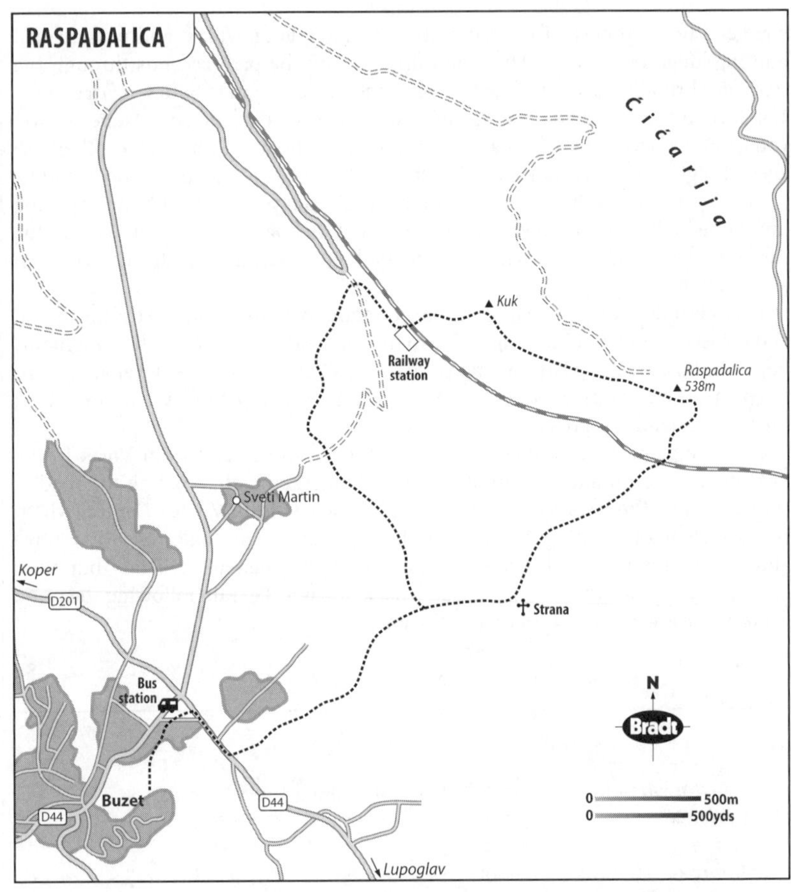

From Mala Vrata in Buzet's old town, follow the unsealed track down to the **bus station**. Turn right on the main road towards Rijeka, then just after the petrol station (look for a sign reading 'Put Raspadalica' – *put* meaning 'route' or 'path') on the opposite side of the road, though it might be in the wrong place), but before the bridge, turn left on to a faint, unmarked path beside the stream bed. Turn right on to a minor road, where you pick up clear trail markings. Follow the road uphill then take a marked footpath on your left, through typical Istrian mixed forest. On reaching a T-junction turn left, then at a broad track turn right, passing a small **votive shrine**. Walk past the farm and church at **Strana**, until around an hour from the bus station you reach the **railway line**. Cross with care, then continue uphill until emerging from the trees at **Raspadalica** (556m), where you are greeted by superb views out across central Istria, including Motovun, perched on its hill above the Mirna Valley.

Raspadalica is the launching point for Croatia's biggest **paragliding championship** in July, and there's also a nice **campsite** up here, a world away from the sprawling campervan-filled campsites of the coast.

Follow the top of the ridge to **Kuk**, before descending and crossing the **railway line** once more near the railway station, and descending past **Sv Martin** to rejoin the route of ascent near the small shrine mentioned above.

3. PAZINSKA JAMA

Start/finish points	Pazin Castle (page 106)
Distance	1.5km
Grade	Easy
Approximate time	45 minutes
Highest altitude	361m
Lowest altitude	230m
Total height climbed	130m
Map	Available from Pazin tourist information office (page 104)
Eating and drinking	Pazin (page 104)
Best season	Spring, summer or autumn, but not after heavy rain
Fees	Adults €5, children €3.50; ticket office at the Vršić Bridge
Further information	w central-istria.com

A short, easy walk from Pazin Castle, down into the forested gorge of the 'Pazin Abyss' before ascending again to the terrace restaurant of Hotel Lovac, from where there are superlative views back over the gorge to the castle. The gorge may become flooded after heavy rain, in which case the route will be impassable and should not be attempted. It's possible to enter and explore the cave, but only with a permit and a guide – see page 107 or ask at the tourist information office.

From the entrance to the castle, walk down Valvasorova ulica to the **Vršić Bridge**, and turn left on to the marked footpath down into the gorge. Descend quite steeply to the **Pazinčica**, which you cross on a small footbridge, then ascend on the other side, following a series of broad switchbacks. The entrance to the cave, as well as the cliff down which the hero descends into the gorge in Jules Verne's novel ***Mathius Sandorf***, is clearly visible. Entering the cave itself without a permit and guide is strictly prohibited (not to mention potentially dangerous), as is leaving the main path and wandering off along the Pazinčica. It is thought that the gorge may have provided inspiration for the entrance to Hell in Dante's ***Inferno*** (Dante is known to have visited Pazin). At the end of the path you reach a grassy terrace in front of the **Hotel Lovac**, where you can enjoy a drink, or a meal, while admiring the view back over the gorge, with Učka rising behind the castle in the distance.

Walk back along the road from in front of Hotel Lovac to the Vršić Bridge and Pazin Castle. Alternatively, if you're game, you can cross the gorge back to the castle by zip line (page 107), which reduces your journey to just a few seconds!

4. PAZIN WATERFALLS

A gentle walk along the valley of the Pazinčica – where the river flows above ground before vanishing into the cliff below Pazin Castle – visiting two large waterfalls and passing the sites of several old mills. The river (and waterfalls) will be less impressive in mid to late summer, and may even completely dry up after an extended period of drought. Walking is along woodland and riverside paths and an unsealed road. This route would also make a nice bike ride, in which case it would be better to ride there and back on the north (right) bank of the river, rather than returning along

Start/finish points	Pazin tourist information office (page 104)
Distance	7km
Grade	Very easy
Approximate time	13/4 hours
Highest altitude	361m
Lowest altitude	240m
Total height climbed	130m
Map	Available from Pazin tourist information office
Eating and drinking	Pazin
Best season	Spring or early summer, when the river is most likely to be full
Further information	More info on this route including GPS route at **w** central-istria.com/en/aktivnosti-activities-aktivurlaub/pjesacenje-walking/Pazinski-krov-short-walk

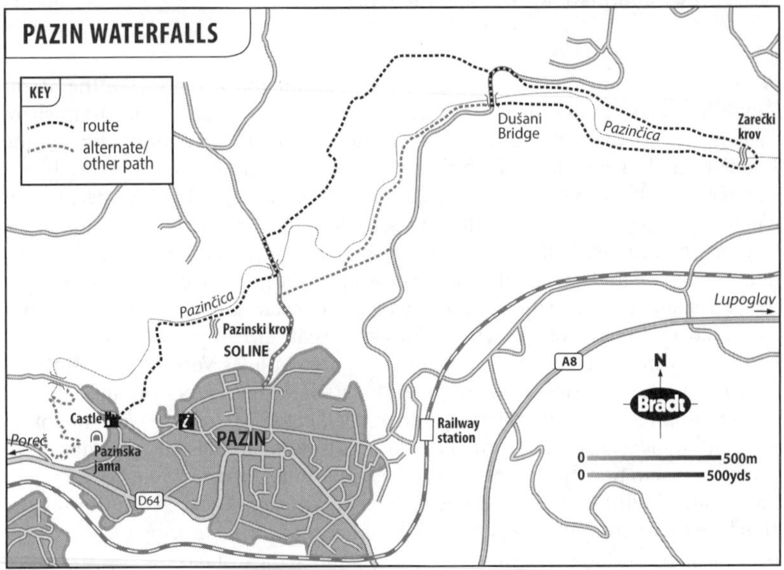

its southern side. In any case confirm at the tourist information office how high the river level is; if you can't cross the river near Zarečki krov, just return along the north bank (or follow the south bank from the Dušani Bridge to Zarečki krov).

From the tourist office walk towards the castle, then just before reaching it follow a track down to the right, veer right passing a ruined stone house on your left and walk under the pylons. Turn left on a clear path, which brings you to the river at the first large waterfall, **Pazinski krov**. There were once four watermills here. Follow the path alongside or close to the river then up to the road, and turn left over the bridge, built at the beginning of the 19th century and nearly washed away by floods in 1993. Turn right after the first house on to an unsealed road, and keep right where this forks. Follow the road round the back of some farm buildings, until arriving at the sealed road at the **Dušani Bridge** (Most Dušani).

Follow the road uphill to the left, then turn right on to a rocky terrace overlooking the river valley (where there's a prominent bit of graffiti carved into the rock). Follow this rocky terrace parallel to the river, then about 50 minutes from Pazin you reach a broad, open area of rock and **Zarečki krov**, a large waterfall that spills over a rock shelf into a pool below.

Zarečki krov is a favourite picnic area (which unfortunately means it's not as clean as it might be) and people come here to swim in the pool below the waterfall. There are some climbing routes here as well, including the roof of the cavern beneath the falls.

To return to Pazin, follow a rocky path through woodland on the south (left) bank of the Pazinčica, until reaching the road again at Most Dušani. Though there's a faint and sometimes overgrown path ahead on the other side of the road, you might instead want to just cross the bridge and return to Pazin the way you came. (You would have to leave the path ahead after about 15 minutes anyway – there's a section on private land which is very poorly kept, including two wooden bridges which feel as though they're about to collapse under you – and turn left on to a road which would lead you to **Soline**, from where you would turn left uphill to arrive in Pazin near the stadium.)

5. RT KAMENJAK

Start/finish points	Premantura (page 65)
Distance	6.5km
Grade	Very easy
Approximate time	2½ hours
Highest altitude	20m
Lowest altitude	0m
Total height climbed	30m
Map	Available from the Javna Ustanova Kamenjak office in Premantura (page 65), or Medulin tourist office (page 64)
Eating and drinking	Premantura
Best season	Late spring/early summer (in particular June, when Rt Kamenjak will be awash with wildflowers and butterflies, and the sun won't roast you, as there's very little in the way of shade)
Further information	w kamenjak.hr

The route, such as there is one, simply involves walking south from the centre of Premantura and following any one of several unsealed roads and tracks down the peninsula to Mala Kolombarica, near its southern tip, and back – and is also popular as a bike ride. There is plenty of scope for exploring the various coves that indent the peninsula's coastline – in which case you'll obviously need to allow more time – or stopping for a swim (though the currents here are very strong, particularly around the southern end of the peninsula, so don't swim out too far, and don't let young kids swim by themselves), and there's a small café/bar at Mala Kolombarica (Safari Bar). Keep an eye out for orchids (of which at least 28 species have been recorded, among the 590-odd plant taxa which have been

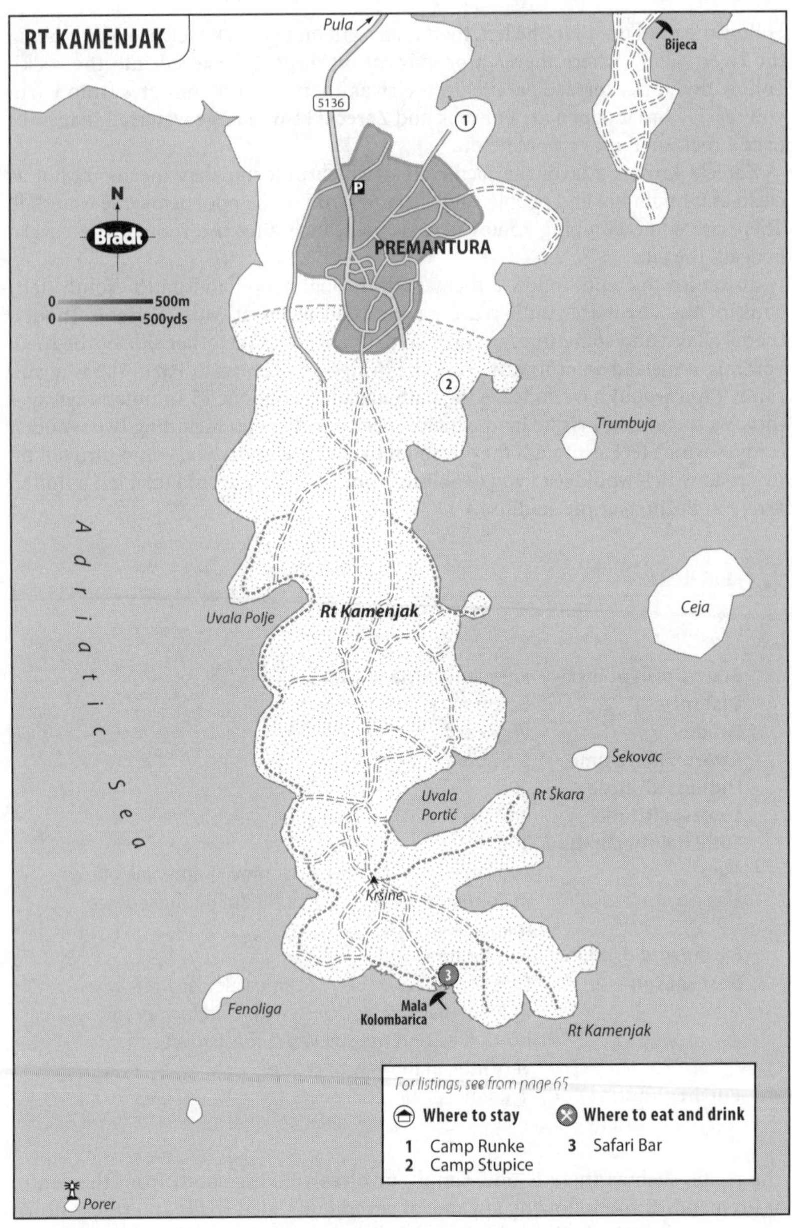

found on the peninsula), butterflies and birds such as sparrowhawk, scops owl and pallid swift. The best time of year for seeing orchids and other wildflowers is spring, with species including bee orchid, late spider orchid, pyramidal orchid and the endemic *Serapias istriaca*. It's worth noting that the black widow spider has also been recorded on Kamenjak. Optimists can keep their eyes peeled for the Endangered Mediterranean monk seal – one of the only sighting of which in Croatian waters in recent decades was off Rt Kamenjak.

6. ŽBEVNICA

Start/finish points	Brest (a small village northeast of Buzet)
Distance	5km
Grade	Medium
Approximate time	1½ hours
Highest altitude	1014m
Lowest altitude	700m
Total height climbed	335m
Map	HGSS Ćićarija (#19)
Eating and drinking	None
Best season	Late spring/early summer or autumn
Further information	w hps.hr/info/hrvatski-vrhovi/cicarija-vrh-zbevnica

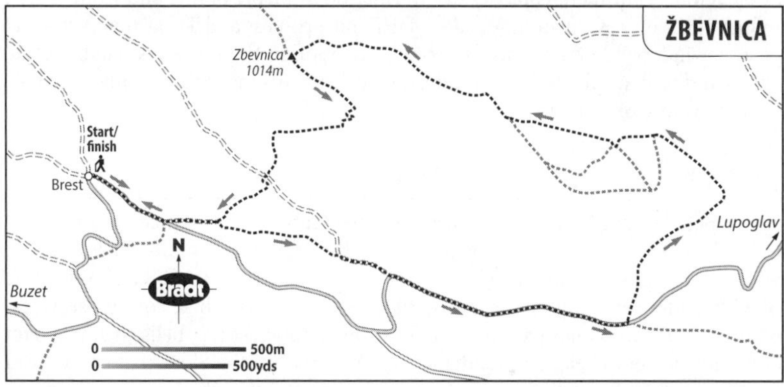

A short hike up to Žbevnica, an isolated hill lodged in the Ćićarija mountains which, as the westernmost Croatian peak over 1,000m, has amazing views. This is the one route included in this guide that is not accessible by public transport – you'll need a car to get to the village of Brest, and the closest you can conveniently get to by bus or train is Lupoglav. Žbevnica lies close to the Slovenian border – one bend in the narrow road up to Brest actually swings through Slovenia for a short distance.

A marked trail leaves the road just southeast of Brest, heading up towards Planinarski dom Žbevnica. Bear right (rather than straight up to the hut) to meet the road again after a sharp bend. Follow the asphalt road east for around 5 minutes then turn left up a rough 4x4 track, cutting off a few corners on paths, then following a well-marked path up over a grassy hillside, with views opening up behind you. Bear right along the top of the hill to reach the summit cairn at Žbevnica. The views are gobsmacking, stretching right across the Mirna valley and beyond. A path continues along the tops and into Slovenia; we however want to backtrack very slightly southeast to pick up a clearly marked path down across the rocky slopes below the summit, where you might see chamois. The path leads down into woodland, to Planinarski dom Žbevnica where you should keep straight ahead to arrive back in Brest.

11

Biking in Istria

Istria in spring and autumn is a very popular destination for biking, especially road cycling, but also off-road. During these seasons the temperature is sunny, mostly dry, not too hot, and the roads are blissfully empty. Cyclists frequently visit as organised groups, sometimes by the busload, often as early as February and as late as November, but there is plenty of information available online and from tourist information offices, including route maps and profiles, and Istria makes a great place for independent cycle tours. Accommodation in the form of small boutique hotels and farmsteads, and the wonderful local cuisine, make this a truly enjoyable area to explore on two wheels.

BIKE RENTAL, SERVICE AND PARTS

Many people bring their own bikes, but they can also be rented in Istria: see individual chapters under *Getting around/By bike*, for where to hire bikes and also where to get them repaired or buy spare parts. There's a list of bike shops, some of which offer servicing, on the Istria Bike website (w istria-bike.com/en/services/bike_shops). Basic bike parts (repair kits, inner tubes, tyres, bells, helmets, etc) are available very cheaply at **Kaufland** in Poreč, and on the Slovenian coast, head for the excellent **Luma Šport** in Piran (w lumasport.com), which has good-quality bikes for rental as well as parts and is very knowledgeable about cycle routes in the area. Most bicycle-rental places will be able to provide you with a local map and suggestions for routes according to your ability.

ROUTES AND MAPS

Istria has a range of well-developed bike routes. Plenty of the many marked routes, both on- and off-road, can be found online (w istria-bike.com), where maps, GPS files and route cards are available for each route as well as useful information on local accommodation, service areas, biking competitions and organised days out. Bike Park Rabac (w istria-bike.com/en/bike_trails/bike-parks) offers a variety of single track routes and facilities for families with kids, as well as services such as bike hire, repairs and transfers.

Six bike maps covering Istria at 1:30,000 scale can be purchased in most shops and kiosks. Poreč tourist offices also have a free biking map available showing 14 routes in a 25km^2 area; this includes basic route cards. The map can be downloaded for free, but few will have printers at home big enough to print an A2-size sheet. To give you a flavour of the cycling available in Istria we present five routes for you here. These cover the very best of the Parenzana old railway trail and three circular routes. Each of the circular routes starts and finishes in Poreč, but could of course be picked up anywhere along the way. For more on the Parenzana old railway route, see page 117.

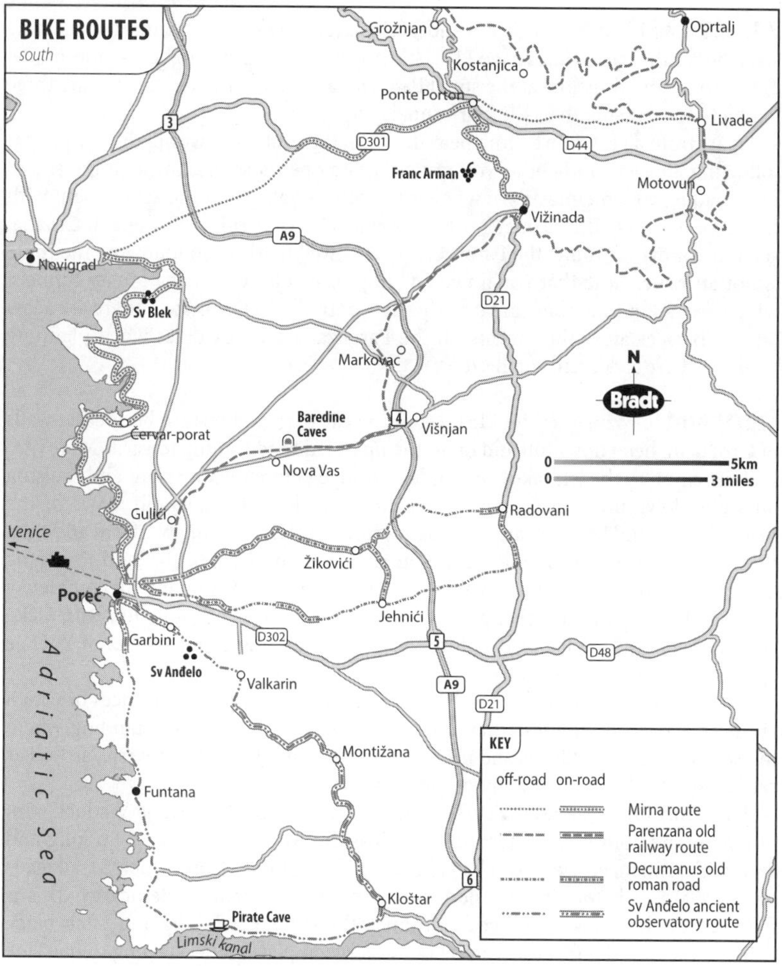

BIKE ROUTES
south

Grožnjan
Oprtalj
Kostanjica
Ponte Porton
Livade
D301
D44
Franc Arman
Motovun
Vižinada
3
A9
Novigrad
Sv Blek
D21
Markovac
N
Bradt
Baredine Caves
4
Višnjan
Červar-porat
Nova Vas
0 5km
0 3 miles
Radovani
Gulići
Venice
Žikovići
Poreč
Jehnići
Garbini
D302
5
D48
Sv Anđelo
Valkarin
A9
D21
Adriatic Sea
Montižana
Funtana
6
Kloštar
Pirate Cave
Limski kanal

KEY

off-road	on-road	
		Mirna route
		Parenzana old railway route
		Decumanus old roman road
		Sv Anđelo ancient observatory route

1. GROŽNJAN TO LIVADE ON THE PARENZANA

Start/finish	Grožnjan (page 115)/Livade (page 114)
Distance	20km
Grade	Easy
Approximate time	2 hours
Highest altitude	290m
Lowest altitude	13m
Total height climbed	<10m
Eating and drinking	Grožnjan and Livade
Viewpoints	Završje, Antonci and Freski viaducts
Public tour day	Mid-December
Repairs	Espo in Poreč (**w** espo.hr; page 86)

ROUTE DESCRIPTION This is a wonderful route along one of the most interesting stretches of the Parenzana (page 117), starting near one of the highest points on the entire route and finishing at the small Parenzana Museum in Livade, crossing three viaducts and passing through four tunnels on the way.

Apart from a very short climb near the start, the route is downhill the whole way, following an easy gradient as you cruise across open terraces, through forest and over viaducts, with fantastic views over the Mirna Valley and the air redolent with the scent of pines. This is one of the most enjoyable bike rides I've done in Croatia. As in the previous route, the Parenzana is very well marked, so following the route is not an issue. Note that you'll need a lamp or headtorch for the longer tunnels, which are not lit (and there are usually a few potholes to negotiate). There are a few big MTB races and other events on the Parenzana – check dates when planning your ride here (w parenzana.net/en).

Startpoint Grožnjan (page 115). From the car park and terrace beside the walls of Grožnjan, head downhill and on to the unsealed road leading towards Motovun. A short climb to the left takes you under a bridge before turning right and cruising blissfully downhill with the wind in your hair. There are splendid views of the Mirna Valley, and back towards Grožnjan, from a raised viewing platform and then from broad terraces near Biloslava. You soon pass under a bridge and reach the first of the tunnels, Kostanjica, which is 70m long and dim (though not completely dark) at its midpoint. Further along you gain good views of Motovun, with Učka clearly visible in the distance, before the square bell tower and houses of Završje appear above the trees ahead.

After crossing an unsealed road you reach Završje station, most traces of which are now hidden by the less-than-attractive ruined building now standing where the station once was. Olives and other crops were once loaded at Završje, as well as cattle hides for the manufacture of footwear.

Two short tunnels follow: Završje I and II, followed by the Završje Viaduct, 62m in length and 20m high. After this you cross the Antonci Viaduct, 80m long and 25m high; enhanced views can be gained from the bridge (from which a trail leads to Zabrdo) just before it, and there's a rest point and picnic table nearby. This is followed by the Freski Viaduct and tunnel, the latter 146m long and pitch-black inside – the gravel and rocks can be rather large in places, and keeping to one side might help reduce the risk of punctures.

Oprtalj station comes next, near the settlement of Grimaldi (the village of Oprtalj itself is a further 3km away up a clear track; page 114). Nothing of the station remains except a grassy terrace, though it originally had a shed and small warehouse. The Parenzana continues downhill through forest and over the Oprtalj Viaduct, then emerges among open fields and terraces before cruising into Livade to arrive at the Parenzana Museum on the opposite side of the road.

Endpoint The Parenzana Museum (Muzej Parenzane; page 114) in Livade has a small collection of documents and other objects from the period in which the Parenzana operated, between 1902 and 1935. Near the crossroads and the road south towards Motovun, the buildings of Livade station are some of the better preserved on the entire route of the Parenzana, and date from 1908 – slightly later than most of the other stations on the route. There's a *konoba* to the right between the museum and the crossroads, where you can sit under a quiet, elder-covered terrace and enjoy an ice-cold glass of Favorit.

2. COAST TO THE MIRNA RIVER AND THE PARENZANA

Start/finish	Poreč (page 83)
Distance	53km
Grade	Medium
Approximate time	4 hours
Highest altitude	326m
Lowest altitude	7m
Total height climbed	452m
Eating and drinking	Ponte Porton, Vižinada (page 115)
Viewpoints	Antenal, St Tomo, and Veli Most Viaduct on the alternate longer route
Public tour day	Third weekend in September, and mid-December for the longer Parenzana tour, and a shorter tour of Buje, Tinjan and Motovun
Repairs	Espo in Poreč (w espo.hr; page 86)

ROUTE DESCRIPTION This route is rewarding for combining a variety of what Istria has to offer: some gentle asphalt and tracks partly along a shoreline and through the once-walled village of Červar Porat; some riverside pathways; a short(ish) but steep, winding climb (or descent in the reverse); and 26km of the old Parenzana railway route (a further 14km for the longer option). While it would be more relaxing to do it in reverse, until the Parenzana is sufficiently well marked to be easy to find in Poreč, it remains easier to pick it up inland.

Startpoint The old railway station. These old buildings are not marked as the old railway station, but locals know them as such and they are sufficiently different in style of stone and construction from their surroundings that they give away their 19th-century Italian origins (distinctive on satellite imagery for their grey slate roofs rather than the usual Istrian burnt sienna tiles). Now partially in disuse, partially a bus garage, a plant nursery and a dwelling, these buildings stretch out along the northern edge of the shore. From here keep left at the wide crossroads and follow the old coastal road – which is cut off to main traffic during the summer – past the popular resorts of Pical and Materada to the old walled village of Červar Porat. Skirting Červar Porat and Autocamp Lanterna, keep on the high road past the old ruins of Sv Blek to join the beautiful coastal road to the mouth of the River Mirna (19km).

From here, below the old lighthouse, head inland on the stone track for the gentle ride along the Mirna to Ponte Porton (14km). Here you can take a longer additional route (see next paragraph) or head south on the asphalt main road, climbing 303m to Vižinada (4km). Stop here for a rewarding lunch after the steep climb. From Vižinada, locate the well-signposted Parenzana route south of the town, which will take you the remaining 26km on a gravel track back to Poreč.

Tip: If you don't fancy the full 14km additional route, I strongly recommend the 3km detour from Vižinada to Veli Most and back, to see this spectacular viaduct of early 19th-century engineering. Don't forget your camera for this one.

Additional route At Ponte Portun, a 14km detour can be taken by keeping to the dirt track 500m north of the River Mirna to Livade. Here you might want to stop at the Parenzana Museum (page 114) or at the most famous **truffle restaurant** in all Istria, Zigante (page 114) – though you'd likely feel underdressed in cycle gear! Heading south from Livade on the asphalt road, you will in fact have picked up the Parenzana rail route. Immediately after crossing the River Mirna again, head southeast (left) to continue on the Parenzana all the way around Motovun, where you might also want to stop for a break (page 111). The Parenzana snakes its way through the countryside at a relatively level height, passing over Veli Most until it reaches Vižinada, and continues on a straighter route to Poreč.

Endpoint The Parenzana ends rather sadly at the back of Stancija Vrgotin 8, at which point you'll rejoin the asphalt road behind the business park and on to the supermarket road. This will take you down to the main car park in town, not far from the old railway station.

3. DECUMANUS MAXIMUS AGRI

Start/finish	Poreč (page 83)
Distance	37km (12km asphalt, 22km off-road 4x4 mud)
Grade	Hard
Approximate time	2 hours
Highest altitude	281m
Lowest altitude	16m
Total height climbed	400m
Eating and drinking	Hotel Filipini (page 88)
Viewpoints	Bačva
Public tour day	None
Repairs	Espo in Poreč (w espo.hr; page 86)

ROUTE DESCRIPTION The Decumanus Maximus Agri was the main east–west Roman road going through the Parentium encampment and leading out to the countryside. It is now a disused 4x4 track mostly consisting of mud, so avoid it after heavy rain unless you're prepared for this. Being mainly under shady trees, the track can retain large puddles even after several days of sun. A circular route combines the southern end of the Staža Sv Maura (Route 142) and part of Zvjezdana Staža (Route 131), but the circular route can also be shortened by taking a north–south asphalt road between Bačva and Ženodraga. As the link between the Decumanus in the old town and how it continues towards Vrvari is obscured by new buildings, it is easier to take Route 142 first and then pick up the Maximus Agri at the far end.

Startpoint The roundabout at Konzum supermarket. From here head west past all the supermarkets and continue straight through the two roundabouts past Stancija Portun towards Kosinožići and Žikovići. At Žikovići, a short cut can be taken south towards Pršurići and Jehnići, where you can join the obvious 4x4 track of the Maximus Agri. Although it is not signposted as Route 141, there is a sign for those coming off the Maximus Agri pointing the way to Route 143, the Eufraziana. This short cut shaves some 17km off the longer route.

To continue on the longer route, the asphalt road takes you less than 1km past Žikovići and then becomes an off-road track. The route continues over the highway and then to Bačva, where you can pick up Route 143 south to Jehnići, or continue northeast on Route 131, the Zvjezdana Staža, through Radovani towards Vrhjani. Two kilometres of asphalt road south take you to the start of the Maximus Agri, from where it is 17.5km west back to Poreč. For those needing a stop on the way back, the Hotel Filipini offers excellent food in a shady atmosphere less than 1km off the Maximus Agri. The Maximus Agri returns to asphalt at the eastern end of Vrvari. Rather than join the busy main road here, head north past the abandoned old school building and take the back road into Poreč.

Endpoint At the back of the commercial zone behind Lidl supermarket.

4. MALI SVETI ANĐEO OBSERVATORY TO THE LIMSKI KANAL

Start/finish	Poreč (page 83)
Distance	46km
Grade	Medium
Approximate time	3 hours
Highest altitude	150m
Lowest altitude	3m
Total height climbed	210m
Eating and drinking	Bistro Aerodrom (Vrsar)
Viewpoints	Mali Sveti Anđeo observatory, Montižani
Public tour day	None
Repairs	Espo in Poreč (w espo.hr; page 86)

ROUTE DESCRIPTION This route takes you past a little-known ancient observatory (Mali Sveti Anđeo), the tiny winery at Braljići, the monastery village of Kloštar (sadly the monastery is long gone), and along the dirt track of the tree-shaded clifftop of the Limski kanal to Vrsar airfield. Thereafter the route lies just inland of the coast back up to Poreč.

Startpoint The car park south of Poreč next to the cemetery. Take the asphalt road east to Garbina, after which it turns to gravel. At 1km past the end of the tarmac, 50m after the woods start, stop and look for an obvious opening on the south side of the gravel track that becomes a single-lane path up the hill. This is the path up to Mali Sveti Anđeo, which is best taken on foot. The gravel track continues to Valkarin and then heads south to join the asphalt road past Starići. At the T-junction turn left up through Dračevac and straight on up to Montižani. (Just before the steep hill up to Montižani is a track on the left at an old concrete water bowser hangar. This track leads after 150m to a *boškarin* farm, if you're interested to see these native Istrian cows.)

After the highpoint of Montižani at 150m above sea level the route sails downhill. At the little village of Braljići is a small local winery, where you can drop in to pick up some local wine. On joining the main road, turn left at the T-junction, and keeping south you'll pass Konoba Gradina. At Kloštar turn west and follow the asphalt road into the woods. This joins the dirt track of the signposted Bike Route 171. Take the southern track to keep closest to the cliffside with a glimpse of the gorge through the trees, and to get to the head of the footpath down to the Pirate's Cave and Bar just up from the water. Further on, the track runs along the southern end of Vrsar airfield, where you can also stop for good pizza at Bistro Aerodrom (052 441 810; 11.00–18.00 daily).

Continue west along Route 171 and past Kapetanova Stancija to avoid the busy main road into Vrsar (page 98) in the summer. Between Vrsar and Funtana the bike route runs a few metres in from the main road through the trees, and after Funtana it joins the coast, then heads over the hill to Zelena Laguna. From here follow the coastal path all the way into Poreč, where the traffic is pedestrian, bicycle or electric tourist train.

Endpoint After popping out at Poreč Marina, continue a few metres to the roundabout and turn right. Follow this road uphill for 250m till you get back to the southern car park.

5. GROŽNJAN TO KOPER ON THE PARENZANA

Start/finish	Grožnjan (page 115)/Koper (page 154)
Distance	47km
Grade	Easy
Approximate time	1–3 days
Highest altitude	290m
Lowest altitude	0m
Total height climbed	95m
Where to stay and eat	Casa Romantica La Parenzana, Kaldanija (page 118), San Rocco, Brtonigla (page 118), Art Hotel Tartini, Piran (page 163), Hotel Marina, Izola (page 159), Koper (page 155)
Viewpoints	Above the Sečovlje saltpans, St George's Cathedral belltower in Piran, waterfront in Izola
Public tour day	Mid-December
Repairs	Luma Šport in Piran (w lumasport.com; page 163)

ROUTE DESCRIPTION This route covers a longer section of the Parenzana (page 117), again starting in Grožnjan but this time heading north and along the Slovenian coast to Koper.

Apart from a few short climbs inland between Portorož and Izola, the route is mostly downhill or level the whole way, with fantastic views as you descend towards the Slovenian border and extended sections cycling beside the sea. There are a few sections along asphalt roads but in only a few cases are they busy with traffic. Like much of the Parenzana, this is a great route for kids – I cycled this route with my then six-year-old daughter, spread over a few days.

Some parts of the route are not as well marked as the section of the Parenzana covered by Route #1, but that's mainly because there are other (asphalt) roads and towns to navigate, rather than staying on an uninterrupted section of the Parenzana.

Fit cyclists will easily cover this route in a day; however, it's much more enjoyable to spread the ride over two or three days and use it as a means to explore the Slovenian coast, as cycling between Piran, Izola and Koper is undoubtedly the

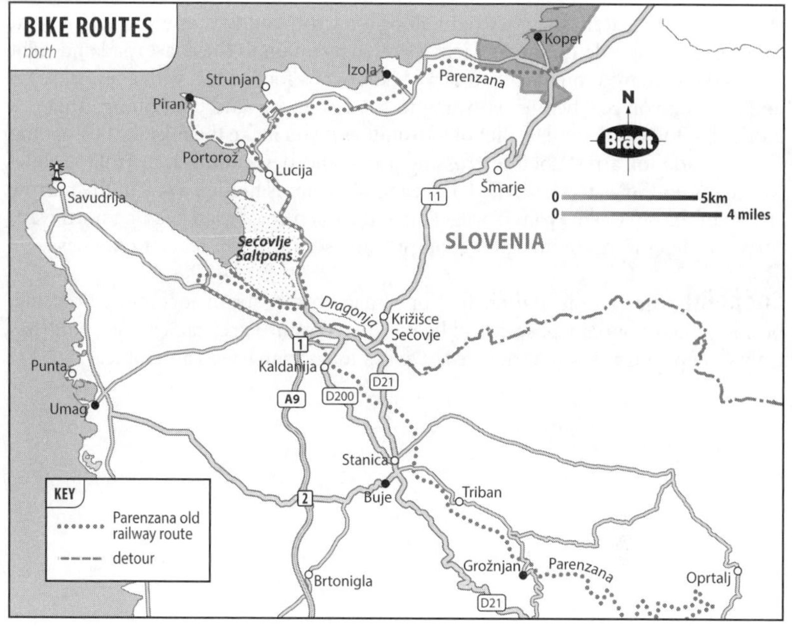

most enjoyable way to see it, and there are some lovely, bike-friendly places to stay (and eat) along the route, in particular Casa Romantica La Parenzana in Kaldanija near Buje (page 118) and San Rocco in nearby Brtonigla (page 118). There are saltpans and nature reserves (page 169) to explore, and the outstanding Magical World of Shells, in Piran (page 166) and the Parenzana Museum in Izola (page 162). Finishing in Koper also puts you conveniently on the railway line to Škocjan and Postojna caves (pages 170 and 176) and Lipica (page 172).

See **w** parenzana.net for more details.

Startpoint Grožnjan (page 115). From the car park and terrace beside the walls of Grožnjan, turn right and follow the asphalt road away from the village, then bear left and head on to the gravel surface of the Parenzana. Go right through a tunnel then cruise across a lovely green landscape, passing a diminutive old station near Triban, before joining the asphalt road before Buje. Go right off the main road before reaching Buje itself, on to another asphalt road past houses then bear right (the route here is a little unclear but if you miss the turning you can follow the main road north from here, towards Kaštel and Dragonja, and pick up the Parenzana again where it crosses this). In Kaldanija, La Parenzana makes for an outstanding place to stay for the night, and its restaurant, in a peaceful garden surrounded by lavender bushes, can be counted one of the culinary highlights of Istria.

There's a lovely downhill cruise to the Slovenian border with spectacular views of the Sečovlje saltpans, then along the coast to Portorož and Piran – this last section is along a main road that can be fairly busy, so you might want to get off and walk in places if cycling with kids. Hotel Tartini in Piran is right on the main square and has a secure storage room for bikes.

From Piran you need to backtrack to Portorož, then after the Hotel Kempinski go left uphill past the amphitheatre, and through the 550m Valeta tunnel (well lit so no need for torches). Cruise downhill again from the other end of the tunnel,

then where the Parenzana goes right along a narrow country lane you might want to make a circular detour and go left, then left again on to the coast road and right across the saltpans (you'll need to carry bikes over a footbridge, with a few steps up and down involved), before returning to the Parenzana and continuing. There's a gradual uphill climb (and hordes of mosquitoes if you make the mistake of stopping in the shade for a rest) before crossing a rise and descending into Izola – Hotel Marina is on the waterfront; the Parenzana Museum is hidden away in the narrow streets of the old town. From Izola get on to the main coast road heading northwest, then turn left off this on to a path alongside the sea until you reach Koper.

Endpoint The railway station in Koper has an old steam locomotive outside, beside which you can pose for obligatory successful Parenzana selfies, and has trains to Postojna or with a change at Divača to Škocjan Caves and Lipica.

12

Diving in Istria

Like any seaside, the beach and its activities are only half of the picture. Under the water is an entire world, which is teeming with life, hiding forgotten stories, and begging our assistance (to survive our excesses). The inherent difficulties of diving (limited air, visibility and warmth) tend to make us more aware of our reliance on the ecosystems we must preserve to survive on this planet. Istria is a good place to explore and learn to respect the relationship between those limits and the freedoms that the sea can offer (weightlessness, omnidirectional movement, calmness). This is because Adriatic waters are warm enough and calm enough, with little significant tidal difference, to make it a good introduction to diving.

Istria's accessibility from western Europe, and particularly for landlocked Austrians and Swiss, makes it a popular destination not only for sunbathing but also for diving, and it is well served by diving centres. Istria's inviting warm Adriatic waters hold a diverse range of wildlife and sites, which have not yet suffered total divers' bleach, especially prevalent elsewhere in the Mediterranean, where the coral and sandy beds of the sea have been scraped by fins, overfishing and debris. In addition, Istria has the second-greatest abundance of wrecks for diving (Vis near Split, in Dalmatian Croatia, has the most), most dating from World Wars I and II, including two of Croatia's top-three largest **shipwrecks**.

The diving season can start as early as Easter, although temperatures will only be around 10–16°C. Water temperatures average 21–29°C at the surface in the summer, and 7–10°C in the winter. At 20–30m the water temperature remains a constant 16–19°C from the summer until the end of the diving season in November. Visibility is best in spring, autumn and winter, when summer plankton and spawning algae clouds are completely absent. The range of underwater flora and fauna (including bottlenose dolphins, seahorses and turtles) is immense, with many indigenous varieties, as discussed on page 208).

This chapter highlights the information you should be aware of if you are considering diving for the first time in Istria. It also lists **eight of the best dive sites** around the peninsula, most of which are accessible to recently qualified open-water-certified divers, with a few requiring more advanced skills for you to aim towards while improving your diving.

PLANNING THE DIVE

DIVE COSTS AND PACKAGES Diving costs with a dive centre range from as little as €20 for a beach dive to around €40 for a boat dive, and from around €40 to €65 for a wreck dive. Many places will do packages, such as a discount for two dives in a day, or up to ten dives in a week, sometimes with limitless shore dives.

All the dive centres offer diving courses at most levels, usually in PADI (Professional Association of Diving Instructors) or with SSI (Scuba Schools

International) and sometimes with CMAS (Confédération Mondiale des Activités Subaquatique) or VDST (Verband Deutsche Sport Taucher). BSAC (British Sub-Aqua Club) instruction and certification is not yet available in Istria. Again prices vary, so it is worth comparing websites or Facebook sites for up-to-date prices: a Discover Scuba afternoon comes to around €75, while a 3–4 day PADI Open Water Diver (OWD) course is around €450. Children from the age of eight can start learning to use scuba gear in shallow water, and take a Junior Open Water Diver course from the age of ten. Some centres also offer wreck-diving speciality courses for around €180 (2 dives).

RULES AND REGULATIONS As with elsewhere around the world, diving in Croatian waters is regulated by several laws. These are overseen by the **Croatian Diving Federation** (Hrvatski Ronilački Savez; w diving-hrs.hr), which grants diving concessions to qualified centres, clubs and individuals. Qualified individuals wanting to dive independently of the dive centres and of local clubs must apply for a concession via the local harbour master (see page 229 for the contact details for some of the main harbours).

Wreck-salvage laws in Croatia are very strict and very simple: nothing may be removed from a wreck. All battlefield casualty wrecks in Croatian waters are war graves, and thus also deemed cultural monuments. Diving to most Croatian wrecks therefore also requires a special permit, which usually costs around €15 and is organised by the local dive centre that has permission to take divers there. Not every dive centre is allowed to go to every wreck.

Wildlife and natural habitat are also protected. It is illegal to even swim in the Limski kanal (page 99; diving is permitted at the mouth of the inlet only) and a permit is required to dive around the Brijuni Islands (page 68). Those dive centres that have permission and permits to dive the various restricted sites are listed in the dives outlined in this chapter.

EQUIPMENT All diving centres will have the basic equipment that you find in most dive centres around the world, and in Croatia they tend to be in good condition. Female wetsuits are increasingly common, but female BCDs (buoyancy control devices) are rare, as are BCDs with integrated weight systems. Even in the summer, diving is usually done in a 5mm full wetsuit, with boots and strap fins. Only some centres have Nitrox.

For those bringing their own equipment, note that it is difficult to get your equipment serviced in Istria. Most dive centres will not do this, especially in the height of the summer, and at the time of writing there is nowhere to buy full dive gear in Istria proper (as opposed to snorkelling gear which is ubiquitous, or spear fishing gear parts). Several dive shops are within an hour's drive of Istria.

Divestore Valmade 58, 52100 Pula, Croatia; +385 52 214 185; e info@divestore.hr; w divestore.hr; 08.30–16.30 Mon–Fri. Distributor for Cressi, but does not service gear. Also has a small shop on Ciscuttijeva 9 around the back of Pula's old town. Divestore's English website is often several months out of date compared with the Croatian version.

Oceanik Polje 21, 6310 Izola, Slovenia; +386 56 401 100; m (Mojca) +386 40 367 377, (David) +386 41 854 118; e info@oceanik-trgovina.si; w oceanik-trgovina.si; 10.00–18.00 Mon–Fri, 09.00–13.00 Sat. Nice little shop with a bit of everything on the east outside of Izola opposite the sea.

Sepadiver Via Colombara di Vignano 6, 34015 Muggia (TS), Italy; +39 40 232573; e info@sepadiver.com; w sepadiver.com; 09.00–12.30 & 14.30–18.30 Tue–Sat all year, & also Mon (same hours) May–Aug. A good range of equipment mostly stocking Apex-Aqualung, Mares & Scubapro, as well as some of their own equipment such as semi-dry suits. Their website does not show all the items in the shop, so it is worth going over personally.

SAFETY Diving safely is the responsibility of every diver. In general, if you've not dived for three years or more, most dive centres will want you to do a refamiliarisation (check) dive or scuba tune-up with an instructor (for around €40). If you've not been diving over the winter, or for a year or so, then your first dive of the season should always be a check dive, especially if you have your own equipment, to ensure that you and your equipment work as you expect them to. Check dives are usually done from the shore in front of the dive centre, as these are the cheapest, and it is easy to go back to the centre if something's not working. Istria's hyperbaric chamber is in Pula (Polyclinic for Hyperbaric Oxygen Medicine Oxy, Kochova 1/a; 052 215 663; m 24hr emergency number (Dr Mario Franolić) 098 219 225; e polilkinika@oxy.hr; w oxy.hr).

WRECK DIVING With over 25 wrecks, Istria is a great place to explore the fascination of wreck diving. Most sites are within 90–100 minutes' boat ride from a dive centre, and over half lie within Croatia's stated recreational dive limit (40m). That said, diving at 20m+ in Croatia is not like diving in the clear blue waters of the tropics or off Egypt, Malta or some of the Pacific islands. Planning the dive and diving the plan are both essential in waters that can have low visibility, even when you are outside the wreck. Navigational and decompression skills are a must, as is a Nitrox qualification if you want to stay down long enough to make the descent worthwhile.

As a result of the higher skillset required to dive wrecks, most centres will require that you are qualified to at least CMAS 2* level (equivalent to PADI rescue diver, SSI Advanced Open Water Diver (AOWD) +40 dives, or the BSAC Dive Leader course even if you have not qualified with all the dives). Dives on some of the simpler, shallower wrecks, such as the HMS *Coriolanus*, might be allowed for PADI AOWD divers once they've dived with a centre a few times and shown their competency. Some centres also require that you show a current (issued within the last year) fit-to-dive medical certificate. If you have not brought one from your usual doctor, then sometimes these can be obtained through a private doctor in Istria. Your dive centre will be able to tell you where to seek one if there are any indications that you need one.

DIVING CENTRES

There are over 25 dive centres in Istria alone. Those listed here are chosen for their spread along the coast and for their access to some of the best dive sites. Most dive centres are open from May to September unless otherwise listed. Key staff at the centres all speak English (as well as Croatian, German and Italian). Dive centres in the northwest tend to offer only PADI courses; those around Rovinj offer SSI courses; while those on the east coast offer a mix of CMAS, PADI and VDST (Verband Deutsche Sport Taucher) courses. Going anticlockwise from northwest to northeast:

Subaquatic Stella Maris Campsite, Savudrijska cesta bb, 52470 Umag; 052 663 220; m 092 261 6168; e subaquatic.umag@gmail.com; w subaquatic.org. The northernmost of all the dive centres, & good for accessing the wrecks of the *Gilda* & HMS *Coriolanus*. Provides PADI courses. A popular centre due to its location & thus not cheap, with the exception of the check dive, which is usually held with a number of divers needing review.

Zeus-Faber Sportski centar Valeta, Lanterna 52465 Tar-Vabriga; 052 405 045; m 098 951

UNDERWATER WILDLIFE AND CONSERVATION

The Adriatic is a rich, fascinating and unique body of seawater. It is unique largely because no more than 4% of the water flow of the northern Adriatic around the Istrian Peninsula escapes into the southern Adriatic (beyond Dubrovnik). Over 75% of the Adriatic's water flow, which is anticlockwise, recycles at Split. On its way round, the water flow picks up more polluted waters from the eastern Adriatic coast and organic matter from the main Mediterranean basin and mineralises it through combination with clean karst-rock waters from Croatian rivers.

As a result of all this, the Adriatic is home to over 70% of all the fish species to be found in the whole Mediterranean, and over 30 of these are found only in the eastern Adriatic due to the karst-rock formations of the region and their abundance of fresh spring water. Seven species of fish found in the Adriatic are endemic (ie: found nowhere else in the world). Sadly, however, overfishing in the last 50 years threatens the extinction of over 60 fish species found in the Adriatic. (See page 6 to learn about which ones not to buy for dinner.)

COMMON SIGHTINGS Crabs, moray eels, goby, cleaner shrimp, sea cucumbers and lobsters are very common. Others include:

Soft corals – ***Alcyonacea*** – particularly **gorgonian sea fans** and sea whips, are common in waters with higher nutrient value (and therefore lower visibility) where they filter-feed off plankton as well as through some photosynthesis in a symbiotic relationship with algae. A large gorgonian colony can be over 1m high and wide, but only 10cm thick. They will be oriented across the current to maximise access to food. Those unable to photosynthesise are more brightly coloured.

Damselfish – ***Chromis chromis*** – when juvenile, are deep cyan blue in colour and only 2–3cm in length. Shoals of 20 or 30 are common at 3–4m depth. Adults are dark brown or black.

Conger conger – **European conger eel** – are like members of the (separate) moray eel family, are found in cracks and crevices. European congers are grey, while moray species tend to be more colourful. Neither congers nor morays are poisonous or dangerous unless provoked (although, if eaten, the flesh of morays eaten can be poisonous if the moray itself has eaten something else poisonous). The European conger can grow up to 3m in length (morays up to 4m).

Bearded fireworms – ***Hermodice carunculata*** – grow up to 15cm long and, if touched, are **poisonous**, causing sharp irritation where bristles enter the skin, and dizziness and nausea in severe cases. Bristles are sometimes successfully extracted using sticking plaster, and the irritation can be relieved by applying neat alcohol or white spirit.

Nudibranchia – these amazing tiny **shell-less molluscs**, often only 1cm long, are abundant for those with the patience to see them. A torch helps in order to highlight their colours in lower visibility. *Flabellina affinis* (fuchsia pink) and *Janolus christatus* (electric blue) are especially common.

LESS COMMON SIGHTINGS

John Dory – ***Zeus faber*** – also known as St Peter's fish, due to its association with St Peter, who is the patron saint of fish. There are many rumours and legends for the origin of the name of the fish, including that the English name is an Anglicism of the French *jaune dorée* meaning 'yellow gilded'. It is a remarkable fish to observe in the water, being large (up to 65cm in length), flat, but broad from dorsal to anal fin, especially if it spreads out the 10 spines on its dorsal fin. The large dark spot on its side is meant to imitate an eye to scare off predators.

PROTECTED FLORA AND FAUNA

Killifish – ***Aphanius fasciatus*** – also known as the south European toothcarp, is a locally protected species, which is more abundant elsewhere in the Mediterranean. It is becoming rare in Croatia due to the destruction of its preferred lagoon habitat.

Orange stony coral – ***Asteroides callycularis*** – are best seen on a night dive when their colours show up brightly in a torch's rays and when these primitive animals feed on the likes of tiny brine shrimp.

Loggerhead turtles – ***Caretta caretta*** – are an extremely rare sight along the built-up and shallow shores of the northern Adriatic, but the clean waters of the eastern Adriatic are their preferred choice. The aquariums at Rovinj and Pula jointly run a **turtle rescue centre** (page 64).

'Black' tree coral – ***Gerardia savaglia*** – is a fast-growing branchy primitive animal, which is beige-yellow when alive and leaves behind a brown-black skeleton. Found below 15m depth and as low as 120m, it has been a popular souvenir – leading to its destruction.

Long-snouted seahorse – ***Hippocampus guttulatus*** – is one of 54 seahorse species, all of which are particularly vulnerable because of their commercial value in traditional Chinese medicine (to counter weak constitution in children, adult male impotence, and bed-wetting!), for curios and for aquariums, for which between 25 million and 150 million are believed to be caught wild every year. Slow moving because of their tiny fins, they are very shy and tend to hide in sea grass, which they cling to with their tails to prevent being swept off by sea currents. Seahorses have been seen at Koversada (page 212), Brseč Pinnacle (page 216), Lanterna dive site near Novigrad, and Karbula, one of the dive sites of Poreč Dive Centre. They can grow up to 15cm in length.

Short-snouted seahorse – ***Hippocampus hippocampus*** – are more commonly seen than long-nosed versions. They prefer muddy-bottomed coastal waters and, because their ability to migrate is limited, when their habitat becomes threatened they do not easily re-establish themselves in a new home. They are also believed to be monogamous, and so a lost or captured partner inhibits further reproduction. The lack of data available on the short-nosed seahorse means that it is difficult to know to what level it is threatened with extinction.

Continued overleaf

UNDERWATER WILDLIFE AND CONSERVATION *continued*

Long-armed purple starfish – ***Ophidiaster ophidianus*** – grows to between 15cm and 40cm in length. Usually found below depths of 5m, they can sometimes appear red or orange.

Fan mussels – ***Pinna nobilis*** – are the largest bivalve molluscs in the Mediterranean, and can grow up to 1m in height. Sadly, a new pathogen found in the Mediterranean in 2016 had killed almost all the fan mussels by 2020. The Pula aquarium has started a Noble Sanctuary to grow and eventually release baby fan mussels back into the local seas. You can follow their progress at w aquarium.hr/nobel-sanctuary.

Neptune grass – ***Posidonia oceanica*** – is endemic to the Mediterranean and only grows in very clean waters. It is thus of course on the decline. It tends to grow in meadows on sandy beds and can grow up to 1.5m in height. Lesser Neptune grass (*Cymodocea nodosa*) is also protected but can be found outside the Mediterranean.

Sea orange sponges – ***Tethya aurantiacum*** – look exactly like an orange. I love this quote by Barnes, Fox and Ruppert in *Invertebrate Zoology* (2004): 'some are known to be able to move at speeds of between 1mm and 4mm per day.'

2986; e info@zeus-faber.com; w zeus-faber.com. Set up in 2004 by brothers Dalibor & Nikola Šolar in response to the overspill from Umag. Located at the mouth of the beautiful River Mirna & near the 19th-century lighthouse on Cape Tooth (Rt Zub) in view of Novigrad's old town, it offers some great locations for beginners & hopes of seeing seahorses & the fabled Zeus faber (John Dory) itself. Offers PADI courses.

Diving Centre Poreč Brulo 4 (parking at Hotel Diamant), 52440 Poreč; 052 433 606; m (Miloš) 091 452 9070; e info@divingcenter-porec.com; w divingcenter-porec.com; Apr–Nov. Miloš & his team pride themselves on providing fun & safe dives, catering particularly for the beginner end of the market during the high season. As a result, the centre's PADI courses are very reasonably priced, & its shore & boat dives are the cheapest in Istria. The house shore dive is a real gem at night, with regular sightings of octopus, plaice, red mullet & feeding fan mussels. Labyrinth is another truly excellent dive of theirs. The centre is a 10min walk from the car park at Hotel Diamant to the dive centre (head left down the path by the tennis courts along the back of the hotel grounds). Off-season between Oct & Easter it's possible to drive to the dive centre.

Starfish Autocamp Porto Sole, 52450 Vrsar; 052 442 119; m (Lydia) 098 335 506, (Christoph) 098 334 816; e info@starfish.hr; w starfish.hr. Starfish's bright yellow 15m boat takes up to 25 divers, & includes an overhead awning for shade & a toilet. It is the only dive centre north of the Limski kanal that is licensed to take divers to the *Baron Gautsch* & *Hans Schmidt*; it also offers 7 other wreck dives. To get to Starfish, take the northern entrance into Vrsar and continue straight on to Koversada. Some 50m before Koversada, turn right towards Autocamp Porto Sole. You can drive up to the dive centre, but will need to leave your car in the camp car park. Provides Nitrox, PADI, TDI/SDI & DSAT courses.

Valdaliso Valdaliso Campsite, Monsena bb, 52210 Rovinj; 052 815 992; m (Stojan) 098 212 360, (Suzy) 099 733 8227; e valdaliso@diving-rovinj.com; w diving-rovinj.com; 15 Apr–15 Oct. This centre concentrates on the more serious end of diving, with a wide range of wreck dives every morning. A medical certificate needs to be shown to dive the wrecks, & this can be obtained from a diving doctor in Rovinj (ask at the dive centre for details). It offers an unbeatable weekly rate for diving equipment. See the dive centre in advance for a car-parking pass into the campsite. Conveniently located only 500m beyond Blu restaurant (page 77) for a nice meal on the beach afterwards. Offers Nitrox & SSI courses.

Puntižela Autocamp Puntižela, 52100 Pula; ☎ (15 Apr–15 Oct) 052 517 474, (16 Oct–14 Apr) +49 9188 305 415; **m** 098 903 3003; **e** info@relaxt-abgetaucht.de; **w** relaxt-abgetaucht.de. This is the only dive centre with access to the Rt Peneda dive site at the Brijuni Islands. Almost all the centre's dives are within 10–20mins by boat, & so the centre often succeeds in providing up to 4 dives in a day (including a night dive). Offers Nitrox, plus SSI & CMAS courses.

Orca Park Plaza Histria, Verudela bb, 52100 Pula; **m** (Olga) 099 831 0667; **e** olga@orcadiving.hr; **w** orcadiving.hr. With easy access from the Park Plaza Histria car park (a 3min walk), this dive centre concentrates on diving rather than courses. It has a large number of varied excellent sites, including drift dives, & wreck dives including, of course, the *Baron Gautsch*, a U-81 German submarine, & the *Maria* wooden 'pirate' ship. Offers several types of PADI courses.

Indie Autocamp Indie, Banjole 96, 52203 Medulin; ☎ 052 573 658; **m** (Robert) 098 344 963; **e** divingindie@divingindie.com; **w** divingindie.com; ⌚ all year. One of the biggest dive centres in Istria, with 3 boats & the ability to handle up to 55 divers. Offers double wreck-dive trips with lunch on their boat (or bring your own lunch). Offers Nitrox & trimix; also PADI, CMAS, SSI courses.

Sv Marina Autokamp Marina, 52220 Labin; ☎ 052 879 052; **m** 091 187 9074, (Valter) 091 474 7481; **e** info@scubacenter.de; **w** scubacenter.de; ⌚ Apr–Oct. Out of the way but worth the drive if you want your dive to feel a bit less like the latest fad in outdoor sports. Great wall diving available on the mouth of the deep Raša Bay. Offers Nitrox, & teaches PADI & CMAS/VDST courses.

Marine Sport Aleja Slatina bb, 51417 Mošćenička Draga; **m** (Robert) 091 515 7212, (Darko) 091 293 2440; **e** info@marinesport.hr; **w** marinesport.hr; ⌚ Easter–Nov. On the east coast of the peninsula, this dive centre has access to some fantastic wall & drift diving. Offers Nitrox, & teaches PADI courses.

1. HMS *CORIOLANUS*

Description	45m British Royal Navy minesweeper sunk in 1945
Depth	15–28m
Location	West of Novigrad: 45°19'239"N, 13°23'406"E
Difficulty	CMAS 2*, AOWD
Visibility	Low in summer, better in winter
Dive centres	Diving Centre Poreč, Starfish

Interestingly, German guidebooks on this wreck site describe the *Coriolanus* as a radio-monitoring ship, while British and Croatian descriptions of it state it was a minesweeper, and some hint that it was a 'spy' ship. Clearly a trip to the British National Archives is in order to get to the bottom of this story. Nonetheless, it was sunk on 5 May 1945 when it hit a floating mine, which had been laid as part of the German defence line.

Although visibility is low to moderate during the main dive season, on a good day, the top of the wreck can be seen from the surface. The wreck is largely uncluttered by fishing nets and it's possible to dive the entire outside of the *Coriolanus* in a 25-minute bottom time, so it makes quite a good introduction to wreck diving.

Overall, the wreck is in relatively good condition, save for the mine explosion hole in its starboard side, and its missing mast and bridge, which were possibly

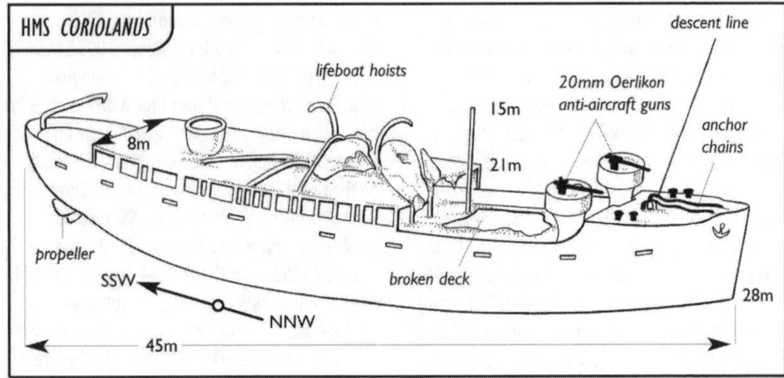

mined after it was sunk so that it would not snag sea traffic. Two mounts with 20mm Oerlikon guns are aft, and one is on the stern of the upper deck. It also carried a 12lb anti-aircraft gun. It is thickly encrusted with shells and coral, and the roof of its mid-deck has caved in. Entry into the wreck is for professionally qualified technical divers only.

2. KOVERSADA WALL

Description	Wall with small caves at the edge of protected waters
Depth	3–30m
Location	North side of the mouth of the Limski kanal
Difficulty	Easy
Visibility	Moderate
Dive centres	Diving Centre Poreč, Starfish, Valdaliso

The Limski kanal itself is out of bounds for swimmers and divers and is home to the greatly sought-after Limski oysters. Being so close to protected waters, Koversada wall, which lies just below the nudist camp of the same name, is rich with yellow and white Gorgonian sea whips, various sponges and moss animals (*bryozoa*). Fish include most of those you'll have for lunch, including John Dory, octopus and scorpionfish. At shallower depths, seahorses have also been seen.

This dive is a good introduction to deep and multi-level diving. The wall is a sheer drop for the first 13m, and then slopes gently to a depth of 30m. Three small caves at 8m, 6m and 5m hide those creatures preferring less light, such as lobsters, conger eels and brittle stars. On the south side of the mouth to the *kanal* is **Saline wall and a wreck** (of a small tourist boat), which are equally rich in flora and fauna, but require a little more navigational skill to dive.

3. *BARON GAUTSCH*

Built in Scotland's Dundee shipyard by Gourlay Brothers & Co, this Austro-Hungarian passenger steamship was launched in 1908 and became the pride of the Austro-Hungarian shipping fleet Austrian Lloyd (today's Italia Marittima) based in Trieste. It sailed the Trieste–Kotor route (in Montenegro), and was leased by the

Description	Luxury passenger steamship sunk in 1914
Depth	28–39m
Location	West of Brijuni, 44°56′4″N, 13°34′7″E
Difficulty	CMAS 2*, AOWD
Visibility	Low in summer, better in winter
Dive centres	Starfish, Valdaliso

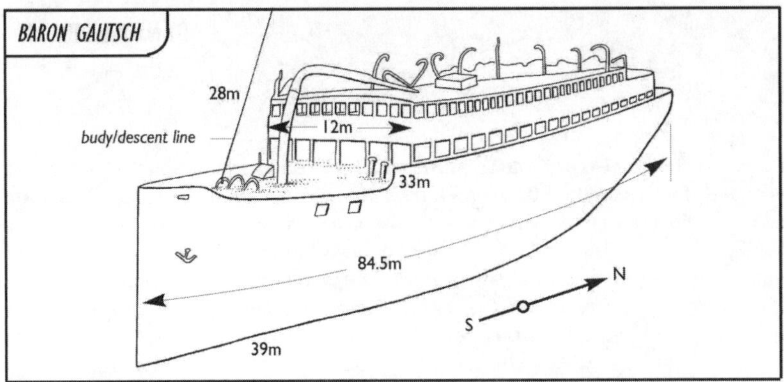

Austro-Hungarian navy in World War I to transport military personnel to Kotor. On a return trip on 13 August 1914, laden with civilian passengers and refugees, the ship hit a mine and sank west of the Brijuni Islands.

Accusations were levelled against the crew for mismanagement (including lifejackets locked away to prevent third-class passengers using them to sleep on), and Austrian Lloyd was sued in the Viennese courts by dependants. Riots in Vienna in 1925 torched the courthouse records of the case, and later in 1939 the offices of the defending lawyer Dr Shapiro, who was Jewish, were ransacked in pogroms. As a result the only remaining official record of the event lies in Rovinj's city archives.

The wreck is a war grave, and has been looted extensively in previous years. After more than 100 years, the wreck today is quite decayed but the overall structure retains its shape. The wreck is marked by a buoy and, as visibility can be low, descent and decompression is by the buoy line. This can get busy in the summer. A double wreck-dive trip to this and to the nearby torpedo boat *Guiseppe Dezza* is offered by Starfish Dive Centre.

Further information on the *Baron Gautsch* can be found at **w** adventuredives.com/barong.htm.

4. BANJOLE ŠPILJA CAVE

This dive is around and beneath a small islet, where three tunnel formations can be dived. The entrance of the shallowest and largest lies at 6m, and emerges after 30m into a crater in the centre of the islet where you can surface into sunlight. This effect lights up the bottom of the seabed below and gives an obvious area to dive towards, making it an excellent introduction to diving with overhead cover.

On exiting the first tunnel, and keeping the islet on your left, head down to 13m where a second tunnel opens on to two galleries with small openings to the sea overhead. A little further along the islet is a third short tunnel. The islet

Description	Cave dive with a fallen roof, emerging into sunlight
Depth	5–30m
Location	West of Rovinj
Difficulty	OWD, lamp recommended
Visibility	Moderate to good
Dive centres	Diving Centre Poreč, Starfish, Valdaliso

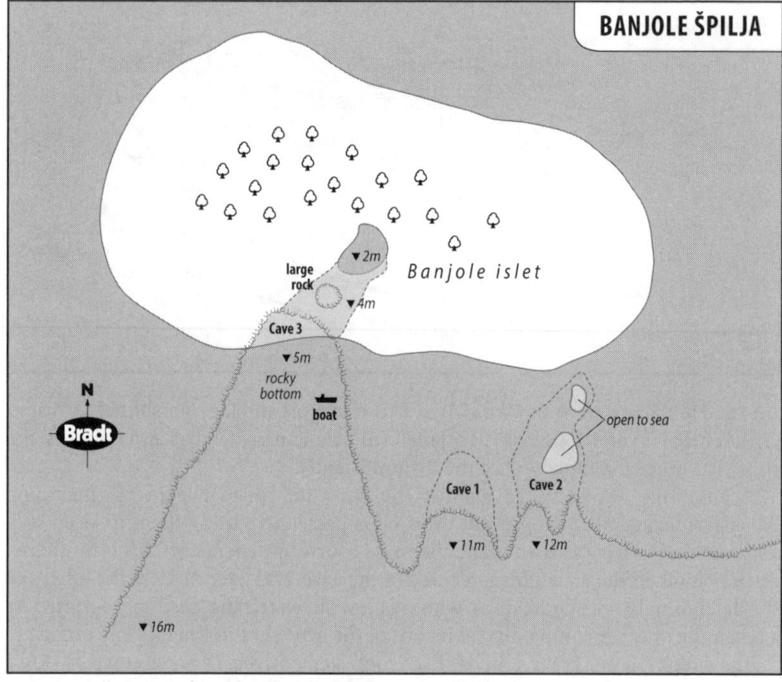

reef continues westward, where at 30m larger shoals of fish can be found and the occasional John Dory. The caves themselves are home to various sponges and sometimes bright red-orange scorpionfish or lurking conger eels.

5. RT PENEDA, BRIJUNI NATIONAL PARK

It is worth making the extra trip to dive at this site, as it is the only place where diving is allowed around the Brijuni Islands National Park. Rt Peneda has one of Istria's nine 19th-century lighthouses (page 16), which can be viewed at the end of the 15-minute boat ride from Puntižela Dive Centre.

Being in the national park, the water here is spectacularly clear and clean, evidenced by the meadows of Neptune grass and the abundance of fish and nudibranch. You should be able to spot almost all of the protected species mentioned in the box on page 208, with the exception of the loggerhead turtle, which requires a much more distant dive.

While the site is a real paradise for underwater photographers, flash is forbidden in this underwater national park due to disturbance that flash can wreak on

Description	A series of walls and tunnels in protected waters
Depth	4–35m
Location	Southernmost tip of Veliki Brijun
Difficulty	Easy
Visibility	Good
Dive centre	Puntižela

threatened species, especially during breeding season. As on other reefs, good buoyancy is important here to avoid killing the coral, especially the protected stony and 'black' tree coral. A night dive here is especially rewarding, revealing feeding octopi, John Dory and bearded fireworms, which can be found in abundance on the soft coral – just don't be tempted to touch their poisonous bristles.

6. FRAŠKERIĆ ISLAND

Description	System of four tunnels with light shafts
Depth	3–26m
Location	Northern side of Otok Fraškerić
Difficulty	Easy
Visibility	Moderate to good in the summer
Dive centres	Puntižela, Orca

This is a good site for beginners wishing to expand their experience with easy wide tunnels lit periodically by overhead sun shafts. The various tunnels lie between 3m and 18m and the reef itself contains numerous other small pocket caves. For many, this is one of the best dives available is Istria, especially for those interested in marine photography. The interplay of light shafts with easy-access caves hosts a wide variety of photographic subject matter in the clearer waters of the more southerly half of Istria.

The site frequently sees catshark and electric rays as well as John Dory, scorpionfish, conger eels, octopi, crabs and lobsters.

7. NIKOLAI'S CAVERN

Description	A small diveable cave along a cliff wall in very clear water
Depth	24–40m
Location	A few minutes south of Marina Autocamp
Difficulty	Medium
Visibility	Good
Dive centre	Sv Marina

Most of the east coast of Istria is characterised by a steep drop-off, which is the continuation of the Učka Mountains towering above it. There are several excellent dives along this coast, one of the best being this high-ceilinged cave, 6m in diameter and 8m in length at 24m depth.

The rough sandy floor makes it easy to navigate and the walls are bright with coral and sponges. Outside the cave, however, has even more to offer, with red Gorgonia sea whips and large deep-red hand corals and all the fish species that these attract. The drop-off south of the cave's entrance almost gives the impression of being in the tropics, if it wasn't for the slightly colder water.

Rocky Dome, a little further south, is another similar dive site. North of these dives is the shipwreck ***Vis***, a Yugoslavian cargo ship, which hit a mine on 13 February 1946. She lies at 38–60m and is only for technical divers.

Across the strait at Rt Pecanj on Cres Island is the January 1914 wreck of the Italian cargo steamship *Lina*. She lies at 20–55m and is thus a possibility for advanced open-water divers.

8. BRSEČ PINNACLE

Description	A spit of sand and a small bay teeming with fish
Depth	7–45m
Location	Below Brseč village
Difficulty	Easy
Visibility	Good
Dive centre	Marine Sport

This spit of sand jutting out below Brseč village shelters a small steep bay in which numerous fish gather and feed in the slight current rounding the spit. Known also as John Dory Bay, the young of this fabled fish are often seen here in the spring. In the summer the bay is known for seahorse sightings. South of the spit are a couple of car wrecks at 25m. North of the spit is a 30m-long wall, rich with anemones and sponges, with a shallow cave at the end. Below the wall is a series of small cliffs reaching down to 45m, in which hand corals, conger eels and lobsters can be seen.

Accessible by both boat and shore, a shore dive offers the opportunity to spend time among the anemones of the bay and their many electric-blue partner cleaner-shrimp (*Periclimenes longicarpus*).

The place to eat after the dive is at Johnson (page 131) at Mošćenička Draga, or at Hotel Draga di Lovrana (page 131) above Medveja.

Appendix 1

LANGUAGE

INTRODUCTION Croatian and Slovene are a phonetic languages – that is, every letter in a word is pronounced, and the pronunciation of any given letter is always the same, making them far more consistent in this sense than English or French. There are, however, a few things that the uninitiated may find difficult or confusing at first, such as consonant clusters, with tongue-twisters like *vrt* (meaning 'garden') or *trg* (meaning 'square') common enough. Also, unlike English (but like most other languages including French and Italian), nouns in Croatian and Slovene have genders (ie: masculine, feminine and neuter), as well as cases (which will be familiar to anyone who has studied a language such as German or Russian, for example).

The following language section contains words and expressions in both Croatian and Slovene. While both languages belong to the South Slavic family of languages and have many similarities, they are much more different to one another than, for example, Croatian and Bosnian, and it's obviously better to switch from using Croatian to Slovene expressions when in Slovenia if you can.

PRONUNCIATION A number of Croatian letters are not found in the English alphabet, and some familiar letters are pronounced differently in Croatian – in particular j (pronounced like an English 'y') and c (pronounced 'ts'). Slovene uses the same alphabet as Croatian, only with five fewer letters.

a	pronounced as the 'a' in father
b	pronounced as the 'b' in bread
c	pronounced as the 'ts' in cats
č	pronounced as the 'ch' in church
ć	very similar to č, but slightly softer, as the 'tj' sound in picture
d	pronounced as the 'd' in dog
dž	pronounced as the 'j' in jam
đ	very similar to the above
e	pronounced as the 'e' in egg
f	pronounced as the 'f' in feel
g	pronounced hard, as the 'g' in give
h	pronounced as the 'h' in hot
i	pronounced as the 'i' in ill
j	pronounced as the 'y' in yes
k	pronounced as the 'k' in king
l	pronounced as the 'l' in loud
lj	pronounced as the 'lli' in million
m	pronounced as the 'm' in mother

n	pronounced as the 'n' in now
nj	pronounced as the 'ni' in onion
o	pronounced as the 'o' in hot
p	pronounced as the 'p' in press
r	rolled slightly
s	pronounced as the 's' in snake
š	pronounced as the 'sh' in shoot
t	pronounced as the 't' in tea
u	pronounced as the 'oo' in pool
v	pronounced as the 'v' in very
ž	pronounced as the 's' in pleasure

There is no q, w, x or y in the Croatian alphabet.

GREETINGS AND GENERAL PHRASES

English	Croatian	Slovene
Hello/Good day (formal)	*Dobar dan*	*Dobar den*
Hi! (informal)	*Ćao!* (pronounced as *ciao* in Italian), *Bok!* or *Bog!*	*Živjo!*
Goodbye	*Doviđenja*	*Nasvidenje*
Bye! (informal)	*Ćao!* (pronounced as *ciao* in Italian), *Adio!* or *Bog!* or *Bok!*	*Adijo!*
Good morning	*Dobro jutro*	*Dobro jutro*
Good evening	*Dobra večer*	*Dober večer*
Good night	*Laku noć*	*Lahko noč*
Have a good trip	*Sretan put*	*Srečno pot*
Yes	*Da*	*Da*
No	*Ne*	*Ne*
Please	*Molim*	*Prosim*
Thank you	*Hvala*	*Hvala*
You're welcome	*Nema na čemu*	*Ni za kaj*
I beg your pardon?	*Molim?*	*Prosim?*
Sorry!	*Oprostite!*	*Oprostite!*
Excuse me (when about to request something)	*Oprostite*	*Oprostite*
Here you are! (when offering something)	*Izvolite!*	*Izvolite!*
Cheers! (as a toast)	*Živjeli!*	*Živeli!*
Do you speak English?	*Govorite li engleski?*	*Govorite angleško?*
I don't speak Croatian	*Ja ne govorim hrvatski*	*Ne govorim slovensko*
I don't understand	*Ne razumijem*	*Ne razumem*
How are you? (formal)	*Kako ste?*	*Kako se imate?*
Fine, thank you	*Dobro, hvala*	*Dobro, hvala*
Pleased to meet you	*Drago mi je*	*Me veseli*
Where are you from?	*Odakle ste?*	*Od kod ste?*
I'm British	*Ja sam Britanac*	*Sem Britanac*
I'm from …	*Ja sam iz …*	*Sem iz …*
Mr	*Gospodin*	*Gospod*
Mrs	*Gospođa*	*Gospa*

NUMERALS

English	Croatian	Slovene
0	*nula*	*nič*
1	*jedan*	*ena*
2	*dva*	*dva*
3	*tri*	*tri*
4	*četiri*	*štiri*
5	*pet*	*pet*
6	*šest*	*šest*
7	*sedam*	*sedem*
8	*osam*	*osem*
9	*devet*	*devet*
10	*deset*	*deset*
11	*jedanaest*	*enajst*
12	*dvanaest*	*dvanajst*
13	*trinaest*	*trinajst*
14	*četrnaest*	*štirinajst*
15	*petnaest*	*petnajst*
16	*šestnaest*	*šestnajst*
17	*sedamnaest*	*sedemnajst*
18	*osamnaest*	*osemnajst*
19	*devetnaest*	*devetnajst*
20	*dvadeset*	*dvasajt*
21	*dvadeset jedan*	*enaindvajset*
22	*dvadeset dva*	*dvaindvajset*
23	*dvadeset tri*	*triindvajset*
30	*trideset*	*trideset*
40	*četrdeset*	*štirideset*
50	*pedeset*	*petdeset*
60	*šezdeset*	*šestdeset*
70	*sedamdeset*	*sedemdeset*
80	*osamdeset*	*osemdeset*
90	*devedeset*	*devetdeset*
100	*sto*	*sto*
110	*sto deset*	*sto deset*
120	*sto dvadeset*	*sto dvasajt*
125	*sto dvadeset pet*	*sto petindvajset*
200	*dvijesto*	*dvesto*
300	*tristo*	*tristo*
1,000	*tisuća*	*tisoč*
million	*milijuna*	*milijon*

TIME, DAYS OF THE WEEK AND MONTHS

minute	*minuta*	*minuta*
hour	*sat*	*ura*
day	*dan*	*dan*
week	*tjedan*	*teden*
month	*mjesec*	*mesec*
year	*godina*	*leto*
What time is it?	*Koliko je sati?*	*Koliko je ura?*

English	Croatian	Slovene
09.25	*devet i dvadeset pet sati*	*devet in petindvajset*
09.30	*pola deset* (or *devet i pol)*	*devet in trideset*
14.00	*dva sata* (or *četrnaest sati)*	*dve* (or *štirinajst)*
At 10.15	*u deset i petnaest*	*ob deset in petnajst*
Sunday	*nedjelja*	*nedelja*
Monday	*ponedjeljak*	*ponedeljek*
Tuesday	*utorak*	*torek*
Wednesday	*srijeda*	*sreda*
Thursday	*četvrtak*	*četrtek*
Friday	*petak*	*petek*
Saturday	*subota*	*sobota*
January	*siječanj*	*januar*
February	*veljača*	*februar*
March	*ožujak*	*marec*
April	*travanj*	*april*
May	*svibanj*	*maj*
June	*lipanj*	*junij*
July	*srpanj*	*julij*
August	*kolovoz*	*avgust*
September	*rujan*	*september*
October	*listopad*	*oktober*
November	*studeni*	*november*
December	*prosinac*	*december*
spring	*proljeće*	*pomlad*
summer	*ljeto*	*poletje*
autumn	*jesen*	*jesen*
winter	*zima*	*zima*
today	*danas*	*danes*
tomorrow	*sutra*	*jutri*
yesterday	*jučer*	*včeraj*
day	*dan*	*dan*
night	*noć*	*noč*
afternoon	*popodne*	*popoldne*
in the morning	*ujutro*	*zjutraj*
in the evening	*navečer*	*zvečer*

GENERAL VOCABULARY

after	*poslije*	*potem*
and	*i*	*in*
beautiful	*lijepo/krasno*	*lepo*
before	*prije*	*prej*
black	*crno*	*črno*
blue	*plavo*	*modro*
cold	*hladno*	*hladno*
difficult	*teško*	*težko*
easy	*lako*	*lahko*
far	*daleko*	*daleče*

English	Croatian	Slovene
fast	*brzo*	*hitro*
from	*iz*	*iz*
green	*zeleno*	*zeleno*
here	*ovdje/tu*	*tukaj*
hot	*vruće*	*vroče*
how?	*kako?*	*kako?*
in	*u*	*v*
large	*veliko*	*veliko*
later	*kasnije*	*kasneje*
left	*lijevo*	*levo*
much/many	*puno/mnogo*	*mnogo*
near	*blizu*	*blizu*
now	*sada*	*sedaj*
of	*od*	*ob*
on	*na*	*na*
or	*ili*	*ali*
red	*crveno*	*rdeče*
right	*desno*	*desno*
slow	*sporo/polako*	*počasno*
small	*malo*	*majhno*
that	*ono/to*	*to*
there	*tamo*	*tam*
this	*ovo*	*to*
to	*u/na*	*k/na*
under	*ispod*	*pod*
very	*jako*	*zelo*
what?	*što?/šta?*	*kaj?*
when?	*kad?*	*kdaj?*
where?	*gdje?*	*kje?*
white	*bijelo*	*belo*
who?	*tko?*	*ki?*
with	*s/sa*	*z*
without	*bez*	*brez*

ACCOMMODATION

apartment	*apartman*	*apartma*
bathroom	*kupaonica*	*kopalnica*
bed	*krevet*	*postelja*
bed and breakfast	*noćenje i doručak*	*nočitev z zajtrkom*
half board	*polupansion*	*polpenzion*
hotel	*hotel*	*hotel*
reservation	*rezervacija*	*rezervacija*
room	*soba*	*soba*
double room	*dvokrevetna soba*	*dvoposteljna soba*
single room	*jednokrevetna soba*	*enoposteljna soba*
swimming pool	*bazen*	*bazen*

BANKS, MONEY, POST AND INTERNET

ATM	*bankomat*	*bankomat*
bank	*banka*	*banka*

English	Croatian	Slovene
currency	*valuta*	*valuta*
exchange office	*mjenjačnica*	*menjalnica*
exchange rate	*tečaj*	*tečaj*
internet	*internet*	*internet*
money	*novac*	*denar*
small change	*sitno*	*drobiž*
post office	*pošta*	*pošta*
Wi-Fi	*Wi-Fi*	*Wi-Fi*

CULTURAL SIGHTS

Baroque	*barok*	*barok*
bell tower	*zvonik*	*zvonik*
bridge	*most*	*most*
castle	*dvorac, kaštel*	*grad*
cathedral	*katedrala*	*katedrala*
cemetery	*groblje*	*pokopališče*
chapel	*kapelica*	*kapela*
church	*crkva*	*cerkev*
citadel/old town	*stari grad*	*staro mestno jedro*
city walls	*zidine*	*mestno obzidje*
cloister	*klaustar*	*križni hodnik*
exhibition	*izložba*	*rastava*
frescoes	*freske*	*freske*
gallery	*galerija*	*galerija*
garden	*vrt*	*vrt*
gate/door	*vrata*	*vrata*
Glagolitic	*glagoljica*	*glagolica*
loggia	*lođa*	*loža*
mill	*mlin*	*mlin*
monastery	*samostan*	*samostan*
monument	*spomenik*	*spomenik*
museum	*muzej*	*muzej*
painting	*slika*	*slika*
palace	*palača*	*palača*
Roman	*rimsko*	*rimsko*
Romanesque	*romaničko*	*romansko*
sculpture/statue	*skulptura/kip*	*skulptura/kip*
square	*trg*	*trg*
street	*ulica*	*ulica*
town/city	*grad*	*mesto*
Venetian	*venecijansko*	*beneško*
village	*selo*	*vas*
wall	*zid*	*zid*

TRANSPORT

aeroplane	*zrakoplov/avion*	*letalo*
airport	*zračna luka/aerodrom*	*letališče*
aisle	*prolaz*	*prehod*
arrivals	*dolasci*	*prihodi*
bicycle	*bicikl*	*kolo*

English	Croatian	Slovene
boat	*brod*	*čoln*
bus	*autobus*	*avtobus*
bus station	*autobusni kolodvor*	*avtobusna postaja*
bus stop	*stanica/stajalište*	*avtobusna postaja*
by train	*vlakom*	*z vlakom*
car	*auto*	*avto*
catamaran	*katamaran*	*katamaran*
departures	*odlasci*	*odhodi*
direct	*direktno*	*direktno*
driver	*vozač*	*voznik*
driving licence	*vozačka dozvola*	*vozniško dovoljenje*
ferry	*trajekt*	*trajekt*
luggage	*prtljaga*	*prtljaga*
motorbike	*motor*	*motorcikel*
on foot	*pješke/pješice*	*peš*
petrol	*benzin*	*bencin*
petrol station	*benzinska stanica*	*bencinska črpalka*
platform	*peron*	*peron*
seat	*sedalo*	*sedež*
railway station/ main railway station	*željeznički kolodvor/ glavni kolodvor*	*železniška postaja/ glavna postaja*
return ticket	*povratna karta*	*povratna vozovnica*
single ticket	*jednosmjerna karta*	*enosmerna vozovnica*
station	*kolodvor*	*postaja*
taxi	*taksi*	*taksi*
ticket	*karta*	*vozovnica*
ticket office	*prodaja karata/blagajna*	*prodaja vozovnic*
train	*vlak*	*vlak*
window	*prozor*	*okno*
One ticket to …, please	*Jednu kartu do …, molim*	*Eno vozovnico do …, prosim*
What time does the train to … leave?	*U koliko sati ide vlak za … ?*	*Kdaj odide vlak za … ?*
Which number?	*Koji broj?*	*Katerih številka?*
Which platform?	*Koji peron?*	*Katerih peron?*

SHOPPING

bakery	*pekarnica*	*pekarna*
bookshop	*knjižara*	*knjigarna*
chemist	*apoteka/ljekarna*	*apoteka/lekarna*
closed	*zatvoreno*	*zaprto*
market	*tržnica/plac*	*tržnica*
open	*otvoreno*	*odprto*
price	*cijena*	*cena*
shop	*dućan/trgovina/prodavaonica*	*trgovina*
I'm just looking, thanks	*Samo gledam, hvala*	*Samo gledam, hvala*
Please could I have …	*Molim vas …*	*Prosim, lahko dobim …*
Do you have … ?	*Imate li … ?*	*Imate … ?*

English	Croatian	Slovene
How much does it cost?	*Koliko košta?*	*Koliko stane?*
Can I help you?	*Mogu li pomoći?*	*Vam lahko pomagam?*
There isn't/aren't …	*Nema …*	*Ni …*

EATING OUT

bar	*bar*	*bar*
café	*kafić*	*kavarna*
menu	*jelovnik*	*jedilnik*
outside	*van*	*zunaj*
restaurant	*restoran*	*restavracija*
table	*stol*	*miza*
terrace	*terasa*	*terasa*
wine list	*vinska karta*	*vinska karta*
I've already ordered, thank you	*Već sam naručio, hvala*	*Sem že naročil, hvala*
Can I order, please?	*Molim vas, mogu li naručiti?*	*Prosim, lakho naročim?*
Can I have the bill, please?	*Molim vas račun?*	*Lahko dobim račun, prosim?*

FOOD

breakfast	*doručak*	*zajtrk*
lunch	*ručak*	*kosilo*
dinner	*večera*	*večerja*
starter	*predjelo*	*predjed*
main course	*glavno jelo*	*glavna jed*
dessert	*desert*	*sladica*
baked	*pečeno*	*pečeno*
boiled	*kuhano*	*kuhano*
bread	*kruh*	*kruh*
cheese	*sir*	*sir*
goat's cheese	*kozji sir*	*koze sir*
eggs	*jaja*	*jajca*
food	*hrana/jelo*	*hrana*
fried/deep fried	*prženo/pohano*	*ocvrte*
grilled	*na žaru*	*na žaru*
homemade	*domaće*	*domače*
organic	*ekološko*	*ekološko*
pasta	*tjestenina*	*testenine*
polenta	*palenta*	*polenta*
rice	*riža*	*riž*
risotto	*rižot*	*rižoto*
black (cuttlefish) risotto	*crni rižot*	črno rižoto
sauce	*umak/sos/saft*	*omaka*
soup	*juha*	*juha*
vegan	*vegan*	*vegan*
vegetarian	*vegetarijanac* (m), *vegetarijanka* (f)	*vegetarijanec* (m), *vegetarijanka* (f)

Meat (*meso*)

bacon	*špek/slanina*	*slanino*
beef	*govedina*	*govedina*
chicken	*piletina*	*piščanec*

English	Croatian	Slovene
cured meat	*suho meso*	*prekajeno meso*
ham	*šunka*	*šunka*
lamb	*janjetina*	*jagnjetina*
pancetta	*panceta*	*panceta*
pork	*svinjetina*	*svinjina*
prosciutto	*pršut*	*pršut*
sausages	*kobasice*	*klobasa*
veal	*teletina*	*teletina*
venison	*srnetina*	*divjačina*

Fish (*riba*) and shellfish (*morski plodovi* or *školjke*)

English	Croatian	Slovene
crab	*rak*	*rak*
cuttlefish	*sipa*	*sipa*
gilthead bream	*orada*	*orad*
John Dory	*kovač*	*kovač*
langoustines	*škampi*	*škampi*
lobster	*jastog*	*jastog*
mackerel	*lokarda/skuša*	*skuša*
monkfish	*grdobina*	*spaka*
mussels	*dagnje*	*dagnje/klapavice*
octopus	*hobotnica*	*hobotnica*
oysters	*kamenice/ostrige*	*ostrige*
prawns	*kozice*	*kozice*
salmon	*losos*	*losos*
sardines	*srdele*	*srdele*
sea bass	*brancin*	*brancin*
squid	*lignje*	*lignji*
trout	*pastrva*	*postrvi*
tuna	*tuna/tunj*	*tun*

Fruit (*voće*) and vegetables (*povrće*)

English	Croatian	Slovene
apple	*jabuka*	*jabolko*
bay leaves	*lovor*	*lovorjev list*
blueberries	*borovnice*	*borovnice*
cabbage	*kupus/zelje*	*kupus/zelje*
cantaloupe	*dinja*	*dinja*
corn	*kukuruz*	*koruza*
courgette	*tikvica*	*bučka*
cucumber	*krastavac*	*krastavac*
fig	*smokva*	*smokva*
grapes	*grožđe*	*grozdje*
lettuce, green salad	*zelena salata*	*zelena salata*
olives	*masline*	*masline*
orange	*naranča*	*pomaranča*
pear	*kruška*	*hruška*
plum	*šljiva*	*šljiva*
poppy seeds	*mak*	*mak*
potato	*krumpir*	*krompir*
French fries	*pomfrit*	*pomfrit*
salad	*salata*	*salata*

English	Croatian	Slovene
mixed salad	*miješana salata*	*miješana salata*
seasonal salad	*sezonska salata*	*sezonska salata*
sour cherry	*višnja*	*višnja*
strawberry	*jagoda*	*jagoda*
Swiss chard	*blitva*	*blitva*
tomato	*pomidoro/rajčica/paradajz*	*rajčica/paradajz*
truffles	*tartufi*	*tartufi*
black truffles	*crni tartufi*	*črni tartufi*
white truffles	*bijeli tartufi*	*beli tartufi*
walnut	*orah*	*oreh*
water melon	*lubenica*	*lubenica*

Cake (*kolač*) and dessert (*desert*)

English	Croatian	Slovene
chocolate	*čokolada*	*čokolada*
ice cream	*sladoled*	*sladoled*
pancakes	*palačinke*	*palačinke*
(apple) pie	*pita (od jabuka)*	*(jabločna) pita*
strudel	*štrudla*	*zavitek*

DRINK

English	Croatian	Slovene
beer	*pivo*	*beer*
bottled	*flaširano*	*ustekleničeno*
draught	*točeno*	*točeno*
cocktail	*koktel*	*koktajl*
coffee	*kava*	*kava*
cappuccino	*kapučino*	*kapučino*
coffee with milk	*kava s mlijekom*	*kava z mlekom*
espresso	*espresso* or *obična kava*	*espresso*
fruit juice	*sok*	*sok*
apple juice	*sok od jabuka*	*jabolčni sok*
orange juice	*sok od naranče*	*pomarančni sok*
milk	*mlijeko*	*milk*
mineral water (carbonated)	*mineralna voda/kisela voda gazirana*	*mineralna voda gazirana*
mineral water (still)	*negazirana voda*	*negazirana voda*
tea	*čaj*	*tea*
herbal tea	*voćni čaj*	*sadni čaj*
tea with lemon	*čaj s limunom*	*čaj z limono*
tea with milk	*čaj s mlijekom*	*čaj z mlekom*
water	*voda*	*voda*
wine	*vino*	*wine*
red wine	*crno vino*	*rdeče vino*
white wine	*bijelo vino*	*belo vino*

LANDSCAPE

English	Croatian	Slovene
beach	*plaža*	*plaža*
cave	*špilja/pećina*	*jama*
pit cave	*jama*	*jama*
coast/shore	*obala*	*obala*
drystone wall	*suhozid*	*suhozid*

English	Croatian	Slovene
forest	*šuma*	*gozd*
hill	*brdo*	*hrib*
island	*otok*	*otok*
lake	*jezero*	*jezero*
meadow	*livada*	*travnik*
mountain	*planina*	*gora*
path	*staza/put*	*pot/steza*
peninsula	*poluotok*	*polotok*
river	*rijeka*	*reka*
rock	*kamen*	*kamnina*
sandy	*pješčano*	*peščena*
sea	*more*	*morje*
spring	*izvor*	*izvir*
stony	*stjenovito*	*skalnato*
summit	*vrh*	*vrh*
valley	*dolina*	*dolina*
waterfall	*slap/vodopad*	*slap*

WEATHER

cloudy	*oblačno*	*oblačno*
dark	*mrak*	*temno*
rain	*kiša*	*dež*
sun	*sunce*	*sonce*
sunny	*sunčano*	*sončno*
wind	*vjetar*	*veter*

PLANTS AND ANIMALS

animal	*životinje*	*živali*
bear	*medvjed*	*medved*
beech	*bukva*	*bukev*
bird	*ptica*	*ptica*
buzzard	*škanjac*	*kanja*
cat	*mačka*	*mačka*
chestnut	*kesten*	*kostanj*
cow	*krava*	*krava*
deer	*jelen*	*jelen*
dog	*pas*	*pes*
eagle	*orao*	*orel*
fish	*riba*	*riba*
flower	*cvijet*	*cvet*
goat	*koza*	*goat*
grass	*trava*	*trava*
horse	*konj*	*konj*
lavender	*lavanda*	*sivka*
oak	*hrast*	*hrast*
pig	*svinja*	*prašič*
pine	*bor*	*bor*
pine marten	*kuna*	*kuna*
plants	*biljke*	*rastlinc*
rabbit	*zec*	*zajec*

English	Croatian	Slovene
sheep	*ovca*	*ovca*
snake	*zmija*	*kača*
tree	*drvo*	*drevo*
wild boar	*divlja svinja*	*divji prašič*

EMERGENCIES

ambulance	*hitna pomoć*	*rešilec*
Be careful!	*Pazi!*	*Pazi!*
Danger!	*Opasnost!*	*Nevarnost!*
doctor	*doktor/liječnik*	*zdravnik/doktor*
Help!	*U pomoć!*	*Na pomoč!*
hospital	*bolnica*	*bolnišnica*
Please call a doctor!	*Molim vas pozovite doktora!*	*Prosim, pokličite zdravnika!*
sick/ill	*bolestan*	*bolan*

Appendix 2

MARINAS AND SAILING CLUBS

MARINAS

The Adriatic Croatia International Club (ACI) w aci-marinas.com. This is a network of 22 marinas across Croatia. The club works to improve cleanliness & maintenance standards in all of its marinas, several of which have been awarded a European Blue Flag – indicating they have received an eco-award for safety & sea cleanliness. The VHF Channel for all ACI Club marinas in Istria is 17.

ACI Marina Opatija (Blue Flag) PO Box 60, 51414 Ičići; 098 398 840; all year. About 2km south of Opatija in Ičići, the ACI Marina Opatija has 302 berths & another 35 places in dry dock. All berths have water & electricity. Facilities include a reception desk, exchange office, restaurant, café, toilets & showers, laundry service, grocery store, nautical gear store, repair shop, a 15-tonne crane, slipway & parking. Fuel is available 2km north in Opatija.

ACI Marina Pomer Pomer bb, 52100 Pomer Pula; 052 573 162; all year. Pomer was expanded in 2016 to include nearly 300 berths & another 30 in dry dock – all with water & electricity. It has a reception desk offering currency exchange, Wi-Fi, shower & toilet facilities, a restaurant, grocery store, laundry facilities, repair shop including a 10-tonne crane, & parking. Fuel is available in Pješčana uvala, which is about 5 nautical miles north & west.

ACI Marina Pula Riva 1, 52100 Pula; m 098 398 837; all year. The marina has 200 berths although it does not offer any in dry dock. The water berths all have water & electricity. The marina has a reception, parking, fuel station, an exchange office, a restaurant & a repair shop with a 10-tonne crane. Pula itself has a wide range of shopping & tourist services (page 50).

ACI Marina Rovinj Vladimira Nazora bb, 52210 Rovinj; 052 813 133; all year. The marina has 196 berths though none in dry dock. Berths have water & power supply. There is also a reception, exchange office, restaurant, toilets & showers, repair shop, 10-tonne crane, parking, grocery store, nautical gear store, & a fuel station nearby. Rovinj has a full range of tourist services (page 71).

ACI Marina Umag (Blue Flag) 52470 Umag; m 098 398 833; all year. Alongside the Adriatic Hotel, Umag's ACI Marina has 475 berths plus another 40 in dry dock. All berths have water & electricity. On site is a reception & exchange office, as well as a grocery store, 50-tonne crane, parking, a repair shop, a fuel station nearby, a restaurant, toilets & showers, & a laundry service.

Marina Admiral Hotel Admiral; Maršala Tita 139, 51410 Opatija; m 091 274 388; w marina-opatija.com; all year. Located at the Hotel Admiral, the marina has 160 berths & 40 more in dry dock. Each has electricity & water. Opatija itself has a full range of tourist services (page 125).

Marina Funtana Ribarska 11, 52452 Funtana; 052 428 500; e funtana@montraker.hr; w montraker.hr; all year. Funtana's marina has 180 berths & 50 more in dry dock. All have electricity & water. The maximum boat draught is 4.5m. The marina has a reception desk, toilets & showers, a café, parking, laundry, ATM, & a repair shop including a crane. In town there are multiple grocery stores, an outpatient clinic, post office, cafés, engine repair, & diving services.

Marina Izola Tomažičeva 4a, Izola, Slovenia; 056 625 400; w marinaup.com; all year. Large marina with 700+ berths, each with water & electricity. The marina also has covered parking, boat charter, an equipment shop, sport facilities, a shopping centre, restaurant & casino, & offers service & maintenance, with the use of a crane. Plenty of accommodation & places to eat in Izola itself (page 159).

Marina Koper Kopališko nabrežje 5, Slovenia; 056 626 100; w marinaup.com; all year. Now merged with Marina Izola as part of MarinaUp, Marina Koper has 68 berths plus 26 dry docks, crane, repairs & petrol station. Plenty of accommodation & places to eat in Koper itself (page 154).

Marina Parentium Trg Slobode 2a, 52440 Poreč; 052 452 210; all year but reception desk only summer 07.00–21.00. The marina lies within the Zelena Laguna resort, approximately 6km from Poreč. It has 184 berths & a maximum boat draught of 5m. All have electricity & water. The marina also has a repair shop with an electrical engineer, a plastics expert, & a joiner among others, plus a 10-tonne crane to hoist boats. There is a restaurant, a grocery store, & toilet facilities on site while nearby there is a hotel, a post office, cafés, some limited shopping, & an ATM.

Marina Vrsar Obala Maršala Tita 1a, 52450 Vrsar; 052 441 052; w montraker.hr; all year. The marina has 220 berths & 40 in dry dock, & can accept yachts up to 50m long with a maximum draught of 14m. The marina has water & electricity at all moorings, video security, fuelling station, ATM, restaurant, showers, parking, 30-tonne crane, repair, shopping, Wi-Fi, laundry service, with diving outfitters, a nautical gear store & nightclubs among other facilities in the vicinity.

Tehnomont Marina Veruda (Blue Flag) Cesta prekomorskih brigada 12, 52100 Pula; 052 224 034; w marina-veruda.hr; all year. Tehnomont is one of the largest marinas in Istria. Its 18 piers have 630 berths with another 250 in dry dock. It has 2 cranes: 1 of 10 tonnes & the other of 30 tonnes. There is video surveillance. The marina can take mega-yachts so long as they don't require more than 4m of draught. In addition Tehnomont has full service repair & maintenance services, 2 restaurants, multiple shower & toilet locations, laundry services, a grocery store, an equipment shop, ATMs, parking, & a fuel station.

SAILING CLUBS

Jedriličarski Savez Istarskih Zupanije (JSIZ) F Barbalića 2, 52100 Pula; 052 210 436. This is an association that manages all the *jedriicarski klub* (JK) yacht clubs in Istria & is based in Pula. It also keeps track of races & regattas, rankings & results.

Hrvatski Jedriličarski Savez (HJS) Osječka 11, Split; 021 345 788; w hjs.hr. Croatian Sailing Association.

JK Alternativa Bernarda Borisia 2, 52452 Funtana; 052 445 188; e mladen.grgeta@pu.t-com.hr

JK Brioni Titova Riva 7, 52212 Fažana; m 098 500 222; e jk.brioni@gmail.com

JK Horizont Poreč Nikole Tesle 16, 52440 Poreč; e jk.horizont@gmail.com; w jk-horizont.hr

JK Uljanik Verudela 9, Pula; m 097 66 26 506; w jku.hr/en

JK Vega Valsaline 31, 52100 Pula; m 099 577 6007; e vega@vega.hr; w vega.hr

PSRD Delfin Kandelerova 25, 52100 Pula; m 052 382 148; w delfin-pula.hr. A sporting & fishing society.

Appendix 3

FURTHER INFORMATION

BOOKS

Guidebooks

Abraham, Rudolf *Islands of Croatia* Cicerone, 2013
Abraham, Rudolf *Slovenia's Juliana Trail* Cicerone, 2023.
Abraham, Rudolf *The Alpe-Adria Trail* 2nd edition; Bradt, 2020
Abraham, Rudolf *Walks and Treks in Croatia* 2nd edition; Cicerone, 2017
Čujić, Boris *Croatia: Climbing Guide* 4th edition; Astroida, 2009
Letcher, Piers *Croatia* 6th edition; Bradt, 2016

History

Alberi, Dario *Istria: Storia, Arte, Cultura* Lint, 1997. At 1,999 pages, this is the most comprehensive book you'll get on Istria, even by Croatian standards, but it is currently only available in Italian.

Bracewell, Catherine Wendy *The Uskoks of Senj: Piracy, Banditry and Holy War in the Sixteenth-Century Adriatic* Cornell University Press, 1992. Not about Istria, but this is the definitive account of the Uskoks, who after being disbanded were outlawed to Žumberak and Ćićarija.

Curta, Florin *Southeastern Europe in the Middle Ages 500–1250* Cambridge University Press, 2006

Glenny, Misha *The Fall of Yugoslavia* Penguin, 1992

Goldstein, Ivo *Croatia: A History* C Hurst & Co, 1999

Mesić, Stipe *The Demise of Yugoslavia: A Political Memoir* Central European University Press, 2004. Personal memoir by Croatia's former president, who was also the final president of the former Yugoslavia before its demise.

Obolenski, Dimitri *The Byzantine Commonwealth: Eastern Europe, 500–1453* Weidenfeld & Nicolson, 1971

Silber, Laura & Little, Allan *The Death of Yugoslavia* Penguin and BBC Books, 1995. Probably the best account of the disintegration of the former Yugoslavia.

Singleton, Fred *A Short History of the Yugoslav Peoples* Cambridge University Press, 1985

Tanner, Marcus *Croatia: A Nation Forged in War* Yale University Press, 1997

Wilkes, John *The Illyrians* Blackwell, 1992. The definitive text on the history of the Illyrians.

Food

Baccia, Paola *Istria: Recipes and Stories from the Hidden Heart of Italy, Slovenia and Croatia* Smith Street Books, 2021

Bogataj, Janez *Recipes from a Slovenian Kitchen* Aquamarine, 2013

Bratovž, Janez *Slovenian Cuisine: From the Alps to the Adriatic in 20 Ingredients* Skyhorse, 2022. Plenty of inspiration here, by the outstanding chef who is widely regarded as the father of modern Slovenian gastronomy.
Pavičić, Liniana & Pirker-Mosher, Gordana *The Best of Croatian Cooking* Hippocrene, 2007

Natural history

Arnold, E Nicolas & Ovenden, Denys W *Reptiles and Amphibians of Europe* Princeton Field Guides, 2002. Worth getting the Princeton rather than the Collins edition as it's paperback and therefore more pocketable.
Gorman, Gerard *Central and Eastern European Wildlife* Bradt, 2008
Polunin, Oleg *Flowers of Greece and the Balkans: A Field Guide* Oxford University Press, 1980
Polunin, Oleg *The Concise Flowers of Europe* Oxford University Press, 1972
Svensson, Lars, Grant, Peter J, Mullarney, Killian & Zetterström, Dan *Birds of Europe* 2nd edition; Princeton University Press, 2010 (also available as *Collins Bird Guide* 2nd edition; Collins, 2010)
Tolman, Tom & Lewington, Richard *Collins Butterfly Guide* Collins, 2009

Language

Hawkesworth, Celia (with Jović, Ivana) *Colloquial Croatian: The Complete Course for Beginners* Routledge, 2005
Norris, David *Teach Yourself Croatian* Teach Yourself, 2003

Literature

Nazor, Vladimor *Veli Jože* (translated by Martin Mayhew) Martin Mayhew, 2022. A fable for the great stoicism of the Istrian people, the story of the kind-hearted giant Veli Jože is Nazor's most beloved work, and was first published in 1908.
Tomizza, Fulvio *Materada* (translated by Russel Scott Valentino) Northwest University Press, 1999. Set in rural Istria, this novel tells the story of a family land feud and a society torn apart, against the backdrop of the Italian exodus following World War II. First published in 1964.
Verne, Jules *Mathius Sandorf* Le Temps, 1885. The epic journey of Count Sandorf, who fights for freedom, ends up in Pazin prison, and escapes via the Pazin Abyss.
West, Rebecca *Black Lamb and Grey Falcon: A Journey Through Yugoslavia* Macmillan, 1942. Still a must-read for anyone interested in southeast Europe.

Art and architecture

Beckwith, John *Early Christian and Byzantine Art* Yale University Press, 1970
Fučić, Branko *Vincent iz Kastva* Kršćanska Sadašnjost, 1992. Account of the Beram frescoes and the medieval painter responsible for them (Croatian/German/Italian text).
Mlakar, Stefan *The Amphitheatre in Pula* Archaeological Museum of Istria, 1984

WEBSITES

Tourism

Buzet Tourist Board w tz-buzet.hr
Central Istrian Tourist Board w central-istria.com
Colours of Istria (Northwest Istria Tourist Board) w coloursofistria.com
Go! 2025 w go2025.eu/en
Croatian National Tourist Board w croatia.hr
Histrica w histrica.com
Istrian Tourist Board w istra.hr
Izola Tourist Board w visitizola.com
Kvarner Tourist Office w kvarner.hr
Ljubljana Tourist Office w visitljubljana.com
Motovun Tourist Board w tz-motovun.hr
Piran & Portorož Tourist Board w portoroz.si
Poreč Tourist Board w myporec.com
Pula Tourist Board w pulainfo.hr
Rijeka Tourist Board w visitrijeka.hr

Rovinj Tourist Board w rovinj-tourism.com
Slovenian National Tourist Board w slovenia.info
Trieste Tourist Office (Turismo FVG) w turismofvg.it
Visit Croatia w visit-croatia.co.uk
Vipava Valley Tourist Board w vipavskadolina.si

Transport

Bus timetables w arriva.com.hr, w arriva.si & w akz.hr
Goopti w goopti.com
HAK (Croatian Automobile Club) w hak.hr
Jadrolinija w jadrolinija.hr
Taxi Cammeo w cammeo.hr
Train timetables (**Croatia**) w hzpp.hr/en
Train timetables (Slovenia) w potniski.sz.si/en
Venezia Lines w venezialines.com

Government departments

Croatian Bureau of Statistics w dzs.gov.hr
Istarska županija w istra-istria.hr
Ministry of Foreign Affairs w mup.gov.hr

Weather

Croatian Meteorological and Hydrological Service w meteo.hr

Outdoors

ACI Club w aci-club.hr
Bike Istria w istria-bike.com
Climb Istria w climbistria.com
Croatian Diving Association w diving-hrs.hr
Croatian Mountaineering Association (Hrvatski planinarski savez) w hps.hr
HGSS (Hrvatska gorska služba spašavanja, Croatian Mountain Rescue Service, and hiking maps) w hgss.hr
Istria Trails w istria-trails.com
Parenzana w parenzana.net
SMAND (hiking maps) w smand.hr

Accommodation

Apartmanija w apartmanija.hr
Croatian Camping Union w camping.hr
Croatian Youth Hostel Association w hicroatia.com
Lighthouses of Croatia w lighthouses-croatia.com

Food and culture

Gourmet Istria w istria-gourmet.com
Istrapedia w istrapedia.hr
JRE Croatia w jre.eu/en/countries/croatia
Manjada (Eat Istria) f eatistria
MDC (Muzejski dokumentacijski centar) w mdc.hr
Milka Šćulac Sennett w milkasculacsennett.com
Smrikve w smrikve.com
Taste Slovenia w tasteslovenia.si

Media

Glas Istre w glasistre.hr
HRT (Hrvatska radiotelevizija) w hrt.hr

National parks, nature parks and reserves

Brijuni Islands National Park w np-brijuni.hr
Postojnska jama w postojnska-jama.eu
Rt Kamenjak w kamenjak.hr
Škocjanske jame w park-skocjanske-jame.si
Učka Nature Park w pp-ucka.hr

Environment

Natura Histrica w natura-histrica.hr
Zelena Istra w zelena-istra.hr

Index

Page numbers in **bold** indicate major entries; those in italics indicate maps.

INDEX OF ADVERTISERS

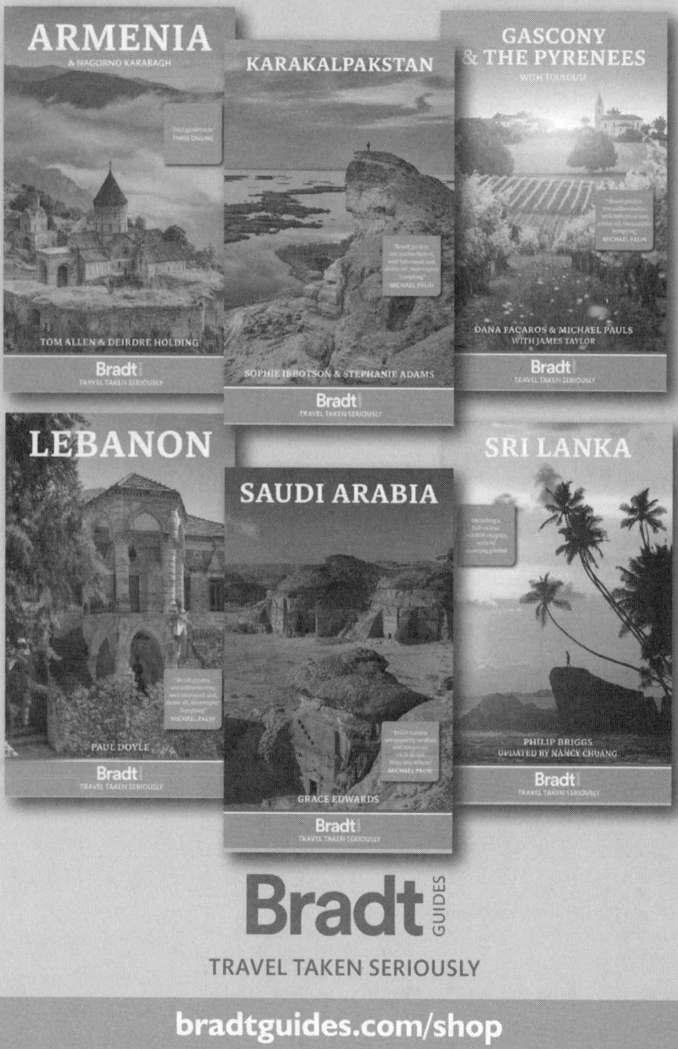